TAPPING REEVE.

# The Bench and Bar of Litchfield County, Connecticut
# 1709-1909

BIOGRAPHICAL SKETCHES OF MEMBERS
HISTORY AND CATALOGUE OF THE
LITCHFIELD LAW SCHOOL
HISTORICAL NOTES

BY

DWIGHT C. KILBOURN

Clerk of Superior Court, Member of the Connecticut Historical Society, Member of the Kansas Historical Society, Vice-President of the Litchfield Historical Society.

THE LAWBOOK EXCHANGE, LTD.
Union, New Jersey
2002

ISBN 1-58477-213-1

*The quality of this reprint is equivalent to the quality of the original work.*

*Printed in the United States of America on acid-free paper*

**The Lawbook Exchange, Ltd.**
965 Jefferson Avenue
Union, New Jersey 07083-8605

*Please see catalogue at rear of this volume or our website* www.lawbookexchange.com *for a selection of our other fine facsimile reprints of legal classics.*

**Library of Congress Cataloging-in-Publication Data**

Kilbourn, Dwight C. (Dwight Canfield), 1837-1914.
The bench and bar of Litchfield County, Connecticut, 1709-1909 : biographical sketches of members, history and catalogue of the Litchfield Law School, historical notes / by Dwight C. Kilbourn.

p. cm.

Originally published: Litchfield, Conn. : D.C. Kilbourn, 1909.

Includes bibliographical references and index.

ISBN 1-58477-213-1 (cloth: acid-free paper)

1. Justice, Administration of—Connecticut—Litchfield County—History. 2. Practice of law—Connecticut—Litchfield County—History. 3. Lawyers—Connecticut—Litchfield County—Biography. I. Title.

KFC3678 .K55 2001
340'.092'2—dc21
[B] 2001038974

# The Bench and Bar of Litchfield County, Connecticut
# 1709-1909

BIOGRAPHICAL SKETCHES OF MEMBERS
HISTORY AND CATALOGUE OF THE
LITCHFIELD LAW SCHOOL
HISTORICAL NOTES

BY

DWIGHT C. KILBOURN

Clerk of Superior Court, Member of the Connecticut Historical Society, Member of the Kansas Historical Society, Vice-President of the Litchfield Historical Society.

PUBLISHED
BY THE AUTHOR
LITCHFIELD, CONN.
1909

To my Brethren
of the
Litchfield County Bar
this book is most
Affectionately
Dedicated

# CONTENTS

# LIST OF ILLUSTRATIONS



**PORTRAITS**

# STATEMENT OF THE CASE

The practice of the law in the English speaking colonies of the new world previous to the organization of Litchfield County is an interesting study of various methods of procedure all founded upon the practice of the mother country. Some were copied from the common law courts, and some from the other courts and in hardly any two colonies was there similarity of practice, while the old common law of England was a general guide to the interpretation of the statute law, with such modifications in the Puritan colonies as the mosaic law suggested to the religious teachers and pastors thereof.

About the time our county was organized, these different modes of practice began to be crystallized into a more established form. There were practically no attorneys, as we now understand the term, "men learned in the law." In many sections there was some influential man who was generally known as "the Squire," and whose opinions ruled the circle of his acquaintance. In this county there were only five or six men who pretended to be lawyers.

Directly after the formation of the county and the establishment of the county court, these men were admitted to practice as attorneys with slight examinations, and with little knowledge of the law, but they were strong-minded and of sterling character, oracles in their own communities, and they very soon brought the decisions of the county court of this county to the front rank of judicature. It was in this opportune period that Tapping Reeve located at Litchfield and unintentionally began that process which eventually overthrew the common law of England, for a common law of our own, and changed the old forms, rules and precedents which had so long prevailed. The close of the Revolutionary War utterly destroyed the doctrine that "the king could do no wrong" and swept away his prerogatives and common laws; and while we now quote the good contained in the "wisdom of ages," we decide questions by Reeves, Swift and Gould, and modern "wise instances."

Ten years ago the compiler of this book conceived the idea of collecting and preserving in a permanent form a mass of material which was then available relating to the legal history and tradition of his native county, and in the midst of his active duties as the Clerk of its courts, has gathered these items and now presents them for your consideration, believing his work to be a somewhat valuable contribution to our earlier history.

The reprint of Chief Justice Samuel Church's Address at the Centennial Celebration of the organization of the county, in 1851, gives a very concise and thorough analysis of the elements which have conduced to give our county great influence in the religious, social, political and legal affairs in both the state and nation. The address, however, was made too early to include Henry Ward Beecher and Harriet Beecher Stowe among the writers and speakers who have done so much to uplift the world's ideas, and wonderfully advance its progress towards its present power and greatness.

The reprint of Hon. David S. Boardman's "Early Lights of the Litchfield County Bar," being the reminiscences of a man ninety years of age, of his colleagues and associates in the earlier years of our county's history, will I am sure be of great interest to every one, and it is worthy of permanent preservation. The original pamphlet containing them has long been out of print, and is very rare. I regret very much my inability to procure his portrait for insertion in this work.

In the re-publication of Sedgwick's address, "Fifty Years of the Litchfield County Bar," I am enabled to bring the biographies of most of the prominent old lawyers down to modern times, prepared by an associate and brother in the legal arena, while Judge Warner's "Reminiscences" completes the chain of those living and practicing at the Bar during his life. Charles B. Phelps published obituaries of a number of his attorney friends in some of the earlier volumes of Connecticut Reports, but as these are easily accessible I have referred to them without republishing.

In the Biographical Notes I have endeavored to include the name of every member admitted to our Bar, or coming from elsewhere to practice, excluding however, those who have been debarred for cause. These notes are not intended to be genealogies or eulogies, but only the legal life briefly told, and they have nearly all been prepared by myself. I deeply regret that there are so many whom I have been unable to trace beyond the mere fact of their admission.

The section on the Law School contains the list of its students alphabetically arranged, with some other interesting matter relating thereto. So many references are made throughout the volume to Judges Reeve, Gould, Huntington, Bacon and others prominently connected with its instruction and management, that I did not think it wise to devote more space to the further history of the Law School.

The Historical Notes include only a few of the many trials and incidents which could be gathered from the Court Records, but in very many cases the account of trials, especially those of a criminal nature, might give pain to some friend or relative of the accused, which I have tried to avoid doing.

Probably no county in the state furnished the Supreme Court in its earlier days, more knotty problems to solve and adjudicate, than Litchfield County, and a full history of its "Leading Cases" would make an interesting volume of itself.

I have obtained all the subjects for illustration which I could and the pictures have been made from originals, many of them from old and faded paintings, as I desired to place in everlasting remembrance the faces of those gone before. In two or three instances I have duplicated, taking another and different portrait for the second picture, after the first one was already in print. If anyone thinks it is easy to collect a hundred pictures of as many persons who have long since deceased, a trial will dispel the illusion.

It is unavoidable that many errors will occur in such a work as this. Great care has been given to make it as nearly accurate as possible, and the compiler will be very glad to have his attention called to any such error, so that in due time proper corrections can be made.

To the very many friends who have aided me in this work, I wish to return my heart-felt thanks for their assistance. I have refrained from making any acknowledgment of quotations or extracts because I have thought that the matter itself would indicate the source from which it was taken. In conclusion I wish to say that I hope the perusal of this book will afford the reader as much pleasure as it has the compiler to prepare it.

Litchfield, May 1, 1909.
D. C. K.

# Centennial Address

# 1851

LITCHFIELD COUNTY

# HISTORICAL ADDRESS

DELIVERED AT LITCHFIELD, CONN.

ON THE OCCASION OF THE

## CENTENNIAL CELEBRATION, 1851

BY


SAMUEL CHURCH, LL. D.

CHIEF JUSTICE OF THE STATE

Hon. Samuel Church, C. J.

# Judge Church's Address

Fellow Citizens:—

I have no leisure now to offer apologies for my unadvised consent to appear before you, in this position, on the present occasion. Declining years, and the constant pressure of other duties, should have excused me.

My residence of sixty-six years from my nativity in this County, and an acquaintance of half a century, of some intimacy, with the events which have transpired, and with the men who have acted in them here, and having been placed within traditional reach of our early history, I suppose, has induced the call upon me to address you. In doing this, I shall make no drafts upon the imagination, but speak to you in the simple idiom of truthful narrative.

Among the most ancient and pleasant of New England usages, has been the annual gathering of children and brethren around the parental board on Thanksgiving day. The scene we now witness reminds me of it. Litchfield County,—our venerable parent, now waning into the age of an hundred years, has called us here, to exchange our mutual greetings, to see that she still lives and thrives, and hopes to live another century.

A little display of vanity on the part of such a parent, thus surrounded by her children, may be expected; but speaking by me, her representative, it shall not be excessive. She must say something of herself—of her birth and parantage—of her early life and progress, and of the scenes through which she has passed. She may be indulged a little in speaking of the children she has borne or reared, and how they have got along in the world. To tell of such as she has lost, and over whose loss she has mourned; and in the indulgence of an honest parent's pride, she may boast somewhat of many who survive, and who have all through this wide country made her name and her family respected.

We meet not alone in this relation, but we come together as brethren, and many of us after long years of separation and absence, to revive the memories and associations of former years.

Some of you come to visit the graves of parents and friends—to look again into the mansions where the cradle of your infancy was rocked, or upon the old foundations where they stood—to look again upon the favorite tree, now full grown, which your young arms clasped so often in the climbing, or upon the great rock upon and around which many a young gambol was performed. You come to enter again, perhaps, the consecrated temples at whose altars the good man stood who sprinkled you with the waters of baptism, and from whose lips you learned the lessons which have guided your footsteps in all your after life.

These are but some of the pages in the history of early life, which it is pleasant after the lapse of years to re-peruse. And now, if the spirits of these dead can pierce the cloud which hides our view of heaven, they look down with a smile of love upon your errand here; and when you shall leave us on the morrow, many of you will feel in truth, as did the patriot Greek, "moriens reminiscitur Argos."

A stranger who looks upon the map of Connecticut, sees at its north-west corner a darkly shaded section, extending over almost the entire limits of the County, indicating as he believes, a region of mountains and rocks—of bleak and frozen barrens. He turns his eye from it, satisfied that this is one of the waste places of the State—affording nothing pleasant for the residence of men. He examines much more complacently the map of the coast and the navagable streams. But let the stranger leave the map, and come and see! He will find the mountains which he anticipated—but he will find streams also. He will find the forests too, or the verdant hill-sides where they have been; and he will see the cattle on a thousand hills, and hear the bleating flocks in many a dale and glen, and he will breath an atmosphere of health and bouyancy, which the dwellers in the city and on the plain know little of. Let him come, and we will show him that men live here, and women too, over whom it would be ridiculous for the city population to boast: a yoemanry well fitted to sustain the institutions of a free country. We will show him living, moving men; but more than this, we will point out to him where, among these hills, were born or reared, or now repose in the grave, many of the men of whom he has read and heard, whose names have gone gloriously into their country's history, or who are now almost every where giving an honorable name to the County of Litchfield, and doing service to our State or nation.

The extensive and fertile plains of the Western country may yield richer harvests than we can reap; the slave population of the South may relieve the planter from the toil experienced by a Northern farmer; and the golden regions of California may sooner fill the pockets with the precious metals;—and all this may stand in strong contrast with what has been often called the rough and barren region of Litchfield hills. But the distinguishing traits of a New England country, which we love so well, are not there to give sublimity to the landscape, fragrance and health to the mountain atmosphere, and energy and enterprise to mind and character.

Not many years ago, I was descending the last hill in Norfolk in a stage-coach, in company with a lady of the West, whose former residence had been in that town. As we came down upon the valley of the Housatonic, with a full heart and suffused eyes, she exclaimed, "Oh, how I love these hills and streams! How much more pleasant they are to me than the dull prairies and the sluggish and turbid waters of the Western country." It was an eulogy, which if not often expressed, the truth of it has been a thousand times felt before.

Our Indian predecessors found but few spots among the hills of this Country, which invited their fixed residence. Here was no place for the culture of maize and beans, the chief articles of the Indian's vegetable food. Their settlements were chiefly confined to the valley of the Housatonic, with small scattered clans at Woodbury and Sharon. The Scaticoke tribe, at Kent, was the last which remained among us. It was taken under the protection of the Colony and State; its lands secured for its support. These Indians have wasted down to a few individuals, who, I believe, still remain near their fathers' sepulchers, and remind us that a native tribe once existed there.

We now see but little to prove that the *original* American race ever inhabited here. It left no monuments but a few arrow-heads, which are even now occasionally discovered near its former homes and upon its former hunting grounds,—and a sculptured female figure made of stone, not many years ago was found in this town, and is now deposited at Yale College.

There are other monuments, to be sure, of a later race of Indians; but they are of the white man's workmanship,—the quitclaim deeds of the Indians' title to their lands! These are found in several of the Towns in the County, and upon the public records, signed with *marks uncouth,* and names unspeakable, and executed with all the solemn mockery of legal forms.—These are still referred to, as evidence of fair purchase! Our laws have sedulously protected the minor and the married woman from the consequences of their best considered acts; but a deed from an Indian, who knew neither the value of the land he was required to relinquish, nor the amount of the consideration he was to receive for it, nor the import or effect of the paper upon which he scribbled his mark, has been called a fair purchase!

The hill-lands of this County were only traversed by the Indians as the common hunting grounds of the tribes which inhabited the valleys of the Tunxis and Connecticut rivers on the eastern, and the valley of the Housatonic on the western side.

The first settlers of this County did not meet the Indian here in his unspoiled native character. The race was dispirited and submissive—probably made up of fugitives from the aggressions of the early English emigrants on the coast,—the successors of more spirited tribes, which, to avoid contact with the whites, had migrated onward toward the setting sun. These Indians were like the ivy of the forest, which displays all its beauties in the shade, but droops and refuses to flourish in the open sunshine.

Previous to the accession of James II. to the throne of England, and before our chartered rights were threatened by the arrival of Sir Edmund Andros, the territory now comprising the County of Litchfield was very little known to the Colonial Government at Hartford. The town of Woodbury, then large in extent, had been occupied some years earlier than this, by Rev. Mr. Walker's congregation, from Stratford. The other parts of the County were noticed only as a wilderness, and denominated the *Western Lands*. Still it was supposed, that at some time they might be, to some extent, inhabited and worth something. At any rate, they were believed to be worth the pains of keeping out of the way of the new government of Sir Edmund, which was then apprehended to be near. To avoid his authority over these lands, and to preserve them for a future and better time of disposal, they were granted, by the Assembly of the Colony, to the towns of Hartford and Windsor, in 1686,—at least, so much of them as lay east of the Housatonic river. I do not stop to examine the moral quality of this grant, which may be reasonably doubted; and it was soon after followed by the usual consequences of grants, denominated by lawyers, *constructively* fraudulent—dispute and contention.

Upon the accession of William and Mary, in 1688, and after the Colony Charter had found its way back from the hollow oak to the Secretary's office, the Colonial Assembly attempted to resume this grant, and to reclaim the title of these lands for the Colony. This was resisted by the towns of Hartford and Windsor, which relied upon the inviolability of plighted faith and public grants. The towns not only denied the right, but actually resisted the power of the Assembly, in the resumption of their solemn deed. This produced riots and attempts to break the jail in Hartford, in which several of the resisting inhabitants of Hartford and Windsor were confined.

It would be found difficult for the Jurists of the present day, educated in the principles of Constitutional Law, to justify the Assembly in the recision of its own grant, and it can not but excite a little surprise, that the politicians of that day, who had not yet ceased to complain of the mother country for its attempts, by writs of quo warranto, to seize our charter, should so soon be engaged, and without the forms of law, too, in attempts of a kindred character against their own grantees. No wonder that resistance followed, and it was more than half successful, as it resulted in a compromise, which confirmed to the claimants under the towns the lands in the town of Litchfield and a part of the town of New Milford. The other portions of the territory were intended to be equally divided between the Colony and the claiming towns.

Thus Torrington, Barkhamsted, Colebrook, and a part of Harwinton, were appropriated to Windsor; Hartland, Winchester, New Hartford, and the other part of Harwinton, were relinquished to Hartford; and the remaining lands in dispute, now constituting the towns of Norfolk, Goshen, Canaan, Kent, Sharon and Salisbury, were retained by the Colony. These claims having at length been adjusted, the western lands began to be explored, and their facilities for cultivation to be known.

Woodbury, as I have before suggested, by several years our elder sister in this new family of towns, began its settlement in 1674. The Church at Stratford had been in contention, and the Rev. Mr. Walker, with a portion of that Church and people, removed to the fertile region of Pomperauge, soon distinguished by the name of Woodbury, and then including, beside the present town, also the region composing the towns of Southbury, Bethlem and Roxbury.

Pomperauge is said to have felt some of the effects of Philip's war—enough, at least, to add another to the many thrilling scenes of Indian depredation, so well drawn by the author of Mount Hope.

New Milford next followed in the course of settlement. This commenced in 1707. Its increase of population was slow until 1716, when Rev. Daniel Boardman, from Wethersfield, was ordained as the first minister. This gentleman was the ancestor of the several distinguished families and individuals of the same name, who have since been and now are residents of that town. His influence over the Indian tribe and its Sachem in that vicinity, was powerful and restraining, and so much confidence had this good man and his family in the fidelity of his Indian friends, it is said, that when his lady was earnestly warned to fly from a threatened savage attack, she coolly replied, that she would go as soon as she had put things to rights about her house, and had knit round to her seam needle! The original white inhabitants were emigrants from Milford, from which it derives its name.

Emigrants from the Manor of Livingston, in the New York Colony, made Indian purchases and began a settlement at Weatogue, in Salisbury, as early as 1720. After the sale of the township in 1737, the population increased rapidly,—coming in from the towns of Lebanon, Litchfield, and many other places, so that it was duly organized in 1741, and settled its minister, Rev. Jonothan Lee, in 1744.

The first inhabitants of Litchfield came under the Hartford and Windsor title, in 1721, and chiefly from Hartford, Windsor and Lebanon. This territory, and a large lake in its south-west section, was known as Bantam. Whether it was so called by the Indians, has been doubted, and is not well settled.

The settlement of the other towns commenced soon after, and progressed steadily, yet slowly. The town of Colebrook was the last enrolled in this fraternity, and settled its first minister, Rev. Jonathan Edwards, in 1795. Rev. Rufus Babcock, a Baptist minister, had, for some time before this, resided and officiated in the town.

One general characteristic marked the whole population; it was gathered chiefly from the towns already settled in the Colony, and with but few emigrants from Massachusetts. Our immediate ancestors were religious men, and religion was the ruling element; but it would be a mistake to suppose that it absorbed all others.

I shall not detain you with an eulogium on Puritan character. This may be found stereotyped every where—not only in books and speeches, but much more accurately in its influence and effects, not in New England alone, but throughout this nation. Our American ancestors were Englishmen, descendants of the same men, and inheritors of the same principles, by which Magna Charta was established at Runny-mede.—They were Anglo-Saxons, inspired with the same spirit of independence which has marked them every where, and especially through the long period of well defined English history, and which is destined in its further developments to give tone and impress to the political and religious institutions of Christendom. So much has been said and written of the Puritans, I have sometimes thought that some believe that they were a distinct race, and perhaps of a different complexion and language from their other countrymen; whereas, they were only Englishmen, generally of the Plebian caste, and with more of the energies and many of the frailties and imperfections common to humanity. If our first settlers here cherished more firmly the religious elements of their character than any other., the spirit of independence to which I have alluded developed another—the love of money, and an ingenuity in gratifying it.

Since the extent and resources of this County have been better known, the wonder is often expressed, how such an unpromising region as this County could have invited a population at first; but herein we misconceive the condition of our fathers. Here, as they supposed, was the last land to be explored and occupied in their day. They had no where else to go, and the growing population of the east, as well as the barren soil of the coast, impelled them westward. Of the north, beyond the Massachusetts Colony, nothing was known; only Canada and the frozen regions of Nova Scotia had been heard of. On the west was another Colony, but a different people; and still beyond, was an unknown realm, possessed by savage men, of whom New England had seen enough; and not much behind this, according to the geography of that day, was the Western Ocean, referred to in the Charter. A visible hand of Providence seems to have guided our fathers' goings. Had the valley of the Susquehanna been known to them then, they would but the sooner have furnished the history of the massacre of Wyoming.

If there were here the extensive and almost impenatrable everglade of the Green-Woods, the high hills of Goshen, Litchfield and Cornwall, and heavy forests every where—these were trifles then in the way of a New England man's calculation, and had been ever since the people of the May Flower and the Arabella and their descendants had been crowding their way back among the forests. These, and a thousand other obstacles, were surmounted, with hardly a suspicion that they were obstacles at all, and every township began ere long to exhibit a well ordered, organized society.

This was no missionary field, after the manner of modern new settlements. Every little Colony, as it became organized and extended from town to town, either took its minister along with it, or called him soon after. He became one with his people, wedded to them almost by sacramental bonds, indissoluble. A Primus inter pares, he settled on his own domain, appropriated to his use by the proprietors of every town, and he cultivated with his own hands his own soil, and at his death was laid down among his parishoners and neighbors in the common cemetery, with little of monumental extravagance to distinguish his resting place. The meeting-house was soon seen at the central point of each town, modestly elevated above surrounding buildings, and by its side the school-house, as its nursling child or younger sister, and the minister and the master were the oracles of each community. The development of the Christian man, spiritual, intellectual and physical, was the necessary result of such an organization of society as this.

The original settlers of this County were removed two or three generations from the first emigrants from England, and some of the more harsh pecularities of that race may well be supposed, ere this time, to have become modified, or to have subsided entirely. If a little of the spirit of Arch-Bishop Laud, transgressing the boundaries of Realm and Church, had found its way over the ocean, and was developed under a new condition of society here, it is not to be wondered at; it was the spirit of the age, though none the better for that, and none the more excusable, whether seen in Laud or Mather—in a Royal Parliament, or a Colonial Assembly.

Less of these peculiarities appeared in Connecticut than in Massachusetts; and at the late period when this County was settled, the sense of oppression inflicted by the mother country, whether real or fancied, was a little forgotten, and of course neither Quakers, Prayer Books nor Christmas were the object of penal legislation. A more tolerant, and of course a better spirit, came with our fathers into this County, than had before existed elsewhere in the Colony, and, if I mistake not, it has ever since been producing here its legitimate effects, and in some degree has distinguished the character and the action of Litchfield County throughout its entire history, as many facts could be made to prove.

Before the year 1751, this territory had been attached to different Counties—most of it to the County of Hartford; the towns of Sharon and Salisbury to the County of New Haven; and many of the early titles and of probate proceedings of several of the towns, before their organization or incorporation, may be found on the records of more early settled towns. The first settlements of estates in Canaan are recorded in Woodbury, and many early deeds are on record in the office of the Secretary in Hartford.

In 1751, the condition of the population of these towns was such as to demand the organization of a new County, and the subject was extensively discussed at the town meetings. As is always true, on such occasions, a diversity of opinions as well as the ordinary amount of excited feeling existed, regarding the location of the shire town. Cornwall and Canaan made their claims and had their advocates—but the chief contest was between Litchfield and Goshen. The latter town was supposed to occupy the geographical center, and many persons had settled there in expectation that that would become the fixed seat of justice, and, among others, Oliver Wolcott, afterward Governor of the State. But at the October session of the General Court in 1751, the new County was established with Litchfield as the County Town, under the name of Litchfield County.

Litchfield County, associated with the thought of one hundred years ago! A brief space in a nation's history; but such an hundred years!—more eventful than any other since the introduction of our Holy Religion into the world. This name speaks to us of home and all the hallowed memories of youth and years beyond our reach,—of our truant frolics, our school boy trials, our youthful aspirations and hopes; and, perhaps, of more tender and romantic sympathies; and many will recall the misgivings, and yet the stern resolves, with which they commenced the various avocations of life in which they have since been engaged. And from this point, too, we look back to ties which once bound us to parents, brothers, companions, friends—then strong—now sundered! and which have been breaking and breaking, until many of us find ourselves standing, almost alone, amidst what a few years ago was an unborn generation.

Litchfield County! Go where you will through this broad country, and speak aloud this name, and you will hear a response, "That is my own, my native land." It will come from some whom you will find in the halls of Legislation, in the Pulpit, on the Bench, at the Bar, by the sick man's couch, in the marts of Trade, by the Plow, or as wandering spirits in some of the tried or untried experiments of life. And sure I am, that there is not to be found a son of this County, be his residence ever so remote, who would not feel humbled to learn that this name was to be no longer heard among the civil divisions of his native State.

The usual officers, made necessary by the erection of the new County, were immediately appointed by the General Court. William Preston, Esq., of Woodbury, was the first Chief Justice of the County, and his Associates were John Williams, Esq., of Sharon, Samuel Canfield, of New Milford, and Ebenezer Marsh, of Litch-

OLD LITCHFIELD, 1851

field. Isaac Baldwin, Esq., was the first Clerk, and the first Sheriff was Oliver Wolcott, of whom I shall speak again. The County Court, at its first session in December of the same year, appointed Samuel Pettibone, Esq., of Goshen, to be King's Attorney, who was, within a few years, succeeded by Reynold Marvin, Esq., of this village, and these two gentlemen were all in this County, in this capacity, who ever represented the King's majesty in that administration of criminal justice.

The tenure of official place in the early days of the Commonwealth, was more permanent than since party subserviency has in some degree taken the place of better qualifications. The changes upon the bench of the County Court were not frequent. The office of Chief Judge, from the time of Judge Preston to the time of his successors, who are now alive, have been John Williams, of Sharon. Oliver Wolcott, Daniel Sherman, of Woodbury, Joshua Porter, of Salisbury, Aaron Austin, of New Hartford, also a member of the Council, and Augustus Pettibone, of Norfolk. I can not at this time present a catalogue of Associate Judges. It has been composed of the most worthy and competent citizens of the County—gentlemen of high influence and respect in the several towns of their residence.

In the office of Sheriff, Governor Wolcott was succeeded by Lynde Lord, David Smith, John R. Landon, Moses Seymour, Jr., and Ozias Seymour, of this village, and the successors of these gentlemen are still surviving.

Mr. Marvin was succeeded in the office of State's Attorney, by Andrew Adams, Tapping Reeve, Uriah Thacy, Nathaniel Smith, John Allen, Uriel Holmes, and Elisha Sterling, whose successors, with a single exception, still survive.

Hon. Frederick Wolcott succeeded Mr. Baldwin in the office of Clerk, and this place he held, undisturbed by party influences, for forty years, and until nearly the time of his death in 1836.

The common Prison first erected was a small wooden building, near the late dwelling house of Roger Cook, Esq., on the north side of East street. This stood but few years, and in its place a more commodious one was built, nearly on the same foundation. The present Prison was built in 1812, and essentially improved within a few years. The first Court House stood on the open grounds a little easterly from the West Park, and may still be seen in the rear of the buildings on the south side of West street. It was a small building, but in it were often witnessed some of the most able efforts of American eloquence. In this humble Temple of Justice, Hon. S. W. Johnston of Stratford, Edwards of New Haven, Reeve, Tracy, Allen, and the Smiths of this County, exhibited some of the best essays of forensic power. The present Court House was erected in 1798.

The early progress of the County presents but a few incidents of sufficient note to retain a place in its traditionary history. The apprehension of savage incursions had passed away, and the people were left undisturbed to carry out, to their necessary results, what might have been expected from the spirit and enterprise which brought them hither. The old French War, as it has since been called, disturbed them but little. Some of the towns in the County, moved by a loyal impulse, and a legitimate hatred of France, as well as hostility to Indians in its service, furnished men and officers in aid of some of the expeditions to the northern frontier.

The pioneers here were agriculturists. They came with no knowledge or care for any other pursuit, and looked for no greater results than the enjoyment of religious privileges, the increase of their estates by removing the heavy forest and adding other acres to their original purchases, and with the hope, perhaps, of sending an active boy to the College. Of manufactures, they knew nothing. The grist-mill and saw-mill, the blacksmith and clothier's shops,—all as indispensable as the plow and the axe,—they provided for as among the necessaries of a farmer's life.

Thus they toiled on, till the hill-sides and the valleys every where showed the fenced field and the comfortable dwelling. The spinning wheel was in every house, and the loom in every neighborhood, and almost every article of clothing was the product of female domestic industry. Intercourse with each other was difficult. The hills were steep, and the valleys miry, and the means of conveyance confined to the single horse with saddle and pillion, with no other carriage than the ox-cart in summer and the sled in the winter. The deep winter snows often obstructed even the use of the sled, and then resort was had to snow-shoes. These were made of a light rim of wood bent into the form of an ox-bow, though smaller, perforated and woven into a net work with thongs of raw-hide, leather or deer skin, and when attached to the common shoe enabled the walker to travel upon the surface of the snow. Four-wheeled carriages were not introduced into general use until after the Revolution. Ladies, old and young, thought no more of fatigue in performing long journeys over the rough roads of the County, on horseback, than the ladies of our times in making trips by easy stages, in coaches or cars.

The County Town constituted a common center, where the leading men of the County met during the terms of the Courts, and they saw but little of each other at other times. The course of their business was in different directions. The north-west towns found their markets on the Hudson River—the southern towns at Derby and New Haven—and the eastern ones at Hartford. In the mean while, and before the breaking out of the war of the Revolution, nearly every town had its settled Pastor, and the schools were every where spead over the territory.

No manufacturing interest was prevalent in the County at first. The policy and laws of the mother country had discouraged this. But the rich iron mine which had been early discovered in Salisbury, and the iron ore found in Kent, could not lie neglected. Iron was indispensable, and its transportation from the coast almost impracticable. The ore bed in Salisbury had been granted by the Colonial Assembly to Daniel Bissell of Windsor, as early as 1731, and produces a better quality of iron than any imported from abroad or found elsewhere at home.

The manufacture of bloomed iron in the region of the ore, commenced before the organization of the County. Thomas Lamb erected a forge at Lime Rock, in Salisbury, as early as 1734,—probably the first in the Colony. This experiment was soon extensively followed in Salisbury, Canaan, Cornwall and Kent, and there were forges erected also in Norfolk, Colebrook and Litchfield. The ore was often transported from the ore beds to the forge in leathern sacks, upon horses. Bar iron became here a sort of circulating medium, and promissory notes were more frequently made payable in iron than in money.

The first Furnace in the Colony was built at Lakeville, in Salisbury, in 1762, by John Hazelton and Ethan Allen of Salisbury, and Samuel Forbes of Canaan. This property fell into the hands of Richard Smith, an English gentleman, a little before the war of the Revolution. Upon this event he returned to England, and the State took possession of the furnace, and it was employed, under the agency of Col. Joshua Porter, in the manufacture of cannon, shells and shot, for the use of the army and navy of the country, and sometimes under the supervision of Governeur Morris and John Jay, agents of the Continental Congress; and after the war, the navy of the United States received, to a considerable extent, the guns for its heaviest ships, from the same establishment.

It will not be any part of my purpose to become the Ecclesiastical historian of the County. This duty will be better performed by other pens. And yet, the true character and condition of a people can not be well understood without some study of their religious state.

I have already suggested, that there was here a more tolerant and better spirit than existed among the first emigrants to Plymouth and Massachusetts. The churches were insulated, and in a manner shut out from the disturbing causes which had agitated other portions of the Colony. I do not learn from that full and faithful chronicler of religious dissensions, Dr. Trumbull, that there was in this County so much of the metaphysical and subtle in theology, as had produced such bitter effects at an earlier time, in the churches at Hartford, New Haven, Stratford and Wallingford. The Pastors were men of peace, who had sought the retired parishes over here in the hills and valleys, without much pride of learning, and without ambitious views. The influence of the Pastor here was paternal; the eloquence of his example was more potent than the eloquence of the pulpit. It might be expected, that by such a Clergy, a deep and broad foundation of future good would be laid,—

a fixed Protestant sentiment and its legitimate consequence, independent opinion and energetic action.

There was here, also, very early, another element which modified and liberalized the temper of the fathers, who had smarted, as they supposed, under the persecutions of an English home and English laws. A little alloy was intermixed in the religious crucible, which, if it did not, in the opinion of all, render the mass more precious, at least made it more malleable, and better fitted for practical use. There was not in this Country an universal dislike of the Chuch of England. We were removed farther back in point of time, as I have said, from the original causes of hostility. We were Englishmen, boasting of English Common Law as our birthright and our inheritance, and into this was interwoven many of the principles and usages of English Ecclesiastical polity. This respect for the institutions of the mother country, though long felt by some, was first developed in the College, and extended sooner and more widely in this County than any where else; so that congregations worshiping with the Liturgy of the English Church were soon found in Woodbury, Watertown, Plymouth, Harwinton, Litchfield, Kent, Sharon and Salisbury, and were composed of men of equal intelligence and purity of character with their neighbors of the Congregational Churches. And yet, enough of traditional prejudice still remained, uncorrected by time or impartial examinations, often to subject the friends and members of the Church of England to insult and injustice. Some of it remains still but too little to irritate or disturb a Christian spirit.

The spirit of emigration, that same Anglo-Saxon temperament which brought our ancestors into the County, and which constantly pushes forward to the trial of unknown fortune, began its manifestitations before the Revolution, and sought its gratification first in Vermont. Vermont is the child of this County. We gave to her her first Governor, and three Governors besides; as many as three Senators in Congress, and also many of her most efficient founders and early distinguished citizens,—Chittendens, Allens, Galushas, Chipmans, Skinner and others. The attitude assumed by Vermont in the early stages of the Revolutionary War, in respect to Canada on the north and the threatening States of New York and New Hampshire on either side, was peculiar and delicate, and demanded the most adroit policy to secure her purpose of independence. In her dilemma, her most sagacious men resorted to the counsels of their old friends of Litchfield County, and it is said that her final course was shaped, and her designs accomplished, by the advice of a confidential council, assembled at the house of Governor Wolcott in this village.

Perhaps no community ever existed, with fewer causes of disturbance or discontent than were felt here, before the complaints of British exaction were heard from Boston. But the first murmurings from the East excited our quiet population to action, and in nearly every town in the County, meetings of sympathy were holden, and strong resolves adopted, responsive to the Boston complainings. The tax on tea and the stamp duty were trifles. The people of this County knew nothing of them, and probably cared no more. The principle of the movement was deeper—more fundamental; the love of self government—"the glorious privilege of being independent!" The excitement was general throughout the Country. Individuals opposed it, and from different, though equally pure motives. Some supposed resistance to the laws to be hopeless at that time, and advised to wait for more strength and resources; others were influenced by religious considerations, just as pure and as potent as had influenced their fathers aforetime; others had a deeper seated sense of loyalty, and the obligations of sworn allegiance. But the County was nearly unanimous in its resistance to British claims, and saw in them the commencement of a Colonial servitude, degrading, and threatening the future progress of the country, in its destined path to wealth and glory. I believe no individual of distinction in the County took arms against the cause of the country.

Our remote position from the scenes of strife and the march of armies, will not permit me to speak to you of battle-fields, of victories won or villages sacked any where in our sight. We were only in the pathway between the different wings of the American army. I have no means of determining the amount of force in men or money furnished by this County in aid of the war. From the tone of the votes and resolves passed at the various town-meetings, and from the many officers and men, Continental and militia, who joined the army, I may venture the assertion, that no county in New England, of no greater population than this, gave more efficient aid in various ways, or manifested by its acts, more devoted patriotism.

Sheldon's was, I believe, the first regiment of cavalry which joined the army. It was raised in this County chiefly, and commanded by Col. Elisha Sheldon of Salisbury. The services of this regiment have been favorably noticed by the writers of that day, and on various occasions called forth the public thanks of the Commander-in-Chief. Among other officers attached to it, was Major Benjamin Tallmadge, afterwards and for many years a distinguished merchant and gentleman of this village, and, for several sessions, a valuable member of Congress in the Connecticut delegation. Major Tallmadge distinguished himself by a brilliant exploit against the enemy on Long Island, for which he received the public approbation of General Washington; and through the whole struggle, this officer proved himself a favorite with the army and the officers under whom he served. Besides these, several other officers of elevated as well as subordinate rank, were attached to the Continental army, from this County. Among them were Col. Heman Swift of Cornwall, Major Samuel Elmore of Sharon, Col. Seth Warner of Woodbury, Major Moses Seymour of Litchfield,

Major John Webb of Canaan, Capt. John Sedgwick and Edward Rogers of Cornwall, Col. Blagden and Major Luther Stoddard of Salisbury, and many others not now recollected.

Contributions in support of the war were not confined to the payment of heavy taxes, but voluntary aid came from associations and individuals in every town. The aggregate can not be computed,—if it could, it would show an amount, which, rich as we now are, I think could not be demanded of our citizens for any cause of patriotism or philanthropy without murmurs, and perhaps, resistance.

Nor was the Patriot spirit confined to men and soldiers,—it warmed the bosoms of wives, mothers and sisters, in every town. An equestrian statue of the King, of gilded lead, before the war, had stood upon the Bowling Green in New York. As soon as the news of the signing of the Declaration of Independence reached New York, this was missing. Ere long it was found at the dwelling-house of Hon. Oliver Wolcott, in this village, and in time of need was melted down into the more appropriate shape of forty thousand bullets, by the daughters of that gentleman and other ladies, and forwarded to the soldiery in the field. Other ladies still, and in other towns, were much employed in making blankets and garments for the suffering troops.

I have no means of determining the number of killed and wounded soldiers belonging to this County.

Mr. Matthews, the Mayor of the city of New York, was for some time detained in this village, a prisoner of war, and it is said that his traveling trunk, and some parts of his pleasure carriage, still remain in possession of the Seymour family. Governor Franklin, the Royal Governor of New Jersey, and a son of Dr. Benjamin Franklin, was confined as a prisoner of war in our jail which was often used to detain English prisoners as well as Tories.

Although the treaty of peace brought peace to other parts of the State, it did not bring it to the whole of this County. One town was left,—not to the continued and merciless inroads of British soldiers and savage Indians, as before, but to the unjust oppressions of Pennsylvania,—Westmoreland, better known to the readers of Indian tragedy by the name of *Wyoming*. Its history is one of melancholy interest. This territory is in the valley and region of the Susquehanna River, and included the present flourishing village of Wilkesbarre. Its extent was as broad as this State. It was supposed to be embraced within our chartered limits, and such was the opinion of the most eminent counsel in England and in the Colony. Under this claim, a company associated about the year 1754, by the name of the Susquhanna Company, and purchased the Indian title to the country, for two thousand pounds, New York currency. This was a voluntary movement,—a people's enterprise, unsanctioned by any direct Legislative act, but unforbidden, and probably encouraged. Within a few years, a settlement was ef-

TEARING DOWN STATUE OF GEORGE III.

fected upon the choice lands of the Susquehanna, chiefly by emigrants from the counties of Windham and New London, with several from this County, among whom was John Franklin of Canaan, the brother of the late Silas Franklin, Esq., of that town, a gentleman whose fortune and history were closely interwoven with the fortunes of that colony. The Authorities of Pennsylvania, though claiming under a later Charter, opposed this settlement, and kept up a continual annoyance until the breaking out of the war with England, and even then sympathized but little with our people there, under the dreadful afflictions which that event brought upon them.

Sad indeed was the condition of the colonists of Wyoming!—persecuted by their Pennsylvania neighbors, and left defenceless to the ravages of British troops and their savage allies! The Legislature of this Colony recognized this interesting band of its own children, and incorporated them into a township, by the name of Westmoreland, in 1774, and annexed it to the County of Litchfield. They would have been protected from the aggressions of Pennsylvania, if the war of the Revolution had not prevented, and the *good Friends* of that Commonwealth would have been compelled to doff the Quaker a while, or quietly to have left our fellow-citizens in peace. Under the protection of their parent power, this little colony now looked for security. They were a town of the Connecticut Colony, organized with Selectmen and other ordinary Town Officers, and semi-annually sent their Deputies to the General Court at Hartford and New Haven; chose their Jurors to attend the Courts of this County, and their Justices of the Peace were magistrates of the County of Litchfield, and all writs and process. served there, were returnable to the Courts of this County, and remain now upon our records. But their security was transient: the war of the Revolution brought down upon them a combined force of British Provincials and Tories, from Pennsylvania, New Jersey and New York, and a large body of Indians, commanded by Brant, a celebrated chief. This whole force was directed by Col. John Butler, of infamous memory.

I have no leisure to describe, in its details, the progress of the tragedy of the Wyoming massacre. Cols. John Franklin and Zebulon Butler were conspicious in their efforts to avert the sad destiny of the citizens. It was in vain. The battle opened on the 3d day of July, 1778, and it closed with the entire destruction of the settlement. Men, women and children, whether in arms or defenceless, were devoted to the bayonet and scalping knife, and such as were so fortunate as to escape, were driven away, houseless and homeless, many of them to be dragged from their hiding places to the slaughter, and others to escape after many perils by the way. That massacre was without a likeness in modern warfare, and a stain upon the English character, for which English historians have found no apology.

"Accursed Brant! he left of all my tribe
Nor man, nor child, nor any thing of living birth;
No,—not the dog that watch'd my household hearth
Escaped that night, upon our plains,—all perished!"

Men, maidens, widowed mothers and helpless infants, flying from this scene of death, are remembered by many still living, passing on foot and on horseback through this County, back to their friends here and to the eastern towns. Such was the fate of a portion of the citizens of our own County. Nine years Wyoming had been a part of us, and after the war was over, Pennsylvania renewed her claims and her oppressions. Our Pilgrim fathers could recount no such afflictions! Our jurisdiction ceased in 1782, after a decision by a Board of Commissioners; but a great portion of those who had survived the conflict with the Indians, gathered again around the ruins of their former habitations, and still refused submission to the claims of Pennsylvania. Col. Franklin was the master spirit of resistance, and upon him fell the weight of vengance. He was arrested, imprisoned, and condemed to death as a traitor. After a long confinement in jail, he was at length released, and survived many years, and was a respectable and influential member of the General Assembly of Pennsylvania, from the County of Luzerne.

The result of the compromise of our claim to the town of Westmoreland, was the acknowledgment, by Congress, of the claim of Connecticut to the Western Reserve, from which has been derived the School Fund of the State.

The war of the Revolution had ceased, and left us an exhausted people. The extravagant hopes of many were disappointed: they felt the present pressure, but anticipated none of the future prosperity and glory in reserve. This disappointment, in a neighboring State, had produced open resistence to the laws,—rebellion! It was a contagious spirit, and such as municipal lines could not confine. Much was feared from it here. A spark from that flame in Berkshire county had flown over into Sharon. One Dr. Hurlbut, an emissary of Shay's, visited that town, in the spring of 1787, to enlist men in his cause. He made some impression. The General Assembly was then in session, and took efficient measures to prevent the spread of the treasonable contagion. Col. Samuel Canfield, of New Milford, and Uriah Tracy, of this village, were sent to suppress it. Several individuals were arrested and imprisoned in the jail of this County; but, as the disturbance in the sister State subsided, the advocates of resistance to the laws were disheartened, the prosecutions were finally abandoned, and these disciples of the treasonable doctrine of resistance were permitted to go at large, punished enough by the contempt which followed them.

Although the resources of our citizens had been consumed by a wasting war and a bankrupt government, the elasticity of our

Col. Samuel Canfield.

former enterprise was not relaxed. Released, now, from Colonial dependence, and free to act without foreign restrictions, the energies of our citizens soon recovered all they had lost. A Constitution of Government, uniting the former Colonies into a great nation, was proposed to the State for adoption; and, in January, 1787, a convention of deligates from the several towns met at Hartford to consider it. The votes of the deligates from this County, upon this great question, stood, twenty-two in the affirmative, and nine in the negative. The negative votes were from Cornwall, Norfolk, and Sharon. Harwinton, New Hartford, and Torrington were divided.

No portion of the country sooner revived under the new impulse, given by the establishment of a National Constitutional Government, than this County. Our resources were varied. Our soil was every where strong on the hills and by the streams. Various sections possessed their peculiarities of production. Wheat was a staple of the western towns. Dairy products were yielded in abundance in the northern and central regions; and, in almost every location, every species of grass, fruit, and grain, indigenous to any northern latitude, by reasonable culture, was found to flourish. We were rich in the most useful mineral in the world, and our streams of purest water afforded privileges every where for converting our ores into iron and our forests into building materials. But we had more—that, without which, all these were worthless; we had an industrious, and what was better, an *economical* and an intelligent yeomanry. We had a few slaves, to be sure; not enough of these, nor enough of a degraded foreign population to render the toil of our own hands, in the fields, or of our wives or daughters, in the kitchen or the dairy, dishonored or disgraceful. Our people were Native Americans! And here is the secret of our prosperity and progress.

In 1784 the first newspaper press was established in this County by Thomas Collier, and was continued under his superintendence for more than twenty years. It was called the "Weekly Monitor." It was a well conducted sheet, and it is refreshing now, after the lapse of many years, to look through its columns, as through a glass, and see the men of other days, as they have spoken and acted on the same ground on which we stand. Mr. Collier was an able writer. and his editorial efforts would have done honor to any journal. It is a Litchfield monitor now, and whoever shall look over its files will see, at a glance, the great changes which have been introduced, in later days, into all the departments of business and of social and political life.

Then, the intercourse between the several towns in this County and the market towns was slow and difficult. The Country merchants were the great brokers, and stood between the farmer and the markets. They received all his produce and supplied all he wished to buy. The thrifty farmer, on settlement, received his annual balance from the merchant. This enabled him to increase his acres. He did not invest it in stocks; of these he knew nothing, except such as he had seen attached as instruments of punishment, to the whipping post in every town.

The merchants, thus employed, almost all became wealthy. A broken merchant in the County was seldom heard of. Among the most successful and respectable of these gentlemen, whom I now recollect, were Julius Deming and Benjamin Tallmadge, of this town; Tallmadge, of Warren; Bacon, of Woodbury; Leavitts', of Bethlem and Washington; Starr, Norton, and Lymans', of Goshen; Battel, of Norfolk; King, of Sharon; Holley, of Salisbury, and Elijah Boardman, of New Milford, afterwards a highly respectable Senator in the Congress of the United States. At that time, Derby was the chief market town for many of the merchants in the southern towns of the County.

The age of Turnpike Roads commenced about the year 1800, and no portion of the country was more improved by them than this County. Before this, a journey through the Green Woods was spoken of as an exploit,—a region now accommodated by the most pleasant road in the County. The roads constructed, about the same time, from New Haven to Canaan, from Sharon to Goshen, and from Litchfield to Hartford, changed very much the aspect of the County and its current of business, and if they have not been profitable to stockholders, they have been invaluable to the people.

The spur given to agriculture by the wars following the French Revolution was felt in every thing. If our farmers have failed in any thing, it has been in a proper appreciation of their own calling. They have yielded a preference to other employments, to which they are not entitled. If we are to have an Aristocracy in this country, I say, let the farmers and business men, and not our idlers, be our Princes!—not such as are ashamed of their employments and withdraw their sons from the field and their daughters from domestic labor. I would have no such to rule over me. But, in spite of some such false notions, agriculture has kept pace even with other branches of industry in the County, as the appearance of our farms and the thrift of our farmers attest. Much of this may be attributed to an Agricultural Society, which was formed here several years ago, and has been well sustained until this time.

I have alluded to the condition of manufactures as it was before the Revolution—limited to iron and confined to the furnace in Salisbury and a few forges in that vicinity; to which may be added, the manufacture of maple sugar, to some extent by the farmers in some of the towns.

Even a few years ago, this County was not believed to be destined to become a manufacturing community. During the Revolutionary War, Samuel Forbes, Esq., commenced a most important experiment in Canaan—the manufacture of nail rods. Before this, nails were hammered out from the bar iron—a slow and expensive process.

There was a slitting-mill in New Jersey, in which nail rods were made, but the machinery was kept hidden from public inspection. Forbes wished to obtain a knowledge of it, and for this purpose employed an ingenious mechanic and millwright, Isaac Benton, of Salisbury. Benton, disguised as a traveling mendicant, obtained admission to the mill, and so critically, and without suspicion, marked the machinery and its operation, as to be able immediately to make such a model of it as to construct a mill, of the same sort, for Forbes. This was the foundation of his great fortune in after life. He afterwards erected another slitting-mill in Washington, (now Woodville.) By these he was able to supply the great demand for this article. This was a great improvement upon the former mode of nail-making, but was itself superseded, some years afterwards, by the introduction of cut nail machinery. Esquire Forbes, as he was afterwards familiarly called by every body, may justly be deemed the pioneer of the manufacturing interests in this County. His efforts were confined, generally, to the working of iron. His forge he extended, and accommodated to the manufacturing of anchors, screws, and mill irons. He introduced this branch of the iron business into this County, if not into the State. It was not long after followed by those enterprising manufacturers, Russell Hunt & Brothers, at South Canaan, by whom the largest anchors for the largest ships of the American Navy were made.

The manufacture of scythes by water-power, was commenced in this County first at Winsted, by Jenkins & Boyd, in 1794. These enterprising gentlemen, with the brothers Rockwell, soon extensively engaged in various branches of the manufacture of iron and steel in Winsted and that vicinity, from which originated, and has grown up to its present condition, one of the most flourishing manufacturing villages in the State.

The furnace, in Salisbury, continued for many years in most successful operation under its active proprietors, and especially its last owners, Messrs. Holley & Coffing, by whose energy and success, the iron interest, in Salisbury, has been most essentially promoted; and it has extended into the towns of Canaan, Cornwall. Sharon, and Kent. Ames' works, at Falls Village, are not equalled by any other in the State.

In speaking of the iron interest, I cannot but allude again to the Salisbury iron ore, which is found in various localities in that town. It stands superior to any other for the tenacity of the iron which it produces, with which the armories of Springfield and Harper's Ferry are supplied, and from which the chain cables and best anchors for the Navy are made. And I am confident, if the machinery of the steam vessels and railroad cars were made exclusively from this iron, and not from a cheaper and inferior material, we should know less of broken shafts and loss of life in our public conveyances.

Paper was first made in this County, at the great Falls of the

Housatonic, in Salisbury, by Adam & Church, as early as 1787, and soon after in Litchfield. The first carding-machine erected, I think, in this State, was built at the great falls in Canaan, about 1802. Previous to this time, wool was carded only by females, at their own firesides.

A general manufacturing policy was suggested by the measures of government, and not long after a more extensive experiment was made in the manufacture of woolen cloths by the late Gov. Wolcott, and his brother Hon. Frederick Wolcott of this place, than had been made in this County before; and although the trial was disastrous to its projectors, it was the parent of the subsequent and present prosperity of the village of Wolcottville.

The same policy has spread into almost every town in the County, and has not only extended the manufacture of iron, from a mouse trap to a ship's anchor, but has introduced, and is introducing, all the various branches of manufactures pursued in this country; and of late, the elegant manufacture of the Papier Mache. Plymouth, New Hartford, Norfolk, Woodbury, as well as the towns before mentioned, have felt extensively the beneficial effects of this modern industrial progress, so that our County may now be set down as one of the first manufacturing Counties in the State; and this confirms what I have said, that here are all the varied facilities of profitable employment, which can be found in any section or region o fthis country. Our young men need no longer seek adventure and fortune elsewhere! Neither the desire of wealth, nor the preservation of health and life, should suggest emigration.

As soon as the war was over, and the Indians subdued into peace, our people rushed again to Vermont, and to the Whitestown and Genesee countries, as they were called; so that, in a few years, let a Litchfield County man go where he would, between the top of the Green Mountains and Lake Champlain, or between Utica and the Lakes, and every day he would greet an acquaintance or citizen from his own County.

And then followed the sale and occupation of the Connecticut Western Reserve. Many of its original proprietors were our citizens; and among them, Messrs. Boardman, of New Milford; Holmes, Tallmadge, and Wadsworth, of Litchfield; Starr and Norton, of Goshen; Canfield, of Sharon; Johnston, Church, and Waterman, of Salisbury. For a time it seemed as if depopulation was to follow. The towns of Boardman, Canfield, Tallmadge, Johnson, Hudson, and several others on the reserve, were soon filling up with the best blood and spirit of our County; and since then, we have been increasing the population of other parts of the States of New York and Ohio, as well as of Michigan, Illinois, and Indiana, so that now there is not one of us who remain, who has not a parent, a brother, or a child, in New York, Vermont, or the States of the West. And we believe that these children of our own raising, have transmitted the impress and image of Litchfield County, to the general condition of society where they have gone, and that they have fixed there a moral likeness which proves its parentage. This emigrating propensity has characterized the Saxon race in all times of its history; and it is still at work, scattering us into every corner and climate, and away to dig for gold and graves in the barrens of California! Notwithstanding this exhausting process of emigration, our population which, in the year 1800, was 41,671, has increased to the number of 46,171.

I do not know that before the Revolution there was a public Grammar School in the County. The preparatory studies of young men, intended for collegiate course, were prosecuted with private instructors—generally, the Clergy; and this course was pursued still later.

Among the clergymen of the County most distinguished as instructors, and in *fitting* young men for college, as it was called, were Rev. Daniel Farrand, of Canaan, Ammi R. Robbins, of Norfolk, Judah Champion, of Litchfield, and Azel Backus, D. D., of Bethlem. This last named gentleman was afterwards President of Hamilton College.

Soon after the war, Academies were instituted, and among the first and best of them was the Morris Academy in the parish of South Farms, in this town, which was commenced in 1790, by James Morris, Esq. Esquire Morris was no ordinary man. He was a distinguished graduate of Yale College, and an active officer in the Revolutionary Army. His learning was varied and practical, and under his direction the Morris Academy became the most noted public school of the County, and so continued for many years. An Academy at Sharon, not long after, acquired a deserved reputation, under such instructors as John T. Peters, Elisha Sterling, and Barzillai Slosson. Many years afterwards an Academy was conducted in Ellsworth Society, in the same town, under the superintendence of Rev. Daniel Parker, which soon attained a high reputation.

Our relative position in the State, and the controlling influence of the cities, have left us without College, Asylum, or Retreats; but our district schools have been doing their proper work, so that Judge Reeve remarked while alive, that he had never seen but one witness in Court, born in this County, who could not read. And these schools have not only made scholars, *but school-masters,* and these have been among the best of our indigenous productions, and have found a good market every where. When Congress sat in Philadelphia, a Litchfield County man was seen driving a drove of mules through the streets. A North Carolina member congratulated the late Mr. Tracy upon seeing so many of his constituents that morning, and enquired where they were going, to which he facetiously replied, that they were going *to North Carolina to keep school.*

A new tone to female education was given by the establishment of a Female Seminary, for the instruction of females in this village, by Miss Sarah Pierce, in 1792. This was an untried experiment. Hitherto the education of young ladies, with few exceptions, had been neglected. The district school had limited their course of studies. Miss Pierce saw and regretted this, and devoted herself and all of her active life to the mental and moral culture of her sex. The experiment succeeded entirely. This Acedemy soon became the resort of young ladies from all portions of the country—from the cities and the towns. Then, the country was preferred, as most suitable for female improvement, away from the frivolities and dissipation of fashionable life. Now, a different, not a better practice, prevails. Many of the grandmothers and mothers of the present generation were educated as well for gentel as for useful life, in this school, and its influence upon female character and accomplishments was great and extensive. It continued for more than forty years, and its venerable Principal and her sister assistant now live among us, the honored and honorable of their sex.

Before this, and as early as 1784, a Law School was instituted in this village. Tapping Reeve, then a young lawyer from Long Island, who had commenced the practice of his profession here, was its projector. It is not known whether in this country, or any where, except at the Inns of Court at Westminster, a school for the training of lawyers had been attempted. No Professorships of Law had been introduced into American Colleges; nor was the Law treated as a liberal science.

Before this, the law student served a short clerkship in an attorney's office,—studied some forms and little substance, and had within his reach but few volumes beyond Coke's & Wood's Institutes. Blackstone's Commentaries, Bacon's Abridgment, and Jacob's Law Dictionary, and, when admitted to the Bar, was better instructed in pleas in abatement, than in the weightier matters of the Law. Before this, too, the Common Law, as a system, was imperfectly understood here and in our sister States. Few lawyers had mastered it. The reputation of this institution soon became as extensive as the country, and young men from Maine to Georgia sought to finish their law studies here.

Judge Reeve conducted this school alone, from its commencement until 1798, when, having been appointed to the Bench of the Superior Court, he associated with him, as an instructor, James Gould, Esq. These gentlemen conducted the school together for several years, until the advanced age of Judge Reeve admonished him to retire; after which, Judge Gould continued the school alone until a few years before his death. It may be said of Judge Reeve, that he first gave the Law a place among liberal studies in this country,—that "he found it a skeleton, and clothed it with life, color, and complexion." This school gave a new impulse to legal learning and it was felt in the Jurisprudence as well as in the Legislation of all the States.

A new subject of study, not known in any other country, had been presented to the legal student here,—the Constitution of the United States and the Legislation of Congress. Uniformity of interpretation was indispensable.

At this institution students from every State drank from the same fountain, were taught the same principles of the Common and Constitutional Law; and these principles, with the same modes of legal thinking and feeling and of administration were disseminated throughout the entire country. More than one thousand lawyers of the United States were educated here, and many of them afterwards among the most eminent Jurists and Legislators. Even after Judge Gould's connection with the school, an inspection of the catalogue will show, that from it have gone out among the States of this Union, a Vice President of the United States, two Judges of the Supreme Court of the United States, forty Judges of the highest State Courts, thirteen Senators, and forty-six Representatives in Congress, besides several Cabinet and Foreign Ministers.

I have said that this school gave a new impulse to legal learning in this country. Soon after its establishment, and not before, reports of judicial decisions appeared. Ephraim Kirby, Esq an able lawyer of this village, published the first volume of Reports of Adjudged Cases, in this country,—a volume which deserved and received the approbation of the profession here and elsewhere. This was soon followed by Reports in Massachusetts and New York.

Standing at this point of time, and looking back over the events of an hundred years, we would recall, not only the scenes which have transpired, but revive our recollections of the men who have acted in them. Memory cannot raise the dead to life again; yet it may bring back something of their presence,—shaded and dim, but almost real;—and through the records of their times we may hear them speak again. To some of these I have made allusion. I would speak of others.

The allusion to the Law School of the County suggests to me a brief notice, also, of the legal profession here, and of its most distinguished members, as well as a further allusion to others of the sons of Litchfield County, distinguished in other professions and employments of life. In speaking of these I must confine myself to the memory of the dead. And here, I feel that I am under a restraint which, on any other occasion, I would resist. I feel this chain which binds me, the more as I look around on this gathering and see some here, and am reminded of others—so many, who have contributed by splendid talents and moral worth, to make our name a praise in the land. As the representative of the County, I would most gladly do them living homage before you all. I regret that I have had so brief an opportunity to make this notice as perfect as it should be,—a favorite theme, if I could but do it justice.

I have not been able to learn much of the Lawyers who practiced in this territory before the organization of the County in 1751. Samuel Pettibone, Esq., of Goshen, and Reynold Marvin, Esq., of Litchfield, (a native of Lyme,) are all of whom I can speak.

Mr. Pettibone lived to a great age and died in reduced circumstances, in 1787. Mr. Marvin was respectable in his profession, and was King's Attorney at the time of the Revolution. His residence was at the dwelling of Dr. William Buel, in this village.

Among the Lawyers of the new County who appeared in its Courts, were Mr. Thatcher, of New Milford, Hezekiah Thompson and Edward Hinman, of Woodbury, Mr. Humphrey, of Norfolk, John Canfield, of Sharon, Andrew Adams, of Litchfield, Mr. Catlin, of Harwinton, and Joshua Whitney, of Canaan. Of these, Messrs. Canfield and Adams became distinguished at the Bar and in public life. Mr. Canfield was the son of Samuel Canfield, of New Milford, one of the Associate Judges of the County. He was appointed a member of Congress under the Confederation, but died before he took his seat. We can appreciate his character when informed that he was the chosen colleague of Johnson, Ellsworth, and Trumbull. Mr. Adams succeeded Mr. Marvin as State's Attorney. He was esteemed an eloquent advocate, and his reputation at the Bar was distinguished. He was well versed in theological studies, and in the absence of his minister, often officiated in the pulpit. He was a member of the Continental Congress, and after the Revolution, became an Associate, and then Chief Justice of the Superior Court.

Before the Revolution there were but few eminent lawyers in the County, and professional gentlemen from abroad attended our courts and were employed in the most important causes. Among these were Thomas Seymour, Esq., of Hartford, and Hon. Samuel W. Johnson, of Stratford, then standing at the head of the Connecticut Bar. A colonial condition was, as it ever will be, unfavorable to the development of forensic talent.

The change in the state of this Bar, after the War, and especially after the settlement of the government, was sudden and great; and, within a few years after this event, no County in the State and but few in other States, could boast of a Bar more distinguished for legal talent and high profession and moral excellence, than this. Reeve, Tracy, Allen, Kirby, Strong of Salisbury, Smith of Woodbury. Smith and Canfield, of Sharon, are names which revive proud recollections among the old men of the County. And while these gentlemen stood before our courts there came to their company a younger band, destined, with them, to perpetuate the high standing of the profession here;—Gould. Sterling, of Salisbury; Benedict, Ruggles, Boardman, Smith, of Litchfield; Slosson, Southmayd,

Swan, Pettibone, and afterward, Miner, Williams, Bacon, and others.

Tapping Reeve was a native of Long Island, and a distinguished gradute of Nassau Hall, New Jersey, and a tutor in that college. He commenced practice here in 1783, and was one of the most learned lawyers of the day in which he lived. He loved the law as a science, and studied it philosophically. He considered it as the practical application of religious principle to the business affairs of life. He wished to reduce it to a certain, symmetrical system of moral truth. He did not trust to the inspiration of genius for eminence, but to the results of profound and constant study, and was never allured by political ambition. I seem, even now, to see his calm and placid countenance shining through his abundant locks, as he sat, poring over his notes in the lecture room, and to hear his shrill whisper, as he stood when giving his charge to the jury. He was elevated to the Bench of the Superior Court in 1798, and to the office of Chief Justice in 1804, and retired from public life at the age of seventy years and died in 1827. He published a valuable treatise on Domestic Relations, and another on the Law of Descents.

Gen. Uriah Tracy was a native of Norwich, and one of the first of the pupils of Judge Reeve. As a jury advocate he obtained a high distinction. His wit was pungent and his powers of oratory uncommon. He was a politician, often a member of our own Legislature; for several years a member of Congress, and he died in 1807, while a member of the Senate of the United States, in which body he was eminently distinguished.

Col. Adonijah Strong, the father of the late Hon. Martin Strong, was unique in genius and manner, of large professional business, sound practical sense, and many anecdotes of his sayings and doings are still remembered and repeated in the County.

Hon. Nathaniel Smith, of Woodbury, a native of Washington, commenced life under discouraging circumstances. He had neither fortune nor the prospect of any, nor early education, to stimulate him. Like many other New England boys, he fought his way to eminence; and eminent he was; and I cannot tell by what process he became so. He, too, was one of the early members of the Law School here. He was not a man of many books. He seemed to understand the law, as did Mansfield and Marshall, by intuition, and to have acquired the power of language by inspiration. His was a native eloquence yet chaste, and "when unadorned, adorned the most." I think he was one of the most profound lawyers and judges of this country. He was a member of the Council, a member of Congress, and was elevated to the Bench of the Superior Court in 1806.

Hon. Nathan Smith was a younger brother of Nathaniel Smith, and though born and reared in this County, his professional and public life was passed in New Haven County, but he often appeared at this Bar. He was less profound than his brother, more ardent, and perhaps more effective as a jury lawyer. He died, while a Senator in Congress, in 1835.

Hon. John Allen was a native of Massachusetts and instructed by Mr. Reeve, and for several years held a commanding position at this Bar.

Hon. John Cotton Smith, of Sharon, was the son of Rev. Cotton Mather Smith, of that town. A graduate of Yale College and of the Litchfield Law School, he soon took a prominent place by the side of Tracy and Nathaniel Smith at the Bar of the County. He was known as a fluent speaker, and of easy and graceful address; he became a popular advocate. For several sessions of the Legislature of the State he was speaker of the House of Representatives. In Congress he sustained an enviable reputation as a presiding officer. Upon retiring from Congress he was soon placed upon the Bench of the Superior Court, from which he was promoted to the office of Governor of the State. From this he retired, and from public life, in 1817. The remainder of his life was spent in doing good, either as President of the American Bible Society, or in discharging the duties of a virtuous citizen in his native town, until his death in 1845.

Hon. James Gould was a native of Branford, a graduate and a tutor of Yale College. He pursued his professional studies with Judge Reeve, and, soon after coming to the Bar of this County, he became associated with him as an instructor of the Law School. Judge Gould was a critical scholar, and always read with his pen in his hand, whether Law book or books of fiction or fancy, for which he indulged a passion. In the more abstruse subjects of the law, he was more learned than Judge Reeve, and, as a lecturer, more lucid and methodical. The Common Law he had searched to the bottom, and he knew it all—its principles, and the reasons from which they were drawn. As an advocate, he was not a man of impassioned eloquence, but clear and logical, employing language elegant and chaste. He indulged in no wit, and seldom excited a laugh, but was very sure to carry a listener along with him to his conclusions. With his brethren, his intercourse was always courteous, and with his younger ones, kind and affectionate. He never gave offense. In his arguments, he resorted to no artifice, but met the difficulties in his way fully in the face, and if he could not overcome them, he yielded without irritation. He was appointed an Associate Judge of the Superior Court in 1816, and retired from the Bench to private life soon after. Judge Gould published an able treatise on the Law of Pleading, in which he was governed by the truth of Lord Coke's saying, "he knoweth not the law, who knoweth not the reason thereof." His volume has received flattering approval from the most learned Jurists in this country and England. Judge Gould died in 1838.

John Cotton Smith.
From Crayon Sketch, 1800.

Noah B. Benedict was the son of Rev. Noah Benedict, of Woodbury, a gentleman of no precocity of intellect or genius, and his first appearance at the Bar did not promise the eminence which he afterwards acquired. He studied, and the Law was the chief subject of his study. He aspired to no higher place than distinction in his profession. He engaged in none of the ordinary business transactions of society, and, as he once told me, he never gave a promissory note in his life. With such an undivided attention to his professional calling, it was not strange that he should reach a high place at the Bar. And he did reach it, and, at the time of his death, no man here stood before him. His example should be a choice model for young lawyers.

Gen. Elisha Sterling, of Salisbury, was a native of Lyme. No one in our profession was more assiduous in its practice than this gentleman. His causes were never neglected in their preparation. The controlling points of every case he discovered quick, and pressed both, in preparation and argument, with zeal. He neglected the study of method and system in his arguments, but, when concluded, nothing had been omitted.

Passing by, on this hurried occasion, a more particular notice of the galaxy of Lawyers, to whom I have alluded, I may be indulged in paying an affectionate tribute to one or two, whose familiar voices still seem sounding in our Court House.

Hon. Jabez W. Huntington earned his high professional character here, where he commenced and continued his practice for several years. He engaged in public life, and returned to his native town of Norwich. He was elected to Congress; afterwards he was elevated to the Bench of the Superior Court, which place he retained until he was appointed a Senator in Congress, in which position he died in 1847. Having been associated with Judge Huntington at the Bar and on the Bench, I can bear true testimony to his superior abilities in both places.

Of my late brother, Leman Church Esq., the proprieties of my connection will not permit me to speak. The deep sensation produced at this Bar, and the grief which tore the hearts of his numerous friends, when he died, is the only eulogy upon his life and character to which I may refer.

I had a young friend, upon whose opening prospects I looked with anxiety and hope. He was of generous heart and liberal hand and stimulated by an honorable ambition, which seemed nearly at the point of gratification, when death came for its victim. This friend was Francis Bacon, Esq., who died in 1849, at the age of 30 years.

Hon. Oliver Wolcott, the younger, late Governor of this State, was also a member of this Bar, and though he engaged in public life soon after his admission, we are entitled to retain his name on our catalogue. I shall not speak now of his life and eminent services. They make a prominent part of the country's history, and have been, within a few years, faithfully written by his near relative. He died in 1833, and I regret to say that his remains lie in our grave-yard, without a monument to mark his resting place. His bust has been presented, on this occasion, to the Bar of this County.

I make the same claim to retain among the names of our departed brethren, that of Hon. Frederick Wolcott, a son of the elder Gov. Wolcott, of this village. He became a member of this Bar in early life, and with high prospects of professional distinction; but he accepted the proffered office of Clerk of the Courts and Judge of Probate for this district, in 1793, and soon relinquished professional duties. For several years he was a prominent member of the Council, under the Charter administration. An intimate connexion with this gentleman, both public and private, justifies the high opinion I have ever entertained of his purity of life and character, his public spirit, and his frank and open bearing. I never pass by the venerable mansion of the Wolcott family, in my daily walks about this village, without recalling the stately form and ever honorable deportment of Frederick Wolcott. The duties of his official stations were discharged with the entire approbation of the community for many years, and until a short time before his death, and amidst the conflicts and overturnings in the political revolutions of the times.

Roger and Richard Skinner, were sons of Gen. Timothy Skinner of this town, and members of this bar. Roger commenced business in this village, and gave assurance, by his early talents, of his future standing; but he was here in the most bitter state of Connecticut politics, and, as he believed, was compelled to escape from unmerited opposition. He removed to the State of New York; soon attained a deserved eminence in his profession and was appointed a Judge of the United States Court, in the Northern District of that State. Richard Skinner removed to Vermont and afterwards became an eminent Judge of the Superior Court, and ultimately Governor of that State.

In the clerical profession, I have remarked before, that there was early manifested a disposition rather to be good than great. The clergy of this County were nearly all educated men; and many of them ripe scholars and profound divines, and if there were not as many here as in some other regions, whose names have been transmitted to us as among the great ones of New England, it has been because the severer calls of parochial duty, and stinted means, and Christian graces, restrained their aspirations after fame. Divinity has furnished the most common theme and employed the most pens. We are all theolgians in New England.

Rev. Joseph Bellamy, D. D., of Bethlem, was probably the first and most eminent of our writers on this subject. He was eloquent and impressive as a preacher, as well as learned and profound as a scholar and writer. He published several theological works upon practical and controversial subjects, besides occasional sermons, which are found in the libraries of Divines, and have been held in high repute, not only among the disciples of his own peculiar opinions, but among others, as well in Europe as in this country; and a modern edition of them has been recently published. Dr. Bellamy was the grandfather of the late Joseph H. Bellamy, Esq., of Bethlem, a gentleman of great moral and professional worth.

Rev. Jna. Edwards was a pupil of Dr. Bellamy in his theological studies, and, although not a native of this County, he resided among us for several years, as the first settled minister of Colebrook, and until he was called to the presidency of Union College, in 1799. He was the author of several volumes of great merit; and among them, a treatise upon the salvation of all men, in reply to Dr. Chauncey; also, a dissertation on the liberty of the will in reply to West, and observations on the language of the Stockbridge Indians.

Rev. Chauncey Lee, D. D., who succeeded Dr. Edwards, as minister in Colebrook, was a native of Salisbury, and a son of Rev. Jonathan Lee, of that town. He was educated for the bar, and commenced practice in his native town. This he soon relinquished for the clerical calling. Very early he published a Decimal Arithmetic and afterwards a volume of Sermons on various subjects. But his most elaborate work, and the one most esteemed by himself, was a poem, entitled "The Trial of Virtue," being a paraphrase of the book of Job. Dr. Lee was a gentleman of some eccentricities, but a very learned divine and impressive preacher.

Rev. Samuel J. Mills, a native of Torrington, and son of the venerable pastor of one of the societies there, is entitled to a more extended notice than I am prepared on this occasion to repeat. Not because he was the author of books, but the author and originator of liberal and extensive benevolent effort. The noble cause of Foreign Missions in this country, is deeply indebted to him as one of its most zealous and active projectors and friends. Another of the most splendid charities of any age or country,—the Colonization Society,—owes its existence to the efforts of this gentleman; and his name will be cherished by the philanthropists of the world, along with those of Howard and Wilberforce.

Rev. Horace Holley, D. D., of Salisbury, was son of Mr. Luther Holley, and one of a highly distinguished and worthy family of brothers. Dr. Holley was first ordined pastor of a Church and Society at Greenfield, in Fairfield County, and was one of the successors of the late Dr. Dwight, in that parish. He subsequently removed to Boston, and became one of the most eloquent pulpit orators among the eminent divines of that metropolis. He afterwards became President of Transylvania University in Kentucky, and died, while yet a young man on ship-board, when on his return from New Orleans to New England. I am not informed that he left any published works behind him, except sermons delivered on special occasions. He was my class-mate in College, and I knew him well.

The Rev. Dr. Backus of Bethlem, Rev. Mr. Hooker of Goshen, and Rev. Dr. Porter of Washington, are remembered as among the most learned Divines of the County.

Of the Medical Profession and the Medical Professors here, my opportunities of information have not been extensive. And yet I have known enough of them to persuade me that a more learned and useful faculty, has not been found elsewhere in the State. Empiricism has always existed, and will exist; and the credulity of some good men will give it countenance. We depend upon a learned medical influence, more than any thing else, to save us from its death-dealing results.

As early as January, 1767, a Medical association was formed in this County, composed of the most eminent physicians then in practice here. Its object was to establish rules of practice and intercourse;—promote medical science by providing for annual consultations and dissertations, and to protect the reputation of the profession and the health of the community, from the inroads of ignorant pretenders to medical science. Among the names of the gentlemen composing this body, I see those of Joshua Porter, Lemuel Wheeler, Joseph Perry, Seth Bird, William Abernethy, Samuel Catlin, Simeon Smith, Cyrus Marsh, Ephraim Gitteau, John Calhoun, &c. One of the earliest physicians of the County was Oliver Wolcott. He was the son of Hon. Roger Wolcott, of Windsor, a former Governor of the Colony. He had served as an officer in the French war, and settled himself in Goshen before the organization of the County, in the practice of his profession. Whether he continued in practice as a physician after his removal to this town is not known; probably, however, his official duties as Sheriff prevented it. He was subsequently honored with almost every official place which a good man would covet,—he was a member of the House of Representatives, of the Council, a Judge of Probate, a Judge of the County Court, a Representative in Congress, a signer of the Declaration of Independence, Lieutenant Governor, and Governor of his native State, and more than all, the father of an excellent family. He is said to have been a man of uncommon diffidence, and distrustful of his own ability. His public communications display sound judgment, and his more confidential correspondence a warm affection and a pure purpose.

Dr. Seth Bird, of Litchfield, probably held the first place among the early physicians of the County. His reputation was wide-spread. For acuteness of discrimination and soundness of judgment he was not excelled.

Dr. Joseph Perry, of Woodbury, was not only eminent in his profession, but, what was unusual in his day, he excelled as a belles-lettre scholar and was a gentleman well read in various branches of science. Later generations produced their eminent and accomplished physicians. Dr. Nathaniel Perry, son of the gentleman just named; Dr. Daniel Sheldon, of this town; Drs. Fowler of Washington, Rockwell of Sharon, Welch of Norfolk Ticknor of Salisbury.

Dr. Samuel Woodward, of Torrington, was not only a physician of high repute himself, but he was almost literally a father of the faculty. Dr. Samuel B. Woodword, late of Worcester, Massachusetts, Dr. Henry Woodward, late of Middletown, and Dr. Charles Woodward, of the same place, were his sons,—born and educated in this County. Few men in any community have attained a more eminent and useful position than Dr. Samuel B. Woodward. Under his superintendance the Insane Hospital, at Worcester, was established and for many years conducted and now sustains a reputation equal with any of the noble charities of this country. The Annual Reports of Dr. Woodward and his other professional writings, and the success of his efforts in the cause of humanity, have earned for him a reputation which will long survive.

Among the Surgeons of note, in earlier times was Dr. Samuel Catlin, of Litchfield, and at a later period, Dr. Samuel R. Gager, of Sharon.

The medical profession in this County has produced some writers of respectability. Dr. Elisha North was for several years a physician of extensive practice in Goshen, and he afterwards removed to New London. He published an approved treatise on spotted fever, which extensively prevailed in Goshen and its vicinity, while he resided there.

Dr. Caleb Ticknor of Salisbury, was brother of the late excellent Dr. Luther Ticknor, of that town, and of Dr. Benajah Ticknor, for many years a surgeon in the navy of the United States; and although a young man when he removed to New York City, about the year 1832, he rose rapidly to a high place in his profession. He published several medical works, the most popular of which was, the Philosophy of Living, which constitutes one of the volumes of Harpers' Family Library.

The Chipman family, a numerous brotherhood, removed from Salisbury to Vermont immediately after the Revolutionary War; it produced eminent men. Nathaniel was an officer of the Revolution. He became Chief Justice of Vermont, and a Senator in Congress. He published a small volume of Judicial Reports and a larger treatise upon the Principles of Government. Daniel Chipman, a younger brother of this gentleman, was a very prominent member of the Vermont Bar. He was the author of a very creditable essay "On the Law of Contracts"; and besides a volume of Law Reports, he published the life of his brother Nathaniel, and also the life of Gov. Thomas Chittenden.

Hon. Ambrose Spencer, late Chief Justice of the State of New York, was born in Salisbury, the son of Philip Spencer, Esq, He was prepared for his collegiate course under the instruction of Rev. Daniel Farrand, of Canaan; studied the law, I believe, with Hon. John Canfield, of Sharon; whose daughter he married.

Hon. Josiah S. Johnston, late an eminent member of the Senate of the United States, from Louisania, was a native of the same town. He was the son of Dr. John Johnston, who removed early to Kentucky. His academical studies were pursued here.

Samuel Moore, of Salisbury, was a profound mathmatician and engaged much in the instruction of young men in what was called the surveyor's art. He published a treatise on surveying, with a table of logarithms. It was the earliest work on that branch of mathematical science published in this country. It introduced the method of computing contents by calculation entirely, without measuring triangles by scale and dividers. It was a valuable treatise, but was nearly superseded by a more finished one by Rev. Abel Flint, in which he borrowed much from Moore.

Ethan Allen is deserving of notice only for his revolutionary services, which are matters of public history. He published a narrative of his captivity as a prisoner of war, and a volume of Infield Theology. He was a native of this county; the town of his nativity has been a matter of dispute, but is not a question worth solving.

We have had Poets, too, besides such as I have mentioned, who deserve a remembrance on this occasion.

Hon. John Trumbull, late one of the Judges of the Superior Court of the State, was born in Watertown in this County, in which his father was a minister. The Progress of Dulness, and McFingal, the most admired of his Poems, were written in early life. They are satyrical productions, and for genuine wit have not been excelled by any modern effort. Judge Trumbull's active life was passed chiefly in Hartford.

William Ray was a Salisbury man, born in 1771, and while a lad developed a taste for poetry but early destitution and misfortunes pressed upon him drove him into the Navy of the United States. He was for some time a captive in Tripoli, and in 1808 he published the Horrors of Slavery, and in 1821 a volume of Poems.

Ebenezer P. Mason was a native of Washington. Very few men gave more early promise of literary and scientific distinction than young Mason. His life and writings were published in 1842, by Professor Olmsted, of Yale College.

VIEW OF THE CENTENNIAL CELEBRATION AT LITCHFIELD—1851.

Washington has been a nursery of eminent men, of whom I cannot now speak without violating my purpose of speaking of the dead, and not of the living.

Mrs. Laura M. Thurston, of Norfolk, permitted to be published by her friends, several poetical pieces of uncommon sweetness and excellence,—the Paths of Life, the Green Hills of my Father Land, and others.

There are but few occasions, and these extreme ones, which call out the qualifications for military life.

Gen. Peter B. Porter was the youngest son of Col. Joshua Porter, of Salisbury, of whom I have spoken before. He was a graduate of Yale College and pursued the study of the law where so many of the noted men of the country have—at the Litchfield Law School. He was among the early emigrants from this County to the Gensee country. He was soon called to occupy places of trust and power in the State of his adoption. He was a member of Congress when the project of the Erie Canal was first suggested, and was one who, with De Witt Clinton, originated that important national work, and is entitled to equal honor with him for its projection. He urged it, when in Congress, as a national work, in a speech of great strength, and asked for the aid of the nation. As a member of the House of Representatives, he was associated with Henry Clay on a Committee to consider the causes of complaint against Great Britain, and drew up the report of that Committee, recommending the declaration of the war of 1812. He thus early ardently espoused the cause of his country, and stood by the side of Tompkins and other patriots, in their efforts to prosecute that war to an honorable result.

He was then a civilian only; but, impatient and mortified at the ill success of our arms upon the northern frontier—his own house pieced by the enemy's shot, on the banks of the Niagara River—he threw off the civil and assumed the military attitude. He raised a regiment of ardent volunteer troops, and at their head, soon contributed to turn the tide of success. His services at Fort Erie and the battles at the Falls, have been repeatedly told by the writers of the country's history. I will not repeat them. So highly were they esteemed by the general Government and the State, that thanks and medals were presented, and before the close of the war he was offered the chief command of the army, by the President. Under the administration of the younger Adams he was offered, and accepted, the place of Secretary of War.

My time confines me to the notice of the most conspicuous of our sons, native and adopted; but there were others, in every town, perhaps of equal merit but with fewer opportunities of display. The list of our members of Assembly, and of men by whose efforts the foundations of society were laid here, and by whom this County has been brought from a repulsive region of mountains and rocks to its present condition of fertility and wealth, would show an aggregate of moral and intellectual worth which no region, equal in extent, has surpassed.

And by whom were all these eminent and excellent men reared and prepared for the stations which they have occupied in society? By fathers, whose own hands have toiled—by mothers, who were the spinsters of the days in which they lived, and who knew and practised the duties of the kitchen as well as the parlor. and to whom the music of the spinning-wheel and the loom was more necessary than that of the piano and the harpsichord.

The spirit of strict economy has marked our progress from the beginning, and by no other could our fathers have left to us this heritage of good! Removed from the profusion, and from what is esteemed the higher liberality of city habits, our County has not fallen behind other kindred communities in encouraging the benevolent operations of these latter days.

A Missionary Society, auxiliary to the Board of Commissioners of Foreign Missions, was established in this County, in the year 1813, and has been in active operation since. This noble charity, since its organization, has received and paid over, as near as I can ascertain, the sum of about $125,000. The benevolent offerings of other denominations—the Episcopalians, Methodists, and Baptists, to the purposes of their respective religious operations, I have no present means of knowing; that they have been equally liberal in proportion to their means, with their Congregational brethren, I have no reason to doubt.

In the year 1817, the Foreign Mission School was established in Cornwall, with the special object of spreading Christian truth and the means of civilization among the heathen.. The origin of this effort, if not accidental, was gradual in its conception and development. Two young natives of the Sandwich Islands were, by the directing, and almost visible hand of Providence, thrown among us and fell under the notice of Mr. Elias Cornelius, in 1815, then a student in Yale College, and since distinguished as a Divine and Philanthropist. The names of these young heathen, as known among us, were Henry Obookaih and William Tenoe. These young men were carefully instructed by Mr. Cornelius, Samuel J. Mills, and Edwin Dwight, with a chief object of preparing them to become Christian Missionaries among their countrymen. They were soon after placed under the care of Rev. Joel Harvey, then a Congregational minister in Goshen; at his suggestion, the North Consociation of Litchfield County, became their patrons. They were, not long after. joined by Thomas Hopoo, their countryman, and all were placed under proper instruction for the great object designed. But a more liberal and enlarged project was conceived; a Seminary in a Christian land, for the instruction of the heathen, joined with the purpose of preparing young men here for missionary service in heathen lands. It was a splendid thought, and the American Board attempted its consummation.

Rev. Timothy Dwight, Hon. John Treadwell, James Morris, Esq., Rev. Drs. Beecher and Chapin, with Messrs. Harvey and Prentice, were authorized to devise and put in operation such a Seminary, and the result was, the Foreign Mission School at Cornwall. Young natives of the Sandwich Islands, and from China, Australasia, and from the Indian nations on this Continent, as well as American youths, were instructed there. The school continued successfully until 1827. The establishment of the Sandwich Island Mission, was one of the important results of this school.

Many years before the modern movement in a temperance reformation was suggested, such a project was conceived in this town and encouraged by the most prominent men here. A Temperance Pledge was signed in May, 1789, repudiating the use of distilled liquors, by 36 gentlemen; and among the names annexed to it, were those of Julius Deming, Benjamin Tallmadge, Uriah Tracy, Ephraim Kirby, Moses Seymour, Daniel Sheldon, Tapping Reeve, Frederick Wolcott, and John Welch—names well known and well remembered here. I believe the first temperance association of modern date, in the County, was formed among the iron operatives at Mount Riga, in Salisbury. The results of this grand effort have been as successful here as elsewhere. If any special cause has operated to retard the final success of this charity, it has been the strangling, death-ensuing embrace of party politicians—the scathing curse of many a good thing. As long ago as 1816, there were distilleries in every town in the County; and in New Milford, as many as 26, and in the whole County, 169! and, besides these, there were 188 retailers of spirits, who paid licenses under the excise laws of the United States, to the amount of $3,760. Whether there be a distillery in the County now, I am not informed; I believe but very few.

I have not attempted to trace the modifications of society here—its progressive changes in modes of opinion and consequent action. It would lead me too far from my object, which has been only to speak of events, and the men who have been engaged in them.

Before the Revolution there was little to excite. There was a common routine of thinking, which had been followed for years—somewhat disturbed, to be sure, by what were called *"new lights"* in religion. But the results of our emancipation from the mother country turned everything into a different channel, opinions and all. A new impulse broke in upon the general stagnation of mind which had been, and made every body speculators in morals, religion, politics, and every thing else. My own memory runs back to a dividing point of time, when I could see something of the *old world and new*. Infidel opinions came in like a flood. Mr. Paine's "Age of Reason," the works of Voltaire, and other Deistical books, were broad cast, and young men suddenly became, as they thought, wiser than their fathers; and even men in high places, among us here, were suspected of infidel opinions. At the *same time* came the ardent preachers of Mr. Wesley's divinity, who were engaged in doing battle with Infidelity on the one hand, and Calvinistic theology on the other. Here were antagonistic forces and influences, which introduced essential changes, and both have been operating ever since, And it would afford an interesting subject of investigation, to trace these influences to their results. The Methodist preachers first visited this County about the year 1787, and organized their first classes in Salisbury and Canaan. This was their first appearance in the State, and, I believe, in New England. In this County they were received with courtesy, and found many to encourage them among those who did not well understand the old divinity.

I might detain you in speaking of the prevalence and effects of party spirit here; but as this, as well as denominational controversy, is unpleasant to me, I forbear. There was a time, about the year 1806, when the spirit was rife here, and led to prosecutions, fines and imprisonment, and a disturbance of social relations, which has never since re-appeared to the same extent.

I need not say any thing of the present condition of the County. This you see and know. Its Railroads, penetrating regions not long since supposed to be impenetrable; villiages rising up in the deep valleys, whose foundations have been hidden for nearly a century; and fertility and thrift, where a few years ago were uncultivated forests and wasting water-falls.

Of what shall we complain? Is it that we do not, all of us, make haste to be rich? Ah! is it so, my brethren? Is there nothing but wealth which can satisfy a rational mind and an immortal spirit?

Of the future we may indulge proud hopes, while we doubt and fear. Progress is the word of modern theorists, but of doubtful import. Innovation is not always progress towards useful results. Of this we, who are old, believe we have seen too much, within a few years, and fear much more to come. Our County is but a small part of a State and Nation, and so our fate stands not alone. We can but look to our political institutions as our ultimate protectors, and I urge upon you all, my brethren, their unwavering support. Our Constitution requires no innovating process to improve it. It demands of us more than a mere political respect and preference—almost a religious reverence. Love for it, in all its parts, in every word and sentence which compose it, should be interwoven into all our notions of thinking, speaking and acting. Disturb but one stone in this great arch—but one compromise in this holy covenant—and the whole must tumble into ruin!

# Early Lights

# SKETCHES

OF THE

# EARLY LIGHTS

OF THE

# LITCHFIELD BAR

BY

HON. DAVID S. BOARDMAN

1860

## PATRIDGE THATCHER.

Patridge Thatcher was the first man who practiced the legal profession in New Milford. He was not educated to the profession, but took up the *trade,* because there were none of the craft hereabout, when this county was organized, which was after he came to middle age. He was a native, I have been told, of Lebanon in this state, and came to New Milford, I know not how long ago. He was, however, a married man at the time. He had no children; but a large number of negroes, whom he treated with kindness enough to put to shame the reproaches of all the abolitionists in New England. He was a man of strong mind, of rigid morality, and religious to the letter according to the strictest sect of orthodox episcopacy. He adored Charles I. as a martyr and he hated Oliver Cromwell worse than he did the evil one. Loyalty, unconditional loyalty, was the prime element of his political creed. Of course, his name was not found in any list of the wicked Whigs of the Revolution, and had he lived in these days, he would most thoroughly have eschewed democracy and abolitionism. On the breaking out of the Revolutionary war, his loyalty necessarily silenced his voice in court, and he died soon after its conclusion. Lawyer Thatcher, as he was always called, was undoubtedly, a very odd, a very honest and a very good man. I wish there were many such men now, both on account of the good example they would set, and the harmless amusement they would afford.

---

## DANIEL EVERITT.

Daniel Everitt was a native of Bethlem and settled in New Milford as a lawyer, some time during the early part of the Revolutionary war, probably as early as '76 or '77, possibly earlier, as from a record I have access to I see he was married to a daughter of the Rev. Nathaniel Taylor on the first of January, 1778, and I remember that he lived here some time before that event. He had not a collegiate education, but was a man of good education and received an honorary degree. He read law with Judge Adams of Litchfield, and I remember to have heard him say, that he occasionaly officiated in Mr. Adams' place as state's attorney, when he, (Adams) was absent in Congress, which he often was, during the war of the Revolution. Mr. Everitt was a man of much wit, boundless extravagance of expression, quick conception, and in command of language and fluency of utterance, unsurpassed, but not a man of much depth of mind nor had he much legal learning: his library extended little beyond Blackstone and Jacobs' Law Dictionary. He had, I believe, a very good run of practice, when the Court *really* opened to do civil business, after the conclusion of the war. His success in this respect was, however, of rather short duration; a number of younger lawyers having about that time commenced practice here, and other circumstances conspired to carry business away from him, and he never recovered it. While studying law I heard him argue a case or two, keeping the Court house in a roar by his wit and sarcasm, but by the time I was admitted, viz. in '95, he had about given up attending Courts at Litchfield, though he was not fifty years of age—and indeed he was, I think, but fifty-seven when he died in 1805. I met him, however, a few times, before Arbitrators and Justices, and had enough to do to parry his home thrusts of good natured wit. Before him I often went, as he tried almost all the Justice cases, which he always did with entire integrity and usually came to a correct conclusion. He represented this town, I think three times in the general assembly, and as a member of the convention which ratified the Constitution of the United States. He was a man of strict honesty, entire moral rectitude of conduct, and a professor of religion. He was, however, much given to sociality, and to that conviviality which some time borders on a kindred indulgence. Mr. Everitt succeeded the late Col. Samuel Canfield as Judge of Probate in this district in 1790, and held that office till his death at the time above mentioned.

---

## TAPPING REEVE.

I saw much of Judge Reeve's practice at the bar for nearly five years, during which time he was engaged in almost every case of importance tried in the Superior Court at Litchfield, and never failed to argue every one in which he was engaged, if argued at all. In the County Court, after I became acquainted with him, he did not practice. His school had become numerous, and he gave up his practice in that Court because (I suppose,) it too much interrupted his course of daily lectures, and knowing as he did that he should have a part in every cause expected to be tried in the Superior Court. And, by the way, trials were then managed and got through with in a reasonable time, and not suffered to be dragged out to the abominable and shameful length which they now are, to the disgrace of the Profession for indulging in it, and of the Courts for permitting it.

I joined Judge Reeve's school in the fall of 1793, and he was not placed on the bench till the spring of 1796, so that I saw him at the Bar during nine sessions of the Superior Court, and never failed to listen to him, if I could avoid it, with unqualified love and admiration through every speech he made, to its conclusion. I say *with love,* for no instructor was ever more generally beloved by his pupils, and indeed entirely so except it was by those whose love would have been a reproach to the object of it. As a reasoner, he had no superior within the compass of my observation of forensic performances. I mean true, forcible and honest reasoning. In sophistry, he was too honest to indulge, and too discerning to suffer it to escape detection in the argument of an adversary.

As a speaker he was usually exceedingly ardent, and the ardor he displayed appeared to be prompted by a conviction of the justice of the cause he was advocating. His ideas seemed often, and indeed, usually, to flow in upon him faster than he could give utterance to them, and sometimes seemed to force him to leave a sentence unfinished, to begin another,—and in his huddle of ideas, if I may so express it, he was careless of grammatical accuracy, and though a thorough scholar, often made bad grammar in public speaking. Careless as he was of his diction and thoughtless as he was of ornament in ordinary cases, yet some elegant expressions and fine sentences would seem, as if by accident, to escape him in almost every speech. But in such cases as afforded the proper field for the display of eloquence, such as actions of slander, malicious prosecutions, etc., and in that part of such cases as usually prompt to exertions of the kind, his hurried enunciation and grammatical inaccuracies, all forsook him, and then he never failed to electrify and astonish his audience. Many of these used to be recited to me by those who had often heard him and it fell to my lot to witness one such occasion. In an action for malicious prosecution, in closing the argument, on entering upon the subject of damages, he burst forth into such a strain of dignified and soul-thrilling eloquence, as neither before nor since, has ever met my ear. The first sentence he uttered thrilled through every nerve of my entire frame to the very ends of my fingers, and every succeeding sentence seemed to increase in overwhelming effect. I was perfectly entranced during its delivery, and for an hour afterwards I trembled so that I could not speak plain. His manner was as much changed as his language, and to me he looked a foot taller than before. The next day I went to him and asked him to commit to writing the concluding part of his speech, to which request he said in the simplicity of his nature, "Why, if I should do that, perhaps I should make it better than it really was, and that would not be fair." We told him (Mr. Bacon was with me,) there was no danger of that, for we knew it could not be bettered. Well, he said he would try, but he did not know whether he could recall it to memory, for there was not a word of it written before hand. A day or two after he saw me in Court, behind his seat, and beckoned me to him and said he had tried to comply with my request, but it was so gone from him that he could make nothing of it.

I believe I have said enough in regard to Judge Reeve as an advocate, and that is the extent of your enquiry. As a Judge, you are acquainted with his reputation, historically, though you probably never saw him on the bench, as he left it nearly thirty-nine years ago, to wit, in May, 1816, to the regret of all admirers of legal learning and lovers of impartial justice.

As I loved and admired Judge Reeve while living, and mourned him when dead, I love to think and talk of him now that I have attained to a greater age than he did, though he reached some eighty-four years, and I feel tempted to obtrude upon you some such leading incidents of his life as I am in memory possessed of, and which cannot be much longer retained.

Judge Reeve was the son of a Presbyterian clergyman and was born on the south side of Long Island. He was educated at Princeton College, where he graduated in 1763 at seventeen years of age as I have heard him say. He was immediately appointed tutor of the grammar school connected with the college, and in that station and as a tutor in the college itself, he remained seven years. He then came to Connecticut to study law, which he prosecuted in the office of Judge Root, then a practicing lawyer in Hartford, and as soon as he was admitted to the bar he settled in the practice at Litchfield. This I suppose to have been in 1772. He had previously married Sally Burr, the eldest child and only daughter of President Burr of Princeton College, and the sister of the celebrated Aaron Burr, who was a pupil of Judge Reeve in the grammar school. The Revolutionary war having commenced within a short time after he came to the bar, there was but little civil business done in the Courts until its conclusion, or nearly so. He therefore early betook himself to giving instruction to young gentlemen who looked forward to the legal profession for support and advancement in life, when the circumstances of the country would allow of its exercise. This employment tended greatly to systematize and improve what stock of legal science he already had acquired, and aided by his uncommonly fine talents and native eloquence early secured to him, the deserved reputation of an able lawyer. About the close, I believe, of the Revolutionary war, either through an acquaintance with the late Judge Sedgwick or otherwise he was introduced to some practice in Berkshire County, and in the celebrated *crim. con.* case of Winchell *vs.* Goodrich, gave such a display of his oratorical powers as astonished the natives, and that, together with the conspicuous part he took with Judge Sedgwick in the great case of General Ashley's negroes, which put an end forever to slavery in Massachusetts, he established a reputation which ensured him business there as long as his avocations at home allowed him to attend to it. This however, I believe, was not very long. The delicate health of his wife, and his great professional business at home induced him to forego any business which called him abroad, and to utterly decline any sort of public appointment whatsoever, during her life. She died to the deep grief of as devoted a husband as ever lived, a few months before it became necessary to fill two vacancies in the Superior Court, occasioned by the death of Chief Justice Adams and the final extinction of mental capacity in Judge Huntington—and to one of those vacancies Judge Reeve was appointed.

I must draw this long letter to a close. It is enough to say, that no act of Judge Reeve's life ever, in the least degree, lessened the admiration and respect entertained for his capacity, integrity and learning, or even diminished the esteem and affection cherished for the spotless purity of his moral deportment through a long life, nor the reverence extorted from all for the deep religious impression which adorned his old age and perfected his character. He was, I presume, in youth extremely handsome.

---

## JOHN ALLEN

John Allen was born in Great Barrington, Mass., sometime, I believe, in 1762, of respectable parents, though not distinguished in society, as I remember to have heard him say that he was the son of a joiner. There were but two children in the family, a son and a daughter, both much distinguished in life for many good qualities, and especially for dignity of manner and deportment, but the *winning* and *amiable* accomplishments all fell to the lot of the female, gaining her many admirers and among others, an husband worthy of her, in that excellent man, Elizur Goodrich of New Haven.. Their father died during the minority of both children. Mr. Allen, having an excellent common school education, though not a classic education, became a teacher, and being impelled by a spirit of adventure, somewhat romantic as he was thought in those days, went suddenly, and without the knowledge of his friends, and while yet a minor, to Germantown near Philadelphia, where he obtained a place as instructor of the young classes of an academic establishment of some note at the time. How long he remained in the above mentioned establishment I do not know, but soon after leaving the place, and I believe almost immediately, he came to New Milford, and taught a school for some six months, and from here went immediately into Mr. Reeve's law school, and after the accustomed period of study was admitted to the bar, and immediately settled in practice in Litchfield, where he spent his life. He confined himself almost entirely to the practice of Litchfield County, though occasionally when called, in consequence of the eminence to which he soon attained in the profession, he practiced in other counties, in some cases of importance, and especially in the Federal Circuit Court, in which, for a few years after the formation of the present Constitution of the United States, some considerable business was done. Mr. Allen, however never went abroad in quest of business, thinking that the very great share of Attorney business which he acquired in being always found in his office, equal, at least in point of profit, to what counsellor business he might obtain by attending Courts in other counties, considering that all the counsellor business flowing from the attorney business which he did, he was sure to be engaged in. From the time I entered the law school in the fall of 1793, I occupied a room in his office, and had free access to his ample library and boarded at the same house with him. During all that time, and all the remaining years of his prosperous practice, which indeed lasted till the apparent commencement of his rapid decline, soon followed by death, he was engaged in almost every case of any importance in the Superior and County Court. He was certainly, a very successful and powerful advocate, equally with the Jury as with the Court, a thoroughly read lawyer, equal in point of legal science to any one at our bar during the fore part of the time I am speaking of, except Tapping Reeve, who had no rival, and in the latter part of the period, James Gould, of whom I need say nothing as you knew him in his meridian light. Mr. Allen always made diligent and faithful preparation of all cases committed to his care, and made himself fully acquainted with every point of law and every accessible point of evidence which could arise in the case, and was therefore usually successful when the case deserved success.

If I knew that you ever saw Mr. Allen, I would omit any attempt to describe his personal appearance, for I am sure any one who ever saw his colossal form and imposing visage, would never need to have him described in order to recall his appearance. He was six feet four or five inches high, very erect and with an attitude and walk well calculated to set off his full stature, and though quite lean, weighed full 230 pounds. His countenance was strongly marked and truly formidable, his eyes and eye brows dark, his hair dark, what little he had for he was quite bald, far back, even before middle age, and indeed his whole appearance was calculated to inspire dread, rather than affection. His manner and conversation were, however, such as to inspire confidence and respect, though little calculated to invite familiarity, except with his intimates, of whom he had a few, and those, knowing the generous and hearty friendship of which he was capable, were usually, much attached to him and ready to overlook all his harsh sallies, imputing them to the "rough humor which his mother gave him." His feelings were not refined, but ardent, generous and hearty. His friendships were strong and his aversions equally so—and as I used to say of him, speaking to others, "his feelings were all of the great sort." He neither enjoyed nor suffered any thing from many of those little incidents which so often affect, either pleasingly or painfully, minds of a more refined texture. As he had no taste for such things, nor, as it would seem, any faculty of perceiving, so he knew no language appropriate to their description, but in respect to those things and principles which he thought worthy of his regard, he lacked no power of language to make himself fully and forcibly understood. For neutral ground, either in morals or politics, he had no taste, and but little less than absolute abhorrence. As a specimen of his feelings and language, better than I can describe, I will give you the laconic answer to an enquiry of him, why he took the *Aurora* the leading democratic paper in the county, then under the guidance of that arch democrat, Duane; he replied it was because *he wanted to know what they were about in the infernal regions.* And after giving this specimen I need make no futher attempt to give you an idea of his humor, manners and language.

After Mr. Allen was married, which was not till he was towards forty years old, and went to house keeping, I boarded at his house at his express solicitation for many years while attending Court; though he took no other one, nor ever named to me any price, nor would he count the money I handed to him when leaving for home, seeming to receive it only because I refused to stay on any other terms. I therefore saw much of him in his family, where his conduct was always dignified, proper and kind. He was proud, very proud, and justly so, of his wife, who was a woman of much personal beauty, polished manners, and great and even singular discretion, and for whom he entertained, I believe, an ardent affection.

Before his marriage and at the age of thirty-five Mr. Allen was elected a member of the fifth Congress, where he distinguished himself at a time when Connecticut was never more ably represented in the House of Representatives, and would undoubtedly have been chosen for as long a period as he would have desired to be a member of that body, but he declined a further election. He was elected an Assistant in 1800, and was re-elected for the five succeeding years, and as such was one of the Judges of the Supreme Court of Errors. For several years, previous to his election to Congress, he had represented the town of Litchfield in the General Assembly. His wife was a grand daughter of the first Governor Griswold. His only son, the Hon. John Wm. Allen of Cleveland, Ohio, has been a member of Congress from that State and is now a very distinguished man there. His only surviving daughter resides also in Cleveland, and is the wife of her brother's immediate successor in Congress. Mrs. Allen, after a rather brief widowhood, accepted the hand of a Mr. Perkins of Oxford in the State of New York, a man of respectability and wealth.

---

## BARZILLAI SLOSSON.

The request, which is the subject of yours of the 4th inst., is too alluring in its nature to be long unattended to. So nearly am I alone in the world that an invitation to hold converse about those of my age and standing in life, and who have now slumbered in the grave for more than forty years, and especially those who were so much beloved and esteemed as were those of whom you solicit my attention, is quite irresistible.

In speaking of Mr. Slosson, I must first observe that I had formed a tolerably correct notion of him before I ever saw him. When I was a boy his father was often at my father's house, intimately acquainted there, and I believe, scarcely ever passed that way without calling and holding a pretty long chat, for he was never in a hurry, and his peculiar turn of mind, abundance of common sense, and great fund of wit, joined to his singularly slow, emphatic and sententious mode of talking, was such as to secure the attention of any one, and especially a boy. He used, occasionally to speak of his children, and especially of his oldest son Barzillai, of whom he was manifestly very proud, representing him to be always at the head of the school when small, and afterwards used to speak with high gratification of his industry and tact at acquiring the higher branches of knowledge without the aid of an instructor, and more particularly the knowledge of the dead languages, of which he knew nothing himself. And this account given by the old gentleman, from intimate intercourse and frequent conversation with his son, when I afterwards became acquainted with him, I found was by no means exaggerated. And to his excellent and accurate common school education, he owed much, very much of his character for exact accuracy and correctness in all that he said and did through life. He was about the best reader I ever heard, wrote a fair, handsome and legible hand, and in the unfailing correctness of his orthography and use of terms, no lexicographer excelled him, and in everything pertaining to mere English, home and common school education, no one appeared to be more thoroughly proficient. And in Greek and Latin I never saw his superior, except old President Stiles, nor with that exception perhaps, his equal, unless it was old Parson Farrand of Canaan, and in the other branches of collegiate education he was, to say the least, above mediocraty. As he entered college not until the senior year, and, I believe, did not even attend during the whole of that year, he could not, of course, expect to shine and did not shine in the college honors depending upon the faculty, but he availed himself of the right to become a candidate for the honors of *Dean Scholar,* and obtained the first premium for excellence in Greek and Latin, in a class of unusually high reputation. This, I suppose, he did merely, out of a laudable pride, for he did not avail himself of the pecuniary reward which would have required him to reside in New Haven; for he went, immediately after his graduation with one of his classmates (Mr. afterwards the Rev. Dr. Smith,) to reside in Sharon, as one of the instructors in the Sharon Academy, then in full and successful operation. He soon after became a student at law, under Gov. Smith's instruction, and the first County Court which sat after his two year's clerkship had expired, being in Fairfield County, he went, there for examination and admission to the Bar. This was I believe at the November Term, 1793. It was not until he began to attend Court at Litchfield, and while I was in the law school there, that I first became personally acquainted with Mr. Slosson though I had barely seen him once or twice before. After my admission to the Bar, being located in adjoining towns, we often met each other before Justices, and consequently before the upper courts. From our frequent meetings and intercourse at Litchfield and elsewhere, I became greatly attached to him, and finally, for a number of years he and I, with Southmayd for our constant companion, always occupied the same room at Catlin's Hotel during every court until his

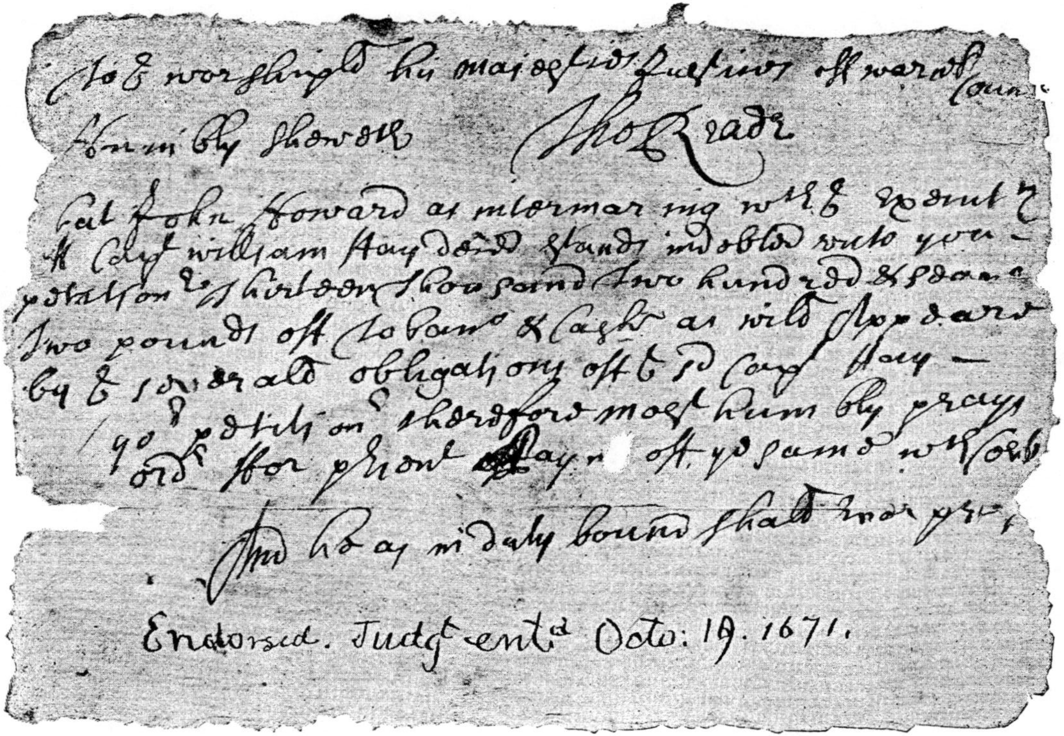

To ye worshipfull his maiesties Justices of Warwick County

Humbly Showeth Tho: Reade

That John Howard as intermarying wth ye Execut[rix]
of Capt William Hayward stands indebted unto your
petition[er] Thirteen thousand two hundred & eleven
Two pounds of tobacco & cask as will appeare
by ye severall obligations of ye sd Capt Hay-
ward yor petition[er] therefore most humbly prays
ord[er] for paym[en]t of ye same wth cost
And he as in duty bound shall ever pray

Endorsed. Judgt entd Octo: 19. 1671.

This writ was obtained by a soldier in the civil war near Warwick C. H., Virginia.
Is a fine specimen of ancient forms.

OLD WRIT.

death and there was the last time I ever saw him in life. Soon after the Court adjourned, hearing of his rapid decline, I set out to visit him, and on the way, heard that he had died the night before. I however went on and stayed with the family until I assisted in burying him. This was in January, 1813, and in that grave I felt that I had buried a sincere, and I am sure, a much loved friend; on whose character and conduct in life I could reflect with melancholy satisfaction, unmarred by a single reproachful recollection or one which I could wish to have forgotten.

Mr. Slosson had been out of health for a very considerable time, and fears were apprehended on his account, in which he fully and rationally participated. So gradual, however, was the operation of his disorder, that he continued his attention to business until some three or four weeks before his death. He attended court at Litchfield, the first and I think the second week of the December term, the month before his decease.

Mr. Slosson's great fondness for ancient literature, rendered him scarcely just in his comparative estimate of that with modern improvements. As a lawyer he was highly respectable in theory and remarkably accurate in practice; as a pleader, I do not remember that he ever had occasion to ask for an amendment, or to alter a title of what he had written. As an advocate he was clear, deliberate, methodical and logical in his deductions. He spoke in much of the peculiarly emphatic manner of his father, above mentioned, though not with his unusual slowness. He was always cool and self-possessed, rarely warming into any high degree of animation, or aiming at effect to appear eloquent, but he never failed to secure a respectful and satisfied attention. Though not one of the most leading advocates of which there are always some three or four at any Bar, he might, at least be estimated an equal to any of the second class of the Litchfield Bar which was then, certainly, a highly respectable one.

Though not an aspirant after public preferment, and from his habitually modest and retiring habits, not calculated to push his way where opportunities offered, he was yet, at the time of his decease, in a fair way of promotion. He was early and often elected to the legislature from his native town, and indeed their usual representative until the October session, 1812, when he was elected Clerk, which in those days was a sure stepping stone to further advancement, and having myself been a witness of the manner in which he performed the duties of that office, for which no man was better qualified, I am sure he established a reputation, which, had Providence permitted, promised a solid and lasting existence.

Mr. Slosson's political opinions were of the genuine Washingtonian, political school. None of your heady, rash, and merely partizan notions found favor with him. He was a constant and honest adherent to the political views then prevalent in this State. He left a widow and two sons—the oldest John William, has been and I believe now is a merchant in Kent. The second son, Nathaniel, a very promising boy, was, I believe soon after his father's death, taken under the care of his uncle, William Slosson, a distinguished lawyer of New York, and was by him educated at Union College and for the Bar, and died soon after his admission.

The foregoing sketch of the leading incidents in Mr. Slosson's life, may be a sufficient indication from which to deduct his true character, but I must indulge myself in adding, that I never knew or heard of a single act of his life, either in youth or mature years, that left even a shade upon his reputation. Cool and deliberate in his temperament, never hurried away by enthusiasm, for enthusiasm never manifested itself in his nature, except in his passion for ancient literature, he was sure to think and act with propriety. He was nevertheless warm and faithful in his attachments, but not so far as to warp his conscientions regard for integrity. He was perfectly just and generous in his intercourse with the world, honest in his predilections and uncompromising in his love of virtue and detestation of vice. In morality his principles were without a taint and his practice through life in conscientious conformity with them. In religion he was a firm and steadfast believer in the great doctrines of the gospel, though not a public professor. His principles were those of true rational Calvanism, unswayed by vindictive zeal or hysterical weakness.

You observed in your letter that you never saw Mr. Slosson. He was a small man, not much, if any, under medium height, but of slender frame and countenance. Though not dark complexioned his countenance was rather dusky, his skin not clear, his features though far from handsome bespoke intelligence and were therefore not disagreeable. His general appearance was more like that of the late Leman Church than any other member of the Bar I can think of, though he was somewhat larger and more erect.

---

## SAMUEL W. SOUTHMAYD.

In the life, conduct and character of Samuel W. Southmayd there were some peculiarities, such as render it a matter of difficulty to describe him in such a manner, as to make them intelligible to one who did not personally know him.

I never saw, or heard of him until I became a member of the law school in the fall of the year 1793, of which he had then been a member about one year, I believe, and of which he continued a constant attendant during the eighteen months which I spent there. He was admitted to the Bar the next term after I was, to wit: September Term, 1795, and passed as good an examination as I ever heard there, or elsewhere, he having been for the full period of three years under Judge Reeve's tuition. He was a native of Watertown, where he settled in practice, and where he spent his life. Like Mr. Slosson, he had an excellent common school education. Beyond that, his acquirements did not extend far in an academic course—enough, however, I believe, to enable him to understand the homely law-latin used in our books. Few have entered upon the practice of law, with a better store of legal learning than Mr. Southmayd, but the place in which he settled was not calculated from its location and the habits of the people, by no means litiguous, to furnish much practice, and he was too honest to promote litigation; and furthermore, he had no legal adversary there except an old gentlemen who never had any more legal learning than was necessary for a Church Warden, and whose ignorance made him the victim of Southmayd's merry witchery and innocent cunning, of both of which he had a superabundance, though he never indulged in malicious, or even very serious mischief, and indeed in none except such as would do to relate for the purpose of making fun in merry company. Anecdotes of that description used to be related in great numbers. As a pleader, Mr. Southmayd was always sure to have all in his drafts which was requisite and pertinent to the object in view, and in all his declarations, affording room for coloring circumstances to be inserted, there was pretty sure to be found, slyly slipped in, some ingenious slang whang, or Southmaydism, as we used to call it. He was not ambitious of arguing cases in Court, but when he did, he always displayed much ingenuity, and attracted respectful attention from the audience as well as from the triers. And before arbitrators, referees and committees a more formidable opponent could hardly be found. And although his practice was not large, and as was observed of Mr. Slosson he was not among the leading practitioners at the Litchfield Bar, he was certainly a very respectable lawyer, upon a par with the foremost of the second class, and much beloved and respected by all whose good opinions are desirable.

As was observed in the outset, there were peculiarities in Mr. Southmayd's private character and deportment, which it is difficult to describe or reconcile. Though of a benevolent disposition and full of good nature and kind feelings, there was yet in him a vein of adventure after intellectual amusement, which, from its very nature, could not be gratified but at the expense of others, and often to such an extent as to render them ridiculous in the view of third persons to whom the results of the adventure was related. I have many times joined most heartily in the laugh at the relation of the result of many such seemingly innocent pieces of roguery, though I could not help condemning the mischief, while participating in its fruits. In all such indulgences, Southmayd never entertained the least malice, for his heart was a stranger to it, but his intense love of fun, and enjoyment of the ridiculous often impelled him to go beyond the line of honest propriety. I used often to reproach him with it, but my admonitions were not well calculated to take effect, when given at the close of a hearty laugh.

From what I have been saying of Mr. Southmayd you would, I presume, be ready to conclude that he was one of the most cheerly and happy of men. But the case was directly the reverse, and during a considerable period of his life, and that too, the most valuable part of it, he was a very unhappy man, indeed, and I have no doubt he had recourse to much of the indulgence of that peculiar propensity I have attempted to describe for the purpose of dispelling a mental malady which for a long time oppressed and preyed upon his heart. He was for many years the victim of the strongest species of hypochondria that ever mortal man was. It never showed itself in long fits of settled melancholy or monomania, but in sudden fits and starts. After hours of cheerful conversation, and while in entire health, he would suddenly complain of great distress, and exhibit unmistakable evidence of great terror and apprehensions of immediate dissolution. One very extraordinary instance I will relate. He and I had been alone many hours, conversing and reading together, and he, not in the least complaining, when he at once sprung from his seat, and with a scream as would have alarmed me, had it been any other person, and pressing both hands upon his breast he exclaimed that he was going to die immediately. I stepped to him and gently and calmly said to him, "don't be alarmed, you are not going to die"—for we never treated him as if he thought his distress imaginary,—and put my hand gently upon him to lead him to the bed, when he raised one hand from his breast and thrusting his finger against the side of his head, declared, with another outcry that something was passing through his head. I persuaded him to lie down, telling him the feeling would pass off in a few minutes, but he continued to groan for some time. I, knowing what would cure him, took up and began to read to him one of Burke's finest essays which lay by me, and turning to a passage of extraordinary eloquence read it; on which he sprung up on end in the bed, and exclaimed "was ever anything finer than that!" I continued on reading, and in the course of half an hour he was well and cheerful as ever. This was the most extraordinary instance I ever saw in him, but those in a degree like it were frequent. He always went to bed an hour or two before Slosson and I did, he saying that he never was able to get sleep until he had gone through a great deal of such feelings as he never would attempt to describe.

Mr. Southmayd was greatly esteemed in his native town, by, I believe, almost every one, both old and young. He was early in life sent to the legislature, and that often, and was so, I know, the last year of his life. He died of lung fever in March, 1813, about two months after the death of his friend Slosson. At the December Term, 1812, the three who had so long occupied the same room in perfect harmony. were, for the last time there together. At the February Term of the Supreme Court, Southmayd and I occupied it, but felt that we were in solitude, and in the next term it seemed to me, most emphatically, a solitude, and more like a family vault than like an abode for living men, and I believe I have never been into it since.

Mr. Southmayd was undoubtedly an honest and honorable man, of uncommon pleasing manners and much beloved, and I never heard that he had an enemy. Indeed the amenity of his manner and the gentleness of his temper almost forbade it.

The family to which Mr. Southmayd belonged was of the Congregational order, and two of his sisters married Congregational clergymen. He, however, joined himself to the Episcopal church of which he was a member after he settled in life, and of which, I believe he was a communicant, but am not sure. He died unmarried, and I believe in the 39th or 40th year of his age.

---

## JOHN COTTON SMITH.

At your request, I now inform you, that the Hon. John Cotton Smith, only son of the Rev. Cotton Mather Smith of Sharon, was born there on the 12th day of February, 1765. It is said that for the first six years of his life his instruction and training was almost wholly conducted by his excellent mother, and to her government and precepts he is said to have attributed much of his extraordinary success in life. His common school education, as exhibited in after life, must have been of the most exactly accurate kind. His classical instruction preparatory to entering college, was commenced at home, and completed under the tuition of the Rev. Mr. Brinsmade of Washington. He entered Yale College in September, 1779, when between fourteen and fifteen years of age, and though young, maintained a high standing in his class, as appeared by the share he had in the exercises of the commencement at his graduation, the appointees being less than one-fourth of the entire class. Immediately after his graduation in September, 1783, he entered as a law student in the office of the Hon. John Canfield in his native town, and there continued until he could be by law admitted to the Bar, which was in the March Term, 1786, a month after coming to twenty-one years of age: and Mr. Canfield, his legal preceptor, having died a few months after his admission to the Bar, a large portion of business for a long time habitually flowing for management to Mr. Canfield's office, he having for many years been one of the ablest lawyers of the County, Mr. Smith's commencement in business was thereby attended by fortunate circumstances, and he improved them with becoming industry, and from the very first found himself in a lucrative practice, which continued to increase until called into absorbing public business. He was first elected to the legislature in 1793 and frequently afterwards; indeed, from 1796 to October, 1800 he was constantly a member, and during the two sessions of 1800 was speaker of the house, and while occupying that station in the October session he was informed by the Goveror that he was elected a member of Congress to fill a vacancy which had occurred for the then approaching last session of the Sixth Congress, and also for the full term of the Seventh Congress; soon after which information, he resigned the chair in the house, and returned home to prepare for assuming his newly assigned duties. It so happened that the extra session to which he had been chosen was that, which, by law, was to be holden at the new City of Washington, whither he repaired and served through that term, and the Seventh Congress; was re-elected to the Eighth and again to the Ninth Congress, at the expiration of the Ninth Congress he declined any further elections to that honorable body. During his congressional career he did not participate much in debate, but his fine talent at presiding was early discovered, and caused him frequently to be called to the chair when the House was in committee of the whole, and he thus presided during some of the most memorable debates which distinguished those days. He was during all but the first session, a member of the committee of claims while in Congress, and during the Eighth and Ninth Congress at the head of that committee, though in the minority. In May, 1809, Mr. Smith was appointed a Judge of the Superior Court, which he resigned in May, 1811, on being elected Lieutenant-Governor; in May, 1813 he was elected Governor, and re-elected to that office until 1818, when, a political revolution having taken place, he retired finally from public life. His administration of the gubernatorial office embraced the greater part of the war of 1812 and 1815, and his duties in all respects were performed with dignity, propriety and grace.

After his retirement to private life much of his time was devoted to religious studies, and his eminent Christian and literary accomplishments being extensively known and appreciated he was selected as the first president of the Connecticut Bible Society on its establishment. In 1826 he was chosen president of the American Board of Commissioners for Foreign Missions, and in 1831 president of the American Bible Society. In 1815 he received the degree of LL. D. As old age pressed upon him his hearing became impaired, and he never would suffer himself to hold public stations when he could not perform all their duties with becoming grace, he resigned all his posts of honor, and on the 7th day of December he died in the 81st year of his age.

In an eulogy delivered before the Connecticut Historical Society by the Rev. W. H. Andrews, then of Kent, soon after the decease of Mr. Smith, giving a concise but eloquent historical sketch of his life and character, stating that he was admitted to the Bar in Litchfield County, and observing that at the time there was no bar in the state which presented a more splendid array of legal forensic talents than this, proceeds to state the standing which he at maturity acquired, in the following words quoted, as he says, from the communication of a well informed competent judge, long acquainted with Mr. Smith at the bar:—"He was esteemed, and justly so, an accurate pleader, and a well read and learned lawyer, and though some of those alluded to exceeded him in force and popularity as an advocate, none of them surpassed, and in my judgment, none of them equalled him in grace of manner and elegance of diction and utterance."

Early in life Gov. Smith married Miss Margaret Everson of Amenia, N. Y., a young lady of many accomplishments, who lived to old age. The issue of this marriage was only one child, William M. Smith, Esq., of Sharon, a gentleman much esteemed for his many virtues and eminent piety. A grandson bearing his name is now the Minister resident of the United States to the court of Bolivia, South America.

---

## NATHANIEL SMITH.

(*From Hollister's History of Connecticut.*)

"I received a line from my friend, General Sedgwick, stating that is was your desire that he would ask of me, in your behalf, to furnish you with some facts in relation to the late Nathaniel Smith, and my views of his character, which might be of use to you in the preparation of the work you have in hand.

"I am of course aware that this application is owing to the accidental circumstance that I am the oldest, if not the only member of the profession now living, who had much personal acquaintance with that truly able and excellent man, or saw much of him in the exercise of his forensic or judicial talents. Judge Smith was indeed one of nature's nobles, and considering the limited range of his early education, he had few equals and perhaps no superior in the profession which he chose, and which he eminently adorned. You are doubtless aware that Judge Smith had only such an education in childhood and youth, as the common schools of the country afforded at the time. It was such, however, as a boy of unusual capacity and industrious habits would acquire from such a source, and such as, under the guidance of uncommon discretion through life, rarely permitted its defects to be disclosed.

"When I first went to the Law School in Litchfield, which was in the fall of 1793, Mr. Smith though not over thirty years old, was in full practice, and engaged in almost every cause of any importance. Indeed, he was said to have established a high reputation for talents in the first cause he argued in the higher courts. It was upon a trial for manslaughter, which arose in his native town, and in which he appeared as junior counsel, and astonished the court, the bar, and all who heard him. Not long afterwards, in the celebrated case of Jedediah Strong and wife, before the General Assembly, (she having applied for a divorce), he greatly distinguished himself again, and thus became known throughout the state as a young lawyer of the first promise; and the reputation thus early acquired was never suffered to falter, but on the other hand, steadily increased in strength until his elevation to the bench.

"During my stay in Litchfield, and after my admission to the bar, I of course saw Mr. Smith, and heard him in almost all the important cases there; and as I was located in the south-west corner town in the county, adjoining Fairfield, I almost immediately obtained some business which, though small, was such as during nearly all my professional life caused me to attend the courts in that county, where I found Mr. Smith as fully engaged and as highly esteemed as in his own county. In New Haven I also knew he had a very considerable practice.

"It is worthy also to be observed, in forming an estimate of Mr. Smith's professional talent and character, that there never at any period was an abler bar in Connecticut, than during his practice. In Litchfield county, were Judge Reeve, Judge Adams, General Tracy, John Allen, Judge Gould, N. B. Benedict, and others; at the Fairfield county bar, were Pierpont Edwards, Judge Ingersoll, and Judge Daggett, constantly from New Haven, Judge Edmonds, S. B. Sherwood, R. M. Sherman, Judge Chapman, and Governor Bissell; and in New Haven, besides the three above named, were James Hillhouse, Judge Baldwin, and others.

"As I suppose it not probable that you ever saw Judge Smith, as he ceased to attend courts in 1819, and died when you was very young, I will observe, what you have doubtless heard, that he was a large and fine appearing man, much of the same complexion of the Hon. Truman Smith, his nephew, with whom you are all so well acquainted; less tall than he, but of rather fuller habit. His face was not only the index of high capacity and solid judgment, but uncommonly handsome; his hair was dark and thin, though not to baldness, except on the fore part of the head, and was very slightly sprinkled with gray. His fine, dark eyes, were remarkably pleasing and gentle in ordinary intercourse, but very variable, always kindling when highly excited in debate, they became almost oppressive. His voice was excellent, being both powerful and harmonious, and never broke under any exertion of its capacity. His manner was very ardent and the seeming dictate of a strong conviction of the justice of his cause; and his gestures were the natural expression of such a conviction. Mr. Smith's style was pure and genuine Saxon, with no attempt at classic ornament or allusion. His train of reasoning was lucid and direct, and evincive of the fact that the whole of it was like a map spread out in his mind's eye from the beginning. His integrity was always felt and dreaded by his opponent. He spoke with much fluency, but with no undue rapidity; he never hesitated for or *haggled* at a word, nor did he ever tire his audience with undue prolixity, or omit to do full justice to his case for fear of tiring them; and indeed there was little danger of it. Though certainly a very fine speaker, he never achieved or aspired to those strains of almost superhuman eloquence with which his old master Reeve, sometimes electrified and astonished his audience, and yet, in ordinary cases, he was the most correct speaker of the two—though Judge Reeve was, and he was not, a scholar. Mr. Smith, though quite unassuming, and often receding in common intercourse and conversation, was, when heated in argument, it must be confessed, often overbearing to the adverse party, and, not only them, but to their counsel. Upon all other occasions, he appeared to be, and I believe was, a very kind hearted, agreeable and pleasant man. To me, he always so appeared, and I have been much in his company.

"Mr. Smith came early into public life, and was frequently elected to the General Assembly from Woodbury. In 1795, he was elected a member of the fourth Congress; and in 1797, he was chosen to the fifth Congress; but declined further election. In May, 1799, he was made an assistant, and was re-elected for the five following years, when he resigned his seat at that board in consequence of the passage of the act in 1803, prohibiting the members of the then Supreme Court of Errors from practicing before the Court. He remained in full practice at the bar until October, 1806, when he was elected a judge of the Superior Court, and continued to fill that office until May, 1819, when the judiciary establishment of that year went into operation; from which time he remained in private life until his death.

"In every public station in which Mr. Smith was placed, he distinguished himself. He did so in Congress, at a time when our representation was as able, perhaps, as it ever has been, and when the character of the house to which he belonged was far higher than it now is. In the Superior Court he was certainly very greatly respected and admired, as an able and perfectly upright judge.

"In private life his name was free from reproach. A strictly honest and pure life, free from any of those little blemishes which often mar the fame of distinguished men, may, I think, be fairly claimed by his biographer to be his due. As a husband, a parent, a friend, a neighbor, a moralist and a christian, I believe few have left a more faultless name."

---

## NOAH BENNET BENEDICT.

In further compliance with your late request, I now place at your disposal some account of the life, character and standing of another highly esteemed member of the Litchfield County Bar.

The Hon. Noah Bennet Benedict was a native of Woodbury, in which he resided during his whole life. He was the son of the Rev. Noah Benedict, long the pastor of the First Congregational Church in that town. Mr. Benedict's early school education must have been correct and good, as its fruits invariably showed itself in after life. He graduated at Yale College in September, 1788, when a little short of eighteen years of age. His legal studies commenced soon after his graduation, which were, I believe, pursued principally, if not wholly, in the office of his brother-in-law, Nathaniel Smith, afterwards so highly distinguished as a jurist, which was near the residence of Mr. Benedict's father. As soon as he arrived to lawful age Mr. Benedict came to the Bar, and for the remainder of his life, to wit: about thirty-nine years, it is believed he never failed to attend every regular session of the Courts holden at Litchfield; and though he never habitually attended Courts in other counties, he occasionally did so for the purpose of arguing a particular case. During the long course of his practice Mr. Benedict had an ample share of business, and for the latter half of that period, he was, especially in the Superior Court, the leading advocate, on one side or the other, in most of the trials either to the court or to the jury. His management of a trial was discreet, his argument sound, sensible, and being aided by the well known and generally esteemed integrity of his character, had their due effect. He never attempted to play the orator or to attract attention by fine turned periods, but contented himself with plain reasoning, of which he was no indifferent master.

At a very early period Mr. Benedict was a member of the legislature. But the political majority of the voters in Woodbury becoming about this time and for long afterwards decidedly democratic, proved an effectual bar to his political promotion, as far as depended upon that town, but by the vote of the State at large he was elected in 1813 one of the twelve assistants, (as they were then styled, who composed the Upper House of the assembly), and was re-elected the two following years; but in the year 1818 an entire political revolution took place in Connecticut, and Mr. Benedict shared the fate of almost every one who held any post of dignity or profit depending upon the public suffrage at large in the State. He was subsequently many years later elected once more to the Lower House. He was also for several years Judge of Probate for the District of Woodbury, an appointment then depending upon the legislature. Mr. Benedict was twice married, but left no living issue. He died in June or July 1831, at the age of sixty, or in his sixtieth year.

In private life Mr. Benedict was entirely unassuming, and a very pleasing companion to all who could relish purity of moral character and conduct, which his whole life was an eminent example: his feelings were peculiarly sensitive and delicate; a loose or profane expression never escaped his lips, and indeed so fastidious was he in respect to the former, that it used to be a matter of amusement with his less scrupulous associates in jocose conversation, to tease his feminine delicacy upon such subjects. Though when alone and unoccupied he had a propensity to indulge in somewhat gloomy reflections, yet he was not averse to participate in facetious conversation when due

Noah Bennet Benedict
From an old Painting.

delicacy was observed. He had a profound respect for religion and was in all respects a *good, a very good man.*

Mr. Benedict was of somewhat less than midling size, of a medium complexion, but his eyes and hair rather dark.

---

## JAMES GOULD.

In compliance, in part, with a request recently received from you, I now send you a brief and imperfect sketch of the literary and professional character, standing and reputation of the Hon. James Gould, who for a very considerable period of time contributed much to the fame of the County and State for legal science, by his talents as an advocate and especially as an instructor and as a judge of the Superior Court; with some account of his person and family. Mr. Gould the son of Dr. William Gould, an eminent physician, was born at Branford in this State in the year 1770. The goodness of his common school education is inferable from the perfect accuracy of it, which showed itself in all he did or said in after life. He graduated when a little over twenty-one, at Yale College, in September, 1791, with distinguished honor in a class distinguished for talents.

The year next following his collegiate course he spent in Baltimore as a teacher. He then returned to New Haven and commenced the study of law with Judge Chauncey; and in September of that year he was chosen a tutor in Yale College, in which office he continued two years. He then joined the Law School of Mr. Reeve at Litchfield and was soon after admitted to the Bar. Immediately after his admission to the Bar he opened an office for practice in that town, where he resided during the remainder of his life.

On his first appearance as an advocate he evinced such an apparent maturity of intellect, such a self-possession, such command of his thoughts and of the language appropriate to their expression, that he was marked out as a successful aspirant for forensic eminence. His progress in the acquisition of professional business was steady and rapid.

Fortunate circumstances concurring a few years before his choice of Litchfield as a field of his professional labors, in the removal by promotion of two very distinguished practitioners at the Bar, opened the way to such a choice, and by like good fortune a similar event removed one of the two only remaining obstructions in that town to his full share in the best business as an advocate, the only business to which he aspired. As a reasoner Mr. Gould was forcible, lucid and logical: as a speaker his voice was very pleasant and his language pure, clear and always appropriate. He never aspired to high strains of impassioned eloquence, and rarely, if ever, addressed himself to the passions of the Court and Jury, but to their understanding only, and was a very able, pleasing and successful advocate. His argument was a fair map of the case, and one sometimes engaged against him, but feeling his superiority, observed, that he had rather have Gould against him in a case, than any other of any where equal powers, because he could perfectly understand his argument, and if susceptible of an answer could know how to apply it. In his practice at the Bar he was always perfectly fair and honorable. Within some two or three years after Mr. Gould commenced practice, Mr. Reeve, the founder and until that time the sole instructor of the Litchfield Law School, accepted a seat upon the bench of the Superior Court. This Court made it necessary for him to give up the school, or to associate some one with him in its management, and to deliver lectures in his absence upon the circuits. The Judge selected Mr. Gould as that associate; and for a number of years they jointly conducted and received the pupils of the School: and on the final retiring of Judge Reeve from any participation in the instruction of the School, Mr. Gould became its sole instructor and so continued until elevated to the bench of the Superior Court in the spring of 1816, when he in turn had to have recourse to temporary aid for the short time he remained on the bench. But a thorough political Revolution having taken place in this State, and a new constitution formed which entirely new modeled the courts of law, Mr. Gould took no further share in public employments: and his health being greatly impaired, he never resumed practice at the Bar, but confined himself wholly to his School during the remainder of his life, as far as severe infirmities would permit. He died, as appears by the College catalogue, in 1838.

In person Mr. Gould was very handsome. Of about medium heighth, or perhaps a little over; but rather less in body and limbs than medium size. His complexion fair, with fine dark eyes and beautiful brown hair; all his features good and in connection indicative of much intelligence and good nature, and his form for symmetry and gracefulness could hardly have been mended; and in all respects, in body, mind and education, he may be fairly styled a finished man. In private and social intercourse he was highly pleasing, facetious and witty.

Soon after his settlement in Litchfield he married the eldest daughter of the Hon. Uriah Tracy, so well known for his long and distinguished service in the councils of the state and nation.

Mrs. Gould in person and mind was a fit wife for such a husband, and partook with him in the happiness of raising a very numerous and promising family of children.

Judge Gould wrote and published a volume of Pleadings, which together with his fame as an instructor, gave him a distinguished name among the eminent jurists of the country.

ASA BACON

Again in compliance with your later request for further sketches of the lives and profesional standing of the former members of the Litchfield County Bar I transmit you a name which, though not decorated by the civic honors annexed to some of them, I think highly worthy of a place in the series.

Asa Bacon, the son of a very respectable and somewhat opulent farmer of Canterbury in this State, was born there on the 8th day of February, 1771. His early school and classical education was had in that and neighboring towns in Windham County so far as was necessary to a preparation for entering Yale College, which he did in September, 1789; and during his collegiate course, sustained a very prominent standing in his class; and by his instructor and class-mates was marked out as one who would make a distinguished figure in the profession in which his talents and turn of mind plainly indicated would be his choice. Immediately after his graduation in September, 1793, he entered the office of Gen. Cleaveland in his native town as a Law-student, and there remained about six months and then joined the Law school at Litchfield, at that time, and for long before, under the sole instruction of Tapping Reeve, Esq., afterwards Judge Reeve, in which he remained until admitted to the Bar in September, 1795, Soon after which, without consulting anybody or taking a single letter of which he might for asking obtained any quantity of the best sort, with characteristic boldness and love of adventure in youth, he left Connecticut for Virginia with a determination of establishing himself in the practice of law in the latter state: an attempt, it is believed never before made by any one from Connecticut. In order to the accomplishment of which object, he found on arrival in Virginia that he had got to obtain a license from a majority of the Judges of the Supreme Court in that state, and that too by visiting them at their respective residences: for they were not in the practice of examining and licensing candidates during the session of the court. This subjected him to the trouble and expense of traveling over a great part of the state; and this being accomplished, he determined to fix himself at Leesburg, the capital of Loudon county, and he accordingly opened an office for practice there; and being aided by a fine and imposing personal appearance and promptness in manners, he succeeded in obtaining a fair and encouraging portion of the business, and there remained for nearly three years, when, on returning to Connecticut to visit his relations, he found the prospects of professional business in his native county to be such as, in connection with a natural preference for Connecticut society to that of Virginia, to induce him to renounce his connection with his new formed establishment and open an office in his native town, and this he did not only with such success as speedily to secure him a fair professional business, but also to induce four young gentlemen to enter his office for legal instruction, upon a plan which he adopted; three of whom were from Massachusetts, and one a member of Congress from the state of New York.

After a prosperous practice of over seven years in Windham County, he received an invitation from the Hon. John Allen, then at the head of practice in the larger county of Litchfield, to remove there and become his partner in business. This he accepted, and was probably in a measure induced so to do from the prospect that Mr. Allen would, on account of declining health, wholly retire from the Bar at no very distant period; and this in fact happened at a time earlier than was desirable. By means of his connection with Mr. Allen, and of a peculiar faculty of his own, Mr. Bacon soon obtained an ample and satisfactory share of the business done at the Litchfield County Bar, and by his faithfulness and zeal in the management of it he retained it for many years to his great satisfaction, for he was very fond of his profession. No man more thoroughly identified himself with the interests of his client, insomuch that he could hardly bring himself to doubt of the justice of his cause, however he might of the legal means of obtaining it; hence his utmost exertions were sure to be put forth for the attainment of it. In untiring industry in the preparation of a cause for trial no man excelled him. He was an able, and when the nature of the case allowed of it, an eloquent advocate. Until some sixty years old he was in full practice, almost never being in any degree diverted from it by political aspirations. But repeated pneumoniac attacks of a threatening nature in the autumn of the year 1832 admonished him of the danger of much public speaking, and induced him to retire from the Bar as soon as it could conveniently be done. While in practice, his untiring diligence in the preparation of his causes for trial, the learning, wit and force of reasoning was so satisfactory to his numerous clients, that it was not remembered that any one who once employed him ever forsook him when in after time he had occasion for legal advice.

After the close of his practice of law, and indeed long before that event, Mr. Bacon paid much attention to pecuniary affairs, and his skill and judgment in the management, led to his appoinment as president of the branch of the Phœnix Bank located at Litchfield, which he held for a number of years. But his cautious policy in the management of it proved unsatisfactory to some of the stockholders, but more particularly with the managers at head quarters.

As a man, a mere private individual, Mr. Bacon will be agreed by all who ever knew him to have been a very peculiar man, both in appearance and in manner. He was full six feet two inches high; well formed for appearance; neither too fleshy nor too spare; and his inexhaustible fund of pleasant wit, judiciously used, made him an agreeable companion to both sexes and all ages: and having in himself an uncommon elasticity of spirits he was fitted to enjoy life

ASA BACON.
EPAPHRODITUS BACON.
MAJ. GEN. FRANCIS BACON.
BACONS
WELLER & CO

and to impart to others its enjoyment in an eminent degree. On many accounts, and indeed on most accounts, Mr. Bacon may be said to be a fortunate man, but on others, had it not been for his peculiar buoyancy of spirits, a very unfortunate man.

In March, 1807, he married Miss Lucretia Champion the only daughter of the Hon. Epaphroditus Champion, of East Haddam, who still survives him; and never was a man through a long married life of half a century, more happy in the conjugal connection. This marriage was blessed by the birth of three sons of uncommon promise, but all of them were cut down in early manhood: not, however, until each had given decided proof of natural and acquired capacity. Three daughters were also the fruit of that mariage, but all died in early infancy.

Quite a number of years since, Mr. Bacon disposed of his property in Litchfield and removed to New Haven, where he spent the remainder of his long and useful life, and died in the full possession of his mental faculties when but two days short of eighty-six years of age. No one ever questioned his integrity. He was a professor of religion, and is believed to have lived in accordance with his profession. He died in the possession of an ample estate, in a great degree the fruit of his discreet management, and out of which, it is but justice to his memory to state, he made a donation to Yale College of ten thousand dollars.

---

## ELISHA STERLING.

Gen. Elisha Sterling of Salisbury, who was for a long time a very respectable member of the Litchfield County Bar, was a native of Lyme in this State, where he received his training and early education, until he became a member of Yale College, of the class which graduated in September, 1787; and that he sustained a good standing in it is evinced by his having an honorary share in its commencement exercises. Immediately after his graduation he assumed the charge of an academy, then recently established in Sharon; and during the two years while it was under his management and tuition, it became very thoroughly established and very extensively and popularly known. While at the head of the academy he pursued the study of Law, and was admitted to the Bar in 1789 or 1790, and immediately opened an office for the practice of his profession in Salisbury, where he continued to reside during the remainder of his life. He was very fortunate in his place of settlement, and soon found himself engaged in lucrative practice, which he pursued with much industry for a long time; and it is believed that very few lawyers have by the mere practice of their profession in Connecticut acquired a larger property than he did. He was at an early period by the County Court appointed Attorney for the State in that County, and by them (to whom alone the right of that appointment then pertained,) annually reappointed for many years, and until a political change in a majority of that Court led to a change in the attorneyship. The propriety of his management as a public prosecutor was never questioned even by his political opponents. As a mere advocate he did not stand at the head of such practice, but did a respectable share of it, and stood high in the secondary rank; and in the entire amount of business, in point of profit, few equaled, and perhaps none surpassed him. In addition to the office of State's Attorney, he for a long time held the office of Judge of Probate for the district of Sharon—an office then depending upon the annual appointment of the legislature, and until, for a like cause above mentioned, he was required to give place to another, of different political principles from his own; and the latter office he held two or three years after he ceased to be, of the then, healthy political faith. He was very often a representative to the General Assembly from Salisbury when the political standing of the town would allow of such a choice, and was a major-general of the militia. At a somewhat earlier period he married a daughter of the Hon. John Canfield, deceased, of Sharon, who for a long time was a distinguished member of the Bar of Litchfield County in former times; and by that marriage he became the father of a somewhat numerous family, nearly all of whom were sons. They were all young men of promise, and on entering into business were well endowed by their father, and it is believed were respectable and prosperous in their several vocations. Gen. Sterling somewhat late in life married the widow of the Rev. Dr. John Elliott, who survived him. Through life Gen. Sterling enjoyed a good state of health, and died when over seventy years of age, in the year 1836, of a sudden illness occasioned by a slight wound in the leg, too much neglected. He was above medium size, of a light complexion and good personal appearance, and his moral and religious habits unimpeachable.

---

## JABEZ W. HUNTINGTON.

In compliance with former requests and of a recent intimation of my own, I now transmit you a brief sketch of the life and character of the Hon. Jabez W. Huntington, son of the late Gen. Zachariah Huntington of Norwich, and grandson of the Hon. Jabez Huntington of that place, the assistant and associate of the first Gov. Trumbull, who was born in Norwich in the year 1787 or 1788. He received his early training and instruction in his native town, which after times evinced to be accurate and good. He became a member of Yale College in September, 1802 and graduated in September,

1806, with the reputation of a good scholar. Soon after his graduation he became a teacher in an academic school under the government of its founder, Esquire Morris of Litchfield South Farms, as then called, now the town of Morris, named after the founder of said school. After about a year thus employed, Mr. Huntington entered Judge Reeve's Law School, in which he continued a diligent student until admitted to the Bar in Litchfield County, of which he soon showed himself to be a worthy member, and in due time a distinguished one; he having commenced the practice of his profession in Litchfield, and there continued it, until its final termination by an office conferred upon him incompatible with its further pursuit. In practice, his whole aim and ambition was to become an advocate, and had no desire to obtain any share of collecting business, though in many hands not less lucrative; and as he was always ready to aid the less ambitious of speaking, he early acquired a very considerable share of the portion of practice of which he was ambitious and which was improving to him. His forte as an advocate was in detecting error in declarations and other parts of pleadings, and in a lucid manner of pointing them out. Upon the whole he was as an advocate clear and accurate, rather than peculiar for the gracefulness of manner or refinement of diction, though his manner was by no means disgusting, and his language entirely free from any approach to vulgarity. His manners were pleasing and popular, and he repeatedly represented Litchfield in the General Assembly and distinguished himself there. He was elected to the 21st Congress, and re-elected to the 22d and 23d Congress; and near the expiration of the last of his Congressional career he was chosen a Judge of the Superior Court, and held that office until 1840, when being chosen a senator of the United States he resigned the Judgeship and accepted the latter appointment, and continued to hold it by virtue of a second appointment until his death in 1847. In all which stations he performed the duties thereof with honor to himself and to the entire satisfaction of the public. His moral character was irreproachable; a professor of religion and an observer of its precepts. Late in life he was married, but it is believed left no issue. Soon after election to Congress he removed to his native town and died there.

---

## PHINEAS MINER.

Phineas Miner, a very respectable and somewhat eminent member of the Litchfield County Bar, was a native of Winchester in that county, and there, and in that region, as far as by the writer hereof known, received his entire training and education in all respects. At an early period in life he commenced the practice of law in the place of his birth, in the society of Winsted, as is believed, a place of a great deal of active manufacturing business and furnishing an ample share of employment for gentlemen of the legal profession, of which Mr. Miner soon acquired an ample share, and at no distant period, an engrossing one, with which he appeared in court from term to term until he felt warranted in the expectation of drawing after him an engagement in all the disputable cases from that fruitful quarter, when he removed to Litchfield and was much employed as an advocate for a number of years, and until his health rather prematurely failed, and he became the victim of great mental and bodily suffering, until relieved by death before reaching the ordinary period at which old age begins to make its effects much perceptible in the human frame. As an advocate Mr. Miner was ardent, impassioned and fluent, but in his apparent great ambition to be eloquent he often made use of figures of speech which a more chastened and correct training in youth would have taught him to avoid, and less wounding to an ear of taste, but the fault apparent to all, was the extreme prolixity of his arguments; but these faults notwithstanding, Mr. Miner was a respectable and able advocate.

Before his removal to Litchfield Mr. Miner was an early and frequent member of the legislature from his native town and after his removal there, a member of the state senate for the fifteenth district, and was also elected to fill a vacancy in the second session of the twenty-third Congress.

Mr. Miner was twice married, but it is believed, left no issue, but of this the writer is uncertain. He led a strictly moral life and was justly esteemed a good man.

---

## LEMAN CHURCH.

One more attempt to comply with your repeated requests. Leman Church, a late member of the Litchfield County Bar, was a native of Salisbury in this county, a son of an opulent farmer of that town, and in it, it is supposed, he received his education, both scholastic and professional; the latter in the office of his half-brother, Samuel Church, afterwards a Judge of the Superior Court, and finally Chief Justice of the same, and after his admission to the bar he opened an office in North Canaan, where he resided during the remainder of his life. Mr. Church was successful in acquiring at an early period a promising share of professional business, which steadily increased, until by the middle of professional life he occupied a stand among the leading advocates at the bar; and towards the close of life there was scarce a cause, especially in the higher Courts, of considerable importance discussed, in which he was not engaged.

In September, 1833, Mr. Church was appointed by the Court, State's Attorney, as successor to his brother Samuel, on the latter's elevation to the bench of the Superior Court, and held that office by annual re-appointments until September term, 1838, when by a political change in the court he was required to yield the place to another; it is believed, however, that he afterwards for a time, re-occupied that place, but not positively recollected.

As a speaker he was cool, unimpassioned and ingenious; he never attempted to affect the passions of those he addressed, and being destitute of passion himself, was consequently incapable of moving the passions of others; he never attempted to be eloquent or made use of a merely ornate expression, his object in speaking was effect, and that wholly directed to his cause and not to himself; in the management of a case he was always cool and self-possessed; no sudden and unexpected turn in the progress of a trial disconcerted him, or appeared to be unexpected by him; no collision at the bar ever appeared to affect his temper in the least. With such a temperament it is obvious that the legal profession, was of all the professions, the one for him, and that in which he was calculated to excel.

Mr. Church was always entirely regardless of personal appearance and dress; he was very small, meager and ill formed, his features quite ordinary, but all this very indifferent appearance was rescued from inattention by a most remarkably attractive and intelligent eye.

Mr. Church was frequently a representative to the Legislature from Canaan, and never failed to make an impression upon that body; and to his sagacious management is attributable the presevation of the Housatonic Railroad from ruin, as a commissioner thereon appointed by the Legislature, with power, together with his associate in office, Mr. Pond, to sell and consequently to destroy the road which seemed to be a favorite object with them for a time.

Mr. Church died in the midst of life as a professional man, July 1849. I am unable to state the particulars of his family.

# Sedgwick's Fifty Years

# FIFTY YEARS

AT THE

# LITCHFIELD COUNTY BAR

## A LECTURE

DELIVERED BEFORE THE

LITCHFIELD COUNTY BAR

BY

CHARLES F. SEDGWICK, ESQ.

1870.

CHAS. F. SEDGWICK

# SEDGWICK'S ADDRESS.

Litchfield, Feb. 9, 1870.

GEN. SEDGWICK:

My Dear Sir—At a bar meeting held this noon the following resolution was offered by E. W. Seymour and unanimously adopted:

*Whereas,* at the next term of this Court Gen. C. F. Sedgwick will have completed a fifty years connection with this bar as a respected member thereof,

*Resolved,* That he be invited to deliver an address in the Court Room at such time next term as may be convenient to him upon some subject connected with his long professional career.

*Resolved,* That a committee of three be appointed to extend this invitation to the General and to make arrangements that may be necessary in case the invitation be accepted,

O. S. Seymour, J. H. Hubbard and Abijah Catlin were appointed a committee for this purpose.

It gives the committee great pleasure to communicate the foregoing proceedings to you and we hope you will gratify us by accepting the invitation. We will at any time confer with you upon the subject of what arrangements should be made.

Yours truly, O. S. SEYMOUR,
For the Committee.

The committee of the Litchfield County Bar have received the annexed letter from General Sedgwick and have agreed upon Wednesday evening, the 13th of April, for hearing the commemoration discourse at the Court Room. Members of the Bar of other Courts and the public generally are invited to attend.

J. H. HUBBARD,
O. S. SEYMOUR,
ABIJAH CATLIN,
Committee.

---

Litchfield, March 14, 1870.

SHARON, March 12, 1870.

JUDGE SEYMOUR:

*Dear Sir*—I received, in due time, yours, written in behalf of the committee of the Bar, and owe you an apology for not giving it an earlier answer. The truth is that I have hesitated to give an affirmative response from a feeling of incompetency to get up any thing which would be of any interest to my kind friends of the Bar whose polite proceedings you communicate. But the respect which I feel for them combined with a feeling of gratitude for the past kindnesses as well as the urgency of many individuals of the profession here as well as in other counties have persuaded me to make the attempt to comply with their wishes, and I will try to get up a commemoration discourse to be read to the Bar at the next term of the Court. As Good Friday will come during the first week of Court I will suggest Wednesday evening of that week for the hearing instead of Thursday, but in this I will conform to the wishes of the committee. If they should fix on any other evening please notify me.

Yours, respectfully,

C. F. SEDGWICK.

## ADDRESS.

The statement that I have been for fifty years a member of the bar of this county, admonishes me of a rapid journey across the stage of life, from its morning to its evening. Those years have sped away, and they have embraced a large portion of the time usually alloted to man as the period of his existence here.

"Large space are they
Of man's brief life, those fifty years; they join
Its ruddy morning with the paler light
Of its declining hours."

They have swept off in their current nearly every one who was active in the proceedings of the courts of this county, at the commencement of that period. It did not then occur to me to consider the question whether I should outlive nearly all my associates at the bar, but of the forty-four members who were then in active practice here, all save three, and they are not now in practice, have preceded me on their journey to the grave. Some have laid their bones in distant parts of the country, but with the exception above named, all have gone to their last account.

I suppose it to be the wish of the bar, as it has been intimated to me, that I should say something of those who were active in conducting the judicial proceedings in this County, fifty years ago. This will imply a notice of the judges, clerks and officers of the court, as well as the legal profession. A wide field is open before me, and I fear the exploration which I shall give it will be of very little interest to my brethren, but such impressions of the men of those times as remain with me, I will endeavor to lay before them.

---

### RE-ORGANIZATION OF THE COURTS.

The Courts had then just been organized under the present Constitution of the State. Under the old government, the Supreme

Court consisted of nine judges, and they were elected annually by the legislature. Under the Constitution, the number was reduced to five, and they held their office during good behaviour, or until they reached the age of seventy years. In like manner, the judges of the County Courts were reduced from five to three. Formerly these judges held the Superior Courts, but under the Constitution, they were holden by one judge. The old Court has embodied as high an order of judicial talent as any other Court in any of the States, and when the appointment of the judges under the new organization was in contemplation, much anxiety was felt among the members of the legal profession lest the character of the Court should deteriorate. Chief Justice Swift was very popular with all classes, and it was thought that his high character as a jurist, and his spotless character as a man, would render it pretty certain that he be retained at the head of the new Court. But the party then in power, known in our political history as the Toleration party, determined to make an almost entire change in the material of the Court, and to man the bench with new incumbents. For the new Chief Justice, they selected the Hon. Stephen Titus Hosmer, of Middletown, who had been a member of the old Court some three or four years, and who, it was claimed, had voted the ticket of the party at the next preceding election. It was laid to his charge that he had done so with the intent of thereby obtaining the position which he was afterwards called to fill. The other judges were John T. Peters, Asa Chapman, Jeremiah Gates Brainard, and William Bristol. Judge Brainard was of the old Court, and it was the intention of the ruling party to put James Lanman in the place; but some of the tolerationists of New London County did not believe him qualified to fill it, and refused to vote for him. Judge Brainard was of the same county, and the federalists naturally rallied upon him in opposition to Lanman, and with the aid of dissentient tolerationists, Brainard was elected. He was the only old federalist on the bench, till Daggett came on, in 1826.

---

## CHIEF JUSTICE HOSMER.

Stephen Titus Hosmer was a lawyer of eminence in his peculiar way. He had no very high standing as an advocate, but as a lawyer, learned in elementary principles his position was a very good one. A gentleman who had heard him, told me that his manner was hard and dry, and his elocution very defective, but in some branches of legal science he had few superiors. He seemed to delight in exploring ancient paths in search of legal principles, and in getting up old legal tracts and dissertations. In the first volume of Day's Reports, there is a note of forty pages of fine print, containing an opinion of Lord Camden, of the English Court of Common Pleas, which has hardly a rival in judicial learning or eloquence. Mr. Day informed me that this was presented him in manuscript by Mr. Hosmer, there being then no printed copy of it on this side of the Atlantic. He was appointed a Judge of the old Court in 1815, but being one of the younger judges, it never fell to his lot to preside on the trial of a case, until his accession to the Chief Justiceship. His career, on the whole, was very successful, both at *nisi prius,* and on the bench of the Supreme Court. His apprehension of the points involved in the case before him, was very quick, and the first intimation he gave on incidental matters occurring in the course of the trial, was a sure indication of what the result would be; and although he would take special pains to say to the counsel that he had formed no opinion, the party against whom he leaned knew that his fate was sealed. His labors in his official duties must have been immense. It fell to his lot to give the opinion of the Court in nearly all the cases tried in the Supreme Court for several years after his appointment, and nearly all the material of the third, fourth and fifth large volumes of the Connecticut Reports are the result of his study of the cases before the Court, and some of them are very learned and labored. His illustrations in the case of Mitchell *vs.* Warner, in the 2d of Connecticut Reports, of the extent of the obligations incurred in the covenants of a deed, explained the subject to me, when I was young, better than anything I had before read on the subject.

It seemed to be his object to render himself as agreeable as possible to the members of the bar, sometimes employing his leisure moments on the bench in furnishing prescriptions for human ailments, such as corns on the toes, and handing them over to such members as stood in need of them. Then he would hand over a formula for making, as he said, the best kind of liquid blacking for our boots. In fact, every thing which he had prescribed, he always designated as *the very best.* At one term of the Court, Phineas Miner, Esq., who had lived a widower for several years, was about being married, which fact was intimated to the Judge. While he sat waiting on the bench for the preparation of some business, he spoke out suddenly, "Gentlemen! Is there a vacant cell in your jail? Won't it be necessary for me to commit Mr. Miner to prevent his doing some rash act?" The laugh was thoroughly turned upon poor Miner, and the whole scene was very enjoyable. He employed all his leisure hours in obtaining all the relaxation which was within his reach. He played on the piano and violin, and sang with great power and effect.

There was no perceptible waning of his powers, physical or mental, during the time of his service on the Court. He retired from the bench at the age of 70 years, in February, 1833, and died, after a short illness, in less than two years thereafter.

JUDGE PETERS.

John Thompson Peters was the senior Associate Judge of the Court, and he held his first circuit in this County. He was a native of Hebron, and a lawyer of respectable standing. His fellow-citizens had often honored him with a seat in the Legislature, and thus he had become tolerably well known in the State. When the United States direct tax was laid in 1813, he was appointed Collector for the first district, removed to Hartford, and held that office when he was appointed Judge. He had been one of the leaders of the Democratic party from its formation; and, as an Episcopalian, had opposed the claims of the "Standing Order" to ecclesiastical priority, and some apprehensions were felt lest his well known views on these subjects might temper his opinions on those questions incidentally involving them. Many fears were entertained as to the stability of ecclesiastical funds which existed in almost every Congregational parish, and those who desired to break them down looked to Judge Peters and his influence with the Court to aid them. But those who entertained such hopes were destined to an early disappointment, as their first experience of his administration on such questions showed him to be disposed to stand firmly on the old paths. He used to tell an amusing anecdote relating to his first trial of such a case in one of the Eastern Counties of the State, where he was appealed to, very strongly, to decide that a promise to pay money in aid of such funds was without consideration. But he told the parties that the law on that subject was well settled, and, in his opinion, founded on correct principles; and that if he had the power, he had not the disposition to change it. It had been the practice of the Congregational pastor of the village, to open the proceedings in Court with prayer, but considering Peters to be a heretic, (I use the Judge's own language,) he had never invited Divine favor for him, but after that decision, every prayer was charged with invocations of blessings upon "*thy sarvent, the judge.*"

He was very severe in meting out the punishments of the law to convicted criminals, generally inflicting the severest sentence that the law would allow. One case was tried before him which excited much remark and some reprehension. A man had been convicted before Judge Lanman of a State prison offence, had been sentenced to four years' imprisonment and had served a part of a year, when he obtained a new trial. He was tried again before Judge Peters, and again convicted. When the time came to pass sentence on the last conviction, his counsel asked for some mitigation on account of the imprisonment already suffered. Said the Judge "He must settle that account with Judge Lanman. He owes me five years' imprisonment in State prison"—and such was the sentence. One prisoner who had received a severe sentence at his hands, after the expiration of his confinement, burned the Judge's barn, and he petitioned the Legislature of the State to pay for it, in 1813, but they declined to make the compensation.

For a few years, the services of Judge Peters on the bench were very acceptable. His decisions were prompt, and generally founded on a sensible view of the matter before him, without any affecttation of learning or display of oratory. His entire candor and fairness were never called in question, and the decay of his powers, which was very apparent towards the close of his career, was observed by the bar with sorrow and regret. I witnessed an affecting scene connected with his experience on the bench, which excited a deep feeling of sympathy. He had a favorite son, Hugh Peters, Esq., whom he had educated at Yale College, and in whom all his hopes seemed to centre. This young man, in connection with George D. Prentice, the noted Editor, had much to do in conducting the New England *Weekly Review*, a paper just established in Hartford, and which was the organ of the party which elected William W. Ellsworth, Jabez W. Huntington, and William L. Storrs to Congress. He had acquired a wide reputation as a writer of brilliant promise, and after a while went to Cincinnati to go into business as a lawyer. On his way across Long Island Sound, he wrote a Farewell to New England in poetry, which was published with great commendation, in most of the newspapers in the country. Soon after his arrival at Cincinnati, his dead body was found floating in the Ohio, several miles below the city, and circumstances were such as to create the belief in some minds that it was a case of suicide. The intelligence of this sad event was brought to Litchfield while the Court of Errors was in session in June, 1831. It was first communicated to Judge Williams, who sat next to Judge Peters; and he, with all possible tenderness, informed the latter. The Reporter, Mr. Day, in giving the report of the case on trial, closing it by saying: "Peters, Judge, having received, during the argument of this case, intelligence of the death of his son, Hugh Peters, Esq., of Cincinnati, left the Court House, *'multa gemens casuque animum concessus,'* and gave no opinion." I witnessed the mournful scene, and I well remember the loud and plaintive groans of the afflicted old man as he passed out of the Court room and down the stairway to his lodgings.

When Chief Justice Hosmer retired from the bench, the Legislature, by a very strong vote, elected Judge Peters' junior, Judge Daggett, Chief Justice. He felt the slight, but did not retire, and held his place till his death in August, 1834. A few weeks longer, and he would have reached the age of seventy years.

---

### JUDGE CHAPMAN.

The next Judge in seniority was Asa Chapman, of Newtown, in Fairfield County. For several years before he received the appointment, he practiced to some extent in this County, and was, of course, well known here. He was the father of the late Charles Chapman of Hartford. He was somewhat taller than the son, and with his bald head, white locks, thin face, and grey eyes, he resembled him not a little in personal appearance, but he had none of that bitterness of manner or spirit which characterized the efforts of the younger Chapman. He was an Episcopalian in religious faith, and he had very naturally fallen into the ranks of the new party, and being well qualified for the place in point of legal ability, he made a very acceptable and popular Judge. He was a man of good humor, genial temper, and great colloquial powers, which he exercised very freely on the trial of cases. If a lawyer undertook to argue a case before him, he soon found himself engaged in a friendly, familiar conversation with the Judge the evident intent of the latter being to draw out the truth and justice of the case. His adminstration was very popular, and his early death was greatly deplored. He died of consumption in 1826, at the age of fifty-six years.

---

### JUDGE BRAINARD.

Jeremiah Gates Brainard, of New London, the father of the poet Brainard, was next in seniority on the bench. He had been a member of the old Court from 1807 and he was elected to the new Court, under the circumstances which I have mentioned. He was a man of no showy pretensions, very plain and simple in his manners, and very familiar in his intercourse with the Bar. He affected very little dignity on the bench, and yet he was regarded as an excellent Judge. He dispatched business with great facility, and implicit confidence was placed in his sound judgment and integrity. He resigned his place on the bench in 1829, his health not being equal to the duties of the office, having served as judge for twenty-two years.

---

### JUDGE BRISTOL.

Of all the judges on the bench, William Bristol of New Haven was the youngest in years as well as in rank. He had not been much known as a lawyer, out of the County of New Haven, and, of course his coming here was looked for with considerable interest. He evidently had a high sense of judicial dignity, his manners on the bench being very taciturn, approaching severeness, very seldom speaking, except to announce his decisions in the fewest possible words, and I doubt if any one ever saw him smile in Court. His decisions were sound and well considered and, upon the whole, his administration was respectable, although he could not be said to have had much personal popularity at the bar.

## JUDGE DAGGETT.

The decease of Judge Chapman and the resignation of Judge Bristol in 1826, created two vacancies in the Court which were to be filled at the session of the Legislature of that year. The same party which had effected the change in the government of the state, and in the constitution of the Court, was still in power, but nearly all the eminent lawyers in the State adhered to the federal party. Probably the most obnoxious man in the state to the dominant party was David Daggett, not so much from personal dislike as from his prominence in the ranks of his party. His talents, integrity and high legal abilitties were conceeded by everyone, but when the legislature assembled, there was probably not a man in the state who looked to his election as a judge.

There were a few men in the state belonging to the toleration party who felt deeply the importance of having a reputable court, and who, on this question, were willing to forego all party consideration. Morris Woodruff, of Litchfield County, Thaddeus Betts and Charles Hawley, of Fairfield County, Walter Booth, of New Haven County, and Charles J. McCurdy, of New London County, were men of that stamp; and it was through the influence of these men, and of others of less prominence, that David Daggett was elected a Judge of the Supreme Court. The same influence, exerted by the same men, secured the election of Judges Williams and Bissell, three years later.

After the election of Judge Daggett was effected, no one seemed to care who the other judge might be, as with Chief Justice Hosmer at the head of the court, and Judge Daggett as an associate, it was felt that it could have a highly respectable character. The Hon. James Lanman received the appointment, but after a short term of service, resigned.

An elaborate sketch of Judge Daggett is given in the twentieth volume of our reports.

---

## THE SUPERIOR COURT, FIFTY YEARS SINCE.

There were sessions of the Superior Court in each year, holden on the third Tuesdays of August and February, and the terms rarely extended beyond two weeks. If they reached to the third week they were deemed to be of extraordinary length. The Superior Court had no original jurisdiction, except as a court of equity. All its actions at law came up by appeal from the County Court, and generally important cases were carried up without trial in the court below. The party wishing to appeal his case would demur, either to the declaration or plea, as the case might be, suffer a judgment to be entered against him, and appeal from it and then

AUGUSTUS PETTIBONE

MICHAEL F. MILLS

JOSEPH F. BALLAMY

WM. G. COE

change his plea in the Superior Court as the exigencies of his case may require. The making of copies in the case appealed was a very profitable item in the business of the clerk. All cases at law wherein the matter in demand exceeded seventy dollars were appealable, and all matters in equity in which the sum involved exceeded three hundred dollars were brought originally to the Superior Court. In criminal matters the jurisdiction of both courts was concurrent, except in crimes of a higher grade which were tried exclusively in the Superior Court. A case was pretty certain to reach a trial at the second term after it was entered in the docket, unless special reasons could be shown for its further continuance.

---

### THE COUNTY COURT—JUDGE PETTIBONE.

The County Court had an important agency in the administration of Justice, fifty years ago. Under the old form of government it consisted of one judge and four justices of the quorum; under the constitution, of one Chief Judge and two associate judges. When I came to the bar Augustus Pettibone of Norfolk was Chief Judge; Martin Strong, of Salisbury, and John Welch, of Litchfield, associate judges. Judge Pettibone had presided for several years in the old court, and although he was a federalist of decided convictions, he was continued in office by the party in power until he resigned the place in 1832. It will be remembered that the judges in this court were appointed annually by the legislature. Judge Pettibone had a high standing as a man of integrity and of sound common sense. His early education was deficient and he made many grammatical mistakes in his charges to the jury, but he had been esteemed, and was a lawyer of respectable attainments. He was a native of Norfolk, where he lived to a very great age. He was tall and slender in person, somewhat round shouldered with hair which was very abundant and which remained so during life. No one could doubt the fairness and good sense of his decisions; and, upon the whole, his career as a judge was creditable to his reputation.

---

### JUDGE STRONG.

Martin Strong of Salisbury, was the senior associate judge. He was a son of Col. Adonijah Strong of that town, a lawyer of the olden time, of whose wit as well as blunders, many stories were rife fifty years ogo. Colonel Strong had four sons all of whom entered into professional life, two as clergymen and two as lawyers. His son, the Rev. William Strong, was father of the Hon. William Strong, of Pennsylvania, recently appointed an associate justice of the Supreme Court of the United States. Our Judge

Martin Strong had been a member of the bar for several years, but had never made a very high mark in his profession—in fact he had never devoted himself very assiduously to the discharge of its duties. He owned a large and valuable farm on the town hill in Salisbury, and his principal business was to attend to that. When he came upon the bench he seemed to have a recollection of a few plain legal maxims, but his methods of applying them to cases was not always the most skillful. He was a man of immense physical dimensions, and when he had taken his seat on the bench, he sat in perfect quiet, until the loud proclamation of the sheriff announced the adjournment of the court. He remained in office till 1829, when William M. Burrall, Esq., of Canaan, took his place.

---

### JUDGE WELCH.

The junior judge of the court was the Hon. John Welch of Litchfield. He was a native of the parish of Milton and a graduate of Yale College in the class of 1778, a class which is said to have produced more eminent men in proportion to its numbers than any other which ever graduated at that institution. Joel Barlow, Zephaniah Swift, Uriah Tracy, Noah Webster and the last Governor Wolcott, with many other distinguished men, were of the class.

Judge Welch never entered either of the professions, but he lived to a very great age. He was appointed a judge of the County Court in the place of Cyrus Swan, Esq., of Sharon, who had resigned his position on the bench of the court in 1819. Judge Welch continued on the bench till he became disqualified by age in 1829. He made no pretentions to legal learning but his decisions were based on a fair impartial view of the questions as they came up. He always gave reasons for the opinion he had formed, always made himself well understood, and his candor, fairness and sound judgment were admitted by all.

---

### JUDGES BURRALL, WOODRUFF AND BOARDMAN.

In 1829, when Judge Welch must retire on account of his age, it was deemed proper by the legislature to make new appointments of both associate judges. Judge Strong had been twelve years on the bench, and in his place William M. Burrall, Esq., of Canaan, was appointed senior associate judge, and Gen. Morris Woodruff took the place of Judge Welch. The court continued thus organized till the resignation of Judge Pettibone, when, not only with the consent, but with the decided approval of both associate judges, David S. Boardman, Esq., of New Milford, was taken from the bar and installed Chief Judge of the County Court, which as then constituted, held a high position in public confidence.

HON. FREDERICK WOLCOTT, CLERK

The Clerk of the Court was the Hon. Frederick Wolcott, who was appointed as early as 1781, and who retained the place till 1835, when he resigned, after a service of forty-four years. He was a son of the second, and a brother of the late Governor of that name, and undoubtedly cherished highly aristocratic feelings and had a great amount of family pride, but his intercourse with the members of the bar was gentlemanly and conciliatory. He was of a noble presence, large and manly in person, and always dressed in the best style of the ancient fashion of small clothes, white stockings, and white topped boots. His knowledge of legal proceedings in the County, ran back so far that no one ever presumed to question his accuracy as to legal forms and precedents. When his resignation was accepted by the Court, a minute, prepared by Judge Burrall, which referred to his long and faithful service, and which contained the statement that no judgment of the Court had ever been reversed on account of any mistake of the Clerk, was entered on the records of the County Court. He was a member of the Governor's Council under the Charter Government, and was coutinued in the Senate for several years, under the constitution.

---

### SHERIFF SEYMOUR

Moses Seymour, Jr., Esq., was Sheriff of the County from 1819 to 1825, but the active duties of the office were performed by his deputy, his brother Ozias, who had been a deputy of the old Sheriff Landon, and who had become well acquainted with the practical duties of the office as they were preformed in our County. He opened and adjourned the daily sessions, called parties to appear in court as their presence was demanded, and, in fact, was the active Sheriff in nearly all the proceedings. He succeeded his brother as Sheriff in 1825, and held the office till 1834.

---

### UNCLE JOHN STONE, MESSENGER

Nor must we omit to mention here, the messenger of that day, good old Uncle John Stone. How long he had held the place before 1820, I know not, but I found him here then, and it took but a very short time to make his acquaintance, and learn his kindness of heart. He had a kind of dry humor, which sometimes showed itself in witty sayings, and sometimes in pungent sarcasms. He was a faithful messenger, an honest man, and to all human appearance, a sincere christian. He retained his place till he fell dead in the public highway, in 1830, in a fit of apoplexy.

---

### BUSINESS OF THE OLD COUNTY COURT

There were three sessions of the old County Court in each year in March, September and December. The September term was generally short, merely disposing of the criminal business, and such other preliminary matters as could not be passed over. The March term lasted three weeks, and the December term from four to six weeks, as the business might demand. The first half day was always taken up in calling the docket. Mr. Wolcott had his files arranged alphabetically, corresponding with the entries on the docket and of these some member of the bar, usually one of the younger, had charge. The Sheriff took his station in the center of the bar, and as the cases were named by the Clerk, the proper entries were made both on the docket and on the file, and then the file was passed to the Sheriff, who delivered it to the party entitled to it, and thus, at the close of the proceedings all the files had passed into the hands of the members of the bar where they remained until the case received final disposition. Three hundred cases were considered as constituting a small docket and I have known as many as nine hundred entered at a single term.

---

ADMISSION TO THE BAR.

When I came to the bar in 1820, there were two grades of lawyers in the State. The first admission only authorized the candidate to practice at the County Court, and a service of two years was required at that bar before he was allowed an examination for admission to the bar of the Superior Court; and I was at the bar of the County Court for a year or more in expectation of undergoing another ordeal in the upper Court. In the meantime the statutes of the State had been revised under the superintendence of Judge Swift and many and material alterations had been made to conform the provisions of the law to the new order of things under the constitutions. The question came before Judge Brainard and he decided that under the revised statutes an admission to the bar of the County Court gave the candidate authority to practice in all the Courts in the State, and that decision was assented to by all the judges.

The matter of examining candidates for admission to the bar was, in those days, an imposing solemnity, and the day for that proceeding was a marked day of the term. All the members of the bar were expected to be present and few failed of attending. The committee of examination occupied the judges seats; the chairman holding the place of the Chief Judge, indicating to each separate member of the committee the subject in which he was expected to examine the candidate, and thus a thorough and searching examination was had. After the examination was closed the candidates retired, and the members of the bar gave their opinions *seriatim* on the question of the admission of the applicant. Sometimes candidates were rejected. It had been the practice in early times to have an entertainment at the close of the examination at the expense of the successful candidates, but this had been dispensed with when I was examined. Stories were told of some eminent members of the bar who, on such occasions, indulged in practices which were not creditable to their reputation for temperance and sobriety. Perhaps it was for this reason that the practice was abolished.

### PRACTICE.

Statutory provisions and the advance of legal science, as well as a more just sense of what is due to the best interest of litigation, have made great changes in the course of proceedings before the Courts, during the last fifty years. Then, it was customary for counsel to take advantage of any trivial omission which could be found in the proceedings, and a case never came to trial until every possible effort for abatement or delay, had been exhausted. Our Statute in relation to amendments had not then received so liberal a construction, nor was it in itself so liberal in its provisions as it now is; and thus opportunity was afforded for the display of much ingenuity in the prosecution of dilatory pleas.

Then, there were no statutory provisions relating to injunctions. All the power which the Court had in that matter being that with which it was invested by the common law as a Court of Equity, and hence, very little will be found in our Reports on this subject, until about 1826, after the Statute authorizing the judges to grant temporary injunctions had been passed. This Statute was introduced into the legislature by Judge Swift, who was a member for several sessions after his retirement from the bench. Since then many cases relating to this branch of jurisprudence, have been before our Courts.

Probably more than half the suits commenced in our County Courts, fifty years ago, were brought to enforce the collection of debts, and in some localities this was a profitable business. The County Court then had jurisdiction in all cases where the matter in demand exceeded the sum of fifteen dollars, and this brought into it a great number of suits now tried by single justices, and accounts for the great diminution in the number of cases now brought here.

Piles of learning were devoted to destruction by the edict of the legislature, admitting parties and other persons in interest to be heard as witnesses. The nicest and most refined legal questions were frequently brought before the Courts for decision in matters relating to the interest of witnesses, but now they are almost forgotten by the most learned of the profession.

---

### THE AUTHORITIES THEN IN USE.

The Statutes then in force were the Revision of 1808, by far the most elaborate and complete of any ever published. It contains a complete history of the legislation of Connecticut on all subjects of statutory enactment from the first, and is still a useful book for study by the profession. The principal labor of its preparation for publication was performed by Thomas Day.

Comparatively few American authorities were cited in our

Courts, then. Mr. Day had published four volumes of Day's Reports, and then had suspended further publication for want of encouragement. The Legislature, in 1815, had authorized the Court to appoint a Reporter, and had given him a salary. Under such an appointment, Mr. Day had commenced publishing the Connecticut Reports, and had published three volumes of them, when he published the fifth of Day, thus filling the gap between the fourth of Day and the first of Connecticut. The N. Y. Reports, by Caine and Johnson, down to the 12th of Johnson, and twelve volumes of the Massachusetts Reports, were out, and these, with our Reports, were about the only American authorities which were cited in our Courts Not a single American elementary work had then been published, except Swift's System and Swift's Evidence. The English Reports from Burrows down, including Douglas', Cowper's, Term, and East's Reports, down to the 12th volume, with Blackstone's Commentaries, which were always on the table, were the staple authorities of the times. I remark in passing, that Judge Reeve said that he considered Cowper's Reports the best that had then been published of the decisions of the Court of King's bench.

But it is time to speak of the warriors in those bloodless forensic battles which were fought on this field, fifty years ago. They are all fresh in my memory, but they have passed from the stage of life. I have delayed this part of my undertaking to the last moment, from the mere dread of entering upon it. I feel it to be a very difficult task to present the lawyers of those days to the profession now, in anything like their just attitude. Men of the highest attainments at the bar are entirely different from each other. Many little things which cannot be detailed enter into the composition of the characters of different men. The same qualities mingle in unequal proportions in different persons and I feel embarrassed in every way as I approach the task of speaking of the professional gentlemen who manned the post of duty on this field, fifty years ago.

There were then, as now, two clases of the profession here. One class had a local practice, being principally engaged in causes arising in their immediate locality. The practice of the other class was co-extensive with the power of their ability and not always confined to the county—of this later class there were several here.

---

## JUDGE GOULD.

The Honorable James Gould had undoubtedly stood at the head of the profession in this state, both as an advocate and a lawyer, previous to his elevation to the bench of the Supreme Court. After his retirement from that position he professed to have retired from practice, and devoted himself principally to giving law lectures to students, but in two cases in this county, and one in Hartford County, he came to the bar and conducted the trials. One was the case of the Phoenix Bank against Governor Wolcott and others, in which the Governor endeavored to avoid payment of a debt for which he was only a surety, on the grounds of usury. It was a proceeding in equity, and the argument of Judge Gould was exceedingly able and elaborate. He occasionally indulged in keen, cutting sarcasms, which pointed strongly to the Honorable defendant who was present. His argument was what Cotton Mather would call *"a luculent commentary"* on the law of usury. The case was decided in favor of the Bank.

The other was a trial to the jury in which a very intimate friend of Judge Gould was a party, and in this case his professional eminence was exhibited in a very striking manner. In his argument he was entirely unimpassioned, and remarkably clear in his illustrations. He stood much of the time with his hand on a book, which stood on one end, on the table before him, and I do not remember that he made a single gesture during the whole time of his argument. He occupied the attention of the court and jury for an hour and a half, and it was the last case he tried. He was a perfect master of the most effective method of delivery. In his written opinions while on the bench there is sometimes an involution of thought and language as well as a prolongation of sentences which renders necessary the strictest attention while reading to work out the true meaning, but in his oral deliveries he had such a perfect mastery of the laws of accent, emphasis and cadence as to make his meaning intelligible to the most careless hearer. The exhibition of his ability in this case was an appropriate closing effort of a long career of high professional eminence.

There were a few other members of the bar, not reaching the eminence of Judge Gould, yet whose practice was co-extensive with the county and extended sometimes into other counties. The names of the following gentlemen now occur to me as belonging to that class: Noah B. Benedict, Asa Bacon, Elijah Sterling, David S. Boardman and Phineas Miner. I have not included the name of Jabez W. Huntington, for the reason that he was then a young man and had not, by any means, reached the high standing which he afterwards attained. He was engaged in very many of the cases tried, but very often as a volunteer in aid of some young beginner who had sought his help, which under such circumstances he was always willing to render. For the same reason I have omitted the late Chief Justice Church because he was then just beginning to obtain a good professional standing, and was called to the bench of the Supreme Court which he afterwards greatly adorned before he had obtained the high rank as a lawyer which otherwise surely awaited him.

### NOAH B. BENEDICT.

From my best recollection of the standing of the first lawyers at the bar in those olden times, I am inclined to award the first place as an advocate to Noah B. Benedict. He had every advantage which a fine personal appearance could give him, not very tall, but well proportioned, with a countenance of great beauty, indicating kindness of feeling and intelligence of mind. His arguments produced conviction in the minds of the triers more by *insinuation* than by *impression.* He was earnest, but seldom impassioned, mild and winning in his manner, and thus worked his way as by stealth to the heart and convictions of the court and jury. I remember a case on trial in which he was opposed by Boardman; and Benedict, who was for the defendant on the trial, contested the points inch by inch as they arose in the case. During an intermission some one asked Boardman how they were getting along with their case. He replied impatiently, "Not very well. Benedict is as ingenious as the devil can make him, and he plagues us to death." He was engaged in nearly all the important cases tried in all the courts, and his practice was extensive in New Haven and Fairfield counties. He attended the session of the Supreme Court at Litchfield in 1831 and argued several cases, but left on account of illness before the term closed. In a short time I heard he was dead. He had reached the age of sixty-one years. In the case of *Fairman vs. Bacon* the last case but one which Mr. Benedict argued, Judge Daggett, in giving the opinion of the court, pays the following tribute to his memory: "I have, in this opinion, made great use of a brief furnished by the late, lamented Mr. Benedict, because I found it presented the argument in that terse, yet luminous view of which that gentleman was so conspicuous, and by which the court were so often instructed and enlightened, and rarely more so than in this, one of his last efforts."

---

### ASA BACON.

Asa Bacon was a native of Canterbury and came to Litchfield as early as 1806, after a short period of practice at East Haven, and, for a while, was a partner of Judge Gould. In 1820 he had become a leading spirit at the bar. He had a fine personal appearance, being tall and well proportioned, and usually richly dressed. The first time I saw him before the jury his head was well cased in powder and pomatum, and a long queue was dangling at his back; but he soon laid aside this conformity to old time fashions, although he was the last member of the bar to do so. He was undoubtedly a very hard student, and his briefs were the result of extensive and faithful study, but was after all an interesting speaker. He would sometimes interlude his arguments with specimens of drollery and flashes of wit, and the expectation that these would be put forth secured a very strict attention from all his hearers. He frequently quoted passages of scripture, and commented upon them, not always irreverently, but sometimes with rather unbecoming levity. He was a mortal enemy of universal suffrage, and once in commenting upon the parable of talents he called the bailee of one talent who had hid it in the earth *a universal suffrage man.* He was a genial, jolly, companionable man, and although not addicted to excessive liberality in his benefactions, still kept himself in good standing while he remained here. When he had reached the age of sixty years he was appointed president of the Branch of the Phoenix Bank, located in Litchfield, and after that was never seen professionally engaged in Court. The last years of his life were spent in New Haven where he died at a very advanced age.

---

## GENERAL STERLING

General Elisha Sterling was a native of Lyme and a graduate of Yale College in the class of 1787. He studied law with the Hon. John Canfield of Sharon, who was his father-in-law, and settled in Salisbury in 1791. He was a man of high order of talent, and had he addressed himself solely to professional points would probably have stood at the head of the bar in this county. But he loved money and gave much of his time to different kinds of business, and acquired great wealth for those times. Notwithstanding this propensity he had an extensive practice and was engaged in most of the cases coming from the northern portions of the county. He was a ready speaker, not very select in the choice of words and not eloquent by any established rule of elocution, but there was a kind of impetuosity in his manner, accompanied by a rapid but distinct utterance of language which gave him popularity as an advocate. He was appointed State's Attorney in 1814, and held the office six years when Seth P. Beers, Esq., was appointed in his place. He retired from practice soon after, and died in 1836, at the age of seventy-two years. His wealth enabled him to indulge the strong taste he had for a handsome style of living and equipage, and in that direction his mind had strong aristocratical tendencies.

---

## JUDGE BOARDMAN

David S. Boardman was a native of New Milford and settled there in the practice of law after his admission to the bar in 1795.

He was a man of retiring disposition, in no way giving showy display of his powers, but he was a finished legal scholar, and was deemed a very safe and prudent professional adviser. He had a very nice literary taste, and the least grammatical blunder by a judge or lawyer attracted his attention and frequently his ridicule. His arguments were pointed specimens of perspicuity, precision and force, but he failed to attract much attention as an advocate through a defect of vocal power. His voice was feeble and could scarcely be heard except by those who were near him. He had a high character for moral rectitude, and his four or five years service at the head of the County Court gave it a dignity and moral power which in other years it had scarcely obtained. Sketches from his pen, descriptive of some of the members of the bar in this County of the last century were published in one of our county papers, some twenty years ago, and they are of the deepest interest to those whose tastes lead them in that direction of historic inquiry. They were originally in letters written to myself, and were afterwards with his consent prepared for the press and published in the paper and in pamphlet form. He was a College classmate of Asa Bacon and they were warm personal friends. He lived to the great age of ninety-seven years.

---

## PHINEAS MINER.

Phineas Miner, the last because the youngest of the class of lawyers to whom I have referred deserves a much more extended notice than I shall be able to give him. His amiable and genial temper as a man seemed to make him very popular as a lawyer. Fidelity to his client and a laborious attention to their interests was a marked trait in his professional career. He commenced practice in Winchester, his native town, and had there acquired a good standing in his profession when he came to Litchfield in 1816. He had an extensive practice and was noted for the diligence with which he pressed every point, however unimportant, which could be made to tell in favor of his client. His arguments were generally extended to a great length, and I have known him to receive a gentle hint from the Judge recommending a condensation of his thoughts. He died in 1839 at the age of sixty years, and Mr. Day, the Reporter, gives a flattering estimate of him in a foot note on the 134th page of the 13th volume of Connecticut Reports.

I am now to speak of a class of lawyers, much younger than those to whom I have already referred, but who had obtained a good standing at the bar fifty years ago.

### WILLIAM G. WILLIAMS.

Of New Hartford, stood as high as any member of this class. He belonged to the eminent and reputable Williams family of Massachusetts, his father being a nephew of Colonel Ephriam Williams the founder of Williams College, and himself the first cousin of Bishop Williams of the Episcopal Church of Connecticut. As a special pleader he had no superior at the bar. He had a tolerably fair standing as an advocate, and was indefatigable in pursuing to the last possible effort any purpose he had undertaken. If he failed in one form of action he would try another, and never gave up till further persistence was hopeless. He commenced business as a lawyer in Sharon, where he married, but after a few years he removed to New Hartford, where he remained during his life. He had scarcely reached the age of sixty years when he died.

---

### JOHN STRONG, JR.,

Of Woodbury, his native town, was a lawyer of very fair standing. I remember once to have heard Judge Boardman say, that if he found John Strong differing from himself on a point, he always doubted the correctness of his own conclusions. He was a ready speaker and had a peculiar habit of looking all over the hall, frequently directly behind himself, while he was addressing the jury. His arguments were clear and logical, and he was always listened to by the court with attention. He had scarcely reached the age of fifty years when he died.

---

### CALVIN BUTLER,

Of Plymouth, had a very good reputation as a lawyer. He also stood well with his fellow citizens of Plymouth, as he was often a member of the legislature, and he was of the convention of this state. He was also a member of the Senate in 1832. He had a part in all cases which came from that town and managed a trial very well. He was earnest in his manner of addressing the jury, and he was in full practice up to the time of his death, when he had reached the age of seventy-two years. He died suddenly, while away from home, and left behind a good record as a faithful lawyer and an honest man.

---

### CYRUS SWAN,

Of Stonington, came to the bar of this county in 1798. He settled in Sharon, and continued in full practice for twenty years. He was appointed a judge of the county court in 1818, and reappointed for the succeeding year, but resigning the office before the close of the term. His health becoming intolerant of sedentary habits and requiring out-door pursuits, he never resumed full practice, although he occasionally appeared in trials where his old friends demanded his aid. His arguments were clear, sound and sensible, and were listened to with attention. His mind was well stored with sound legal maxims and his aim seemed to be to make a sensible application of these to the case in hand. He died in 1835 at the age of sixty-five years.

---

### ANSEL STERLING.

A younger brother of the General, with whom he studied law, settled first in Salisbury, but in 1808 went to Sharon, where he spent his life. His talents were diversified, addicting himself readily to any pursuit which was a source of money making, in which he was very successful. As a lawyer, his forensic ability was of high order, nor was he deficient in legal science. His language flowed readily and rapidly, and sometimes his appeals to the jury were very effective. He was a member of Congress for two terms, and did not conceal his disappointment that he was not nominated for the third. That compliment was afforded him two years later, but he was defeated by Orange Merwin whom the federalists had placed on their ticket. He died at the age of seventy-two years, leaving a large estate and a numerous family.

---

### JOSEPH MILLER,

Of Winsted, who died recently in Michigan at a very advanced age, was a man of moral talent and of a higher order of legal acquirements than he usually had credit for. After the removal of Mr. Miller to Litchfield, his practice was large and continued to be so for several years. His arguments were short, compact and logical, and were listened to with attention and interest. In middle life he removed to Michigan, where he had a prosperous career.

---

### WILLIAM M. BURRALL,

A native, and through life a resident, of Canaan, was a lawyer of very extensive practice in one branch of business. He commenced a great many cases to the court, but never argued one on the final trial. He would sometimes argue motions for continuance, or for other purposes, and his success on such occasions showed that he had underrated his own powers. Although he did not argue his cases he was the master spirit in managing all the details of the trial, in what order witnesses should be called, and the points of testimony brought out. His associates depended greatly on his skill in conducting this part of the proceedings. He had a kind, affable and winning way in his social intercourse, and his offices were employed in adjusting and settling legal controversies. He acted as committee and arbitrator in more cases than any other member of the bar of his time, and if a desire to make himself as indifferent as possible to all parties sometimes seemed to hold him back from decisive action, he always, in the end, showed true firmness and integrity. He was an associate judge of the County Court from 1829 to 1836, and after that chief judge for ten years. He died at the age of seventy-seven years.

---

COLONEL WILLIAM COGGSWELL,

Of New Preston, a very worthy and respectable gentleman, was a member of the bar and was very seldom absent from the courts, He never engaged in the trial of a case, and very seldom spoke to the bench, but he was always a busy man in the court room. He was one of the electors who cast the vote of Connecticut for John Quincy Adams for President in 1824. He died before he had reached a very advanced age.

---

SETH P. BEERS.

When I came to the bar in 1820, Seth P. Beers, Esq., was in full practice. He was appointed State's Attorney soon after, but resigned in three years, having been appointed Commissioner of the School Fund, which office he held for twenty-five years. I have heard him say that some terms of the Court he had commenced as many as one hundred and fifty cases, and he was very thorough in all matters committed to his trust. His talents as an advocate were respectable; his briefs being very full and his knowledge of every minute point being very complete. It is hardly necessary to speak further of him as he lived down to a period within the memory of most of those who are present.

---

PERRY SMITH,

Of New Milford, held a somewhat prominent place at the bar and his practice was extensive. So many different estimates have been

SETH P. BEERS

made of Mr. Smith's real qualities, that it is difficult to speak of him with any very strong assurance of correctness. That he had talents and friends the success he achieved both as a lawyer and a politician render certain, but those who remember the time of his professional experience, here, know that he had enemies, and such would be the natural result of the unrelenting bitterness with which he pursued his adversaries in his efforts before the courts. There was a bitterness in his invectives, a persistence in his persecutions, an implacability in his enmities, which gave a decided character to his professional career, and which insured him the enmity of all against whom his efforts were directed. He was always listened to with a kind of inquisitiveness as to what new fountain of bitterness he would open, or what new invectives he would invent to pour out upon his adversary. These were sometimes directed against the opposing party, and upon the whole he incurred a great amount of hatred. I am only speaking of what occurred in court, and expressing the opinion which we would form in witnessing his professional conflicts. It cannot be doubted that he had many friends and supporters outside of this scene of action and it is not likely that he was as warm and constant in his friendship as he was bitter and unrelenting in his hatreds. After his election to the United States Senate he retired from the bar and was very seldom seen here.

---

## ROGER MILLS

Of New Hartford, was at one time a partner of Mr. Williams, of whom we have already spoken, from whom he differed in every respect except that both held the position of honorable and worthy gentlemen. Mr. Mills was slow in his conception of thoughts, slow in all the movements of mind, and very slow in his delivery of his arguments, and yet when all his duties in a case were accomplished it would be seen that he had made a creditable effort and that he was far from being a lawyer of indifferent pretensions. His son of the same name succeded him in the practice of law at New Hartford, but has since moved to Wisconsin where he has had a successful career.

---

## MICHAEL F. MILLS

Of Norfolk, was a somewhat prominent member at the bar, not because he had very much legal ability, but because he had the tact to make much show out of little substance. He never attempted to argue cases in the higher courts, but on the trial of motions as they came before the Courts, he was very prominent. We all thought well of Uncle Mich. as we used to call him and so did the people of Norfolk, for he was always a prominent man in the affairs of the town. He was a member of the legislature in 1830 and 1831, and there made himself conspicuous in the same way he did before the courts. He lived to a very advanced age.

---

### CHARLES B. PHELPS

Settled in Woodbury soon after his admission to the bar, nearly sixty years ago. He continued in practice while he lived. He died suddenly, from a disease of the heart, at the age of seventy-two years. He held a respectable position as a lawyer and for two years was a judge of the County Court, while that court was holden by a single judge. All who knew him have a very pleasant memory of his genial hnmor, pertinent anecdotes, and witty and pungent sayings. The younger members of the bar were delighted with his company and all deeply deplored his sudden death.

---

### MATTHEW MINOR

Of Woodbury, was a lawyer of good classical education and respectable legal attainments. He had a native diffidence, which prevented him putting himself forward, very often on the trial of cases, but when his powers were brought out he made a respectable show. He belonged to one of the eminent families of Woodbury and for personal qualities was very much respected.

---

### NATHANIEL P. PERRY

Of Kent, was a quiet, unobtrusive, conscientious man. He was the only lawyer in that town during the greater part of his professional life, and did a good local business. He was very diligent in the pursuit of his profession and generally argued the cases that he commenced. He was a member of the Senate for two successive years and died at the age of about sixty years.

---

### HOLBROOK CURTIS

Was a native of Newtown but practiced law in Watertown. He was a judge of the County Court for two years was frequently a

JUDGE C. B. PHELPS

member of the legislature, where he had a good share of influence. He was usually chairman of the committee on divorces and his reports in such cases were very interesting. He was a man of good common sense and acquitted himself creditably as a judge, but his powers failed with his advancing life and he lived for several years in comparative obscurity.

---

### ISAAC LEAVENWORTH AND ROYAL R. HINMAN.

There were two lawyers in Roxbury fifty years ago, Isaac Leavenworth and Royal R. Hinman, who made a considerable show of business before the courts, but who retired from practice in the course of a few years. Mr. Leavenworth went into other business in New Haven where it is said he has been very successful and is still living at a very advanced age. Mr. Hinman held the office of Secretary of State for eight years, and published several pamphlets containing the statistics of many of the most prominent families in the state.

---

### JOSEPH H. BELLAMY

Of Bethlehem, deserves more than a passing tribute. He was a grandson of the celebrated divine of that name and was a man of great moral worth. He never had a very extensive practice as a lawyer, but was much imployed in various branches of public business. He was frequently a member of the legislature, and once represented the sixteenth district in the Senate. He died in middle life, and all, of all names and parties, pay him the tribute of an affectionate and respectable remembrance.

---

### THEODORE NORTH

Of Goshen, his native town, removed to Chenango County, N. Y., about 1823. He graduated at Williams College in 1806 with the highest honors of his class. He was a remarkably well read lawyer, and had a respectable standing as an advocate. He attained to eminence in his profession in the State of New York. He died some twenty years since.

### YOUNG MEMBERS OF THE BAR.

In 1820 there were several young members of the bar who had just commenced practice, some of whom afterwards became eminent, and two of them, Truman Smith, and his cousin Nathaniel B. Smith still survive. Besides these there were George Wheaton, Leman Church, David C. Sanford, Nathaniel Perry of New Milford, and William S. Holabird. These all lived to a period within the memory of many now in practice here. Perry died at an earlier date than either of the others and left a family, but he was still a young man when he was called away. Sanford became judge of the Supreme Court and was greatly respected for his eminent fitness for the place. Wheaton was celebrated for the great skill with which he prepared his cases for trial, and his arguments, homely in style, and commonplace in method, were listened to with great attention. They were often charged with dry shots of wit which told upon his adversary and excited merriment with the bar.

---

### LEMAN CHURCH

Obtained quite a celebrity for his legal acumen and sharp points of character. If a lawyer is to be deemed successful in proportion to the number of cases in which he wins he was far from being a successful lawyer. I am inclined to think that the spirit of forensic combativeness, which seemed to possess the whole man, led him sometimes to advise groundless prosecutions and to encourage groundless defences. He wanted to fight, no matter whether for the right or wrong, and the consequence was that he lost more cases in proportion to the whole number in which he was engaged than any other lawyer at the bar. Still, nobody could deny that he possessed eminent shrewdness and sagacity as a lawyer, as well as forensic ability of very high order.

---

### WILLIAM S. HOLABIRD.

A native of Canaan, practiced in Colebrook, but spent most of his life in Winsted. He possessed talents which might have given him prominence and distinction as a lawyer had he devoted himself strictly to professional avocations, but he addicted himself more to other pursuits than to that. He was Lieutenant Governor for two years, and for a short time United States Attorney for the District of Connecticut, and I never heard any complaint of his want of fitness for either position. He experienced various fortunes in his worldly affairs, being sometimes poor and sometimes rich. At

TRUMAN SMITH

his death, which occurred soon after he reached the age of fifty years, he left a handsome estate to his family.

There were a few young members of the bar in 1820 who died after, a short career, some of whom were probably never heard of by the members of this generation. Their names now occur to me: Homer Swift of Kent; Philo N. Heacock of New Milford; and Chauncey Smith of Sharon. These started in professional life with ardent hopes and fair prospects of success, but their career was soon cut short by death.

---

GEORGE S. BOARDMAN,

Son of the Hon. Elijah Boardman of New Milford, was admitted to the bar in 1821. He was a young man of decided promise and was a special favorite of his uncle Judge Boardman. When I visit New Milford I observe, still standing, the brick fire proof office which his father built for him, but he lived only a few months after taking possession of it, and his death was greatly lamented throughout the community. His efforts at the bar gave proof of decided talent and he had made himself a special favorite among the members.

---

CONCLUSIONS.

The whole history of this bar for the last fifty years, teems with pleasant recollections. As a whole, it has a reputation for high toned integrity and professional comity among its members which is very much to its credit. If there have been instances of professional delinquency, they have been so rare as to have made no mark on the record of the times.

I have now spoken, to as great an extent as the time will allow, of the men who flourished in this temple of justice fifty years ago. I have no time to give expression to thoughts which come up, with great urgency for utterance, upon such an occasion as this, or to review the history of the last fifty years in any other relation than those which appertain to the administration of justice here. The progress of human affairs during that period, towards their final consummation, has been marked with great changes and vicissitudes. What shall be their development during the fifty years to come, can be of very little personal interest to me. I cherish the hope that this bench will continue to be occupied by judges of integrity, ability and of high judicial aptitudes, and that this bar will continue to be adorned with members whose pure lives and eminent attainments shall make their position one of honor and usefulness.

Standing here alone, the only member of this bar who has been in practice for fifty years, I take pleasure in expressing to my brethren of more recent experience the deepest gratitude for the pleasant and friendly relations they have permitted me to enjoy with them during the whole of our acquaintance. By their kind amenities and the favor of the judges, the rays of my evening sun have fallen upon me softer than did those of my noonday. These precious remembrances will remain with me as long as I have consciousness, and in conclusion I say to my brethren, not as a thoughtless wish, but as an honest prayer—may God bless you, each and all.

# Warner's Reminisences

# REMINISCENCES

OF THE

# LITCHFIELD COUNTY BAR

DELIVERED AT THE

CENTENNIAL BANQUET

NOVEMBER 18, 1898

BY

HON. DONALD J. WARNER

DONALD J. WARNER

# Reminiscences of Litchfield County Bar.

Mr. Chairman and gentlemen of the Bar. I thank you all sincerely that I am permitted to be present on this occasion, and the effort would require better language than I can express to tell you of my gratitude at your kind reception.

If I understand the purport of what is expected of me on this evening it is that I shall give my reminiscences of the Bar, of the sayings and doings of the dead who have passed before me. As a preliminary matter I wish to call your attention to an earlier period in my life in relation to the great inroads made by the Legislature of the State of Connecticut upon the ancient laws. Fifty years ago last April, through a rupture in the democratic party in Salisbury to which I belonged, a faction, I ought to say, not being identified with either, but attending to my own business rather than to any political aspirations, I was urged to stand for the nomination for representative to the House; I did so, was elected and became a member of the Legislature which held its session in May, 1849. Fortunately or unfortunately I was elected, in my 29th year, although at that time I was considered a very youthful man to legislate for the people of the State of Connecticut. Lafayette Foster, the distinguished gentleman, state senator and judge of the Superior Court, was the Speaker of the House; Hon. Charles J. McCurdy afterwards minister to Austria and a judge of the Superior and Supreme Courts, was Lieut. Governor and presided over the Senate. I was highly honored, without any solicitation on my part, by being appointed on the Judiciary Committee. Of course I had to go to the tail end of it, a very proper place for me,——

Mr. Huntington:—But that tail wagged the dog.

Mr. Warner:—Well, I will tell you about the dog later. In the year 1847, three distinguished men in this state had been appointed a committee to revise the statutes of the state. That committee consisted of Governor Minor, afterwards a Superior Court judge, Judge Loren P. Waldo and Francis Fellowes, a lawyer, keen and shrewd, of Hartford, on that committee. The very first thing that was referred to our judiciary committee was the report of this revision committee, and our very first subject were the details of that report. They appeared before us at our first sitting. And allow me to say right here, that chief-justice Butler of Norwalk, then state senator, was the chairman of that judiciary committee. The revision committee had drafted one or two laws which they wished the judiciary committee would see were offered in the Legislature and passed so that it might be incorporated in the revision which would be published that year.

This was only an act permitting and authorizing, in a suit between parties, that the party in question should have the privilege of calling upon the opposite party as a witness to testify to the facts that he might inquire about. Judge Waldo was also on the judiciary committee, repesenting Tolland. The distinguished William W. Eaton was his colleague in the House. I, being the first at the tail end of the committee, was called upon after the discussion to give my opinion. The opinion which I gave I had a long time under consideration in relation to the law of witnesses and parties interested being permitted to testify. Chairman Butler called upon me to give my opinion. I said distinctly, (it was in the presence of the revision committee also) that I was opposed to any such law. They had said to me it was a copy of an Act that had been passed in the State of New York, a recent statute there, and I gave my reason as being opposed to it, one great reason was this, that an honest party might be compelled by a scoundrel to testify to a fact that would be damaging to him unless he had the same ability to testify himself. And I was in favor of going further, I was in favor of passing an Act which would sweep away and wipe out that century-old doctrine and permit every man, party or interested witness in any form, to tell his story before a court and jury, that justice might be done. I said further "look over your Connecticut reports and you will find decision after decision where questions have gone up to the Supreme Court to ascertain whether there was a shred of interest in the witness that testified before the court. I said to them "we have the action of account in which witnesses are permitted to testify; we have the action of book debt in which all parties may testify, and how many cases will you find in the reports in this state where the question is laid before them whether an action which was brought in book debt did not properly belong in an action of general assumpsit.

Well, the next gentleman was the late Hon. John P. C. Mather of New London who sat at my right. He concurred with me, and so it went around from lawyer to lawyer and laymen, we had an excellent layman there, he did royal work, and it was passed unanimously with the exception of Judge Waldo, who said: "I am in favor of the law, but we tried it last year in the Legislature and it could not pass and the people are not ready for it, and I have concluded that the next best thing to do is to adopt the law of New York." Well, there was then in the House a man named Peck of New Haven, a brilliant man, a lawyer by education and a leader of the Whig side; there was Trumbull, later Governor, there was the elder Charles Chapman who were leaders from Hartford, there was Chauncey Cleveland, Ex-Governor, a power anywhere, his name and his fame are known to you all; there was William W. Eaton also. Well, I was finally instructed by the chairman, Judge Butler to draw up a bill and have it presented. I drew the bill which was introduced in the House or Senate, I forget which. It immediately passed the judiciary committee, and was introduced into the House, and also in the Senate. It lay upon the table sometime there and the matter was often cussed and discussed. Judge Dutton came to me while in the House and said to me "Mr. Warner, every member of the Superior and Supreme Court is opposed to this law, it is such a radical change that they think a great injustice, wrong, fraud and perjury will be perpetrated in the administration of justice." I said "Well, I can't help that, I am in favor of it." So it went along, and one day Judge Dutton came to me in my seat and said to me "Mr. Warner do you intend by that Act that a criminal should testify in Court?" "By no means, sir." Dutton said "Well, he has a right to." I said "No, sir." Well, we looked at it and he explained it to me, to my astonishment I felt as if I had done a very wrong thing, that I had disgraced myself by drafting a bill that extended the law to criminals, and I looked at it and it convinced me that he was right. I immediately went to Chapman in his seat and told what Judge Dutton said and I told him I thought it permitted of such an interpretation. He replied "well, it does, now what shall we do?" After a thought, he said "Warner, draw an amendment, when it comes into the House, just move an amendment to the bill." Well, I drew the amendment and soon after that Chapman came to me hurriedly and said "that bill has only passed the Senate by the casting vote of the Lieut.-Governor, don't you introduce that amendment, don't say a word, unless objection is made in the House, and then you can offer the amendment." The bill came into the House passed by the Senate and the usual formal vote was gone through with and the bill passed in the House. Chapman came around to me and said he "Well, Warner, it went through like grease." Thus was passed the law which made a radical change in the administration of justice and permitted interested parties in criminal as well as civil cases, to testify in their own behalf. That law I consider one of the wisest laws that was ever passed by this Legislature and the roll of honor for it stands to Connecticut, and I thank God that some of its labor belonged to Litchfield County.

The very next term of the Superior Court in Litchfield County after that session of the Legislature was held in August and presided over by Judge Church, a native of Salisbury and one of the best lawyers on the bench. There was an interesting criminal trial on the docket, a lawyer of prominence from New York and Judge Seymour were the prisoner's counsel. The defendant had put in his evidence when Judge Seymour arose and said to his Honor, "here is a statute passed by the last Legislature, I am not clear in my own mind as to the proper interpretation of it, whether it will permit the prisoner to testify or not, but I am of the opinion that he has that right, and I submit the question to your Honor for the purpose of determining." The Judge with considerable acerbity of feeling animadverted upon the passage of that law as cutting up root and branch of the old principle which had come down to us and which no one had conceived ought to be changed. He thought it would introduce fraud and perjury and all those things which go to outweigh and destroy justice as administered by the court. Then Seymour, after the judge had decided that the prisoner had the right to testify, said to the States Attorney "Then I offer you this prisoner to testify, I don't propose to put him on the stand for he might say something which might inadvertently injure his case" and that was a shrewd act on his part. The States Attorney declined to accept it and the prisoner did not testify.

Now there was another radical change and overthrow of the common law principle, and that was that no plea in abatement of a suit brought in an action of tort should bar the prosecution of it, which was in effect that the right of action for personal injuries survived. In other words, that the executor or administrator of a person that had deceased could continue an action commenced by the deceased. Well, that was a charitable act, but too radical for many of the lawyers, but it passed the Legislature and no one has seen fit since to have it repealed.

Now I will tell of an incident which I heard which shows the workings of the old law. There was a distinguished lawyer by the name of Loomis in Bridgeport, a merry fellow full of fun, and there was also Dwight Morris. This was before the passage of the law of the survival of actions for personal injuries and before the law allowing criminals to testify. There was a wayward son down in Bridgeport who had an old, warm, kindhearted father. This wayward son had cost the old man many hundreds of dollars and great grief. He had recently committed some tortious act and he was prosecuted criminally and convicted and then prosecuted civilly for damages and his body was attached, and the poor old father gave bonds for his appearance at Court.

This worthless son was a merry-go-round fellow and he began to have some feelings for his old gray-headed father, who was in great grief and sorrow and in great affliction; his money was nearly expended on his boy who was so wayward. Well, Dwight Morris was the junior counsel who was most familiar with the case that had to be tried at the approaching term, and this rollicking fellow came into his office one day and talked over the case and the facts in it, how much they could do and what circumstances would mitigate the damages. He said "Well, now, Morris, supposing I should die before that case comes on; would that have any effect on the case?" Morris said "Why, yes, that would end the case." This son then replied "By God, I guess I had better die first." Morris said "I think that is a damned good idea." A few days before the session of the Court Dwight Morris hurried into Loomis's office and said "My God, Loomis, I guess I have committed murder." "Why?" "Why our client is dead, he has committed suicide; he came into my office and said he guessed he would die if it would end the case," and in a foolish manner I said "Why, it would be a damned good idea." Well, the case went out, the poor old man's money was saved, and he lost his son.

It is a well-established fact that in the law repealing that old common law which prohibited an interested witness to testify, Connecticut was the pioneer. And that Westminster Hall in England from which we received our common law adopted that very act that was passed by the Legislature of 1848. And from there it has extended all over the United States.

Brethren, I commenced reading law in March, 1841, under the instructions of Hon. John H. Hubbard at Lakeville, and I spent a portion of my time under his advice at Litchfield so that I might have the advantages of attending Court there, and under the instruction of the Hon. Origen S. Seymour, that venerable and great man. I completed my studies with Mr. Hubbard and was admitted to the bar at the August term, 1843. Now as it was expected of me that I should speak of the lawyers who are gone, that I knew when I was first admitted to the bar, I shall go in routine and start with my native town.

Before I come to those that I knew, I wish to speak about another man, one of the pioneers of law in the town of Salisbury, because he was the ancestor of a very distinguished race of people, the ancestor of that prominent man, a judge of the Supreme Court of the United States who went from the State of Pennsylvania and died a few years ago. Adonijah Strong was one of the roughest pieces of granite, I suppose, that ever existed. He had a strong powerful mind, he was full of wit and humor, he was illiterate, but he had great common sense and he had great force and ability and effect upon the court and jury, as I have learned by tradition. Adonijah had a peculiar voice, it is said, and he had a good old wife by the name of Nabby, and a great many stories are told about him. He was a strong man and belonged to the Congregational Church and a great supporter of it. There was another colonel there, a distinguished man, Col. Joshua Porter. He was the ancestor of distinguished sons, one of them was a cabinet officer under the presidency of John Quincy Adams. Now about the time that the Methodist people organized a society in Salisbury there was a great deal of opposition to them. I guess there was more objection to them than the Salvation Army has seen in these later days. They held a meeting in my old school district on Ore Hill, and Col. Strong and Col. Porter had made up their minds that they would go over there, but not for any very religious purposes. Well, they each had a peculiar reputation. Col. Strong had the reputation of imbibing considerably and eating heartily. Col. Porter had another reputation, but I will let you guess what that was. It is spoken of in the Scriptures. Well, the clergyman who was to officiate on that occasion had been advised and Col. Strong's character was portrayed and so was Col. Porter's. They went in and sat down, and, as I said, for not very worthy purposes, and after a while the clergyman was speaking about the characteristics of different individuals, and he said "where is that wine-bibber and a glutton?" Col. Strong got up and said "here I am, sir!" and sat down. The next thing the preacher said when speaking of the wickedness of the world, "and where is he." Col Porter sat still. Strong said "Col. Porter, get up and answer to your name as I did?"

Now I will come to those whom I knew in Salisbury. There was John G. Mitchell of Salisbury, I believe he was born in Southbury. He came from a very pious parentage and was admitted to the bar, and came to Salisbury at an early age. He was not an educated man academically speaking, he was rough in his manners, uncouth, but he always maintained a reputation of a man of the highest integrity, but that is common among laywers in Litchfield County. Everybody esteemed him. He had in his office a very few books, old and musty, but he was a trial justice and judge of probate after the establishment of the Salisbury district. He was also connected in merchandise with Mr. Walton under the firm name of Walton & Mitchell, and he lived to an advanced age. He was rough and uncouth, but he had great redeeming traits. Late in life he came under the influence of a revival in the village in Lakeville and became a very religious man to the astonishment of everybody.

He was frequently called upon to speak in Methodist and religious meetings, he attended faithfully always, and in one of them he spoke of how they should work and toil to bring men into the fold. He said "brethren and sisters, you know the sharks follow the ship, now cast your nets out among them and you may bring in a lawyer as they brought me in." On another occasion he was speaking of the power of God, and talked well about it and wound up by saying "why God could take and throw me right through this meeting house, but he won't do it."

There was another old lawyer there when I was admitted to the bar in 1843 who gave me a great deal of good advice? He advised me one day as a lawyer "if anybody offers you anything, take it, if it is nothing but a chew of tobacco." I recollected that and always took one.

Then there was Philiander Wheeler, a Yale College graduate, an educated man, a keen bright man, full of wit and humor, quick and happy in repartee, but after I came to the bar he never attended the courts at Litchfield, neither did Mitchell, but tried cases before justices and arbitrators. One day he was called in over in Canaan as an adviser to the justice in the trial of a man by the name of

JOHN H. HUBBARD

Rockwell who was prosecuted for murdering his brother. Leman Church was the defendant's counsel and the Hon. John H. Hubbard was another, and the prosecuting attorney I think was Elmore, and it was a protracted case, and one forenoon the lawyers had a set-to as to the admissibility of evidence or some question that arose before them, and there was a great deal of controversy between the lawyers, and after very much had been said they adjourned and went to dinner. The lawyers sat around the table and Wheeler came in and sat down. The landlord came and asked him what he would have, he wanted to know if he would take some of the goose. "No" he said "I have had that all the morning and I don't want any."

There was an old lady who possessed some property in Salisbury, whom they called Aunt Polly. She was litigious in her character and she applied to every lawyer to sue somebody and when one would refuse she would go to another and finally she got a writ out for one of her neighbors and brought it before the Court. Wheeler defended the person that she had brought the suit against and he would stir up Aunt Polly until she become violent and quick-tempered. She had her money in specie tied up in one corner of her handkerchief, and he became so intolerable, as she thought, towards her that she jumped up and she just flung this specie at his head and it hit him, but didn't hurt him very much. He picked it up and put it in his pocket. No sooner had he done that, than Aunt Polly went for him and downed him over his chair and the lawyer on the other side said "stick to him, aunt Polly." That was a scene in court in the early days.

I come now to speak of a man to whom I feel greatly indebted, and I wish I could pay a better tribute to his character than I am able to, and that is the Hon. John H. Hubbard. He was a native of Salisbury and in his early struggles he had formidable opposition to contend with. In early life he was feeble and unable to work and finally he chose this profession, and by dint of educating himself by hard study and teaching school winters he was admitted to the bar in the year 1826. He had a great opposition politically, it was the day of anti-masonry when the feelings of people were very much excited upon that question arising out of the alleged death of one Morgan in the State of New York. He adopted the views of the anti-masonic party and was opposed by strong men and he had a terrible struggle, but he held his own. He had that persistent indomitable never-die principle in him that carried him along and he became a distinguished lawyer of the bar of Litchfield County. He is a living example to young men, no matter what the circumstances may be, if he is persistent, if he is studious, if he bends his efforts in that direction with an inflexibility that is not to be beaten, he will in the end conquer. I owe a debt of gratitude to that man for he drilled me in the principles of the law to such an extent that he said when I went to the office of Judge Seymour so as to be present when the courts were in session and learn some thing of its practice, that I was able to be admitted as soon as my time of study should expire. He became a member of Congress and represented the 4th district. He was states attorney for the county for how many years I don't now remember.

I will now speak of another gentleman, a lawyer in Salisbury, Roger Averill. He was a graduate of Union College, tall, erect and well proportioned, dignified in manners and a lawyer of fair ability. He practiced in Salisbury for some years, but the field was not sufficiently wide and he moved to Danbury and practiced there, until he was made Lieut.-Governor during a portion of the time of the distinguished war governor, Gov. Buckingham. He was my opponent in many cases that we tried and he early taught me an important lesson in table pounding. In a case we were trying before a justice I became quite vehement and brought my fist down on the table so strong and so often that he commiserated me and felt sorry for me, and he kindly placed a law book upon the table on the spot where I had been hammering and said "Brother Warner, I am afraid you will injure your hand, the book is softer." That took all the starch out of me.

Another gentleman by the name of Norton J. Buel was a native of Salisbury. He studied a portion of his time under the venerable Charles F. Sedwick, and the latter portion of it under Judge Church when he was practicing in Salisbury. He moved to Naugatuck in the first place and afterwards to Waterbury, but he frequently tried cases in this county and at this bar. He was a successful lawyer and a gentleman, and one who acquitted himself with great ability as a lawyer.

Moving along East, we come to North Canaan and we find John Elmore, he was a native of the town and I understood he was a very popular young man when he started in business, he was surrounded by many friends, he was very genial and a hale fellow well-met, everybody liked Jack Elmore, and he was on the hightide to become a successful lawyer, but his convivial habits dragged him down.

Leman Church, who was a half brother of Samuel Church, was a native of Salisbury, and he attended the law school of Judge Gould at Litchfield. He located at North Canaan about the same time that Elmore did. Instead of having many friends to aid him he had to encounter the opposition of the prominent men of the place. I asked years ago an old gentleman who was familiar with North Canaan why it was that they all stood by Jack Elmore and not by Church. Well, he said, Elmore was a congenial man, he was a pleasant man, he had all the social elements in him that were attractive. While they never saw Church, he never met us anywhere and if he did, why there was no congeniality between us, they were all opposed to him in the town, I mean the prominent men;

but he studied his books and thought deeply. He would occasionally have a case, and bye and bye his star began to rise, and though he could not and did not command the love, yet he commanded the respect of the people by dint of his great talents and power. I considered Leman Church one of the ablest lawyers and the best equipped on all occasions that I ever met. He had a keen, quick perception, he had that continuousity of purpose; he did not pander to please the multitude nor to the applause of the individual. He ploughed a straight furrow along his own course, and he attained the highest position at the bar at an early age. He had the keenest blade of satire, wit and humor, it abounded with him; at repartee he was never at a loss, nor upon any question that the judge might propound to him whether he ever had the case under consideration or not; and always acquitted himself with the highest ability. I speak thus of him because I was so situated when I first came to the bar, the other lawyers being older, I was forced to call upon Leman Church, and he aided me and always assisted me in any case for which I might call upon him. Physically he was tall, frail in appearance, he had a hunch with his head slightly deformed, a shrivelled face, lean and gaunt, and his apparel was always neat but of the coarsest character. His feet were clad in heavy brogan shoes, but the redeeming feature of his countenance was his eye, and such an eye would convince you gentlemen when cast upon you as being that of a man of powerful intellect. Now to speak of his ability as a lawyer. Porter Burrall, the son of William Burrall, a Canaan man, a highly educated man was president of the Housatonic Railroad. Some of its directors lived in the city of New York and some question arose in relation to the management of the road and there were lawyers in New York who had the question under advisement and they had expressed opinions in relation to it. There was a final meeting appointed for the further discussion and the determination of the question involved. Burrall called upon Church and told him he wanted to have him to go down to New York City and attend that Director's meeting. Church said in his peculiar voice "I am not going down among those dandy lawyers they think they know everything, and I am not going." However, Burrall had great faith in him and insisted upon his going, and he finally went down, clad like a clod-hopper and he sat down in that convention. The opinions of these distinguished New York Lawyers were called for and finally Mr. Burrall said, "Mr. Chairman, I wish my friend Mr. Church of Canaan might be permitted to speak." Well Church got up, a most inferior looking man, you can't find one to compare with him in that respect, but he went at the question under discussion and laid them out so broad and clear and so perfectly lucid that he established them, and his views were finally adopted. He could not bear a fop, he could not bear what he called a Miss. Nancy, or vaporism of any kind, he went too far perhaps in that respect, but he had a happy gift of puncturing bubbles and I will give you one or two instances of it. Now you know that when young men come to the bar and make their first appearance before a Jury, they wish to make an impression and sometimes be classical and ornate. There was brother Hitchcock who lived in Winsted, a man for whom I held the highest respect, and whose memory I revere. He and Judge Granger and myself were great friends. Hitchcock was a partner of Holabird. They had a very important case to be tried at Litchfield. Hitchcock had made great preparations in the case, and it was among his first efforts at the bar in the way of argument and trial, and he familiarized Granger and myself with the case and we felt a very deep interest in his behalf. Hitchcock in the course of his argument animadverted upon one principal witness in the case against him, he was a very important witness for the other side, and it was very important for Hitchcock's client that the Jury should not take his word or the testimony he gave before the Court. In the course of his argument Hitchcock said, alluding to that witness, "why, gentlemen of the jury, he is the very 'folliculus,' in this case." A little further along he said "He is a Jupiter Tonans, gentlemen of the Jury." When Leman Church came to answer that he said "Now, gentlemen of the Jury my young friend here, brother Hitchcock has attempted to mislead you; why he has talked about one Miss Polly New Rose gentlemen of the jury, have you seen any such witness on this stand?" "Not satisfied with that, he has imposed upon you again, he has talked about a witness here by the name of Jew Peter Toe Nails." As soon as we could, Granger and I took our hats and went out. Another case we had in the Superior Court in which Leman Church was interested, we had medical experts in, and a learned Doctor by the name of Fuller from New Haven was there as a witness against the interests of Church's client. He went along very learnedly, as such physicians do, and when Church came to cross-examine this witness he commenced by saying "well, now, Dr. Fooler" and he took the wind out of him pretty effectually.

Another illustration of his mode of examining a witness. There was a great controversy in years gone by between Jedediah Graves and Sylvanus Merwin, father-in-law and son-in-law, about a man who went and took up the tombstones of his children and offered them for sale on an execution for a judgment.

Graves was a pompous sort of fellow, he was a trial justice in the town of New Milford and he was called upon to testify to what was said before him on a trial. He went along well and easily and was turned over to Church for cross-examination, and Church in his questions began to imply that he was going outside of the truth. After a while the witness stopped and says "Squire Church, I have a realizing sense of the obligations of my oath, I have administered them and I protest against your insinuations." Church said "Squire Elliott, if you have got through with your peroration, please answer my question."

Now I come to speak of that distinguished man in North Canaan, Miles Toby Granger. He was a graduate of Wesleyan University at Middletown in this state. He was a school teacher on a plantation down in Mississippi, teaching the sons and daughters of the surrounding plantations, and during that time he studied law in Mississippi and was admitted to the bar in that state. He came back to Connecticut and went into the office of Leman Church and studied law with him for the purpose of obtaining a knowledge of Connecticut laws and was admitted to the bar after 1843. He was the greatest wit, humorist and wag of the bar, he was the very Mark Twain of the bar. His sayings, his wit and his humor might be read as Innocents at Home instead of Innocents Abroad. He was skilled in doggerel poetry as he called it. He would see the ludicrous and ridiculous in persons and things that no one but he thought of, and he would bring it out to the great amusement of his hearers. His very first argument in the Superior Court was in poetry. It was the case of Dunham vs. Dunham. Dunham brought a petition for a divorce against his wife, he was a widower when he married, and she was a widow. They were both very old and infirm, their spouses were dead and they desired companionship, and so they inter-married. Jack Elmore brought the petition and in that petition he set up as a ground, a fradulent contract. Judge Ellsworth, a very grave man and a deacon of the church in Hartford was holding Court. Granger led off in the argument for the defense and Church was to close the debate. His whole argument was in poetry, but I remember nothing but the last verse, which was this:

"Now all his hopes in ruins lie,
Crushed by this prolapsus uteri."

He was a great fellow for giving names to persons. He dubbed me by the name of Elder, and it has been carried on to this day, and I believe I had been so addressed since I have been here. Why he did it I don't know, whether an elder of the Methodist Episcopal church or some other persuasion I havn't any idea, he never explainded it to me. He was full of his jokes and quirks, it made no difference whether it was foe or friend, but it was all in good nature. Well, you all know his history in later life when he was highly honored, represented his town in the Legislature, in the Senate and represented the 4th district in Congress after his retirement as a Judge.

Col. Jacob B. Hardenberg, he was a native of Kingston, N. Y. He was a good lawyer, a soldier and a warrior at Gettysburg under Col. Pratt. I might well say of him "he was the bravest of the brave."

Now I come to one of my first students, George Washington Peet. He was a native of Salisbury and read law in my office and completed his studies in the law in the Harvard Law School. Soon after his admission he located in South Canaan in the office of Judge Burrall and commenced practice there, and afterwards at Falls Village. From his maternal ancestry he inherited the power of acquisitiveness which was but little diluted by what he inherited from the paternal side. And only semi-occasionally did he commit waste by profuse expenditure. He was a unique character. Peet was a nervous, excitable, confident, energetic, bold man. He went in pursuit of money and he got it. He was not devoid of wit and by it occasionally entertained us. We boys were playing tricks upon each other, as I presume they are now, the younger members. Hitchcock had a good deal of that in his makeup, and one day at the Court in Litchfield in warm weather Peet was down there with his linen coat on, and in those days the clerk had on his desk a wafer box with little red wafers, we didn't have mucilage then, but we used red wafers to stick things on, and Hitchcock got out a lot of these every little while, then would wet one of them and go around and slap Peet on the back and stick on a wafer, and soon got him pretty well pasted. Peet was marching around in different places making an exhibition of his back, and finally he found people were laughing at him. Peet would ask, "well, what are you laughing at" and then they would laugh the more. Finally someone asked "What the devil have you got on your back, Peet?" Peet was very indignant and accused Hitchcock of trying to make him the butt of this bar.

As I said, Granger gave names to everybody. There is a place in South Canaan called Dogtown, and years ago there was a tavern there and the place of trial of many cases. That was Peet's stamping ground, and Granger and others met him there, and so Granger gave him the name, not of the constellation exactly, but he called him Attorney *Serious,* the dog-star, the brighest star in dog-town.

I pass along to Norfolk. There was Michael Mills. He was a tall, lean lank, bony man, high cheek bones and rather tawny face. Granger called him the Sachem of Norfolk.

Then comes William K. Peck, Jr., he was a native of Harwinton; his parents moved with him to Salisbury when he was a young boy. He studied law in my office and commenced practice in Norfolk. He was very fond of making public speeches when ever an opportunity presented. Abolitionism and temperance were his favorite topics and he availed himself of every opportunity to make speeches, and in that respect, so far as capability of addressing popular sentiment at his age of life, he had decided talent. Granger called him Duke of Norfolk. When he contemplated settling in Norfolk, one of the good deacons of Norfolk came over to see me to inquire about him and informed me that Mr. Peck had referred

GIDEON HALL

him to me and wanted to know what sort of a man he was. I told him he was exactly adapted to Norfolk. He said "what do you mean?" I replied "in the first place he is a very moral man, a man of excellent moral character; in the second place he will be an admirable successor of Michael Mills in his physical make-up, he has a peculiar tawny brown hair, high cheek bones, and in another respect he is a black republican" as they called them then. The old deacon laughed and said he guessed he was the man. So he settled there and I believe acquitted himself with ability. After he had been there a while he removed to Michigan where I have heard he became a successful lawyer. I felt proud of him as a student in my office.

Now I come to Winsted. William S. Holabird was a native of South Canaan. He was physically a large, tall, splendidly made-up man, imposing in appearance and presence, and he was the great democratic leader of the bar. He was a politician and he was a man around whom the young democratic lawyers liked to gather. He had excellent conversational powers and they were always interested in his conversation. He was really one of the instructors in political matters among the democratic lawyers, and he was then in active practice. He had some bitterness in his make-up, but his friendship was as strong as his hatred was deep and unforgiving.

Gideon Hall was an opponent, and as a lawyer and in politics they were diametrically opposed. Holabird was vindictive sometimes, and his hatred extended down too far.

Now I come to another unique character, and that was Gideon Hall. He was a lean, tall, gaunt man, he was in full practice, and continued in practice until he was appointed Judge of the Superior Court. He was a hard worker, diligent; his contests were elaborate, many and severe. Hall and Holabird were opponents always in politics and lawsuits, never associated. Hall was very prolix in the conduct of trials, and remarkably so in his arguments before the court and jury. The one hour rule had not been passed when he practiced. Hall would occasionally make attempts at oratory in his trials, and here is an illustration of it. He had a suit in court for his client, the plaintiff in the case. It was a contest over a piece of rocky land of no value comparatively speaking. During the trial he was often talking about the littleness and smallness of the case, and it was so alluded to in the argument by the counsel for the defense. This was a sort of an exordium or peroration in which he said it was not available on account of the super-abundant fecundity of its soil, but because it was ancestral estate and had come down from a long line of colonial ancestors.

In relation to Hall, there is one thing which shows the estimation of the bar. This story was told to me by the late George C. Woodruff of Litchfield. A lawyer of this county had a suit in court, a young lawyer and he had associated with him George C.

Woodruff. It was a case asking for the appointment of a committee in chancery which was to be tried out of term-time, and the question arose who should be that committee. Of course, if the parties agreed on the committee, the court would sanction it, otherwise the court would have to decide and appoint whom it thought best. Negotiations were made between the opposite counsel, Woodruff on one side and Hubbard and Granger on the other side, and Hubbard and Granger suggested Hall as a good one for the committee-man. The young man went to see Mr. Woodruff and told him that they proposed to have Hall appointed committee, and Woodruff said to him "don't you have him, why he will get things all mixed up in his report so that we shall not get head or tail to it." The young man reflected and said "Mr. Woodruff, that may be just what we want." Well, it turned out so, it was mixed and Woodruff won his case.

I come now to the friend of whom I have spoken, Roland Hitchcock. He was a native of Burlington. He read law in Holabird's office and he was admitted to the bar in about 1844, and became a partner of Holabird and practiced law in Winchester until appointed as Judge of the Superior Court. I always liked the man, and so well did I know him that his peculiarities never interfered with our friendship. He at times exhibited much wit and humor and enjoyed the funny side of things and contributed his share to the merriment of the bar. There was a streak of melancholia in his nature which always made him sorrowful. It lasted him through life, and in the last few years of his life, had a woeful effect upon him. He was testy and often irritable in trials. As an illustration of that I remember a case in which Granger and myself were on one side and Hitchcock on the other before a committee at Canaan. Hitchcock's client was one Hart, a notable character and who was easily stirred up. In the course of the trial Granger, knowing Hart's peculiarities would stir him up and he would rattle along and interrupt the trial so that Hitchcock would sometimes get mad at his client and he would once in a while issue an expletive on the subject. He was very fixed in his opinions of the law and unchangeably so at times. He was through and through an honest man and administered justice impartially in the courts where he was judge.

I go now to Barkhamstead and speak of the late Hiram Goodwin. He was in full practice, his clientage was not only in his town, but extended to the adjoining towns in this and Hartford County. I considered him an able lawyer. He conducted his trials with skill and his arguments were clear and logical. As a judge of the County Court he gave satisfaction.

I come now to New Hartford. Roger H. Mills was in practice there many years before I came to the bar. He was of fine appearance and high standing at the bar. He was a member of the Senate in the Legislative session of 1848 at the time these radical

HON. ROLAND HITCHCOCK

GEO. WHEATON

BIRDSYE BALDWIN

laws were made and I think he opposed both of those enactments. He was a very accomplished man, pleasant, scholarly, but the field was not wide enough for him and so he moved to Wisconsin, and after a while died there.

Jared B. Foster was his successor there. He came to the bar after 1843, and he is entitled to great credit, for he read law while making and mending boots and shoes in Colebrook. He was a merry, good fellow, he became well equipped in the principles of the law and quickly acquired its practical parts. He represented the town in the Legislature with ability and he succeeded Hitchcock as judge of the Litchfield County Court and discharged his duties with ability. He was eminently social and a hale fellow well-met. We used to address him as Jerry. Granger dubbed him Jerry Red. For many years he was a sufferer from rheumatism and it finally brought him to his grave.

Goshen. Nelson Brewster. His law business was local. He lived two years in Litchfield and he tried a few cases and he was a bank commissioner several times. Birdseye Baldwin, a unique character was his contemporary in Goshen, a kindhearted man of limited practice and of great simplicity of character. He was very fond of whist. Granger and Hitchcock at court whenever they were in session entertained him very often very royally, in the amusement of which I was a witness. Oftentimes I was a partner of Granger, and Baldwin and Hitchcock were partners. If Hitchcock and Granger turned up a trump they would pass their trumps one to the other under the table and pick out all the best cards and hand back the poor ones. Finally Baldwin would get up and exclaim, after losing all the games, "well, it does beat the devil."

I now come to Cornwall, to George Wheaton. He was of humble origin, born in East Haven. When I was a boy, I learned that he was of most extraordinary ability, illiterate, he murdered the Queen's English, but one of the most skilful and adroit lawyers at the bar in his day and time. Wheaton was a great lawyer in my judgment. He had one peculiar gesture and that was this, he never laughed and hardly ever smiled. As an illustration of his cunning and shrewdness and his aptitude for hitting the party against him I will mention an instance. There was a suit brought against the Housatonic Railroad for damage to property injured by the cars. Peet and myself were defending the Railroad Company and Granger and Wheaton were counsel for the plaintiff. One of the witnesses, Charles Emmons, an employee of the railroad, was a very important witness and his testimony was crucial in behalf of the defendant. Of course the case being against a railroad corporation it had to be put to a jury. This witness Emmons was a very honest man and a christian gentleman, and if he could make the jury believe as they ought to believe, that his testimony was truthful, then the case should be decided for the defendant. In the course of the argument, in commenting on the testimony of the witness Emmons, I dwelt upon the purity of his life and character, his christian character. When Wheaton came to wind up the case he said "Brother Warner says this Emmons is a Christian. Well, I aint going to dispute that, but if the company finds out that that is his character, they will discharge him very quick."

Another instance comes down by tradition. Church frequently came in contact with Wheaton. He was called down there to defend a man in some case before a justice, and Wheaton commenced the argument of his case. He had his book of Connecticut reports and he stated to the Court what the law was and he would read from this book and so he read from the brief of one of the lawyers. Church said, "Wheaton, let me take that book." Wheaton said, "go get your own law, brother Church."

Church of course told the judge he was reading from the brief of the attorney, not from the opinion of the court or the judge who decided the case. Wheaton replied "I didn't say I did, I said I read what is the law there, and I believe it to be good law, and if the Supreme Court has said otherwise, they will over-rule that decision." He was a communicant of the Congregational Church in Cornwall. Now there was a religious revival in that town long years ago and there was a man there by the name of Daniel Scoville. During that revival he attended these meetings very faithfully and appeared very much interested in them. There was a bitter hatred between this man and Wheaton. Wheaton had law suits against him frequently and they were conducted sharply by Wheaton as against him. Some of Wheaton's fellow members went to him and said, "Why this man is so much interested in the supject of religion I think that you ought, as a member of the church, to go to him and encourage him in some form and show forgiveness on your part." So one evening Wheaton went up there and while Scoville was in the attitude of praying and said "If there is any mourner here who has any feeling against me or I have any against him, God forbid that I should in any way bar his coming to God." Well, he had a client there who waited until Wheaton came out and then he said "Wheaton, you know that law suit we have got there against him, now I want that fought right up." Wheaton replied "Oh! he'll fight all right."

Then there was Julius B. Harrison. He was a native of Cornwall, he read law with Wheaton and came to the bar after 1843 and practiced a while in Cornwall and moved to New Milford where he died. He was state's attorney for the county, he was a very diligent man, very ambitious and he rapidly rose in his profession. He was repetitious in his arguments, and that was the only criticism I ever heard made, for he was certainly logical, and had he lived to the ordinary age, I have no doubt he would have been one of the leaders of the bar.

JARED B. FOSTER

Another man from Cornwall was Solon B. Johnson, and many of you no doubt remember him. He was a tall, large-framed person, I don't know what year he came to the bar, and he was editor of the Litchfield Sentinel, and his editorial articles were read with a great deal of interest; there was a great deal of wit and humor and sarcasm contained in them. He died early in life, he was of a peculiar nature and character, a loveable man in a great many respects. He had a peculiar stolid appearance at times, whether put on or natural, I don't know. If unnatural it was very successful consumation. The last term that Judge Minor held of the Superior Court prior to his resignation, having accepted the nomination for member of Congress from the 4th district, there was a gentleman came up to Litchfield, an entire stranger. He was in everybody's office, he was in the court room. He was a queer sort of a man, talking with everybody and with Judge Minor and you couldn't help being interested to know who he was. He came across Solon Johnson and Johnson tried to get rid of him. He was all the while teasing Johnson to take drinks with him, and Mr. Johnson declined and kept declining. Finally, after much urging Johnson says "my friend, there is a drug store down here and we will go down there and get something that is pure and good." Well, they went down to the drug store and a pint bottle was brought out with the very purest kind of whiskey they had and a tumbler was set down, and this stranger told Mr. Johnson to take a drink. Johnson took up the bottle, looked at the cork, smelled of it and says "that's all right" turned it up and drained the bottle. The stranger looked at him aghast, expecting him to fall dead every minute. Johnson looked at him, smiled and said "Well, aint you going to take something?"

Now I come to Frederick Chittenden. He was in practice when I came to the bar, a high tempered man of great knowledge. He had many conflicts with those with whom he came in contact. He was of an irrascible temper, but a good-hearted, generous likely man, very well read in the law, but depended a great deal upon his natural abilities; it took but very little to excite him, he was very beligerent in the trial. There was a lawyer from Kent, Henry Fuller, who came to the bar after myself. They had a contest and Chittenden was so excited he struck him on the head. Well, there was an interruption, and after the adjournment Chittenden came in and laid his cane down upon the table and he said he would preserve order in the court room.

John G. Reed was a native of Salisbury and read law with me. His father and mother were Scotch. His father, the late Dr. Adam Reed was a celebrated Divine. He was educated at Williams College, he practiced law in Kent a short time, moved to Ohio, enlisted in an Ohio regiment in the civil war, and when he returned from that, he removed to Chicago and there distinguished himself as a lawyer before the higher courts upon mere questions of law. He was not what you call a jury lawyer.

Well, brethren and gentlemen of the bar: The bell tolls and my hour has expired. I look back to the time when life was new and bright before me and everything seemed fair and good to see. I stand here now and remember all these friends of so long ago As I stand here alone of all those I knew in my early days. whom I have seen fall around me like leaves in the wintry weather.

"I feel like one who stands alone,
In some banquet hall deserted;
Whose lights are dead,
Whose joys are fled,
And all but he departed.

# Historical Notes

# HISTORICAL NOTES

OF

# COURTS, BAR LIBRARY AND

# PROMINENT OFFICIALS

---

Compiled By

DWIGHT C. KILBOURN

CLERK

DWIGHT C. KILBOURN

# HISTORICAL NOTES.

Upon the establishment of Litchfield County in 1751, the General Assembly was pleased to order two terms of the County Court to be held therein, one on the fourth Tuesday of December, and the other on the fourth Tuesday of April in each year, and also one term of the Superior Court to be held on the last Tuesday save two, in August of each year.

In this Superior Court there was but one Clerk for the whole Colony who went with the Judges from place to place as the sessions were held, and kept the records all together in Hartford, where those prior to 1798 can now be found in the Secretary of State's office.

The following is the record of the first court held in Litchfield County:

"At a County Court held at Litchfield within and for the County of Litchfield on the fourth Tuesday of December A. D., 1751.

Present: WILLIAM PRESTON, *Chief Judge.*

JOHN WILLIAMS<br>SAMUEL CANFIELD<br>EBENEZER MARSH } *Esqrs. Justices of quoram.*

Isaac Baldwin was appointed Clerk and sworn.<br>
Mr. John Catling, County Treasurer and Excise Master.<br>
Mr. Joshua Whitney of Canaan in said County, Attorney.

"At the same Court John Davies of Litchfield in the County of Litchfield plt. versus John Barrett of Woodbury in sd County deft. The parties appeared and the deft. exhibited pleas in abatement of the pltf's writ which being overruled the parties then joyning in a demurr. to the declaration as on file, the Court is of Opinion that the Declaration is sufficient in the Law and thereupon it is considered that the plt. shall recover of the Deft. the Sum of £1200 money. Damages and costs of Court allowed to be ———.

The deft. appeals from the judgment of this Court to the Superior Court to be holden at Litchfield on the second Tuesday of August next, and the plat. with Mr. Samuel Darling of New Haven before this Court acknowledged themselves bound to the Treasurer of sd County in a recognizance of £200 money to prosecute their said appeal to effect and answer all damages in case they make not their plea good."

The following is the Record of the first Superior Court held in Litchfield County, and to be found in Hartford.

At a Superior Court holden at Litchfield on Tuesday ye 11th, day of August Anno Dommi 1752 anno ye Regni Rt. Georgii Secunde Vigestum Sexto.

Present, ye

Honbl. THOMAS FITCH, *Esqr. Chief Judge.*

| | |
|---|---|
| WILLIAM PITKIN<br>EBENEZER SYLLYMAN<br>SAMUEL LYNDE | *Assistant Judges.* |

This Court was opened by Proclamation and adjourned till Two of ye clock of ye afternoon, and then opened according to adjournment.

Persons returned to serve as jurors were:

| | | | |
|---|---|---|---|
| WILLIAM MARSH<br>JOSHUA GARRETT<br>THOMAS CATLING | Litchfield | NATHAN BOTCHFORD<br>JOHN HITCHCOCK<br>PARTRIDGE THATCHER | New Milford |
| TIMOTHY MINOR<br>GIDEON WALKER<br>BENJAMIN STILES | Woodbury | NATHAN DAVIS<br>JACOB BENTON<br>SAMUEL PHELPHS | Harwinton |

The first recorded judgment is that of:

| | | |
|---|---|---|
| WILLIAM SHERMAN<br>and<br>ROGER SHERMAN | of New Milford vs. | JOHN TREAT<br>of<br>New Milford |

At the May session of the General Assembly 1798 it was enacted that the Superior Court Judges appoint a Clerk for each County and that the Records thereafter be kept in their respective Counties, but that the then existing records be kept at Hartford.

In obedience of this law the Judges appointed Frederick Wolcott, Esq. of Litchfield, Clerk for Litchfield County, and the first term of the Superior Court having its records at Litchfield, was held at Litchfield on the Third Tuesday of August 1798 and was "Opened by proclamation."

The record is as follows:

STATE OF CONNECTICUT:

At a Superior Court holden at Litchfield within and for the County of Litchfield, on the Third Tuesday of August A. D. 1798,

PRESENT:

The HON. JESSE ROOT, Esq. *Chief Judge*

| | |
|---|---|
| HON. JONATHAN STURGES<br>HON. STEPHEN M. MITCHELL<br>HON. JONATHAN INGERSOLL<br>HON. TAPPING REEVE | *Assistant Judges.* |

FREDERICK WOLCOTT, *Clerk.*

THE SUPERIOR COURT AT LITCHFIELD, APRIL TERM, 1909

CLERK, D. C. KILBOURN　SHERIFF, F. H. TURKINGTON　JUDGE, WM. H. WILLIAMS　STENOGRAPHER, L. W. COGSWELL　J. P. WOODRUFF

The Attorneys in active practice in 1798 were the following:

At Litchfield:
TAPPING REEVE
ELIJAH ADAMS
JOHN ALLEN
ISAAC BALDWIN
URIEL HOLMES
DANIEL W. LEWIS
EPHRAIM KIRBY
REYNOLDS MARVIN
ROGER SKINNER
AARON SMITH
URIAH TRACY
FREDERICK WOLCOTT.

At Canaan:
JOHN ELMORE

At Goshen:
NATHAN HALE
NOAH WADHAMS

At Kent:
BARAZILLA SLOSSON

At New Milford:
DAVID S. BOARDMAN
SAMUEL BOSTWICK
DANIEL EVERETT
PHILO RUGGLES

At Norfolk:
EDMUND AIKEN
AUGUSTUS PETTIBONE

At Plymouth:
LINUS FENN

At Roxbury:
RUFUS EASTMAN.

At Salisbury:
JOSEPH CANFIELD
ELISHA STERLING
ADONIJAH STRONG

At Sharon:
JUDSON CANFIELD
JOHN C. SMITH
CYRUS SWAN

At Southbury:
SIMEON HINMAN
BENJAMIN STILES, JR.

At Washington:
DANIEL N. BRINSMADE
WILLIAM COGSWELL

At Watertown:
ELI CURTISS
SAMUEL W. SOUTHMAYD

At Winchester:
PHINEAS MINER

At Woodbury:
NOAH B. BENEDICT
NATHAN PRESTON
NATHANIEL SMITH

The following members of the Bar are now (April 1907) residing in the County: Those with a * are not in active practice.

Litchfield:
J. GAIL BECKWITH, JR. *
FRANCIS BISSELL *
WHEATON F. DOWD
JOHN T. HUBBARD
DWIGHT C. KILBORN
WILLIAM L. RANSOM *
ELBERT P. ROBERTS
THOMAS F. RYAN
GEORGE M. WOODRUFF
JAMES P. WOODRUFF

Bethlehem:
WALTER M. JOHNSON *

Cornwall:
WILLIAM D. BOSLER
LEONARD J. NICKERSON

Goshen:
CHARLES A. PALMER *

Norfolk:
ROBBINS B. STOECKEL

New Hartford:
- Frederick A. Jewell
- H. Roger Jones, Jr.
- Frank B. Munn

New Milford:
- John F. Addis
- Frank W. Marsh
- Henry S. Sanford
- Fred M. Williams

North Canaan:
- Samuel G. Camp
- Geo. A. Marvin
- Alberto T. Roraback
- J. Henry Roraback
- J. Clinton Roraback

Plymouth:
- Henry B. Plumb *
- E. Leroy Pond
- Fred A. Scott

Salisbury:
- Howard F. Landon
- Donald T. Warner

Sharon:
- Willard Baker

Thomaston:
- Albert P. Bradstreet
- E. T. Canfield
- Frank W. Etheridge

Torrington:
- William W. Bierce
- Bernard E. Higgins
- Walter Holcomb
- Peter J. McDermott
- Willard A. Roraback
- Homer R. Scoville
- E. T. O'Sullivan
- Gideon H. Welch
- Thos. J. Wall

Watertown:
- C. B. Atwood *
- S. McL. Buckingham

Winchester:
- Wm. H. Blodgett
- C. E. Bristol *
- Jas. P. Glynn
- Samuel A. Herman
- Richard T. Higgins
- Samuel B. Horne
- Wm. P. Lawrence *
- Wilbur G. Manchester
- Geo. A. Sanford
- Frank W. Seymour
- James P. Shelley
- Wellington B. Smith
- James W. Smith

Woodbury:
- James Huntington
- Arthur D. Warner

The following persons who have been connected with this Bar either by admission or residence, are not now residing in the County. but are supposed to be alive and residing elsewhere.

John Q. Adams,
Negaunee, Mich.

Louis J. Blake,
Omaha, Neb.

Edward J. Bissell,
Fond-du-Lac, Wis.

John O. Boughton,
Stamford, Conn.

David S. Calhoun
Hartford, Conn.

Uriah Case,
Hartford, Conn.

John D. Champlin,
New York City.

Chester D. Cleveland,
Oshkosh, Wis.

Frank D. Cleveland,
Hartford, Conn.

George W. Cole,
New York City.

WILLIAM L. RANSOM.

STEWART W. COWAN,
Mount Vernon, N. Y.
S. GREGG CLARK,
New Jersey.
E. T. CANFIELD,
Hartford, Conn.
SPENCER DAYTON,
Phillipa, West Va.
LEE P. DEAN,
Bridgeport, Conn.
E. C. DEMPSEY,
Danbury, Conn.
WILLIAM H. ELY,
New Haven, Conn.
JOHN R. FARNUM,
Washington, D. C.
V. R. C. GIDDINGS,
Bridgeport, Conn.
W. W. GUTHRIE,
Atkinson, Kansas.
ROBERT E. HALL,
Danbury, Conn.
CHARLES R. HATHWAY,
So. Manchester.
MARCUS H. HOLCOMB,
Southington, Conn.
JOHN D. HOWE,
St. Paul, Minn.
EDWARD J. HUBBARD,
Trinidad, Col.
FRANK W. HUBBARD,
New York, N. Y
FRANK L. HUNGERFORD,
New Britain, Conn.
WALTER S. JUDD,
New York City.
WILLIAM KNAPP,
Denver, Col.
FRED M. KOEHLER,
Livingston, Mont.
FRANK D. LINSLEY,
Philmont, N. Y.
Rev. A. N. LEWIS,
New Haven, Conn.
THEODORE M. MALTBIE,
Hartford, Conn.
T. DWIGHT MERWIN,
Washington, D. C.
NATHAN MORSE,
Akron, Ohio.
FRED E. MYGATT,
New York City.
WM. P. MULVILLE,
New Canaan.
WM. H. O'HARA,
New York City.
E. FRISBIE PHELPS,
New York City.
FRED A. SCOTT,
Hartford, Conn.
MORRIS W. SEYMOUR,
Bridgeport, Conn.
ORIGIN STORRS SEYMOUR,
New York City.
GEORGE F. SHELTON,
Butte, Mont.
GEORGE E. TAFT,
Unionville, Conn.
F. R. TIFFANY,

---

JOHN Q. THAYER,
Meriden, Conn.
FREDERICK C. WEBSTER,
Missoula, Mont.
REV. EDWIN A. WHITE,
Bloomfield, N. J.
JOHN F. WYNNE,
New Haven, Conn.

## GOVERNORS.

Governors of Connecticut who were members of this bar.

| | | | |
|---|---|---|---|
| Gen. Oliver Wolcott | 1796-1798 | Oliver Wolcott, Jr. | 1817-1823 |
| John Cotton Smith | 1813-1817 | Wm. W. Ellsworth | 1838-1842 |

Charles B. Andrews 1879-1881

### JUDGES.

Members of this bar who have been Judges of the Superior Court. Those starred, members of the Supreme Court of Errors.

| | |
|---|---|
| Roger Sherman,* | 1766-1789 |
| Andrew Adams,* | 1789-1798 |
| Chief Justice, 1793. | |
| Tapping Reeve,* | 1798-1815 |
| Chief Justice, 1814. | |
| Nathaniel Smith, | 1806-1819 |
| John Cotton Smith,* | 1809-1811 |
| James Gould,* | 1816-1819 |
| John T. Peters, | 1818-1834 |
| Samuel Church,* | 1833 -1854 |
| Chief Justice, 1847. | |
| Wm. W. Ellsworth,* | 1842-1861 |
| J. W. Huntington,* | 1834-1840 |
| David C. Sanford,* | 1854-1864 |
| Origen S. Seymour,* | 1855-1863 |
| Gideon Hall, | 1866-1867 |
| Miles T. Granger,* | 1867-1876 |
| Origen S. Seymour, | 1870-1874 |
| Chief Justice, 1873. | |
| Roland Hitchcock, | 1874-1882 |
| Charles B. Andrews,* | 1882-1901 |
| Chief Justice, 1889-1901. | |
| Augustus H. Fenn,* | 1887-1897 |
| Edward W. Seymour,* | 1889-1892 |
| A. T. Roraback,* | 1897 |

### CLERKS.

The following members of the bar have been Clerks of the Superior Court.

| | |
|---|---|
| Frederick Wolcott, | 1798-1836 |
| Origen S. Seymour, | 1836-1844 |
| O. S. Seymour, | 1846-1847 |
| G. H. Hollister, | 1844-1845 |
| G. H. Hollister, | 1847-1850 |
| Elisha Johnson, | 1850-1851 |
| F. D. Beeman, | 1851-1854 |
| Henry B. Graves, | 1854-1855 |
| F. D. Beeman, | 1855-1860 |
| William L. Ransom, | 1860-1887 |
| Dwight C. Kilbourn, | 1887- |

### ATTORNEYS FOR THE STATE.

The following members of the bar have been Attorneys for the State, or King's Attorney.

Joshua Whitney, 1752.
Samuel Petibone, 1756.
Reynold Marvin, 1764.
Andrew Adams, 1772.
John Canfield, 1786.
Tapping Reeve, 1788.
Uriah Tracy, 1789.
John Allen, 1800.
Nathaniel Smith, 1806.
Elisha Sterling, 1814.
Seth P. Beers, 1820.
Samuel Church, 1825.
David C. Sanford, 1840.
Leman Church, 1844.
John H. Hubbard, 1845.
Leman Church, 1847.
John H. Hubbard, 1849.
Julius B. Harrison, 1852.
Gideon Hall, 1854.
Charles F. Sedgwick, 1856.
James Huntington, 1874.
Donald T. Warner, 1896.

### SHERIFFS.

The following have been the Sheriffs for Litchfield County from its organization:

DONALD T. WARNER.

| | | | |
|---|---|---|---|
| Oliver Wolcott, | 1751-1771 | Henry A. Botsford, | 1866-1869 |
| Lynde Lord, | 1771-1801 | George H. Baldwin, | 1869-1878 |
| John R. Landon, | 1801-1819 | John D. Yale, | 1878-1881 |
| Moses Seymour, Jr., | 1819-1825 | Charles J. Porter, | 1881-1884 |
| Ozias Seymour, | 1825-1834 | Henry J. Allen, | 1884-1895 |
| Albert Sedgwick, | 1834-1835 | Edward A. Nellis, | 1895-1903 |
| Charles A. Judson, | 1835-1838 | C. C. Middlebrooks, | 1903-1907 |
| Albert Sedgwick, | 1838-1854 | F. H. Turkington, | 1907- |
| L. W. Wessells, | 1854-1866 | | |

## COURT HOUSES.

The first Court House of the County was built at Litchfield in 1751-52. It stood on the public square directly in front of and about one hundred and fifty feet distant from the site of the present one. It was a very plain looking building about twenty-five feet wide by thirty-six long and fifteen feet posts. In it was a huge stone chimney and a monstrous fire-place. It was in existence as a part of one of the stores of the village until the great fire of 1888. It cost as near as can be ascertained from the County Treasurer's books £3343 4s 9d. The tax paid by each town was as follows:

| | L | s | d | | L | s | d |
|---|---|---|---|---|---|---|---|
| Litchfield, | 284 | 10 | 9 | Canaan | 302 | 0 | 0 |
| Woodbury | 1124 | 11 | 11 | Cornwall | 103 | 0 | 0 |
| New Milford | 328 | 7 | 6 | Goshen | 189 | 0 | 8 |
| Kent | 297 | 14 | 0 | Torrington | 115 | 17 | 4 |
| Sharon | 56 | 0 | 0 | Harwinton | 129 | 12 | 7 |
| Salisbury | 307 | 10 | 0 | New Hartford | 105 | 0 | 0 |

The second Court House was located on the same site now occupied by the present one, it was given to the County for that purpose by Moses Seymour. It was built in 1789 at a cost to the County of five thousand dollars; and whatever it cost over that was made up by private contributions. It was designed by William Spratt an English Architect whose original drawing of it is now in existence.

After many years it was believed that the spire was unsafe and it was taken off and the one shown in our cut of it was added which ruined the whole effect of the front.

It was a veritable temple of justice, the interior being like a church all in one large high room with a jury room in one corner and a gallery at one end with stairs leading up to it. It took a large amount of wood to fill the immense fire-places and keep it warm during the sessions in the winter. The judges sat on a raised platform at one end with a pulpit-like desk in front of them and looked down with great majesty and dignity upon the arena in front and beneath them.

After a number of years (in 1818) an arrangement was made by and between the town of Litchfield and the county officials whereby the town was permitted to divide the high room and make an upper and a lower room; the courts to use the upper one and the town the lower room and this arrangement continued to the time of its destruction by fire June 10, 1886. The expenses of repairs and maintaining were divided between the town and county.

It has been often remarked that this old court room was one of the pleasantest in the State and although devoid of every modern convenience, it was a delight to lawyers and judges to practice therein. From its windows the finest of landscapes greeted the eye, the beautiful lakes encircled by emerald hills and the mountain peaks beyond towering into the blue sky, the fertile and well tilled farms on every side made a natural panorama that soothed the weary brain of the tired lawyer. The great Franklin stoves filled with Mt. Tom hickory wood made snapping sparkling fires. The graceful arching over head the quaint wooden benches and painted carvings, all delighted the eye and by their simple effects aided the judges and worn-out jurors in solving the intricate problems they were called to try.

The jury room in the cold bleak north-west corner was not a parlor. A big sheet iron stove for wood, a dozen wooden benches, and a plain table was the make-up of this trysting place; there was little prospect of comfort for an all night session of a disagreeing jury and they seldom lingered patiently about. Their verdicts generally were rendered altogether too speedily for the poor prisoner in the box or the fellow who lost his case.

The States Attorney's room was entirely wanting. In those primitive times those officials carried their all in their heads and pockets and what the attorney failed to do in his last argument the Court carefully supplemented in his charge. The practice in the criminal cases was largely a degree of eloquence and if the testimony was weak the advocate was strong and never failed to mention what the witnesses ought to have said.

The Clerk's office was also absent and he was permitted to rent at his own expense an office in some other building and keep the records and files wherever he chose. The judge's room was not thought of in the olden days. Why should he need one? No findings of facts were required of him and when the sheriff adjourned the court his duties ceased.

On the morning of the 11th of June, 1886 nothing remained of this old building where so many memories clustered but the two great chimneys. The fire fiend in its ruthless track had swept everything away.

Directly after the fire in 1886 attempts were made to divide the County or divert the Court to other places, and the town of Litchfield began to erect another Court House which was practically

COURT-HOUSES
WINSTED 1889
LITCHFIELD 1886-1887
LITCHFIELD 1888
LITCHFIELD 1798-1886
NEW MILFORD 1889

completed about the 1st of August 1888. It was a wooden structure somewhat like the former one with good arrangements for court, clerk, jury, judges and attorneys rooms. On the morning of the 8th of August 1888 before it had been turned over to or occupied by the County this also lay in ashes.

Immediately the town took action towards building another Court House and appointed a committee consisting of Hon. Charles B. Andrews, Dr. Henry W. Buel, Henry B. Graves, Esq., with Jacob Morse and Garner B. Curtiss, selectmen of the town. The result of their action is the present building at Litchfield built of stone and practically fire proof with excellent accomodations for all court purposes and presented to the County by the town and accepted by the county commissioners in behalf of and for the county on the 11th of March, 1890.

Meanwhile the agitation about dividing the county and court business continued until finally it resulted in an act of the legislature allowing courts to be held at Litchfield, Winchester and New Milford upon the two latter towns providing suitable accomodations. Whereupon the town of Winchester leased to the county such a building with suitable accomodations for the courts of the county on the 9th of August, 1887 and the town of New Milford also leased such building and accomodations on the 15th day of August, 1887 and the courts are now held at each of said places practically holding court wherever it is most convenient to try the cases.

In 1905 the town of Winchester increased the Court accomodations by adding four large spacious rooms and fire proof vault with metal fixtures, making this Court building one of the best in the State for its purposes.

In 1907 a bill was presented before the General Assembly of Connecticut, ordering the removal to Winchester from Litchfield, of the civil records and files of the Superior Court, with the seal and Clerk, making Winchester practically the main office of the Court. It also provided for the removal of all the files of the Common Pleas Court and seal, to the Winsted Court House. The bill, however, failed of passage.

## SELECTING JURYMEN.

The Statutes of Connecticut provide for the selection of jurymen for the several towns, and also prescribe the number to which each town is entitled.

Various ways of selecting these men have been provided in former years, but the present method seems to have been more nearly satisfactory than any of the past ones.

The Selectmen of each town are required to forward to the Clerk of the Superior Court during the month of May the names of twice the number the town is entitled to. The Judges at their annual meeting in June appoint two Jury Commissioners to act with the Clerk of the Superior Court, who is by Statute a Jury Commissioner, who meet on the second Monday of July and select one half of the names returned by the Selectmen. These names, so selected, are printed on slips of paper, and those of each town are placed in a box by themselves, and are the names of the men liable for jury duty from each town for the year from the following September first. When a petit jury is required, the Clerk draws them without seeing the name, from such towns as he desires, in the presence of a Judge and a Sheriff.

## ABOUT JURIES.

This important part of the Court deserves a very honorable mention. The juries of this County have been composed of the very best class of men; men of good judgment and sterling common sense, seldom carried away with the oratory or pathos of the advocate or losing sight of the issues of the case.

There are some incidents related of jury trials that tend to show that they are but men and liable to some of the caprices of human nature. The common style of voting blank upon a case by one or more of them on the first ballot is of very little consequence only showing that some people do not form conclusions as rapidly as others.

That the jurymen do not always agree with the Court is illustrated by a case in which Judge Carpenter in charging the jury remarked "Now gentlemen, if you believe this incredible story you will convict the prisoner, but if you do not believe it you must acquit him." The jury after a long consultation disagreed. Upon receiving further instruction in which the incredible story was discredited still more strongly, they again retired and after mature deliberation they still disagreed. Another strong instruction, retirement and disagreement, when they were discharged from further consideration of the case. It was ascertained they stood eleven for conviction and one for acquittal.

In another case wherein a man sued an officer for false imprisonment it was admitted that the officer was liable and the judge charged the jury that they were the ones to assess the damages. The offense was where an officer arrested a drunk and put him in the town lockup over night, intending to try him in the morning; before the trial however the man's friends hearing of his condition went to the lockup opened the door and carried him away. After being out a long time the jury returned much to every ones surprise a verdict for the defendant. The explanation that the jury gave was that the man was rescued by his friends before the officer had had a reasonable time to prosecute the offense.

A man was prosecuted for an assault and battery of rather an aggravated nature; he claimed it was done in self defense. It was

EDWARD W. SEYMOUR.

shown that the parties had an altercation and the accused followed up the complainant and pounded him. The prisoner admitted it, but claimed he was obliged to follow up for fear that the other man would, as soon as he got a little distance from him, turn around and shoot him. The Jury pondered a long while, then returned to the Court Room for instructions. The foreman said they wished to know how far the law allowed a man to follow up another with a sled stake in self defense.

### WITNESSES.

Of course our Courts had all sorts of witnesses to deal with from the garrulous man who knows everything, to the reticent man who knows nothing and has forgotten that.

A few specimens are preserved in the traditions of our elders.

A child was asked if he knew the nature of an oath and he replied "No sir." Then the kind hearted judge leaned over the side of his desk and smilingly asks "My son don't you know what you're going to tell?" "Yes, sir," said the boy, "that old bald headed lawyer over there told me what I must say." "Administer the oath, Mr. Clerk."

A witness in a criminal case haled from a unsavory place called "Pinch Gut;" he was duly sworn and upon being asked his name, gave it. The next question was "Where do you reside?" No answer came. The question was repeated twice and the last time with great severity. The witness turned with dignity to the judge and said, "Must I answer that question?" "Why not?" said the Court. "Because" said the witness "I have been told that no man was obliged to criminate himself."

Witnesses are often ridiculed for making evasive answers to attorneys' questions but perhaps they do not always fully understand the query. The following is a question asked by a learned attorney in the trial of a tax case, taken from the Stenographer's notes:

Q. "What I want to ask you is whether comparing his land with the other lands that you have been swearing about here, you have sworn to some 30 other farms, and in comparison, that is, I mean whether, how should you take them in comparison, how should you consider them, if you take that as a basis, they are assessed for $3,000. Taking that as a basis for your comparison, how should you start?"

### STENOGRAPHER.

In 1884 the General Assembly passed an act providing for the appointment of a Stenographer for the Superion Court in each of the Counties. About 1886 Mr. Leonard W. Cogswell was appointed for this County and has held the position since that date.

Leonard W. Cogswell, Esq., the official stenographer is a na-

LEONARD W. COGSWELL.

tive of Litchfield County, and was born in New Preston, in July 1863, and enjoyed all the lights and shadows of a farmer's son on a rugged farm upon the side of Mt. Bushnell. He polished up an education received at the districe school and Village Academy by a term at Claverack College at Hudson, N. Y. In 1884 he quit the farm and went to New Haven and learned short hand. In 1886 he was appointed official Stenographer of Litchfield County, and holds the same position for Windham County. His services are in great demand during the sessions of the Legislature, by the Committees thereof.

He was admitted to the Bar of New Haven County in June, 1897, and resides in New Haven. In the preparation of this memoir we are indebted to him for the preservation of the remarks at the Banquet, and for poetical selections herein.

STUDENT'S LIFE.

At the Bar Dinner in 1901 Judge Roraback in his remarks gave a few reminisences of his student days which are worthy of preservation as illustrating how lawyers were made in the country offices. Upon being introduced by the Toastmaster he responded as follows:

Mr. Toastmaster, and gentlemen of the Litchfield County Bar: I hardly expected to make a speech, but the reference that was

ALBERTO T. RORABACK.

made by my distinguished friend, Donald J. Warner carries me back to the month of April, 1870. That is almost 32 years. I then commenced the study of Blackstone in his office. Well, I pounded away at Blackstone for five months, and learned it pretty thoroughly. As I remember it, if it had been set to music I think I could have sung it. It was pretty dry work and pretty hard work. But one morning D. J. came in, and he says, "Roraback, you have been pounding away at Blackstone some time, would'nt you like a change?" Well, I hardly knew what was coming, whether it was a change from Blackstone to Chitty, or what it was, but I looked up at him, and I said I thought I would. "All right," he said, "I have got a client for you." I could hardly believe it. A real client with a case? It was the first ray of light, the first gleam of hope in those long months; to have a client, a real live client. He brought him in. I wish you could have seen him. He was colored. His trousers were stuck in the tops of his boots, he was out at the seat of his pants, but he was a client; my first client. It was my first case, and I was happy. The case was returnable before Daniel Pratt, a Justice who had his office in the village of Salisbury. I went to work to prepare my case, and at the time stated for the trial I was there with my client. I made the great, supreme, and sublime effort of my life. There was'nt any attorney for the plaintiff. I appeared for the defense. It was'nt necessary that the plaintiff should be represented. The magistrate occupied that position, and when I had finished my argument he made his. It was very effective; just $36.22 for the plaintiff and costs. Well, of course I felt crestfallen. I came down to the office the next morning, and Donald J. the elder came in, and he asked me how I got along with the case. I had to tell him I got beat. Thoroughly beaten. And he said to me, "Oh, well, never mind that. You will come across those little misfortunes once in a while in your practice of law, but, of course, you won't get any pay." "I did, I got my pay." "You did? How much did you get?" "$6." "$6," Donald J. says, "that is better than a victory; I have been defending that cussed nigger in season and out of season for the past twenty-five years, and I never received a cent," and he grasped me warmly by the hand, and he says, "Roraback, you will be a success." That was case No. 1, My first case.

Case No. 2 was the case of Julius Moses vs. Virgil Roberts. Virgil Roberts was an old farmer that lived down on the Gay St. road, as I remember it. When the case came to trial D. J. said to me that I had better come along down and write the evidence. So I went along down and wrote the evidence, and when the evidence was all in D. J. spoke to me over across the table and he says, "Roraback, you get up and make the opening argument." I was demoralized, for gentlemen, sitting on the other side was Gen'l. Charles S. Sedgwick. You never saw him, most of you, but he was a man that stood six feet four in his stockings, and weighed 250 lbs. I am afraid I made very poor work of it with that great giant on the other side. I was afraid. I verily believe if the old General had stamped his foot and yelled "scat," I would have gone through the window and forever abandoned the idea of studying law. But we fought it out. I got up and made my argument, and then the old General got up and made No. 2, and then Donald J. Warner made the closing. Talk about wit, and talk about sarcasm, talk about eloquence, I learned the lesson right there and then that it was not the avoirdupois of the lawyer that wins cases. Gen. Sedgwick was three score and ten. He lived along a few years, and wrote a little pamphlet on his experiences in fifty years at the Litchfield County Bar. He was then state attorney.

## BAR LIBRARY.

The matter of having a Bar Library at the Court House was attended to at an early date. The following action of the Bar is an interesting Record.

"At a meeting of the Bar December 29, 1819.

The following Report of a Committee having been read was adopted. "To the Bar of the County of Litchfield. The Subscribers having been appointed by said Bar, a Committee to enquire into the expediency of commencing a Law Library for the use of the Bar, (and if deemed expedient to devise some mode by which it may be obtained), having attended to the subject beg leave to report in part, That the Bar now owns six volumns of the Statutes of Massachusetts, the two volumns of the revised edition of the Statutes of New York, published in 1813, and the two volumes of the Statutes of Vermont published in 1808; that there now remains unexpended the sum of Seventeen Dollars formerly raised by the Bar for the purpose of purchasing Statutes of other States.

And further report that it is expedient that there be raised by the Bar the further sum of One Hundred and Fifty-six Dollars to be paid and apportioned to the members thereof as follows:

| | | | |
|---|---|---|---|
| Elisha Sterling | $6.00 | Jabez W. Huntington | 5.00 |
| Jno. G. Mitchell | 3.00 | Samuel Church | 5.00 |
| Reuben Hunt | 2.00 | Wm. M. Burrall | 5.00 |
| W. S. Holabird | 3.00 | Michael F. Mills | 4.00 |
| Calvin Butler | 4.00 | Holbrook Curtiss | 4.00 |
| Chas. B. Phelps | 5.00 | Nathaniel B. Smith | 3.00 |
| Nath'l. Perry, Jr. | 2.00 | Roger Mills | 4.00 |
| R. R. Hinman | 4.00 | Philo N. Heacock | 2.00 |
| Perry Smith | 6.00 | Homer Swift | 3.00 |
| Nath'l. Perry | 4.00 | Geo. Wheaton | 3.00 |
| Cyrus Swan | 5.00 | Phineas Miner | 6.00 |
| Asa Bacon | 7.00 | Philander Wheeler | 3.00 |

| | | | |
|---|---|---|---|
| Leman Church | 4.00 | Wm. Cogswell | 3.00 |
| Joseph Miller | 5.00 | Ansel Sterling | 5.00 |
| Wm. G. Williams | 5.00 | Theodore North | 4.00 |
| Noah B. Benedict | 7.00 | Seth P. Beers | 6.00 |
| John Strong | 2.00 | Matthew Minor | 3.00 |
| Jos. B. Bellamy | 4.00 | Isaac Leavenworth | 4.00 |
| David S. Boardman | 6.00 | | |

And that said sums of Seventeen and One Hundred and Fifty-six Dollars with such further sum as the Court may appropriate from the County Treasurer for that purpose, be applied to the purchase of the Law Books hereinafter mentioned, or such other Books as the Bar may hereafter direct, viz:

Kirby's Reports, Root's Reports, Day's Cases in Error, Connecticut Reports, Swift's Evidence, Swift's System, Chitty's Pleadings, Lane's Pleadings, Phillip's Evidence, Johnson's Reports, Massachusetts Reports.

All of which is respectfully submitted,

Signed per order,

S. P. Beers, *Chairman.*

The books mentioned in this report were purchased and are now in the Library at Litchfield. The only provision for the increase of the Library which I find is an admission fee of Five Dollars from a new attorney, until 1874, nor do the books in the Library show additions of any account.

In 1874, it was Voted As a standing Rule of the Bar, that each member pay to the treasurer thereof the sum of One Dollar each, yearly, to be expended in the purchase of Books for the benefit and use of the said Bar. Said payments to be made at the annual meeting in each year.

In 1877 the Legislature enacted a Bill providing for the formation of County Law Library Associations. The County Commissioners were to pay in their discretion each year on the first of January a sum not exceeding Three Hundred Dollars, for the support thereof. The Litchfield County Law Library Association was duly organized and received money from the County Treasurer for one year, after which the discretion of the Commissioners did not mature, and payments ceased, for some years. In 1897 an act was passed making the payment obligatory of one hundred and fifty dollars to each of the libraries at Litchfield, Winsted and New Milford, since which time a good supply of law books may be found in each Court House.

At the session of the Legislature of 1907 an act was passed requiring the County Commissioners to pay each library four hundred dollars a year.

At New Milford large accessions came from bequests of Bros. Henry S. Sanford and James H. McMahon.

JAMES H. MCMAHON.

In 1906 Bro. McMahon left by his will the sum of $1,200 to be equally divided between the three libraries, which was available in 1907, and has been paid to the committees.

In each Court House may be found a first class working library with some of the Reports of other States.

In 1900 the Bar voted that all the law books of the Bar Association be presented to the Litchfield County Law Library Association, so that all the books are under one management.

AARON WHITE FUND.

Another branch of these libraries is purchased by the income derived from a bequest of Aaron White, a lawyer who by his will left to each County Law Library one thousand dollars for certain classes of books.

The following account of Mr. White who deceased in 1886, taken from a newspaper, will no doubt be of interest in this connection and is worthy of preservation.

A Boston *Globe* correspondent tells the following story of Aaron White of Quinnebaug:—

Aaron White has figured in his life as the most eccentric man in this locality, and one who is widely known in Massachusetts,

Connecticut and Rhode Island. He was born in Boylston, Mass., October 8, 1798, and was the eldest of ten children, seven boys and three girls, nine of whom are now living. He entered Harvard college, graduating in a class of sixty-eight members in 1817. Of his classmates only seven are now living. Mr. White, in recounting incidents of his college life, shows a wonderful memory. Among his classmates were the late Hon. Stephen Salisbury of Worcester, the Hon. George Bancroft, the Hon. Caleb Cushing, whom he considered the most talented man he ever met; Samuel Sewall, now living in Boston; Dr. John Green of Lowell, the Rev. Dr. Tyng of the Episcopal church, now living in Phildelphia; John D. Wells of Boston, one of the greatest anatomists of his day, and Professor Alva Woods, formerly president of the Transylvania college in the South. living in Providence. When the "Dorr War" broke out Squire White was living in Woonsocket. "Governor" Dorr, being at the head of the controvesy, called upon Mr. White, for advice "as a friend and acquaintance," which resulted in frequent visits between them. This resulted afterwards in both White and Dorr being obliged to leave the state, both going to Thompson, Conn. Soon after, Mr. White secretly got Dorr into New Hampshire. The authorities in Rhode Island used a warrant for the arrest of Squire White, in which he was called the "commander-in-chief" of the forces that opposed the state. They called on Governor Chauncy Cleveland of Connecticut for assistance, which was refused. They afterwards called on Governor John Davis of Massachusetts to arrest White when he came to Dudley, Webster or Worcester, but Governor Davis as in the case of Governor Cleveland, refused to grant the request. Both governors were in sympathy with Dorr and White. The Rhode Island authorities then threatened to send an armed force to kidnap Squire White at his home in Quinnebaug. Governor Davis then issued a warrant for White's arrest if seen in Massachusetts, but this warrant was not intended to harm Squire White, for it was to run only thirty days from its date. The result was that Squire White remained unmolested in his quiet home on the banks of the placid Quinnebaug. He is a lawyer and his business has been such as settling estates, drawing up wills, giving advice, etc., and he has always been considered a safe man to consult on such business. When he was in his prime he was six feet in height, lightly built and very long-limbed, weighing 160 pounds. He is nearly blind, his eyesight having been failing for some five years.

In his college days he, with Caleb Cushing, collected several rare coins. Later he engaged in collecting old-fashioned coppers. When the government called in the old coppers in 1863 or thereabouts, issuing new ones, and for three years afterwards, he was most active in picking them up. His reason for going into this business was that he thought it very profitable. He visited the mint at Philadelphia, making arrangements with the officers to take these coppers and give him new pennies in return, the government to pay all expenses in shipping to and from his home. This business, which he has carried on for some fifteen years, as a whole has netted him a large amount of profit. He has some instances sold copper coins of rare date for from $1 to $3, and in one case he received $5 for a rare copper. He paid from forty to forty-four cents per pound, "good, bad and indifferent," selecting the good ones from them and shipping the rest to the mint. In his trips he visited the principal cities and large towns in New England, collecting many thousand coins as a result.

After the death of Mr. White in 1886, his executors found many barrels of copper cents—of the "not rare" ones. About four tons of these coins were redeemed by the Sub-Treasury at Washington.

### EXTRACTS FROM AARON WHITE'S WILL.

Fourth.—Out of the residue of the estates so given in trust as aforesaid, to pay to the Treasurers of the present eight Counties in the State of Connecticut, to each the sum of One Thousand Dollars in lawful money, to be by them received in trust, as funds for the procurement and maintenance of County Bar Libraries in their respective Counties, in their several County Court Houses, for the sole use of the Judges and Clerks of Courts therein, Members of the Bar, and their students at law while in the offices of said Bar members, in their respective Counties; which funds or the annual income thereof, as said Bar Members may direct, shall be expended under their direction in the purchase of Books of History, and Books of Moral and Political Philosophy.

And in case said residue last mentioned be not sufficient for the payment of all said legacies to said Counties in full, then said residue, in equal portions to said Counties for the purposes aforesaid shall be deemed a fullfilment of their trust. Such payment to be made within three years from the time of my decease."

### CENTENNIAL.

At a meeting of the Litchfield County Bar held at the Court House in Litchfield on the 4th day of January 1851 the following preamble and resolution was adopted:

WHEREAS, During the present year a century will elapse since the organization of the County of Litchfield; and

WHEREAS, A Centennial celebration of that event has been under consideration, Therefore

RESOLVED, That Chas. B. Phelps, O. S. Seymour, John H. Hubbard, Gideon Hall, G. H. Hollister, J. B. Harrison and J. B. Foster Esquires, be a Committee of the Bar to call a meeting of citizens of the County to consider that subject and to take such

F. D. Beeman

order thereon by appointment of a Committee of arrangements or otherwise as shall be thought best.

F. D. Beeman, *Clerk*.

In pursuance of these proceedings the Centennial Celebration of August 1851 was held. Several thousand people were present. Judge Samuel Church delivered the Historical address which is reprinted in this volume. Horace Bushnell the sermon and John Pierpont the poem.

DAVID DAGGETT.

At a meeting of the Bar of Litchfield County during the August Term 1834, a Committee was appointed to prepare an address to the Hon. David Daggett, Chief Justice of the State, on the occasion of the near approach of his term of judicial service, which Committee reported to the Bar the following address, which was by order of the Bar communicated to the Hon. David Daggett, and together with the reply thereto was ordered to be recorded upon the records of the Bar.

"To the Hon. David Daggett, Chief Justice of the State of Connecticut. Sir:—The members of the Bar of the County of Litchfield, having heard from a communication which you made to the Legislature of the State at its last session that your judicial term of office service will expire by Constitutional limitation during the present year, and consequently not expecting to meet you again in your official character, beg leave to express to you the high sense which they entertain of the ability, integrity and impartiality, which you have manifested upon the bench, and to thank you cordially for the uniform kindness and courtesy with which you have treated them when they have had occasion to appear before you to discharge the arduous duties of their profession. In taking leave of you we cannot but recollect that it is now rising of forty years since you first formed a connection with the Bar of this County, and that you were long associated in practice with Adams, Reeve, Smith, Tracy, Allen, Kirby, Benedict, Slosson and Southmayde, whose bright names are inscribed on our records and whose memory will be cherished so long as learning, talent and virtue shall command esteem; nor can we forget that your labors may be traced in the very foundations of the judicial system of Connecticut, nor that you have exercised a happy influence in adorning that system with various learning, and in bringing it to its present matured condition.

We tender you our best wishes that the residue of your days may be as happy as your life has been heretofore distinguished and honorable.

Per order of the Bar,

Phineas Miner, *Chairman*.

Geo. C. Woodruff, *Clerk pro tem*,
Litchfield, August 29th., 1834.

The following is the reply made by the Hon. David Daggett to the foregoing address.

"To the members of the Bar of Litchfield of the County of Litchfield:

Gentlemen:—I have received with high satisfaction the address signed by Phineas Miner and George C. Woodruff, Esquires, your Chairman and Secretary, which you did me the honor to communicate to me this day.

In taking leave of a Bar so distinguished, by the illustrious names inscribed on its records, it is impossible that I should not entertain a grateful recollection of the memories of those who are now away from all earthly scenes, and also cherish a lively affection and respect for those who now occupy with such honor their places.

If my official conduct on the bench deserves the commendation bestowed upon it, much of it is justly due to the gentlemen of a Bar ever characterized by ability, integrity, industry and learning. Of your courtesy towards me and your gentlemanly deportment towards each other while engaged in the conflicts of the Bar, I cannot speak in terms sufficiently expressive of the feelings of my heart. They will be recollected with grateful affection. How much such an intercourse between the Bar and the bench tends to alleviate the burdens of the judicial station, can be known only by those who have had the pleasure to witness it.

I pray you to accept my fervent wishes for the prosperity and happiness of you individually, and my cordial thanks for this expression of your esteem and respect.

David Daggett.

Litchfield, August 28th., 1834.

A true copy. Attest,

Wm. P. Burrall, *Clerk*.

COURT EXPENSES.

In the earlier part of the century the Judges were given a certain sum per day and their dinners.

Among the vouchers of the past the following bill of Court expenses appears.

The State of Connecticut:

To Isaac Baldwin, Dr.

Superior Court, February Term, 1810.

| | |
|---|---|
| To ninety nine dinners for the Court | $49.50 |
| To 21 bottles of wine at 10s | 35.50 |
| To Brandy, Sugar, etc., 17 days at 4-6 | 12.75 |
| To pipes and tobacco | .50 |
| To Segars | .25 |
| To paper | .25 |
| | $98.75 |

GIDEON H. WELCH.

# THE COUNTY COURT.

Prepared by the late Wm. F. Hurlbut, Clerk.

The first Court organization in Litchfield County was the County Court, and for several years it was the principal trial court,—having criminal jurisdiction in all cases except those punishable by death, or imprisonment in the State Prison for life,—and civil jurisdiction in law and equity where the matter in demand did not exceed three hundred and thirty-five dollars, but a right of appeal to the Superior Court existed, in cases where the *ad damnum* exceeded two hundred dollars, or the title to land or right of way was in question, also raising or obstructing the water of any stream, river, creek or arm of the sea by erection of a dam, etc., which gave litigants the power to prevent a determination of causes by the County Court, and which the defeated parties availed themselves of to such an extent that most cases passed through both courts with a trial of facts in each, with the result that public opinion considered the County Court of but little practical value. Therefore the legislature of 1855, abolished it and transferred all causes therein pending to the docket of the Superior Court, causing that Court to be loaded with such a mass of business that it was impossible for a case to be tried within two years after being brought. This congestion of the docket of the Superior Court coupled with the inconvenience of travel to Litchfield (then the only County Seat) caused the organization in 1872 of the District Court for the First Judicial District, the district being composed of the towns of Barkhamsted, Bridgewater, Canaan, Colebrook, Cornwall, Kent, New Hartford, New Milford, Norfolk, North Canaan, Salisbury, Sharon, Washington and Winchester. This Court continued to exist until 1883 when the remainder of the County desirous of enjoying the privilege afforded by it, the name was changed to the Court of Common Pleas and its jurisdiction extended to the entire County with sessions holden at Litchfield in addition to Winchester, New Milford and Canaan.

This was practically a revival of the old County Court with civil powers enlarged to cover causes demanding one thousand dollars damages but with no right of appeal to the Superior Court nor any criminal jurisdiction.

The Court of Common Pleas has been a popular court transacting a large majority of the litigation of the County with less expense to the State and to parties than the same could have been done by the Superior Court.

## JUDGES OF THE COUNTY COURT.

William Preston, Woodbury 1751-1754
John Williams, Sharon 1754-1773
Oliver Wolcott, Litchfield 1773-1786
Daniel Sherman, Woodbury 1786-1791
Joshua Porter, Salisbury 1791-1808
Aaron Austin, New Hartford 1808-1816
Augustus Pettibone Norfolk 1816-1831
David S. Boardman, New Milford 1831-1836
William M. Burrall, Canaan 1836-1838
Ansel Sterling, Sharon 1838-1839
Calvin Butler, Plymouth 1839-1840
Ansel Sterling, Sharon 1840-1842
William M. Burrall, Canaan 1842-1844
Abijah Catlin, Harwinton 1844-1846
Elisha S. Abernethy, Litchfield 1846-1847
Holbrook Curtiss, Watertown 1847-1849
Hiram Goodwin, Barkhamsted 1849-1850
Charles B. Phelps, Woodbury 1850-1851
Hiram Goodwin, Barkhamsted 1851-1856

## JUSTICES OF THE QUORUM.

John Miner, Woodbury 1704-1716
John Sherman, Woodbury 1708-1714
John Sherman, Woodbury 1723-1728
Joseph Miner, Woodbury 1725-1739
William Preston, Woodbury 1740-1751

## THE FOLLOWING IN LITCHFIELD COUNTY.

Thomas Chipman, Salisbury 1751-1753
John Williams, Sharon 1751-1754
Samuel Canfield, New Milford 1751-1754
Ebenezer Marsh, Litchfield 1751-1772
Joseph Bird, Salisbury 1753-1754
Noah Hinman, Woodbury 1754-1759
Elisha Sheldon, Litchfield 1754-1759
Increase Moseley, Woodbury 1755-1780
Roger Sherman, New Milford 1759-1762
Daniel Sherman, Woodbury 1761-1786
Bushnell Bostwick, New Milford 1762-1776
Joshua Porter, Salisbury 1772-1791
Samuel Canfield, New Milford 1777-1790
Jedediah Strong, Litchfield 1780-1791

WILLIAM F. HURLBUT

| | | | |
|---|---|---|---|
| Heman Swift, Cornwall | 1786-1802 | Birdseye Norton, Goshen | 1809-1812 |
| Aaron Austin, New Hartford | 1790-1808 | Augustus Pettibone, Norfolk | 1812-1816 |
| Nathan Hale, Canaan | 1791-1809 | Uriel Holmes, Litchfield | 1814-1817 |
| David Smith, Plymouth | 1791-1814 | Moses Lyman, Jr., Goshen | 1815-1817 |
| Daniel N. Brinsmade, Washington | 1802-1818 | Oliver Burnham, Cornwall | 1816-1818 |
| Judson Canfield, Sharon | 1808-1815 | Cyrus Swan, Sharon | 1817-1819 |
| Martin Strong, Salisbury | 1819-1820 | | |

ASSOCIATE JUDGES.

| | | | |
|---|---|---|---|
| Martin Strong, Salisbury | 1820-1829 | Morris Wodruff, Litchfield | 1829-1836 |
| John Welch, Litchfield | 1820-1829 | Hugh P. Welch, Litchfield | 1836-1838 |
| William M. Burrall, Canaan | 1829-1836 | | |

The Judges of the District Court were Roland Hitchcock, two years; Jared B. Foster, three years; Florimond D. Fyler, four years and Donald J. Warner, two years; of the Court of Common Pleas Donald J. Warner, six years; Alberto T. Roraback, four years; Arthur D. Warner, three and one half years; Alberto T. Roraback, five months (when he was appointed to the Superior Court bench) and Gideon H. Welch now (1907) holding the office.

The Clerks have been of the County Court

Isaac Baldwin, 1751-1793 Frederick Wolcott, 1793-1836

Of the District Court and Court of Common Pleas

Wm. F. Hurlbut, twenty-two years Walter S. Judd, two years

Wheaton F. Dowd, from 1901

JUDGE PRESTON'S MONUMENT IN WOODBURY

# Trials

# NOTED TRIALS.

Although the Courts are organized to remedy private wrongs and as such their proceedings are not matters of general history, yet these are sometimes of such a public nature and relate so closely to the general weal and welfare that they are properly a part of Court history, while of course Criminal trials are public property. Some of these have passed through the Courts of highest adjudication and are very important.

The Attorney in preparing his brief in an action cannot have avoided noticing how often his references quote from some Litchfield County decision, especially in the earlier cases.

Those earlier Blackstones of our jurisprudence, Reeve, Gould, Church and Seymour laid their work on the deep foundations of the philosophy and truths of natural justice and common sense.

The early part of our records are of appeals from the County Court, motions for new trials, foreclosures, and a good many cases of Insolvency proceedings and cases of equitable nature. Very few trials of fact occur; the judgments were rendered mostly after decisions upon demurrers, pleas in abatement and such preliminary pleadings, upon the determination of which we now have a right to answer over, and have a trial on the facts.

In the Criminal prosecutions, if the accused by any chance was acquitted he was discharged by paying the costs of his trial, and till 1835 the sentences of imprisonment were made to Newgate, now known as the Copper mines in Simsbury.

We append herewith a few of the memorable trials, and have probably omitted others of equally as valuable and important significance. The abstracts are necessarily very brief and condensed.

The first recorded case upon the books of the Superior Court is that of

Abner Wheeler, of Bethlem
vs.
Joshua Henshaw, of New Hartford.

In which the plaintiff recovered $642.75 damages and costs taxed at $49.86.

The first divorce granted was Lucy Mix of Salisbury against Thomas Mix.

These mixings and unmixings have formed a large per cent. of the judgments during the century.

### THE SELLECK-OSBORN MATTER.

One of the most important trials and probably one that in its general results affected the State, especially the political part of it more than any other that has ever occurred in the State, was the Selleck-Osborn trial 1806-1807.

Benjamin Talmadge, Esq., was a Colonel in the Revolution and at the close of hostilities settled in Litchfield where he was a very prominent citizen and for many years a member of Congress. Frederick Wolcott, who for more than forty years was the clerk of the County and Superior Courts, brought a suit against one William Hart of Saybrook and at the August Term of this court 1805 recovered $2,205.00 damages. The case was taken to the Supreme Court and affirmed. Execution was issued and paid in full in 1806.

Selleck Osborn and Timothy Ashley were then publishing a newspaper in Litchfield called the Witness and made comments upon the judgment reflecting severely upon the integrity of the Court.

Whereupon the Superior Court prosecuted them as follows: "James Gould, Esq., Attorney for the State for the County of Litchfield specially appointed by this Court in this behalf filed an information before this Court, therein representing that Selleck Osborn and Timothy Ashley both now resident in Litchfield in County intending to bring the Superior Court of judicature of this State into disrepute and contempt and especially to induce a belief among the good people of this State that said Court in proceeding to and rendering judgment in a certain cause in which Benjamin Talmadge and Frederick Wolcott, Esquires were plaintiffs and William Hart, Esq., was defendant, and that the jury who attended said Court in finding a verdict in said cause were influenced by partial, dishonest and corrupt motives, did at Litchfield aforesaid on the 4th day of September 1805 with force and arms most unjustly wickedly and maliciously print and publish and cause to be printed and published of and concerning said Court and jury and of and concerning the proceedings in said cause in a publick newspaper called the Witness a certain false and scandalous libel purporting to be a statement or report of the aforesaid action of the evidence adduced therein and of the proceedings therein had which said information is as on file."

The defendants plead to the jurisdiction of the Court to which the attorney demurred and the Court decided that it had jurisdiction. It then went to the Court for trial on their plea of not guilty. They were found guilty and fined two hundred and fifty dollars each. Osborn in his statement of the numerous trials says that this one cost him $605.98. The libel suit of Julius Deming against him $346.46 and for slandering Thomas Colier he paid $522.00.

Osborn and Ashley were also fined in the County Court one hundred dollars for libelling Julius Deming a prominent merchant of Litchfield. Mr. Ashley paid his part but Mr. Osborn would not pay and was taken to jail. This aroused the Jeffersonians all over the County and State, they calling it a political martyrdom and on the 6th of August 1806, they gave him a great ovation forming a grand procession with cavalry and military parade passing by the jail where he was confined and saluting him with great honors. A part of the celebration was an address delivered in the meeting house by Joseph L. Smith, then a young lawyer of Litchfield. He made remarks reflecting upon the Superior Court, consequently in due course of time the State's Attorney, Urial Holmes, Esq., issued an information against him for uttering "the following false, malicious, scandalous and defamatory words, viz: 'The Courts of justice (meaning the aforesaid Courts of justice in this State) have regarded the face of man in judgment. If the Republicans shall retake the property which the Federal Courts (meaning the aforesaid Courts , magistrates, judges and justices of this State) have taken from them (meaning the said Republicans) it will be but a poor apology for the Federalists that they obtained it by false witnesses perjured judges and packed juries." Also "Osborn is imprisoned for publishing that of a Federal justice which is true of every Federal justice in the State."

Smith first plead not guilty, then the Court allowed him to change his plea to a demurrer. The Court found the information sufficient and fined Smith two hundred and fifty dollars and costs, one hundred and twenty three dollars and sixty four cents.

The clerk adds to the record, "The delinquint was delivered to the custody of the Sheriff of said County."

Smith's connection with the Court was not altogether agreeable after that, but he was soon appointed Major in the United States Army and was a Colonel in the War of 1812 after which he was United States Judge in Florida. He was the ancestor of the confederate General E. Kirby Smith.

## BLASPHEMY.

At the August Term of the Court in 1809 William Leavenworth, Jr., was informed against for blasphemy in the town of Plymouth. The information stated "Who did in the presence and hearing of sundry of the good people of the State then and there assembled, blaspheme the name of God the Father and of the Holy Ghost, and deny and reproach the true God and His government of the world by wickedly and blasphemously uttering and speaking the words following, viz: 'I am the Holy Ghost and here is the Holy Ghost,' he the said William speaking of himself and meaning that he, said William was the Holy Ghost."

The accused was arrested, brought before the Court and plead not guilty, and after a trial was acquitted by the jury and the Clerk adds, "The said William was discharged by order of Court without the payment of costs."

This was a new departure, it having been customary for the prisoner to be obliged to pay the costs whether convicted or acquitted.

The following remarkable proceeding appears upon the record of our Courts, but the account herein given is from Gen. Sedgwick's History of Sharon.

### A WRONG VERDICT STANDS.

At a regimental training in Sharon on the 20th day of Sept., A. D. 1805 an altercation occurred between Zenas Beebe of Sharon and Aner Ives of Kent which was consummated by the stabbing of Ives by Beebe with a bayonet, inflicting a mortal wound of which he died at the end of a week. There were mitigating circumstances in the case which relieved Beebe from the charge of wilful murder, but it was a clear case of manslaughter. By a singular blunder of the foreman of the jury he was pronounced not guilty of any offense. The jury had agreed upon the verdict to be rendered to be "not guilty of murder, but guilty of manslaughter." The foreman rendered the first part of the verdict but stopped there. The subsequent proceedings in the matter are copied from the records of the Court.

"After the verdict was rendered the foreman informed the Court that the verdict which the jury had intended to return and had agreed on was—that the said Beebe was not guilty of murder, but by mistake he had omitted to return and state the whole finding of the jury, and desired to be directed by the Court whether the verdict and the whole finding of the jury as agreed upon by them, and as he designed at first to have stated the same, would then be made and returned.

On consideration it was adjudged by the court that the verdict of the jury as returned and recorded by them could not be explained or altered."

Beebe was defended by two of the ablest lawyers in the State Nathaniel Smith of Woodbury and David Daggett of New Haven.

At the Term of the Superior Court holden February, A. D. 1820, Beebe was tried for an assault with intent to kill Amasa Maxam and found guilty. He was sentenced to confinement in the Old Newgate prison for two years but died before the expiration of his sentence.

### A SINGULAR INFORMATION FOR SLANDER.

In 1814, Elisha Sterling, Esq., then Attorney for the State for the County of Litchfield presented to the Court his information against a very prominent man of the County who was at that time Brigadier General of the State Militia.

The complaint was for libel upon his deceased father-in-law made by the General in the form of a "Funeral Order" and sent to one of the inferior officers of his regiment directing him to conduct the funeral. The order is too wicked and vulgar to be published entire but a few extracts from it will show its general purport.

### A FUNERAL ORDER.

I have this day been informed that old                    is dead, and I being out of health cannot attend the funeral. I therefore give you this order and empower you to conduct it in the following order and I will pay the expense. First get a coffin made of Pepperidge Plank three inches thick and duftail it strong together with large Iron Spikes, Hoop it thick with Bars of Iron, make a winding sheet with sheet iron, braze it well Top and Bottom, make a Muffler with two hundred pounds of German Steel. Place a large Iron Screw on the top of his head extending through the Jaws so that the old fellow cannot open his mouth, next place on a mule dressed in Regimentals with old sword and Epaulette which he wore at the time the British invaded New York, when he run and left his men twenty rods behind. . . . .

Raise four red or crimson Flags, place (certain neighbors) as pall bearers to blow Rams Horns, dress (other neighbors) in Indian Stockings and Wampum and make them carry around Winkum or Cyder Brandy in large iron kettles to treat the procession, start by the shouting of Rams Horns until the walls fall in ( ) as they did in Jericho. Draw Him to , then blast a grave into a solid rock ten feet deep, put him in head downwards, place bars of iron thick across the grave, take a sledge, drive in stones, cement them with Plaster of Paris, so that the old Devil cannot get out, as he would make Quarrells and Disturbance until the Day of Judgment. Go to and get one hundred and fifty barrells of tar or pitch and twenty barrells of brimstone and burn around the door to keep off the devils until you perform this my order. . . . . . . .

The information concludes as follows:—

"All of which was false, willful and malitious and done to blacken the memory of the said deceased and cast a stigma on his memory and on all others connected with him and excite his children to a breach of the peace and expose them to the hatred and contempt of the good people of this State; all which wrongdoings of the said are against the peace and dignity of this State contrary to law and a high crime and misdemeanor and of evil example to others in like manner to offend. Said attorney therefore prays the advice of the Honorable Court in the premises.

Elisha Sterling."

The indorsement is as follows:—

"James Gould and Noah B. Benedict assigned as counsel for the delinquint. Plea not guilty. On the jury for trial. The delinquint changing, pleads guilty.

The Court adjudge that delinquint is guilty and that he pay a fine of $75 into the treasury of this State and the costs of this prosecution and stand committed until judgment be complied with.

J. W. H., Clerk pro tem."

RABELLO TRIAL.

In the spring of 1835 a most horrible murder was committed in New Preston. A young lad of twelve years of age, son of Mr.

Ferris Beardsley, was brutally murdered by a wandering fellow, a Portuguese by birth, for some fancied insult, claiming that the boy stepped on his toes. The trial commenced in August 1835 before Judges Waite and Williams. The prosecuting attorney for the State was Leman Church assisted by George C. Woodruff, Esq., and the Court appointed Truman Smith and O. S. Seymour for the prisoner. The trial lasted several days and on the eighteenth of August 1835 the jury returned a verdict of not guilty by reason of insanity. The prisoner was committed to jail for safe keeping and remained there a number of years but was afterwards committed to State Prison for safe keeping. He became a raving maniac and died in prison only a few years since. It was at that time a noted case and one of the earliest ones, now so common, of offering expert evidence on insanity.

The proceedings of the trial were published in pamphlet form.

BENNET WARD MURDER.

On the 23rd of November, 1846, Bennet Ward went into a store kept by W. B. Lounsbury, he was somewhat intoxicated, became noisy and violent, threatened to whip several persons who were in the store, and began to throw fire among the dry goods that were disposed about the store. Among those present was George W. Smith. Ward finally proposed to whip him, and Smith seized a stick of wood from the wood box, and struck him over the left side of the head, causing a fracture in the skull five inches in length. He then kicked him out of the store and he fell upon the stoop. He got up however and wanted to fight, but the door was shut upon him. He then went about a quarter of a mile, to an out house of David J. Stiles and staid there two nights, when he went into Mr. Stiles' house, and soon became insensible. In this condition he re-remained till his death, which occurred fifty-six hours after the blow was received. A post-mortem examination showed there was concussion and compression of the brain, besides a chronic inflammation resulting from an old injury. Smith was arraigned for murder, February Term 1847. Hon. John H. Hubbard, State's Attorney and Hon. Charles B. Phelps, appeared for the State and Hons. Leman Church, G. H. Hollister and William Cothren appeared for the accused. After an interesting trial, Smith was acquitted, on the ground that he acted in self defence.

LUCIUS H. FOOT MURDER.

On the morning of March 4th., 1856, Lucius H. Foote, a taverner of Woodbury, was found brutally murdered, under the horse sheds of the Episcopal Church in the center of the town, and his whole body frozen stiff, showing that he had been killed the evening before. Circumstances strongly pointed to Edward E. Bradley, as being the perpetrator of the crime. He was arrested on this suspicion, and after a hearing before Justice Bull, bound over, without

WILLIAM COTHREN.

bail to the next Superior Court to be held at Litchfield. A Grand Jury was summoned, and a true bill for the crime of murder was found. The trial of the accused on the indictment commenced at Litchfield on the 14th., of April, before Judges William L. Storrs and Origen S. Seymour and a Jury, Hon. Gideon Hall, State's Attorney, Hon. Charles B. Phelps and William Cothren, Esq. appeared for the State, and Hon. Charles Chapman of Hartford, Gideon H. Hollister and Henry B. Graves, Esqrs. appeared for the prisoner. Not only very nice questions of circumstial evidence, but other intricate questions of law, were involved in the case, and the trial excited a more general interest than any case which has been tried in this county. On the tenth day of the trial the presiding Judge charged the jury, and on the eleventh day, they having failed to agree on a verdict, after having been sent out for several times, the papers were taken back, the jury discharged, and the prisoner remanded to jail. The jury stood five for conviction of murder in the second degree and seven for acquittal.

At the September term of the Court the case came on again for trial. It was commenced October 3rd., 1856 before Hon. David C. Sanford and Hon. John D. Park, presiding Judges with a jury. After a careful and laborious trial for twelve days, the jury again disagreed and were discharged.

On the 14th of April, 1857 he was again arrainged for trial before a jury with Hon. William W. Ellsworth and Hon. Thomas B. Butler as presiding Judges, and after a trial of fourteen days the jury again disagreed. Soon after this result the State's Attorney entered a *nolle prosequi* and the accused was discharged. Mr. Cothren published a complete report of the trial.

### MATTHEW MORRIS MURDER.

On the 17th of July, 1861, Woodbury was again startled by the announcement that another murder had been committed there. Matthew M. Morris a very respectable citizen became engaged in a quarrel with one Charles Fox, was stabbed by Fox and the knife at the last thrust, entirely severed the main artery under the collar bone on the right side, called by the doctors the vena cava. Fox immediately hid his knife in the corner of the yard where it was found the next morning, almost covered with blood. Fox took his scythe and started for Roxbury, but was detained by a neighbor till Sheriff Minor arrested him.

After an inquest, Fox was bound over for trial to the September term of the Superior Court, 1861. Judge Ellsworth presided over that Court. Gen. Charles F. Sedgwick and Wm. Cothren, appeared for the State, and Gideon H. Hollister and Henry B. Graves, Esqrs., for the defence. After the evidence on both sides had been introduced the judge called all the counsel to the bench, and told them that in his judgment the crime amounted to manslaughter and no more; and that if it pleased them to agree to that view and would waive argument, he would immediately so charge the jury. The counsel cheerfully acceded to the suggestion of the distinguished judge, who immediately charged the jury in accordance with his views. The jury retired, and in a few minutes returned with a verdict of manslaughter, and Fox was sentenced to ten years imprisonment in the Connecticut State Prison.

### DRAKELY MURDER.

Again Woodbury was the scene of a sad murder. On the night of August 10th., 1886 Robert Drakely shot his wife through the heart after she had retired for the night. He was a young man, not twenty years old and had been married only a few weeks and was, as he claimed, jealous of his wife for the attentions she bestowed on a small child that boarded with them. He was of a good old family of very respectable people but had become dissolute and dissipated and committed the act while in a drunken frenzy. He was bound over to the Superior Court by Justice Skelly and taken to the jail at Litchfield. At the April term, 1887 of the Court the Grand Jury indicted him for murder in the second degree. In September, 1887 he was arraigned and plead not guilty. He was tried before Hon. David Torrance and a jury. The prosecution was conducted by Hon. James Huntington, State's Attorney and Arthur D. Warner, Esq.; the defense by Henry B. Graves and William Cothren, Esq. The defense was that the accused from various reasons was not mentally or mortally responsible for his acts. After an exhaustive trial and the charge of Judge Torrance the jury retired and in about ten minutes returned with a verdict of guilty. He was sentenced to State Prison for life and died a few years after commitment.

### BERNICE WHITE, MURDER.

In the early part of 1850 the people of Colebrook and vicinity were startled by the report that Bernice White, an elderly gentleman living near Colebrook River, had been murdered. In a short time four men were arrested for the deed, named William Calhoun, Lorenzo T. Cobb, Benjamin Balcomb and Henry Mennasseh, the latter a half breed Indian. After the preliminary hearing they were bound over for trial to the Superior Court at Litchfield. A Grand Jury found a true bill against each of them and they were brought to trial at the August Term 1850. There was so great a crowd of witnesses and interested spectators that the Court was obliged to adjourn to the Congregational Church to hold the trial. Two Judges presided, Chief Justice Church and Judge Storrs. Calhoun and Balcomb being minors, Charles Chapman, Esq., of Hartford was appointed guardian *ad-litem* of Calhoun and Origen S. Seymour for Balcomb. Upon their arraignment Balcomb plead guilty and the rest not guilty of murder in the first degree.

HENRY B. GRAVES

After a long trial Calhoun and Mannasseh were found guilty and Cobb was acquitted. The guilty ones were sentenced to be hung on the second Friday of July, 1851. One of them, Cobb, died in jail and the other three finally had their sentences changed to imprisonment in State Prison for life. After serving there some years Balcomb died in prison and Calhoun and Mennasseh were pardoned out, it having been fairly proved that they had no hand in the actual commission of the deed but were only accessories after the fact. Calhoun died somewhere in the west and Mennasseh died in the Farmington town house. He is said to have been the last of the Tunxis Indians.

### WILLIAM H. GREEN TRIAL.

The trial of the Rev. William H. Green of Cornwall for murder excited a very general interest.

In 1865 Mr. Green resided in Centerville, N. Y., in the character of an itinerant Methodist preacher, and about that time he married a woman with whom he lived several months occupying with her the parsonage of the parish wherein he preached. In 1866 he abandoned this wife and married a young widow who had a small amount of property amounting to some twelve or fifteen hundred dollars. In the spring of 1867 he came to Connecticut and took the stump for P. T. Barnum who was then running for Congress on the Republican ticket. He was esteemed a very powerful preacher and his political arguments were eloquent and convincing, he also lectured on temperance and was an evangelist and held revival meetings in different places. After a time he joined his second wife's brother in West Cornwall and engaged with him in the general country store business. Mrs. Green was in feeble health with consumption and grew rapidly worse. On the evening of May 6, 1867 she was attacked with spasms and died just after midnight. From certain suspicious circumstances and subsequent conduct of Green, suspicion was aroused to the cause of her death. About the middle of June her body was exhumed and the stomach and liver sent to Prof. Barker of New Haven for examination who found traces of strychnine in those organs. Green was arrested and sent to Litchfield for safe keeping without a mittimus and of course was not locked up. While under keepers here his brother-in-law called upon him and informed him of the result of the analysis. Green concluded that his residence at the jail was not desirable at least on his part and made his departure therefrom unknown to the authorities and was for a few days in parts unknown. In a few days he reported at West Cornwall where he was formally arrested and attempted to save the State the trouble and expense of three trials by cutting his throat with a pocket knife in which he was not entirely successful. He was bound over to the Superior Court for trial and in November 1867 was tried for the crime and convicted of murder and sentenced to be hung on December 4th., 1868. His case was carried to the Supreme Court and a new trial granted him on the ground of newly discovered evidence. In January 1869 he was again before the Superior Court and the new trial resulted in a disagreement of the jury, but in September of that year the third trial was had and the jury returned a verdict of guilty of murder in the second degree. He was sentenced to State Prison for life September 25, 1869, where he died.

### JAMES LE ROY.

The career of James LeRoy, who received in 1850 at the age of twenty-five years his third commitment to the State Prison for the term of fifteen years upon his plea of guilty to seven different burglaries committed in or near Winsted and New Hartford in the years 1849 and 1850, is in many respects a remarkable one. From his boyhood he seemed to have nothing but a criminal instinct. When arrested in 1850 he was placed under keepers who fell asleep and he not enjoying their society departed from them. He had hand cuffs on and disliking them, proceeded to one of the scythe shops, broke into the shop and set one of the water grindstones running, and ground the shackles from his wrists and then secreted himself so that he was not found by the officials for several days, although they were constantly on the alert for him. After his release from the Connecticut State Prison he was engaged in practical observations in the management of prisons in other States and in 1877 under the name of James Whiting was sent to prison for theft for three and a half years, and died in prison. He made in 1850 a confession of his exploits which was published.

### WOLCOTTVILLE BURGLARS.

On the night of November 1876 the warehouse of the Union Manufacturing Company in Torrington was broken into and a large quantity of manufactured goods carried away. The burglars stole a hand car from the section house and started towards Bridgeport on the Naugatuck Railroad track. When it passed through Waterbury the watchman at the depot informed Superintendent Beach of the passage of the car. Mr. Beach immediately had an engine fired up and started in pursuit, and just before reaching Ansonia at about half past four in the morning the engine struck the hand car and threw it from the track. Stopping the engine they found fifteen pieces of woolen goods scattered about, but the occupants of the hand car had fled, but were tracked in the snow and soon arrested. They were lodged in Litchfield jail and had their trial before this Court December 6, and 7, 1876 and Franklin Johnson, William C. Davis and William C. Davis, Jr. were convicted of the crime and received State Prison sentences. It was a case that excited great attention partly on account of the mode of capture and the novel method of transit. The whole evidence

Augustus H. Fenn

was purely circumstantial and the defense was not only denial by the accused but a fairiy proved alibi presented. The skillful prosecution conducted by the State's Attorney Huntington and G. H. Welch, Esq. with the adroit defenses presented by H. B. Graves and the large attendance at the trial makes it a noted case.

LIQUOR TRIALS.

. From the Litchfield Enquirer of April 29, 1880 we take extracts which will illustrate the great battle which was fought in our Courts in the prosecution for the illegal sale of intoxicating spirits at about that date:

"With all its victories in the moral field, temperance has heretofore met defeat or but partial success in the Courts. Even in high teetotal times, when the people were electing Prohibition Governors and Prohibition Legislatures, we have seen rum-seller after rum-seller brought before juries, their guilt conclusively proved, yet escaping justice by acquittal or disagreement. The old prohibitory Statute of 1854 in this County at least was an utter failure. Of the dozens we have seen tried under the act we can recollect but one conviction. Under Local Option there has been a marked change, particularly of late years, and especially since the popular feeling against the liquor traffic has been intensified by the Blue Ribbon movement. There can be no doubt, too, that Litchfield County is very fortunate in her State's Attorney, an officer who never shirks or slights his duty, whether it is a rum-seller, or a sheep stealer that is brought to the bar of the Superior Court for trial. Of late years, therefore we have seen several convictions bv juries, but in this County, rum and justice have never been brought face to face so sharply and with such decisive defeat—indeed such utter rout, demoralization and capture of the liquor interest—as the past week has witnessed." After stating the trial of a certain case which was most strongly contested by State's Attorney Huntington, H. P. Lawrence and W. B. Smith for the prosecution and H. B. Graves and A. H. Fenn for defense but resulted in conviction of the parties, the article continues: "The prisoner was very much overcome and went home completely broken down and took to his bed seriously if not dangerously ill. On Thursday the Winsted Temperance men began to reap the benefit of their victory. Dealer after dealer came up to make such settlement as he could. The terms were the same to all. All costs must be paid and an obligation given that they would quit the traffic. On Friday afternoon the Court adjourned for the Term with the following record of progress for about six days work on liquor cases:

Three convictions with fines and costs amounting to about $500 and one hundred and six cases settled for $2,664.11 and one man in jail.

Messrs. Forbes, Holmes, Lawrence, W. B. Smith and others are to be highly commended in their wonderfully successful assault of what has so long been considered the last strong-hold of the liquor traffic, the Glorious uncertainty of the law!"

### MASTERS VS. WARREN.

One of the important civil cases tried in this Court came from Warren.

Nicholas Masters, while riding horse-back in the eastern part of the town, was thrown from his horse by reason of its breaking through a small wooden sluice or bridge and received serious injuries, having his neck nearly broken and for some years carried his head turned partly around and also received some other minor injuries of not so serious or permanent a nature.

His attorneys, Graves and Hollister, brought suit against the town of Warren for damages, claiming ten thousand dollars, the writ returnable to the September term, 1856. A long exhaustive trial before a jury was had at the November term, 1857 in which the plaintiff recovered thirty-five hundred dollars. Some very interesting questions came up during the trial regarding the taking of depositions by the defendant without notice to the plaintiff and also in the charge of the judge to the jury of a statement made by the judge of matter outside of the evidence. An appeal was taken to the Supreme Court of Errors by the defendant claiming a new trial which the Supreme Court did not grant and final judgment was rendered against the town at the April term, 1858 for three thousand five hundred and eighty-seven dollars and fifty cents damages and costs.

The story is told in connection with this case that Dr. Buel one of the expert witnesses for the plaintiff testified that he examined the plaintiff and found him suffering from tortochlorosis of the neck. Mr. Hollister in his argument indulged in the high sounding word frequently, portraying the sufferings of his client during his lifetime from such a terrible complaint. One of the defendant lawyers soon after met Dr. Buel and asked him what that big word he used meant. "Stiff neck," was the answer. "Why didn't you say so in Court said the lawyer. That word cost the town $1500."

### ROBBINS VS. COFFIN.

In 1883 an action from Salisbury wherein Samuel Robbins sued the administrator of the estate of George Coffing.

The points of law involved were important and the amount involved was about $70,000, an unusually large sum for this Court and the attorneys engaged were of the highest rank in the State.

George A. Hickox, who then edited the Litchfield Enquirer, reports it as follows: "The management of the case by the noted counsel on each side respectively, was looked on with much interest. Judge Warner made an excellent opening argument for the defendants, on whom the burden rested to prove their various defenses. Then followed John S. Beach, with a very clear quiet statement of the plaintiff's claim. Most interest was naturally felt

MILES T. GRANGER.

in the argument of Ex-Governor Hubbard, who followed Mr. Beach. The elegant forcible style of his address showed all the polish of his first class literary work, and the weight of his oratory was made doubly effective by his remarkable power as an actor. It was worth while studying the use he made of an old pair of steel spectacles he wears, to damn the defendants claims or enforce his own. The way they fell on the table was made to express the extreme of confidence or the extreme of disgust. They came down with the weight of a sledge hammer in emphasizing the one or the other view. His mode of handling a law paper spoke volumes. Indeed we have heard as fine rhetoric and as fine oratory in a law court, but never combined with such acting. Mr. Perkins closed the case with a very telling exposition of the evidence in connection with the position of the defendant." The jury returned a verdict for the plaintiff to recover $67,633.33 damages and costs.

In connection with Brother Hickox's discription of the conduct of the trial it may be proper to add that this was the last argument in a law court that "Dick" Hubbard ever made.

### HIGGIN'S ESCAPE.

One of the most interesting and exciting matters that have arisen in modern years, related to the escape of Richard Hadley a prisoner while being transported to the State Prison in Wethersfield in the year 1883.—Higgin's alias was Richard Hadley.

The following extracts from the papers of the time will give full details as well as some interesting history:

When James R. Higgins escaped from the wagon in which he was being taken from Litchfield to Wethersfield to serve out a ten years sentence for burglarly it was supposed that he had been furnished with a key to his handcuffs by his counsel, Henry H. Prescott of Litchfield. A. T. Roraback of Canaan, W. B. Smith of Winsted, and Dwight C. Kilbourn of Litchfield were appointed a committee to obtain evidence to be presented to the court at Litchfield touching Mr. Prescott's connection with the affair. Mr. Smith, of the committee, was at Wethersfield on Tuesday and obtained the following statement from Higgins:—

I first met Harry H. Prescott of Litchfield soon after I was arrested, in Litchfield jail. He was my attorney in the superior court in that county. When I called him into the case he agreed to help me to get away from jail, and I was to give him $250. Not having any money I was to give him some stolen bonds as security. The bonds were stolen from the savings bank at Woodbury, this state, and the total amount was $7,500. I put into Prescott's hands $6,400 in bonds. The understanding was that if I got out he should have the bonds. He was to give Paddy Ryan and others who came from New York to assist me in breaking jail all the points about jail, also the use of his office, and in short was to act as a general go-between to aid me in escaping from jail. The understanding was that Prescott was not to negotiate the bonds and was to keep the matter quiet until Howard, my pal, who was arrested with me, and I had escaped. Prescott told me that he went to New York to see Ryan at 154 East Twenty-third street, and that Ryan was afraid to have anything to do with him in the matter. Later he told me that he had been to New York again, but did not see Ryan. Soon after Prescott brought me a letter that was sent to him by Ryan and written by Farley, one of the Ryan gang. The letter inquired whether Prescott was all solid and to be trusted. After reading the letter I burned it in the jail stove. I sent a letter through Prescott to Ryan saying that Prescott was straight and to be trusted.

The following Sunday, after he had been to New York, Prescott came to me and stated that he had taken the bonds to the bank parties and had got something over $400 for them. As I had objected to his doing anything about the bonds until I had made my escape, I was angry when I found that he had given them up. At that time he gave me $15 and in a day or two gave my wife $200. I could not get anything more out of him. I afterwards found that he received about $1,200 for the bonds, but I could not get anything more out of him. My friends of the Ryan gang did not appear and I found that I had to depend upon my own resources. I continued to find fault because Prescott would not give me more money, and at last he said to me, about two weeks before court opened, that if I would keep still he would get me a key that would fit my handcuffs, and I could escape either when on the way from jail to the court house, or when I was being conveyed to the state prison if I was convicted. Howard and I talked it over and concluded to make the attempt to escape when we were being conveyed to or from the court room. Prescott brought us four handcuff keys that fitted my handcuffs and two small keys, like dog-collar keys; also two files. I had the four handcuff keys in my pocket all the time during the trial. The two other keys I filed and gave to Howard. One of the files I kept until I escaped, the other I left in the jail. When Prescott gave me the keys he told me that he knew that four of them would fit any handcuff in the jail. They did fit without any filing. When we were taken to the court room to plead Howard was handcuffed to me and the sheriff took my right wrist in his nippers. While we sat in the dock, Prescott came up to us and said: "Why did you not escape on the way over?" I told him that Howard might have got away, but I could not. Prescott replied: "That's right. You had better wait and get away together." While I was in the Litchfield jail Prescott gave me a revolver loaded with five cartridges, also ten cartridges afterwards. He gave them to me in my cell, I think on the afternoon of the day I was sentenced. I wanted the revolver and he did not want to give it to me until after I had received a visit from my wife, so that it would appear as if she had

Wellington B. Smith.

furnished it to me if it was discovered. I asked him if he had it with him, and he said he had. I then asked him to let me see it. After making me promise to give it back to him, he let me take it. I examined it and then handed it back. At 4 o'clock Thursday evening, after I was sentenced, he gave me the ten cartridges. The revolver was a "Young America" or "Young American," I don't remember which. It was double-acting, had five chambers, and was of 32 caliber. I did not know where he got it. I don't remember whether he told me he got the keys from a man in Litchfield, or whether he said he was going to get them of some man there. I understood that the man was an officer or had been one. The last time I saw Prescott before my escape was when he gave me the ten cartridges on Thursday. He then cautioned me not to use the revolver, shook hands with me and wished me good luck. After my escape I pawned the revolver in Baltimore. I had it tied between my legs the Saturday morning when they started to take me to Wethersfield. I was on the back seat of the last wagon, which the sheriff was driving. Howard was in the first wagon with the deputy.

Mr. Prescott was present while the latter part of this statement was made, and afterwards cross-examined Higgins without materially shaking his statement of the case."

### MICHAEL BION CASE.

One of the most important cases of our Courts, considering it in all of its features, was the case of Michael Bion from the town of North Canaan.

In 1871 Lyman Dunning's store at East Canaan in the town of North Canaan was burglarized, and a woodchopper named Michael Bion was arrested and convicted of the crime and sentenced to two years in State Prison. He behaved himself well, receiving the due credit therefor and was discharged at the expiration of his sentence with no great love for Mr. Dunning.

In 1874 a bag containing gun powder was placed near the house of the next neighbor of Mr. Dunning occupied by the congregational minister and was exploded in the night time setting the house on fire, but doing no great damage. The two houses looked alike and it was supposed that the intention was to place the powder at Mr. Dunnings house. Bion was charged with this deed and arrested and after a hard fought trial convicted and sentenced to ten years in State Prison mainly by the active agency of Mr. Dunning which did not increase Bion's affection and he made threats of violence against Mr. Dunning. Upon his discharge from prison he was induced to return to France his native country. About five years after this he was discovered working under an assumed name in the vicinity of Pine Plains only a few miles distant from East Canaan. Mr. Dunning fearing further injury from him got out a sureties of the peace complaint, obtained a warrant and when he found him in Connecticut had him arrested and brought before a justice who placed him under bonds in the sum of five thousand dollars. Bion could not furnish such bond and on the 19th day of November 1889 was lodged in Litchfield jail. He employed attorneys who instituted habeas corpus proceedings to release him and by various stages the matter came before the Supreme Court of Errors at the May Term 1890 and the report of the case occupies twenty pages of the 59th volume of the Connecticut Reports. The Court found no error in the judgment complained of and Bion still remained in the Litchfield jail. Afterwards an arrangement was made by the French Consul by which Bion was released and returned to France.

### THE BORJESSON MURDER TRIAL.

Only one sentence of death passed by this Court during the Century was carried into effect and this was upon Andrew Borjesson a native of Sweden who was residing in New Milford. On the first of August 1890 in the night season Borjesson went to the house of Homer Buckingham and climbing on the roof of the ell part of the house entered the room of a Swedish girl named Emma Anderson, a servant of Mr. Buckingham's and murdered her.

Mr. Buckingham hearing the noise in the room, went out of his house and saw Borjesson upon the roof of the house from which he jumped and ran off into the woods, and going to the girls room found her lying upon the floor in a pool of blood, her neck cut from ear to ear on the back side with other wounds upon her body. The murderer was arrested and bound over to the Superior Court and a true bill was found against him on the 9th of October 1890. He was tried before the Superior Court in December and a verdict of guilty found against him December 31st 1890, and sentenced to be hung January 29th, 1892. His counsel made most strenuous efforts for his reprieve getting depositions from relatives in Sweden concerning his sanity. All efforts failed. It was a cool deliberate murder and there was no public sympathy or extenuating circumstances. The sentence was duly carried into effect in the jail yard at Litchfield. The scenes connected with the execution outside of the jail enclosure, were of a disgraceful character but everything connected with it officially were solemn, orderly and proper. The citizens of the village were exasperated and shocked and made such an appeal to the public sense of propriety that the Legislature enacted the law that all future executions of the death penalty should be had within the State Prison.

### GOSHEN TAX CASE.

In 1894, June Term, a very interesting case was tried at Winsted being an appeal from the decision of the Board of Relief of

CHARLES J. PORTER.

Town of Goshen, about abatement of Taxes. The amount involved was trifling, but the principle was important enough for a two weeks contest with a very large number of witnesses and several attorneys. A local bard reports the trial as follows:

## GOSHENIA.

A famous tax-case once was tried,
By the staid old land of Goshen;
One Fessenden Ives was taxed too high,
At least, that was his notion.

He said his land was cold and wet,
And hard-hacks covered the ground.
The once fertile soil was sterile and cold
And yellow charlicks abound.

His barn was like sweet charity
That covereth a multitude of sin:
The outside was neat and fair to the eye,
But old rotten timbers within.

He's assessed too high, the rest too low,
And there's a plot to take his gold,
'Tis wrong to do so after years of toil,
Thus to rob him when he's old.

The town appeared by Huntington and Warner,
By Webster, Welch and Judd,
While Ives employed Hubbard, Hickox and Burrell
To shed his opponent's blood.

The air was fragrant with sweet breath of June,
Outside were the birds and bees:—
The Judge's desk was strewed with flowers,
Hardhacks, charlick and cheese.

The stenographer dreams of hardhack on toast,
Of ivy, rocks, alders and birch,
As the lawyers try to win their case
The other side trying to smirch.

The case dragged on its weary length,
Watched by Goshen ladies fair,
While poor old Kilbourn, the portly clerk,
Sat fast asleep in his chair.

For ten long days they fussed and fumed,
With witnesses goaded to tears,
While the costs were doubtless large enough,
To pay the taxes a hundred years.

EDWARD A. NELLIS.

THE MANNERING CASE.

Edwin Mannering a resident of Roxbury died on February 19, 1893, the result of taking a dose of Epsom Salts for medicinal purposes in which as afterwards discovered was a quantity of strichnine. The coroner made a very full investigation which resulted in the arrest of Mrs. Mannering for the crime of poisoning her husband. It was admitted that strichnine had been kept in the house for the purpose of poisoning foxes, and it was shown that she had purchased strichnine from a neighboring druggist a short time before his death. She was bound over for trial to the Superior Court and a true bill was found against her by the Grand Jury. The trial occurred at Litchfield in November 1893, lasting six days and resulted in her acquittal.

It was perhaps the most sensational trial ever held in this Court. The prisoner was led into Court leaning upon the arms of two friends and one or two physicians were constantly near to administer stimulants which was occasionally necessary. Several ladies of the village of Litchfield interested themselves in her trial by attending Court every day arrayed in all the sombre blackness of mourning habiliments. It seemed like a stage play rather than a cold blooded matter of fact trial. Her attorney left no art or artifice untouched to arouse the sympathies of the Court and jury. A distinguished jurist remarked that it was the most artistic trial he ever witnessed.

LEONARD J. NICKERSON.

### NORMAN BROOKS, WILL CASE.

Norman Brooks a farmer living in Winchester died on the 28th of July 1895, aged 78 years. He left a widow but no children and had a small amount of property. After his death a will was offered for probate which was made on the 15th of January 1895 in the office of Warner & Landon at Salisbury. From the probate of this will his widow appealed to the Superior Court. Upon the trial of the case in the Superior Court the claim was made that the will in question was not made by Norman Brooks but by some one personating him and that the disposition of his property given in this will was entirely different from repeated declarations he had made and also that there was a previous will which corresponded with these declarations. The contestants had his body exhumed and the witnesses to the will were present to identify or not identify the person. It was also claimed that one E. M. Clossey whose wife was a relative of the deceased and with himself were the principal beneficiaries of the disputed will was largely instrumental in the production of this will. That he went with Mr. Brooks who was quite an infirm man on one of the coldest days in January to Salisbury to get the will made although he was not actually present at its execution. The case came to trial before the Superior Court and a jury at Winchester at the April Term 1896, and after a protraced trial the jury found that there was undue influence exerted upon the testator in making a part of said will to wit, that part which gave the residue of the estate to said Clossey and also of that clause which gave him power to sell all the real estate and that said paragraph was null and void but confirming and establishing the rest of the will. The case was appealed to the Supreme Court of Errors at the October Term 1896. Upon a motion for a new trial for a verdict against evidence.

In the record of the case the evidence is printed in full, occupying 269 pages.

After a full hearing before the Supreme Court the motion for a new trial was denied.

### HAYES MURDER TRIAL.

In February 1901, John T. Hayes, a young man of Winsted, shot and killed Winnifred F. Cooke, a young lady he had fallen in love with, because she would not elope with him and marry against the wishes of her father. The tragedy occurred at the Gilbert Home in Winsted on the 11th of February, where the lady was employed as a teacher. He, after shooting her shot himself three times in his head—but failed to kill himself—and was held for trial in the Superior Court. The trial came on at Litchfield at the October Term, before Judge Elmer and lasted four weeks, when the Jury returned a virdict of, on the 8th of November of guilty of murder in the second degree, and he was sentenced to imprisonment for life. The defense was insanity from hereditary causes and four expert physicians were present all through the trial, and testified from a supposed state of facts—which it took nearly two hours to read. Two of them pronounced him not responsible and the other two thought him responsible, for which important evidence the state allowed nearly two thousand dollars, while the jury paid no attention to them at all, but on their first ballot stood eight for first degree and three for the second degree and one blank. After twelve hours confinement in the jury room they all agreed to bring in a verdict of murder in the second degree, which the court accepted. It was the most expensive trial on our cost book. The total expenses being a little over seven thousand dollars.

HADDOCK CASE.

One of the most important cases regarding the property rights of husband and wife, and also one that has made great confusion in the divorce laws of the country, was decided in the United States Supreme Court, April 12, 1906, and can be found in Vol. 201 of said Reports beginning at page 562. This case had its inception in this Superior Court, December 1881, and is known by the legal profession as the case of Haddock vs. Haddock.

The facts are briefly as follows: The Haddocks were married in 1868 in New York, where both parties then resided. The very day of the ceremony they separated, and never lived together. In 1881 Mr. Haddock having resided in Connecticut for three years, obtained a divorce from his wife Harriet Haddock, at the December term, on the ground of desertion. The service of the writ was by publication in the Litchfield Enquirer and a copy sent by mail to the defendant at Tarrytown, N. Y. where it was supposed she resided. This divorce was granted December 6, 1881, and the decree was signed by Hitchcock, Judge. At that time the plaintiff was poor but he afterwards acquired considerable property, and also married another wife by whom he had children. In 1894 the first wife brought suit against him in New York for a divorce from bed and board and for alimony. Constructive service was made of this process and she obtained a decree. As there was no personal service the judgment for alimony was ineffectual. In 1899 she brought another suit against him, and obtained personal service on him, and was allowed a decree for alimony for $780. a year. The defendant in this last suit plead for one of his answers the Connecticut divorce in 1881, but the New York courts disallowed it. Haddock appealed to the United States Supreme Court on the ground that the decree denied full faith and credit to the judgment of the Connecticut courts, but the Supreme Court upheld the actions of the New York courts and sustained the judgment, five judges in the affirmative and four dissenting. The discussion and explanation of this seemingly inconsistent decision require thirty pages of fine print in the Report.

HENRY J. ALLEN.

RICHARD T. HIGGINS.

COUNTY CORONER.

Previous to 1883 all sudden deaths that occurred in the county were reported to the Clerk's office only by the returnes of a jury of inquest. A very great many of such deaths were never reported, and those that were, showed some remarkable verdicts.

In 1883 the Legislature enacted a law for the proper return and preservation of these untimely deaths. Each county was to have a coroner who should be appointed by the Judges of the Superior Court at their annual meeting, and who should hold office three years, and until another was appointed in their place. The county coroner had power to appoint an able and discreet person learned in medical science to be medical examiner in each town in the county. The medical examiner was to examine the cause and manner of each sudden death and make his report thereon to the county coroner who was to keep a record of such deaths. The medical examiner's reports were to be placed on file with the clerk of the Superior Court.

The first County Coroner in Litchfield County was Col. Jacob Hardenburgh of Canaan, who held the office until his decease on April 4, 1892. Richard T. Higgins of Winchester was appointed to succeed him, and has held the office from that time until the present.

FRANK W. ETHERIDGE.

HEALTH OFFICERS.

In 1893 the Legislature enacted a law for the appointment of a County Health Officer, who was to be an attorney-at-law and be appointed by the judges of the Superior Court, and hold office for four years. The statute prescribes that he shall cause the execution of the laws relating to public health and the prevention and abatement of nuisances dangerous to public health, and of laws relating to the registration of vital statistics, and co-operate with, and supervise the doings of town, city and borough health officers, and boards of health within his county. He is clothed with all the powers of a grand juror and prosecuting officer for the prosecution of violations of laws relating to such matters.

The appointee was Walter S. Judd, of Litchfield. The second was William F. Hurlbut of Winchester, in 1894, and the third was the present incumbent, Frank W. Etheridge, who has held the office since 1896.

ARTHUR D. WARNER.

MARCUS H. HOLCOMB.

ATTORNEY GENERAL.

In 1897 the Legislature of Connecticut enacted a law for the election of an Attorney General. In November 1906 Marcus H. Holcomb a member of this bar, but residing in Southington and practicing law both in that town and in Hartford was elected to that office.

# THE FIRST LAW REPORTS.

Judge Church in his address mentions the fact that the first Law Reports in this country were published at Litchfield soon after the establishment of the Law School, by Ephraim Kirby, Esq. who was then a prominent and successful attorney at Litchfield.

A manuscript copy of part of these reports has been preserved by some of his descendants, and has been placed in the room of the Historical Society at Litchfield, by whose courtesy I have been able to reproduce in this work the first page of the "Symsbury" case.

I am also enabled to give a picture of this eminent man from a photograph of a painting presented to St. Paul's Lodge, F and A. M. of Litchfield, by Col. E. K. Russell U. S. A., a grandson of Col. Kirby.

I also republish the preface to the Reports, together with a short memoir of its author and a list of the books composing his Law Library.

PREFACE.

The uncertainty and contradiction attending the judicial decisions in this state, have long been subjects of complaint.—The source of this complaint is easily discovered.—When our ancestors emigrated here, they brought with them the notions of jurisprudence which prevailed in the country from whence they came.—The riches, luxury, and extensive commerce of that country, contrasted with the equal distribution of property, simplicity of manners, and agricultural habits and employments of this, rendered a deviation from the English laws, in many instances, highly necessary. This was observed—and the intricate and prolix practice of the English courts was rejected, and a mode of practice more simple, and better accommodated to an easy and speedy administration of justice, adopted.—Our Courts were still in a state of embarrasment, sensible that the common law of England, "though a highly improved system," was not fully applicable to onr situation; but no provision being made to preserve and publish proper histories of their adjudications, every attempt of the Judges, to run the line of distinction, between what was applicable and what not, proved abortive: For the principles of their decisions were soon forgot, or misunderstood, or erroneously reported from memory.—Hence arose a confusion in the determination of our courts;—the rules of property became uncertain, and litigation proportionably increased.

In this situation, some legislative exertion was found necessary; and in the year 1785 an act passed, requiring the Judges of the Superior Court, to render written reasons for their decisions, in cases where the pleadings closed in an issue at law.—This was a great advance toward improvement; still it left the business of reformation but half performed:—For the arguments of the Judges,

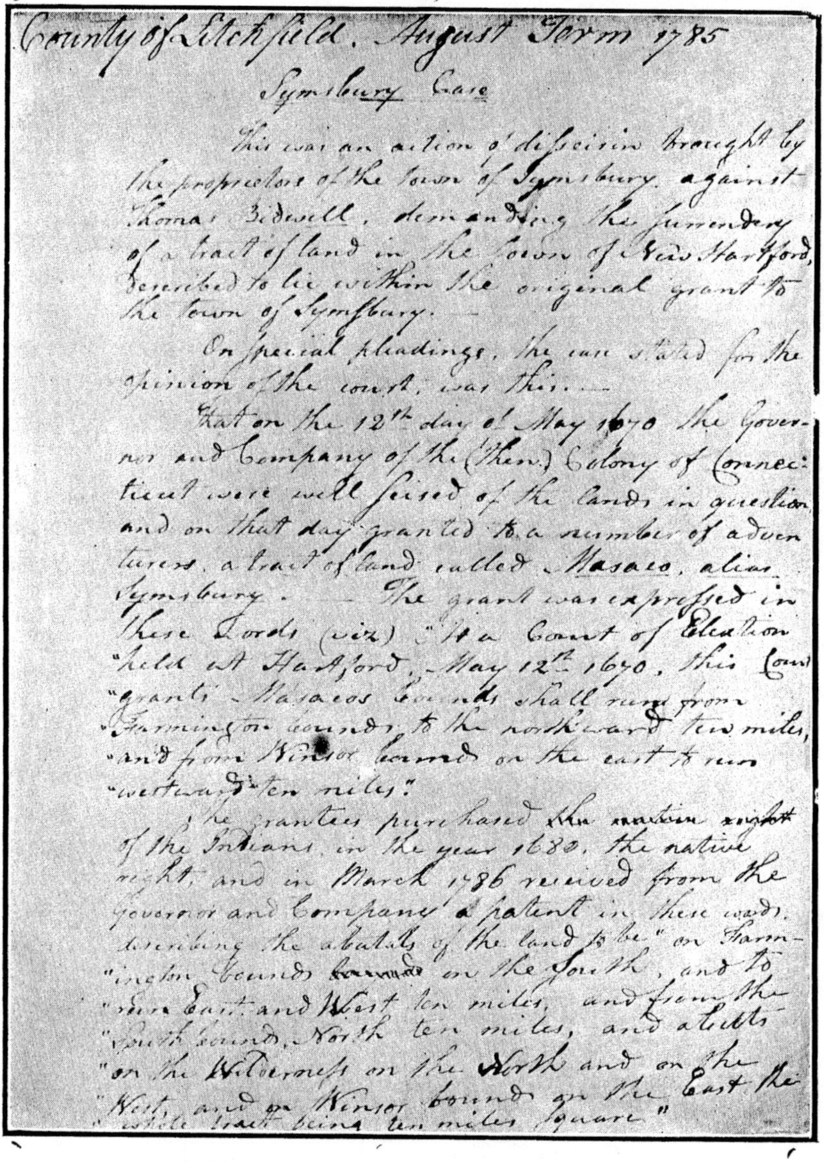
County of Litchfield. August Term 1785

Symsbury Case

This was an action of disseisin brought by the proprietors of the town of Symsbury against Thomas Bidwell, demanding the surrender of a tract of land in the town of New Hartford, described to lie within the original grant to the town of Symsbury. —

On special pleadings, the case stated for the opinion of the court, was this. —

That on the 12th day of May 1670 the Governor and Company of the (then) Colony of Connecticut were well seised of the lands in question, and on that day granted to a number of adventurers, a tract of land called Masaco, alias Symsbury. — The grant was expressed in these words (viz) "At a Court of Election "held at Hartford, May 12th 1670. this Court "grants Masacos bounds shall run from "Farmington bounds to the northward ten miles, "and from Winsor bounds on the east to run "westward ten miles."

The grantees purchased ~~the native right~~ of the Indians in the year 1680, the native right, and in March 1786 received from the Governor and Company a patent in these words, describing the abuttals of the land to be "on Farmington bounds ~~bounds~~ on the South, and to "run East and West ten miles, and from the "South bound, North ten miles, and abutts "on the Wilderness on the North and on the "West, and on Winsor bounds on the East the "whole tract being ten miles square"

REPRODUCTION OF KIRBY'S MANUSCRIPT.

without a history of the whole case, would not always be intelliigible; and they would become known to but few persons; and being written on loose papers, were exposed to be mislaid, and soon sink into total oblivion.—Besides, very many important matters are determined on motions of various kinds, where no written reasons are rendered, and so are liable to be forever lost.

Hence it became obvious to every one, that should histories of important causes be carefully taken and published, in which the whole process should appear, showing the true grounds and principles of the decision, it would in time produce a permanent system of common law.—But the Court being ambulatory through the State, the undertaking would be attended with considerable expence and interruption of other business, without any prospect of private advantage; therefore, no gentleman of the profession seemed willing to make so great a sacrifice.—I had entered upon this business in a partial manner, for private use; which came to the knowledge of several gentlemen of distinction.—I was urged to pursue it more extensively;—and being persuaded that an attempt of the kind (however imperfect) might be made in some degree subservient to the great object, I compiled the Volume of Reports which is now presented to the public.—Could any effort of mine induce government to provide for the prosecution of so necessary a work by a more able hand, my wishes would be gratified, and my labour in accomplishing this, amply repaid.

In these Reports, I have endeavored to throw the matter into as small a compass as was consistent with right understanding of the case:—Therefore, I have not stated the pleadings or arguments further than was necessary to bring up the points relied on, except some few instances which seemed to require a more lengthy detail of argument.—As the work is designed for general use in this state, I have avoided technical terms and phrases as much as possible, that it might be more intelligible to all classes of men.—Some cases are reported which are merely local, and have reference to the peculiar practice of this state; these may appear unimportant to readers in other states; but they were necessary to the great object of the work.

I am sensible that this production is introduced to the world under sircumstances very unfavorable to its reputation.—But, however different I might be, under other circumstances, I feel an honest confidence in this attempt to advance the common interest of my fellow-citizens;—and that, so obvious are the difficulties which occur in almost every stage of the business, that to detail them in a preface would be offering an insult to the understanding of my readers.—The candid and generous, if they read the Reports, will doubtless find frequent occasion to draw into exercise those excellent virtues; and as to readers of an opposite disposition, I have neither wishes or fears concerning them.—If any one should experience disagreeable sensations, from the inelegance of this performance, let him rest assured he cannot more sincerely regret its faults than I do."

Having persued Mr. Kirby's "Reports of Cases adjudged in the Superior Court, from the year 1785 to 1788," it appears to us that the Cases are truly reported.

RICHARD LAW.
ELIPHALET DYER.
ROGER SHERMAN.
WILLIAM PITKIN.
OLIVER ELLSWORTH.

### EPHRAIM KIRBY.

Ephraim Kirby was born in Litchfield in 1756, as appears by the records of the town. His birth is also claimed to have been in the town of Washington, Conn. on the site of the residence of the late Hon. O. H. Platt. He was a farmer boy, but at the age of nineteen on the arrival of the news of the Battle of Lexington he shouldered his musket and marched with the volunteers from Litchfield to the scene of conflict and was present at the Battle of Bunker Hill. He remained in the field until independance was won, except when driven from it by severe wounds. He was in nineteen battles and skirmishes, among them Brandywine, Monmouth and Germantown, where he received thirteen wounds, seven of which were saber cuts on the head inflicted by a British soldier at Germantown, where Kirby was left for dead upon the field. Mr. Kirby studied law in the office of Reynolds Marvin, Esq., who had been King's Attorney before the war, and who was a prominent member of the bar. In 1787 he received the degree of M. A. from Yale College. After his admission to the bar, he married Ruth Marvin, daughter of his preceptor. Col. Kirby took a prominent part in the political matters of the day, and in 1791 was first elected representative to the Legislature, and was re-elected at thirteen semi-annual elections, and was several years, candidate for the office of governor.

On the election of Jefferson to the Presidency, in 1801. Col. Kirby was appointed supervisor of the national revenue for the State of Connecticut. Upon the acquisition of Louisiana, the President appointed him a judge of the then newly organized territory of New Orleans. Having accepted the station, he set out for New Orleans; but he was not destined to reach that place. Having proceeded as far as Fort Stoddard, in the Misisissippi territory, he was taken sick, and died October 2d, 1804, aged forty-seven—at a period when a wide career of public usefulness seemed opening upon him. His remains were interred with the honors of war and other demonstrations of respect. Col. Kirby was a man of the highest moral and well as physical courage—devoted in his feelings and aspirations—warm, generous and constant in his attachments—

EPHRAIM KIRBY.

and of indomitable energy. He was, withal, gentle and winning in his manners, kindly in his disposition, and naturally of an ardent and cheerful temperament, though the last few years of his life were saddened by heavy pecuniary misfortunes. As a lawyer, he was remarkable for frankness and downright honesty to his clients, striving always to prevent litigation, uniformly allaying irritation and effecting compromises, and only prosecuting with energy the just and good cause, against the bad. He enjoyed the friendship of many sages of the Revolution, his correspondence with whom, would form interesting materials for the history of his time.

Col. Kirby, was a prominent member of the Masonic fraternity. He was one of the early Masters of St. Paul's Lodge of Litchfield, and for many years was its secretary. He was a beautiful penman, as is evidenced by the records of St. Paul's Lodge. He was largely instrumental in forming the Grand Lodge of the State of Connecticut, and was one of its early officials. He was also a prominent Royal Arch Mason, and was a delegate to the convention which organized the general Grand Chapter of the United States, and was its first General Grand High Priest. When he left Litchfield to accept the position of Judge of the territory of Louisana, he gave to St. Paul's Lodge, Litchfield, his library of miscellaneous books, which have been carefully preserved by the Lodge as a memorial of him, and are now placed in the fireproof building of the Historial Society.

He also sold his law books to Seth P. Beers and I am enabled to give the conveyance with the list of books, which will show the library of a prominent practising lawyer of a century ago.

List of Law Books sold to Seth P. Beers by my husband Ephraim Kirby and delivered to said Beers by me in pursuance of written directions from my said husband which directions bear the date of July the 5th A. D. 1804.

| | Vols. | | Vols. |
|---|---|---|---|
| Blackstones Commentaries | 4 | Powel on Devises | 1 |
| Dunscombs trial per pais | 2 | Woods Institute | 1 |
| Beacon Abridgm't | 5 | Coke on Littleton | 1 |
| Jacobs Dictionary | 1 | Woodesons Lectures | 3 |
| English Statutes | 6 | Bacon on Awards | 1 |
| Goddphin on Executots, etc. | 1 | New York Atty Vade Mecum | 1 |
| Fosters Crown Law | 1 | Schifflers Practice | 1 |
| Bullen Nisi Prius | 1 | Barlamiqui on Nat. Law | 1 |
| Powel on Mortgages | 1 | Historical Law Tracts | 1 |
| Morgans Essays | 3 | Compleat Attorney | 1 |
| Attorneys Vade Mecum | 2 | Stats. England abridgd | 1 |
| Comyn's Digest | 5 | Stiles Practical Regr. | 1 |
| Cokes Institute 2 Part | 1 | English Pleader | 1 |
| Hawkins Plea of ye Crown | 2 | Clerks Tutor | 2 |

| | Vols. |
|---|---|
| Every man his own Lawyer | 1 |
| Office of Justice | 2 |
| Douglass on Wills | 1 |
| Law of Evidence | 1 |
| Dagges Criminal Law | 3 |
| Statutes of Vermont | 1 |
| Benthams Defence of Usury | 1 |
| Adye on Court Martial | 1 |
| Beccaria on Crimes | 1 |
| Acts of 1st Session of Congress | 1 |
| Acts of 3d Session of 5th Congress | 1 |
| Acts of 1st Session of 6th Congress | 1 |
| Acts of 1st Session of 1st Congress | 1 |
| Saxbys Customs | 1 |
| Holts Reports | 1 |
| Strangers Reports | 2 |
| Burrows Reports | 5 |
| Wilsons Reports | 3 |
| W. Blackstone Reports | 2 |
| Browns Reports | 1 |
| Douglass Reports | 1 |
| Dainfords Reports | 1 |
| Salkelds Reports | 2 |
| Lutwyches Reports | 1 |
| Cokes Reports | 7 |
| Crokes Reports | 3 |
| Kebles Reports | 3 |
| Plowdens Reports | 1 |
| Ventries Reports | 1 |
| Carthews Reports | 1 |
| Hobarts Reports | 1 |
| Cowpers Reports | 1 |
| Vernons Reports | 2 |
| Vesey's Reports | 2 |
| Pre Chancery | 1 |
| Fincks Reports | 1 |
| Hardwicks Reports | 1 |
| Vaughan's Reports | 1 |
| Siderfins Reports | 1 |
| Thos. Raymond Reports | 1 |
| Littletons Reports | 1 |
| Yelvertons Reports | 1 |
| Dyer's Reports | 1 |
| Moore's Reports | 1 |
| Palmer's Reports | 1 |
| Jenkins Reports | 1 |
| Fitzgibbons Reports | 1 |
| Saville's Reports | 1 |
| Peere Williams Reports | 3 |
| Atkins Reports | 3 |
| Livins Reports | 2 |
| Ambles Reports | 1 |
| Lord Raymonds Reports | 3 |
| Comberbach's Reports | 1 |
| Bulstrode's Reports | 1 |
| Comyns Reports | 1 |
| Chipman's Reports | 1 |
| Kirbys Reports | 1 |

(Signed)
RUTHY KIRBY.

# Signers

ROGER SHERMAN.

# Signers of the Declaration of Independence.

---

## ROGER SHERMAN.

One of the signers of the Declaration of Independence, was admitted to the practice of the law in 1754 by the Litchfield County Court.

He was born in Newton, Mass., April 19, 1721, and received a very limited education, and learned the trade of a shoemaker. His father, William Sherman, dying when Roger was twenty years old, he soon after removed to New Milford, Connecticut, and lived with his brother William who had been settled there on a farm for about three years. The first notice of Roger Sherman on the town records of New Milford is Feb. 6, 1744. He became a large land owner and was very prominent in all the town affairs, a deacon in the church, and clerk and treasurer of the Eccl. Society. He and his brother also had a general store, and he lived very nearly on the site of the present Town Hall, which in later years has been named "Roger Sherman Hall." The old store building is said to be still in existence.

He was a very industrious and studious man. In 1745 the General Assembly appointed him a County Surveyor of New Haven County, which then included New Milford; this office was pecuniarily of more value in those days than it has been in later years, for one of his surveys he received nearly 84 pounds; many of the plans and maps of his surveys are to be found in the New Milford Land Records made by him in his own hand.

Soon after the formation of Litchfield County in 1751 he studied law, and in 1757, three years after his admission to the bar, he was appointed County Judge, and a Judge of the Quorum. He was also a representative to the General Assembly several sessions. Removing to New Haven in 1761, he was chosen the Governor's assistant, and also a Judge of the Superior Court, which office he held twenty-three years.

He was elected a member of the first Continental Congress which met September 5th, 1774 in New York, and continued a member of Congress for nineteen years, the last two being in the Senate, of which he was a member at the time of his death, July 23, 1793.

As a member of the Continental Congress, he was one of the committee to draft the Declaration of Independence, which he signed on July 4, 1776.

Thomas Jefferson says of this distinguished statesman, "I served with him in the old Congress in the years 1775 and 1776. He was a very able and logical debater in that body, steady in the principles of the Revolution, always at the post of duty, much employed in the business of the committees, and, particularly, was of the committee with Dr. Franklin, Mr. J. Adams, Mr. Livingston and myself for preparing the Declaration of Independence. I had a very great respect for him."

John Adams also wrote, "Destitute of all literary and scientific education, but such as he acquired by his own exertions, he was one of the most sensible men in the world. The clearest head and steadiest heart. He was one of the soundest and strongest pillars of the Revolution."

Chief Justice Ellsworth said that he made Mr. Sherman the model of his youth.

The honor and fame of Roger Sherman does not rest entirely upon his being a signer of the Declaration of Independence. In the early formation of this government, he took an active and important part. He was a member of the Convention which framed the Consutution of the United States, and it was undoubtedly due to his wise and sagacious counsel and cool impartial judgment, that the Convention was held together until the great work was accomplished. Very many of its peculiar provisions, which are now considered so important, originated with him. This compilation cannot go into the history of the Convention in detail, but those wishing further light on the subject of the part taken in it by Roger Sherman, will do well to consult Hollister's History of Connecticut, where it is discussed at length.

A competent authority says, that "he is the only man who signed four important fundemental documents of our government, viz: The Articles of Association in 1774; the Declaration of Independence in 1776, which he assisted in drafting; the Articles of Confederation in 1778, and the Federal Constitution in 1788.

### OLIVER WOLCOTT.

The other signer of the Declaration of Independence in whom Litchfield County is interested, was Oliver Wolcott, who was the first sheriff of the County upon its organization in 1751.

The following taken from Kilbourn's History of Litchfield is a pretty concise sketch of this distinguished man.

"The Honorable Oliver Wolcott, son of His Excellency, the Hon. Roger Wolcott, Governor and Chief Justice of Connecticut, was born in Windsor, December 20, 1726, and was graduated at Yale College in 1745. In early manhood he commanded a company

Gen. Oliver Wolcott.

of volunteers in the Northern Army, in the war against the French. Having pursued the usual course of medical studies, he established himself as a physician in Goshen, and was there at the date of the organization of the County of Litchfield, October, 1751. The Legislature appointed him the first High Sheriff of the new County, and he immediately took up his abode in this village, and continued to reside here until his decease, a period of forty-six years. In 1752 he erected the "Wolcott House" in South street, where during the Revolutionary War, King George's leaden statue was melted into bullets, to be fired at his own troops.

With a commanding personal appearance, dignified manners, a clear and cultivated intellect, and a character for integrity far above the reach of suspicion, it is not to be wondered at that he became a favorite of the people with whom his lot was cast. Besides holding the office of Sheriff for over twenty years, he was chosen a Representative to the Legislature five times between the years 1764 and 1770, inclusive; a member of the Council or Upper House from 1771 to 1786. Judge of the Court of Probate for the District of Litchfield from 1772 to 1795; Judge of the Court of Common Pleas from 1773 to 1786; and member of the Continental Congress from 1775 to 1784 (except two years). He was one of that memorable band of patriots and sages who, on the 4th of July, 1776, affixed their names to the Declaration of Independence. In the early part of the war of the Revolution, Judge Wolcott was commissioned as a Brigadier General, and Congress appointed him a Commissioner on Indian Affairs for the Northern Department, with General Schuyler and others. In May, 1779, he was elected by the Legislature and commissioned by Governor Trumbull as Major General of the Militia of Connecticut, to succeed General James Wadsworth, resigned. In these important and responsible stations, he rendered the country essential service. On the field, in the camp, at the rendezvous, in the department of the Commissary of Supplies—in fact, wherever he could render himself useful—he was found, ever prompt in planning and efficient in executing. At the same time he was an active member of the Committee of Safety; and, when at home, was equally zealous and conspicuous in the local affairs of the town—officiating as Moderator, Selectman, Committeeman, etc. Indeed, no man in the State, at this period, discharged so many and varied public duties. A considerable share of the reputation which Connecticut required for promptness in furnishing men and means for the army, is due to General Wolcott. Certainly, to no other individual in the western counties could Governor Trumbull or General Washington appeal for aid, with the certainty of success, as to him.

In 1786, he was elected to the office of Lieutenant-Governor of the State, and was annually re-elected for a period of ten years. In May, 1796, he was chosen Governor, to which distinguished position he was again elevated at the annual election in 1797. He was now seventy years of age. His naturally robust constitution began to feel the weight of care and responsibility which had been so long pressing upon it. He departed this life at his residence in Litchfield, December 1, 1797, aged 71 years.

Joel Barlow, in his great national poem, *The Columbiad,* thus refers to his zeal and efforts in the cause of Independence;

"Bold WOLCOTT urged the all-important cause,
With steady hand the solemn scene he draws;
Undaunted firmness with his wisdom joined,
Nor kings nor worlds could warp his steadfast mind."

Governor Oliver Wolcott was of and had a very distinguished family. His son, Oliver, Jr., was Secretary of the United States Treasury under President George Washington, and Governor of this State for ten years. Another son, Frederick, was clerk of County and Superior Courts for years, and the founder of the village of Wolcottville, now the business portion of Torrington. One of his daughters married Hon. William Moseley, M. C., of Hartford, and another married Lieutenant-Governor Goodrich, of Hartford.

His sister, Ursula Wolcott, married Governor Matthew Griswold, and was the mother of Governor Roger Griswold. Thus her father, brother, husband, son and nephew were all governors of Connecticut, a fact which cannot probably be said of any other lady who has lived in the State or the United States.

---

## THE COUNTY JAIL

The history of the legal matters of the County would be incomplete without a reference to the County Jail. This institution is situated on one of the most prominent sites in Litchfield at the corner of North and West streets. The original jail was located on the brow of East Hill, on the exact spot now occupied by the Center school house. At the excavation of the ground for the cellar for the school house some of the original foundation work was discovered, and in some of the stone work were found staples and rings indicating that occasionally a prisoner might have been chained up. It is said to have been a crude, but strongly built structure of hewn logs. Adjoining it a large old-fashioned house was erected in which the jailer lived and kept a hotel, the prison being in the rear. This building appears to have been built in 1786, at a cost of about nine hundred pounds, sterling.

LITCHFIELD COUNTY JAIL

The front part of the present jail was erected in 1810-11, at an expense of $11,245.78, and was built of brick, which were made of clay dug on the road between Torrington and Litchfield, just east of "Seymour's meadow." The bricks were very hard and builders have said that it was much easier to dig through the granite foundations than through the brick.

A wooden building for a kitchen was afterwards added on the northern side, and the present arrangement of cells in the middle building was made about sixty years ago.

In 1895, the accommodations not proving adequate, a county meeting was held and an addition ordered to be constructed on the west end of the original building, which was done at a cost of about $25,000.00. The old part had cells for seventeen inmates and this addition provided cell room for twenty-eight, with cages for five more, with washroom, bathroom and other needed accommodations. It is now heated by steam and furnished with city water, and is lighted with gas from its own private plant.

In the early days the keeping of the prisoners was let out to the highest bidder and the keeper (now called the jailer) made what he could out of the prison work and also kept a hotel in the building. This system prevailed until about 1865, when the sheriff, as one of the prerogatives of his office took possession and ran the institution himself. The price allowed for board of prisoners has varied; at the present time it being $2.25 per week, paid by the State.

One of the large rooms in the third story was used as a public hall. The Masons and other societies used it for their meetings and at other times it was used as a schoolroom. The compiler of these sketches has attended school there.

A large workshop is located in the second story of the new part, in which many of the prisoners are employed caning chair seats, manufacturing brooms, and such other employments as is allowed to prison labor.

A large elm tree, seen in the cut at the southeast corner of the jail yard, is known as the "Whipping post elm," on which formerly prisoners were publicly whipped; the last whipping occurred about seventy-five years ago.

# Law School

# THE LITCHFIELD LAW SCHOOL

---

## CATALOGUE

OF

## SCHOLARS

---

INTERESTING MEMORANDA

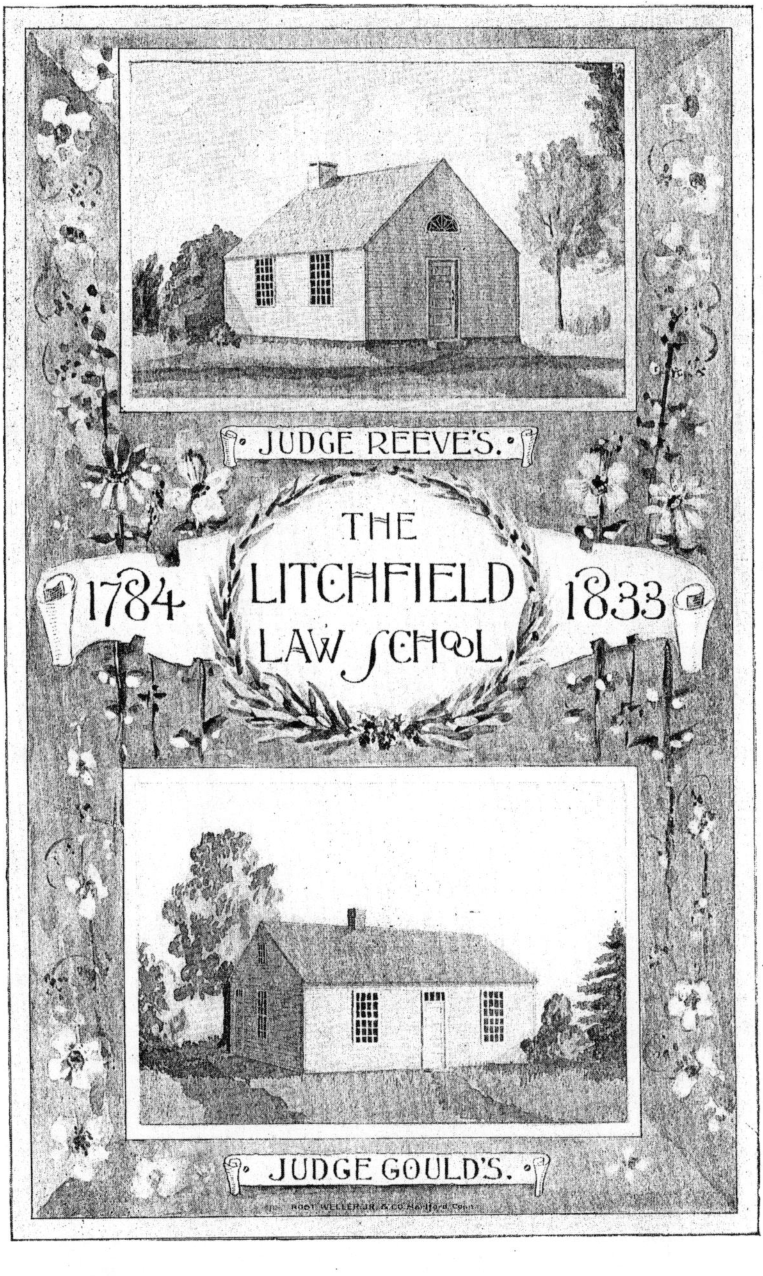
JUDGE REEVE'S.
THE
LITCHFIELD
LAW SCHOOL
1784
1833
JUDGE GOULD'S.
ROOT WELLER JR. & CO. Hartford, Conn.

# THE LITCHFIELD LAW SCHOOL.

The following article appeared originally in the February (1901) number of *The Law Notes,* published by The Edward Thomson Co., of Northport, L. I. It was written by Charles C. Moore, Esq., a native of Winchester, and a former member of this bar, now one of the editors of the American and English Encyclopedia of Law, published by the above-named company. The article has been slightly abridged for this work. In its preparation Mr. Moore was largely aided by the late Chief Justice Charles B. Andrews:

"One who looks through the records of the town meetings of Litchfield from 1765 to 1775 will find that there were discussions on the Stamp Act, the Boston Port Bill, and other acts of Parliamentary aggression, as clear and well defined as the debates in that town meeting where Samuel Adams and Harrison Gray Otis were the principal speakers. The child Liberty would not have been born in the Boston town meeting had not the Litchfield town meeting and other like town meetings throughout the colonies prepared the atmosphere in which alone that child could breathe. Litchfield was the principal station on the highway from Hartford to the Hudson; and a depot for military stores, a workshop, and a provision storehouse for the Continental Army were there established during the Revolution. Many distinguished royalist prisoners were sent there, and a military atmosphere pervaded the place. General Washington was a frequent visitor, and so were other general officers of the American forces, including Lafayette, who, when he visited the United States in 1824, went to Litchfield to renew old memories with some of his former comrades in arms. The leaden statue of King George the Third which stood on the Battery in New York was conveyed to Litchfield, and in an orchard in the rear of the Wolcott house it was melted into bullets for the patriot army. All through the struggle with the mother country Litchfield was a hotbed of patriotism, and when the first law school in America commenced its regular systematic course of instruction there in 1784, the ambitious village had among its citizens numerous men of exceptional intelligence and culture. One of them was Andrew Adams, who had been a member of the Continental Congress and was afterward a judge of the Supreme Court. Oliver Wolcott was there. He also had been a member of the Congress, had signed the Declaration of Independence, and was afterward Governor of the State. Ephraim Kirby, who a few years later published the first volume of law reports ever published in America, Major Seymour, who had commanded a regment at the surrender of Burgoyne; Benjamin Tallmadge, perhaps the most noted cavalry commander of the Revolution; Julius Deming, a very prominent and successful merchant and financier, and many others of like character were residing in the town. Into this community in the year 1778 came Tapping Reeve, a young lawyer just admitted to the bar, to settle in the practice of his profession. Born in Southold, Long Island, in 1744, the son of Rev. Abner Reeve, a Presbyterian clergyman, he was graduated at Princeton College in 1763, and was immediately appointed teacher in a grammar school in connection with the college. In that station and as a tutor in the college itself he passed seven years. He then came to Connecticut to study law, entering the office of Judge Root, who was then a practicing lawyer in Hartford, and some years later a judge of the Supreme Court. From Hartford he came to Litchfield. He had just previously married Sally Burr, daughter of President Burr of Princeton, and sister of Aaron Burr. Until the conclusion of the Revolutionary War there was but very little civil business done in the county at Litchfield, and Mr. Reeve betook himself to giving instruction to young gentlemen who looked forward to the legal profession for support and advancement when quieter times should come. This employment tended greatly to enlarge and improve his stock of legal learning, and led the way for him to begin in 1784 a systematic course of instruction in the law and to regular classes. The Law School dates from that year. It continued in successful operation and with annual graduating classes until 1833. The catalogue contains the names of one thousand and fifteen young men who were prepared for the bar subsequent to the year 1798, most of whom were admitted to the practice in the court at Litchfield. The list of students prior to that date is imperfect, but there are known to have been at least two hundred and ten. More than two-thirds of the students registered from states other than Connecticut. Maine sent four, New Hampshire fifteen, Vermont twenty-seven, Massachusetts ninety-four, Rhode Island twenty-two, New York one hundred and twenty-four, New Jersey eleven, Pennsylvvania thirty, Delaware eighteen, Maryland thirty-nine, Virginia twenty-one, North Carolina twenty, South Carolina forty-five, Georgia sixty-nine, Ohio four, Indiana, Mississippi and Tennessee each one, Kentucky nine, Alabama three, and Louisiana seven. There were four from the District of Columbia and one from Calcutta. The greatest number who entered in any single year was fifty-four in 1813.

"Lawyers now living in the original states will recognize the names of many men conspicuous in the juridical annals of their state. Aaron Burr studied law at Litchfield. John C. Calhoun entered the Law School in 1805; only a few rods from the school building was the house where Harriet Beecher Stowe was born in 1811, and Henry Ward Beecher in 1813; and a short hour's walk would have brought the young Southerner to the spot where John Brown was born in 1800, in the adjoining town of Torrington. Two of the graduates became judges of the Supreme Court of the United States—Henry Baldwin and Levi Woodbury; fifteen United States Senators, fifty members of Congress, five members of the United States Cabinet, ten governors of states, forty-four judges of state and inferior United States courts, and seven foreign ministers. Georgia is especially well represented. Among the names of judges of that State we notice Eugenius A. Nesbit, who wrote the elegant dissertation in Mitchum *v.* State, 11 Ga. 615, on the privilege and duty of counsel in arguing a case to a jury, in connection with the proper limitations of the freedom of debate—an opinion copied almost verbatim in Tucker *v.* Henniker, 41 N. H. 317, with an omission of quotation marks so singular and flagrant as to have occasioned comment by the profession.

"The course of instruction was completed in fourteen months, including two vacations of four weeks each, one in the spring, the other in the autumn. No student could enter for a shorter period than three months. The terms of instruction were (in 1828) $100 for the first year and $60 for the second, payable either in advance or at the end of the year.

"In the library for the Law School at Yale University may be found several bound volumes of manuscript which apparently contain the entire lectures of Judge Reeve. They are in the handwriting of his son, Aaron Burr Reeve. But marginal reference interlineations in his own hand make it certain that these volumes have all been revised by Judge Reeve himself. The tradition is that they are the manuscripts which he used in his lectures during the last years that he taught. An inspection of these volumes shows that the course of instruction given at the Litchfield Law School covered the entire body of the law. They speak of the law generally—in reference to the sources whence it is derived, as customs and statutes, with the rules for the application and interpretation of each. Then follows Real Estate, Rights of Persons, Rights of Things, Contracts, Torts, Evidence, Pleading, Crimes, and Equity. And each of these general subjects is treated under various subsidiary topics, so as to make the matter intelligible and afford the student a correct and adequate idea of, and basis for, the work he will be called upon to perform in the practice of his profession. Judge Reeve conducted the school alone until 1798, when, having been elected a judge of the Supreme Court, he associated James Gould with him. They had the joint care of the school until 1820, when Judge Reeve withdrew. Mr. Gould continued the classes until 1833, being asissted during the last year by Jabez W. Huntington. Judge Reeve remained on the bench until he reached the limit of seventy years in 1815. The last part of the term he was chief justice. He died in 1823, in the eightieth year of his life. He left an only child, Aaron Burr, who graduated at Yale in 1802. Aaron Burr Reeve married Annabelle Shedden, of Richmond, Va., in 1808. He died in 1809. He left an only child, Tapping Burr Reeve, who graduated at Yale, but died unmarried in 1829, and thus the family became extinct. Mr. Gould became a judge of the Supreme Court of Connecticut, and was the author of the celebrated work on Pleading. He died at Litchfield in 1838. The course of instruction at the school must have been incomparably more exhaustive than would be possible at the present day, for the obvious reason that there was so much less to learn. In 1784 there were no printed reports of decisions of any court in the United States. Substantially the entire body of the law was to be found in the English reports. It is said that Judge Gould had systematically digested for his students "every ancient and modern opinion, whether overruled, doubted, or in any way qualified." But vast bodies of law of which the modern student must learn something were unknown to the curriculum of the Litchfield Law School, and many principles latent in the common law were just beginning to be developed. Lord Mansfield resigned his office of Chief Justice in 1788, after presiding in the King's Bench over thirty years. Prior to his time the greatest uncertainty had prevailed on questions of commercial law. "Mercantile questions were so ignorantly treated when they came into Westminster Hall," says Lord Campbell in his Lives of the Chief Justices, "that they were usually settled by private arbitration among the merchants themselves." There were no treatises on the subject and few cases in the books of reports. Thus in Helyn *v.* Adamson, 3 Burr. 699, decided in 1758, it was first distinctly ruled that the second indorser of an inland bill of exchange was entitled to recover from the prior indorser upon failure of payment by the drawee, without making any demand on or inquiry after the drawer. In 1770 it was held that the indorser of a bill of exchange is discharged if he receives no notice of a refusal to accept by the drawee. (Blesard *v.* Hirst, 5 Burr. 2670.) And not until 1786, in Tindal *v.* Brown, 1 Term Rep. 167, was it finally determined that what is reasonable notice to an indorser of non-payment by the maker of a promissory note, or acceptor of a bill of exchange, is a question of law and not of fact. Of course there was no American constitutional law when the school was founded, though some of the states had already adopted constitutions. The first book on corporation law was that of Kyd, published in London in 1793, but it was chiefly made up of authorities and precedents relating to municipal corporations; and Willcock on Corporations, also an English treatise was still more limited in its plan. There was no American text-book on corporations until the first edition of Angell and Ames was published in 1831. At that time the need of such a book had become very urgent, but in the early years of the Litch-

JUDGE JAMES GOULD

From a Crayon now owned by Hon. A. T. Roraback.

field Law School there must have been extremely few private business corporations in this country. Not until Louisville, etc., R Co. *v.* Letson, 2 How. (U. S.) 497, decided in 1844, did corporations become competent to sue and be sued as "citizens" of a State, regardless of the citizenship of the corporators. A "fellow servant" was a total stranger in legal nomenclature: Priestly *v.* Fowler, 3 M. & W. 1, was decided in 1837; Murray *v.* Railroad Co.,1 McMull. (S. Car.) 385, in 1841; and Farwell *v.* Railroad Co., 4 Met. (Mass.) 49, in 1842. The term "contributory negligence" had not been coined: Butterfield *v.* Forrester, 11 East 60, was decided in 1809; Davies *v.* Mann, 10 M. & W. 546, in 1842, and the phrase is not used in either case. Civil actions for damages for death by wrongful act were not maintainable. The law of insurance was virtually the creation of Lord Mansfield, but the volume of insurance law was comparatively insignificant for several decades. On the other hand, there was an abundance of real estate law and of law concerning executors and administrators and trustees generally. In those days the executor *de son tort* was more in evidence than at present, although even now he has so much vitality in some jurisdictions that it would not be wise for the practioner to characterize him as Judge Lumpkin did in Shotwell *v.* Rowell, 30 Ga. 559, "*de son* fiddlestick!" and cry, "Away with him!" The principles of equity jurisprudence had secured a firm footing, and at this day they are administered in the Federal courts as they were expounded in the High Court of Chancery in England when the Constitution was adopted in 1789. Judge Gould was a master of the common-law system of pleading, which was extolled by some of its eulogists as the perfection of human reason. During the period of the Law School the noble science of pleading became burdened with so many refinements and fictions that it fell into disrepute; the celebrated Rules of Hilary Term were adopted in 1834, and we have since substituted very generally for the technicalities of the common-law system what we term a plain and concise statement of causes of action and of defenses, administering law and equity in one suit, and sometimes peradventure evolving a judgment as incongruous as the one examined in Bennett *v.* Butterworth,, 11 How. (U. S.) 669, or exhibiting the chaos of pleadings and proceedings tabulated by the reporter in Randon *v.* Toby, 11 How. (U. S.) 493. Speaking of the reformed procedure, how many lawyers are aware that the chief merit of the Code system was recognized and recommended for adoption by the preceptor of Judge Reeve, founder of the Litchfield Law School? The first volume of Root's Connecticut Reports was published in 1798. The reporter was Jesse Root, afterward, as above stated, a judge of the Supreme Court, with whom Tapping Reeve had studied law in Hartford. We will close with a quotation from the introduction to that volume: "Are not the courts of chancery in this State borrowed from a foreign jurisdiction, which grew out of the ignorance and barbarism of the law-judges at a certain period in that country from whence borrowed? And would it not be as safe for the people to invest the courts of law with the power of deciding all questions and of giving relief in all cases according to the rules established in chancery, as it is to trust those same judges as chancellors to do it? Those rules might be considered as a part of the law, and the remedy be made much more concise and effectual. Further, would not this remedy great inconveniences and save much expense to suitors, who are frequently turned round at law to seek a remedy in chancery, and as often turned round in chancery because they have adequate remedy at law? These are serious evils and ought not to be permitted to exist in the jurisprudence of a country famed for liberty and justice, and which can be remedied only by the interposition of the legislature.' "

## THE LITCHFIELD LAW SCHOOL.

At the annual dinner of the Story Association, of Cambridge Law School (Mass.) in 1851, the following reference was made to the Litchfield Law School:

Judge Kent gave the sentiment:

" The first-born of the law schools of this country—the Litchfield Law School. The Boston Bar exhibits its rich and ripened fruits. By them we may judge of the tree and declare it good."

Hon. Charles G. Loring, of the class of 1813, reponded:

" I do not remember," he said, " to have ever been more forcibly reminded of my younger days, than when looking around on my young friends in the midst of whom I stand. It recalls the time when I, too, was a student among numerous fellow students. It will, probably, be news to them and many others here, that thirty-eight years ago, which to many here seems a remote antiquity, there existed an extensive law school in the State of Connecticut, at which more than sixty students from all parts of the country were assembled—every State then in the Union, being there represented. I joined it in 1813, when it was at its zenith, and the only prominent establishment of the kind in the land.

"The recollection is as fresh as the events of yesterday, of our passing along the broad shaded streets of one of the most beautiful of the villages of New England, with our inkstands in our hands, and our portfolios under our arms, to the lecture room of Judge Gould—the last of the Romans, of Common Law Lawyers; the impersonation of its spirit and genius. It was, indeed, in his eyes, the perfection of human reason, by which he measured every principle and rule of action, and almost every sentiment.

"Why, sirs, his highest visions of poetry seemed to be in the refinement of special pleadings; and to him a *non sequiter* in logic was an offense deserving, at the least, fine and imprisonment, and a repetition of it, transportation for life. He was an admirable English scholar; every word was pure English, undefiled and every sentence fell from his lips perfectly finished, as clear, transparent and penetrating as light, and every rule and principle as exactly defined and limited as the outline of a building against the sky. From him we obtained clear, well-defined and accurate knowledge of the Common Law, and learned that allegiance to it was the chief duty of man, and the power of enforcing it upon others, his highest attainment. From his lecture room we passed to that of the venerable Judge Reeve, shaded by an aged elm, fit emblem of himself. He was, indeed, a most venerable man, in character and appearance, his thick, gray hair parted and falling in profusion upon his shoulders, his voice only a loud whisper, but distinctly heard by his earnestly, attentive pupils.

"He, too, was full of legal learning, but invested the law with all the genial enthusiasm and generous feelings and noble sentiments of a large heart at the age of eighty, and descanted to us with a glowing eloquence upon the sacredness and majesty of the law. He was distinguished, sirs, by that appreciation of the gentler sex which never fails to mark the true man, and his teachings of the law in reference to their rights and the domestic relations, had great influence in elevating and refining the sentiments of the young men who were privileged to hear him. As illustrative of his feelings and manner upon this subject, allow me to give a specimen. He was discussing the legal relations of married women; he never called them, however, by so inexpressible a name, but always spoke of them as 'the better half of mankind,' or in some equally just manner. When he came to the axiom that 'a married woman has no will of her own,' this, he said was a maxim of great theoretical importance for the preservation of the sex against the undue influence or coercion of the husband; but although it was an inflexible maxim, in theory, experience taught us that practically it was found that they sometimes had wills of their own—*most happily for us.*

"We left his lecture room, sirs, the very knight errants of the law burning to be the defenders of the right and the avengers of the wrong; and he is no true son of the Litchfield school who has ever forgotten that lesson.

"I propose, sirs, the memories of Judge Reeve and Judge Gould —among the first, if not the first founders of a National Law School in the United States—who have laid one of the corner stones in the foundation of true American patriotism, loyalty to the law."

## THE FOLLOWING IS A COPY OF A STUDENT'S LETTER.

Litchfield, October 28th, 1830.

DEAR FRIEND:—

Having received your letter just as I was on the wing for this place, I was unable to answer it then; but avail myself of these first moments of calm after the bustle and confusion incident to the settling down into my nest, to turn my thoughts to that brood in which I found myself when my eyes were first opened to *legal light*, and when I first inhaled the legal atmosphere which from its mistiness gives to those who breath it, (at least so I presume) the well known name of *petty fogs* (you will perceive an analogy in the derivation of this word to that of *lucus* a non *lucendo*, or *Pared* a non parcendo) & from which like yourself I have absconded, being now big enough to take care of myself.

Really, Ned, since my arrival I have been as busy as a hen with one chick—I have been obliged to furnish my room, with whatever I need, from the bellows to the lamp wick. We are obliged to board *here*, at one house and lodge at another. They give you a room, with bed and bestead, et tout ca, at the rate of one dollar a week you furnish your wood, your servant, carpet if you don't wish to go without, lamps, oil, &c., &c.

You see & hear no more of the family than if you were the sole occupant of the premises.

Upon your return from breakfast your room is swept, bed made, things set to rights, as if done by magic, you never see how. I have a fine room at Parson Jones', who is very obliging and would be more so if able, and I board at Mrs. Reeve's, a very agreeable, pleasant, old lady. We pay her, I believe two dollars and a half a week. Our board and lodging and contingencies will run us up to about five dollars a week, which I think is pretty well on to the brogue for a country town. And this is independent of the lectures. Judge Gould is so much overcome with his late family bereavement that he is unable to lecture himself. His son, however, delivers them in his stead. As far as I can judge they will be very *valuable*, independent of their intrinsic merit; I will be obliged to write up at least three reams of finely ruled foolcap. The lecture lasts for an hour and a quarter each day, examinations once a week. Litchfield appears to be a very pretty place, and I think I shall like it well. I attended an evening or two ago an exhibition of the young ladies' seminary at this place of which you speak in your letter. There were several very handsome and interesting young demoiselles. The court room in which it was held was excessively crowded and two or three fainted, one young lady upon receiving her premium. At one end of the room men, boys and girls were all heaped up together, and ever and anon, you would hear some sturdy bum resounding against the floor, its luckless owner having incautiously pushed it out beyond the line of equilibrium.

I understand from Mrs. Reeve that all the marriageable young ladies have been married off, and that there is at present nothing but young fry in town, consequently that it will not be as gay as usual. The young ladies, she tells me, all marry law students, but as it will take two or three years for the young crop to become fit for the harvest, you need apprehend no danger of my throwing up my bachelorship.

The road from Poughkeepsie here is, I think, the most tedious I ever travelled, you see nothing but rocks and stones. Considering the roughness of the country and the scarcity of *land* I am not at all surprised the yankays depend for their livlihood upon their *wits*. I wish I had it in my power to exercise a watchful care over B. as you have enjoined me. "Ah me! forsooth, he is a *sorry* weight." His pa I suspect is afraid of some *singular maneeurvre* on his part and dare not trust him from his paternal eye. He did not accompany me, as in all probability you know, but I do not yet despair of his coming. In such expectation I shall not write him, for I think it very possible he may arrive this evening, if so he shall write you a P. S. He and his father had not fully considered the subject when I left.

It is growing dark and I must conclude before tea (for I expect this evening to be very busy copying notes) and this I cannot do, without assuring you that it will give me the greatest pleasure to see you here. I have a double bed. I will give you half, and as long as Coont. is the land of cakes you will not starve. The excursion will, no doubt, be agreeable and advantageous to your health. You can come by the way of New Haven or Poughkecpsie. When you write to the office remember me to them and to all enquiring friends.

Direct, Litchfield, Connt.

The following extracts from a letter written by Augustus Hand, while a student at the law school, will further illustrate the conduct of the institution:

"Litchfield, Jan. 30th, 1829.

"My Dear Father:—

* * * Let me tell you how I spend my time. I rise between 7 and 8, make a fire and scrub for breakfast, from thence to lecture, where I remain until between 10 and 11. Thence to my room and copy lectures till 5 p. m. (Save dinner time at 1 p. m.) thence to O. S. Seymour's office with whom I read law until half past 9 p. m., then again to my room, write till between 12 and 1 o'clock, then draw on my night-cap and turn in." Exception—Monday we spend from 6 to 9 in the Law School Debating Society, over which

I have the honor—I never brag). Friday at 3 p. m. attend an extra lecture on criminal law, and also hear an argument in the "Moot Court" and decision by the judge. On Saturday at 2 p. m. attend a severe three hours examination on the studies of the week by Jabez W. Huntington, Esq. Aside from these exceptions the first day is a correct specimen. As to the lectures and their utility I will refer you to the preface of the catalogue mailed with this. I can only say that their daily practical use to a lawyer can only be appreciated by those who have enjoyed them. Without any doubt, they give the same talent—a powerful superiority. The whole is comprised in between 2500 and 3000 pages. Of these I have written about 1200 and 1300 and should I remain here till May and enjoy my present excellent health there will be no difficulty in copying the whole, having access to Seymour's volumes (for what I do not take in the office), who has attended two courses and has them complete. This is, however, business between ourselves for these lectures are secured to the Judge, being the labor of his life in the same manner as a patent right. So we talk less and write faster. This Seymour with whom I study is the son of the sheriff of the county, nephew of our State Senator, a graduate of Yale, a bachelor of 26 or 27, of most sterling mind and manners, with a brain completely identified with the study of the law in its most theoretical and scientific part. From a natural weakness of the eyes he does not allow himself to study evenings and therefore invited me to read to him. This offer, knowing his fame, &c., I readily accepted, his office being next door but one to mine, and he being altogether such a man as "studies learning to use it." We take up the title in a lecture and progress with it till it is finished, reading (about) between ten and twenty pages an evening, he giving me a thorough insight into it as we proceed—allowing me without reserve, to tease him with as many questions as I please and now and then reading a report of some cases adapted to the subject. Before the lesson he examines me in the preceding lesson from memory. * * * The law here is a study. There are one or two lawyers in the vicinity who make 4 or 5000 dollars a year. I pass every day by the door of one worth about $150,000.00, about one-half of which he made in law. This "Huntington" who examines is a bachelor rather above forty who studies, thinks and talks law sleeping and waking. He never "pettifoggs," but pleads in the higher courts and writes opinions for other lawyers in every section of the country. He will sometimes become so animated in discussing a question which arises on the examination, that he can hardly keep his seat. Friday, the 11th inst., it came my turn for the second time to come on to the "Moot Court." A short time after my admission my name came on opposed to Mr. Halsted, of N. J. (in alphabetical order), who was an old student. I tried to cross the Rubicon but like a poor, stuck-in-the-mud I could not ford.

Frightened out of my wits, surrounded by a literary fog in the midst of my "nothing," I quoted from an author (Swift) with whom the Judge had a personal quarrel, this with being on the wrong side of the question fired me. This time I resolved to retrieve. A most intricate question on the doctrine of relation and estoppel was handed M. Brown of N. J. and myself by Sq. Sanford of this place. The next day we had a very learned decision luckily in my favor. * * *

Your affectionate son,

AUGUSTUS HAND

## THE LAW SCHOOL BUILDINGS.

The pictuhe of the Reeves Law School building appended here, shows it as now (1908) appears after the restoration as far as possible to its original condition. The Litchfield correspondent of the *Waterbury American* describes the situation as follows:

Litchfield, Nov. 19—Tapping Reeve, the founder of the Litchfield Law School, famous as having been the first law school in the United States, was the son of a Presbyterian minister and was born on the South side of Long Island. He was educated at Princeton, where he graduated in 1763, at the age of 17 years. For seven years he remained as a tutor at Princeton, then came to Connecticut and practiced law in the office of Judge Root of Hartford and as soon as he was admitted to the bar he settled in Litchfield about 1772. He had previously married Sally Burr, daughter of President Burr of Princeton College, and sister of Aaron Burr, who studied in the school, and who was a frequent visitor in his family.

In 1782, the number of students who wished to study in Reeve's office had become so large, that he built the small house shown in the picture, in the corner of his yard, on South Street, the place now owned by Charles H. Woodruff of New York and Litchfield. To this school came students from all parts of the country, many of the men who gained renown in the practice of law and in other professions, being graduates of this school.

Judge Reeve continued to use this building until his death, and in 1846 the building was sold to Henry Ward, who purchased a lot of land on the brow of West Hill and placed the building there, fitting it up as a small house. In 1886 the property was bought by Mrs. Mary C. Daniels and her son, Prof. Charles F. Daniels of New York, who made it their summer home for many years. Prof. Daniels died a few years before his mother and upon Mrs. Daniel's death it became necessary to sell the property.

D. C. Kilbourn began planning to have the old building preserved, and to that end a committee was apponted by the Litchfield County Bar, with Mr. Kilbourn as chairman. He went before the Legislature at its session of 1907 with the proposition that the state buy it and keep it as state property. This proposal was, however, rejected. Thereupon the executor was obliged to sell the place at auction, and Mr. Kilbourn bought it for about $2,700. He immediately began restoring the old part and to do this he had the original law school building detached from the additions which had been put on by Mr. and Mrs. Daniels.

The building was moved to the extreme west end of the lot and has been restored both inside and out as far as possible to its original appearance. At the time of the Ward purchase of the house, it was lathed and plastered. This has been taken off, leaving the original wide pine boards with which it was ceiled, which still show inkstains, and in some places penciled names. One of the original outside doors was found in a mutilated condition, and this has been framed into the wall, and forms the frame of a large crayon portrait of Judge Reeve. The old small-paned windows, which appear in the picture are the same as of old.

When taking off the plastering and lath, several old boards were found literally covered with names and inscriptions, done by jack-knife artists in those old school days, when human nature was much the same as now. Many of these names are to be found in the catalogue of the school in Mr. Kilbourn's possession. Some of the names are W. T. Gould, 1818; N. Billings, New London; Boardman, 1820; William Petit, Marietta, Ohio; 1810; J. B. Skinner, A. Bates, Samuel W. Cheever, F. E. P., R. McE., E. P. S., Jones, (in monogram.)

An interesting question is how the building was heated, as no trace of a fireplace was found. Did they sit in the room with no fire, as the churches of those days were unheated.

It is Mr. Kilbourn's present intention to make, if possible, some arrangement by which the old building can be kept as an interesting relic, and the members of the Litchfield County Bar are getting much interested to have this done.

It should be understood, in this connection, that the picture of what has been called "The First Law School of America" which has appeared from time to time in the state papers, is not a picture of the first law school building, but of the second one, which was built by Judge Gould later. He came to Litchfield and was associated with Judge Reeve in his school, and after Judge Reeve's death he carried on the school, putting up the building sometimes called the first school in the yard of his property, now the Hoppin house, on North street. The school was carried on in that building, to be sure, but it was not the first building. It has been standing about a mile west of the village, and used as a negro tenement, but is fast falling to pieces. There is no doubt that the interest of Mr. Kilbourn in the real "first law school building" has been the means of saving this historic building, and preserving it for the benefit of future generations.

JUDGE REEVE'S RESTORED LAW SCHOOL BUILDING

## THE LITCHFIELD LAW SCHOOL.

A catalogue of this school was published in 1828 of those attending from 1798. A supplement was added bringing the names down to 1831. In 1849 it was reprinted including the names to the close of the school in 1833.

In January, 1900, Hon. George M. Woodruff again reprinted the catalogue, adding some pictures and matter relating thereto.

The various notices and prefaces are herewith reprinted and fully explain themselves.

In the former catalogues the names are arranged by classes, in this they appear alphetically,

It is believed that these names all appear upon the Bar Records, it being the rule that all students should be entered thereon. Upon our records there are a great many names not appearing in this catalogue, being students who were studying with other attorneys. That none of the law school students previous to 1798 appear here is probably from the fact that our bar records begin at that date.

## ADVERTISEMENT TO FIRST EDITION 1828.

The committee to whom has been referred the publication of this catalogue, deem it proper to prefix a few observations in relation to the institution, and the course of instruction therein prescribed.

The Law School was established in 1782 by the Hon. Tapping Reeve, late Chief Justice of this State, and continued under his sole direction until the year 1793, when the Hon. J. Gould was associated with him. These gentlemen continued their joint labors until 1820, since which period Judge Gould has lectured alone. From its commencement, it has enjoyed a patronage, which distinguished talent, combined with legal attainment, justly merited. It has been composed of young men from every section of the Union, many of whom have since been eminently conspicuous, both as jurists and as statemen. And, indeed, even now, notwithstanding the nuermous legal seminaries which have been established throughout our country, this school maintains its proud pre-eminence. This, it is believed, it to be attributed to the advantages, which the mode of instruction here prescribed, possess over the system usually adopted in similar institutions.

According to the plan pursued by Judge Gould, the law is divided into forty-eight titles, which embrace all its important branches, and of which he treats in systematic detail. These titles are the result of thirty years severe and close application. They comprehended the whole of his legal reading during that period, and continue moreover, to be enlarged and improved by modern adjudications. The lectures, which are delivered every day; and which usually occupy an hour and a half, embrace every principle and rule falling under the several divisions of the different titles. These principles and rules are supported by numerous authorities, and generally accompanied with familiar illustrations. Whenever the opinions upon any point are contradictory, the authorities in support of either doctrine are cited, and the arguments, advanced by either side, are presented in a clear and concise manner, together with the lecturer's own views of the question. In fact, every ancient and modern opinion, whether over-ruled, doubted, or in any way qualified, is here systematically digested. These lectures, thus classified, are taken down in full by the students, and after being compared with each other, are generally transcribed in a more neat and legible hand. The remainder of the day is occupied in examining the authorities cited in support of the several rules, and in reading the most approved authors upon those branches of the law, which are at the time the subject of the lectures. These notes, thus written out, are, when complete, comprised in five large volumes, which constitute books of reference, the great advantages of which must be apparent to every one of the slightest acquaintance with the comprehensive and abstruse science of the law. The examinations, which are held every Saturday, upon the lectures of the preceeding week, consist of a thorough investigation of the principles of each rule, and not merely of such questions as can be answered from memory without any exercise of the judgment. These examinations are held by Jabez W. Huntington, Esq., a distinguished gentleman of the bar, whose practice enables him to introduce frequent and familiar illustrations, which excite an interest, and serve to impress more strongly upon the mind the knowledge acquired during the week.

There is also connected with the institution, a *Moot Court* for the argument of law questions, at which Judge Gould presides. The questions that are discussed are prepared by him in the forms in which they generally arise. These courts are held once *at least* in each week, two students acting as counsellors one on each side. And the arguments that are advanced, together with the opinion of the judge, are carefully recorded in a book kept for that purpose. For the preparation of these questions, access may at all times be had to an extensive library. Besides these courts, there are societies established for improvement in forensic exercises, which are entirely under the control of the students..

The whole course is completed in fourteen months, including two vacations of two weeks each, one in the spring, the other in the autumn. No student can enter for a shorter period than three months. The terms of instruction are $100 for the first year, and $60 for the second, payable either in advance or at the end of the year.

JUDGE GOULD'S LAW SCHOOL BUILDING

This building was built by James Gould as his law office about 1795. When he associated with Judge Reeve in law school he used his office for his lectures. It stood in his yard on the West side of North street. It was abandoned at the close of the Law School about 1835, and soon after the death of Judge Gould was sold and removed a mile West of the village on the Bantam road and converted into a dwelling house. For many years it was occupied by a colored family, and for five or six years has been unoccupied. It is now a ruin.

The photo from which this picture was made was taken in 1898.

GEORGE C. WOODRUFF

Compiler of this Catalogue, 1828.

This catalogue extends only as far back as 1798. Previous to that period, it is believed that the whole number exceeded four hundred; no record, however, has been preserved. The names of the students are placed in the order in which they entered, without any regard to the length of time they continued as members of the institution. The committee have endeavored to notice those who have distinguished themselves; but as this has been done merely from recollection, they have no doubt passed by many, who have conferred honor upon their country and their profession.

Litchfield, Jan. 1, 1828.

## CATALOGUE.

### A

| | | |
|---|---|---|
| Abeel, George | New York | 1823 |
| Adams, Charles | Massachusetts | 1812 |
| Adams, Joseph T. | Massachusetts | 1820 |
| Adams, John | Massachusetts | 1822 |
| Adams, John T. | Connecticut | 1833 |
| Aiken, Charles | New Hampshire | 1832 |
| Albro, John A. | Massachusetts | 1821 |
| Alden, Cyrus | Massachusetts | 1808 |
| Alden, Hiram O. | New Hampshire | 1823 |
| Allen, Alexander M. | Georgia | 1801 |
| Allen, Zimri R. | Vermont | 1811 |
| Allyn, J. T. | Maryland | 1821 |
| Alston, William W. | South Carolina | 1818 |
| Alston, William J. | South Carolina | 1824 |
| Ames, Samuel | Rhode Island—Chief Jus. R. I. | 1824 |
| Andrews, William | Massachusetts | 1812 |
| Andrews, William T. | Massachusetts | 1812 |
| Anderson, Franklin | Maryland | 1813 |
| Anderson, John | Maryland | 1815 |
| Ashley, Chester | New York—U. S. Senator | 1814 |
| Aspinwall, Thomas L. | New York | 1810 |
| Atwater, Frederick | New York | 1814 |
| Atwater, Russell | New York | 1815 |
| Austin, Charles | Massachusetts | 1812 |
| Austin, Ralsamon | Connecticut | 1801 |
| Austin, Senaca | Vermont | 1820 |
| Averill, Elisha | Connecticut | 1814 |
| Averill, William H. | Connecticut | 1817 |
| Ayer, Zaccheus | Georgia | 1817 |

## B

| | | |
|---|---|---|
| Babbitt, Roswell | New York | 1833 |
| Bacon, David | Connecticut | 1806 |
| Bacon, William J. | New York | 1823 |
| Baker, Joshua | Louisiana | 1821 |
| Baker, Walter | New Hampshire | 1812 |
| Balcom, Everett | Massachusetts | 1818 |
| Baldwin, Birdsey | Connecticut | 1806 |
| Baldwin, Charles | New York | 1801 |
| Baldwin, Charles | Connecticut | 1810 |
| Baldwin, Ebenezer | Connecticut | 1810 |
| Baldwin, Henry | Conn.—Judge Sup. Ct. U.S. M. C. | 1798 |
| Baldwin, Roger S. | Conn.—Governor. U. S. Senator | 1812 |
| Baldwin, Samuel S. | Connecticut | 1800 |
| Banks, William C. | Georgia | 1818 |
| Barclay, David, Jr | Virginia | 1832 |
| Barnes, Enos H. | Virginia | 1826 |
| Barnes, Joseph | Massachusetts—Judge Penn. | 1801 |
| Barnes, Lauren | Connecticut | 1806 |
| Barnwell William | South Carolina | 1826 |
| Bartram, Daniel S. | Connecticut | 1799 |
| Bates, Anson | Connecticut | 1820 |
| Battle, Josiah B. | Connecticut | 1798 |
| Baxter, Eli H. | Georgia—Judge Circuit Court | 1818 |
| Baxter, Horace | Massachusetts | 1812 |
| Beach, Erasmus D. | Massachusetts | 1832 |
| Beebe, Levi S. | New York | 1830 |
| Beecher, Truman | Connecticut | 1816 |
| Beers, David B. | Connecticut | 1829 |
| Beers, Frederick | Connecticut | 1809 |
| Beers, Seth P. | Conn.—Com. of School Fund | 1803 |
| Belden, Hezekiah | Connecticut | 1798 |
| Bell, Harvey | Vermont | 1812 |
| Bell, James | Vermont | 1824 |
| Bellamy, Joseph H. | Connecticut | 1808 |
| Bennett, Milo L. | Conn.—L.L.D, Judge SupCt. Vt. | 1811 |
| Beverly, James | District Columbia | 1813 |
| Beverly, William | District Columbia | 1813 |
| Bigelow, Horatio | Massachusetts | 1810 |
| Bigelow, Silas | Massachusetts | 1814 |
| Billings, Noyes | Connecticut—Lieut.-Governor | 1820 |
| Bingham, F. W. | New York | 1830 |
| Bissell, Edward | Connecticut | 1828 |
| Bissell, John, Jr. | Connecticut | 1826 |
| Bishop, Jonathan P. | Maryland | 1814 |
| Bixby, Alfred | New Hampshire | 1821 |

| | | |
|---|---|---|
| Blackwell, David | Kentucky | 1813 |
| Blake, Eli W. | Connecticut | 1817 |
| Blake, Francis A. | Massachusetts | 1817 |
| Bond, Nathaniel P. | Georgia | 1819 |
| Bond, William | Maryland | 1811 |
| Bonestall, Virgil D. | New York | 1830 |
| Bonnel, Joseph | Delaware | 1815 |
| Boardman, George S. | Connecticut | 1819 |
| Boardman, William W. | Connecticut—Member Congress | 1816 |
| Bolles, Job S. T. | Georgia | 1822 |
| Booth, James, Jr. | Delaware—Chief Justice | 1810 |
| Bosson, Charles | Massachusetts | 1811 |
| Bostwick, Charles | Connecticut | 1798 |
| Boyle, James | Connecticut | 1833 |
| Brace, John P. | Connecticut | 1812 |
| Brace, Thomas K. | Connecticut | 1802 |
| Bradley, Benj. H. | Connecticut | 1818 |
| Bradley, Edwin B. | Connecticut | 1827 |
| Brayton, George A. | Rhode Island | 1825 |
| Breckenridge, John | Maryland | 1821 |
| Brimsmade, Daniel B. | Connecticut | 1803 |
| Bronson, Frederick | New York | 1824 |
| Broome, Jacob | Delaware | 1809 |
| Brookes, Whitefield | South Carolina | 1814 |
| Brown, Charles R. | Connecticut | 1813 |
| Brown, Franklin | New York | 1827 |
| Brown, George | New York | 1814 |
| Brown, Nicholas, Jr. | Rhode Island | 1811 |
| Bruyn, Andrew D. W. | New York—Member Congress | 1811 |
| Buffet, William P. | New York | 1813 |
| Buchanan, William S. | Pennsylvania | 1824 |
| Bulkley, Joseph | Cnnecticut | 1810 |
| Bullard, Royal | Massachusetts | 1810 |
| Bull, Epaphras W. | Connecticut | 1826 |
| Bunker, Charles | Massachusetts | 1822 |
| Bunnell, James F. | New York | 1827 |
| Burgess, W. Arnold | Rhode Island | 1821 |
| Butler, Chester P. | Pennsylvania—Mem. of Cong. | 1818 |
| Butler, David B. | New Jersey | 1825 |
| Burrall, William P. | Connecticut | 1828 |

## C

| | | |
|---|---|---|
| Calhoun, John C. | South Carolina—L. L. D., V. P. Mem. of Cong.; Senator; Sec. of State and of War | 1805 |
| Camp, Ralph G. | Connecticut | 1824 |

Cambrelling Stephen ........North Carolina ...............1813
Campbell, Collin ..........South Carolina ...............1809
Campbell, George L........New York ....................1826
Campbell, John ............South Carolina ...............1820
Cantelou, Peter L. ..........Georgia ....................1813
Cantelou, William B........Georgia ....................1813
Canfield, Ezra ............Connecticut ..................1801
Canfield, Henry J..........Connecticut ..................1808
Cardwell, John W..........South Carolina ...............1823
Carroll, Charles H.........New York—Member Congress..1817
Carroll, Willam ...........Indiana ......................1823
Castor, Dyer ..............Pennsylvania ................1825
Catlin, George ............Penn.—Indian portrait painter..1817
Catlin, George S...........Conn.—Member of Congress....1827
Catlin, Grove .............Connecticut ..................1806
Chase, Harvey ............New Hampshire ..............1800
Chase, Moses .............New Hhampshire .............1798
Chase, Samuel ............New York ....................1818
Champion, Epaphroditus ...Connecticut ..................1805
Champlin, Christopher .....Rhode Island..................1810
Chambers, Joseph .........Pennsylvania ................1820
Chambers, Benjamin L.....Maryland ....................1822
Chamberlin, Mellin ........Maine .......................1819
Chandler, Anson G.........Maine .......................1818
Chandler, John A. .........Maine .......................1818
Chandler, Hannibal ........Virginia ....................1832
Channing, Henry W. ......Connecticut ..................1809
Chapin, Moses ............Mass.—Judge N. Y. Courts.....1813
Chapman, Charles .........Connecticut ..................1818
Chester, Henry ............New York ....................1815
Chester, Stephen M........Connecticut ..................1813
Cheever, Samuel ...........Massachusetts ...............1812
Child, Abiel ..............Connecticut ..................1821
Childs, Timothy, Jr........Massachusetts—Mem. Congress.1814
Chittenden, Frederick ......Connecticut ..................1824
Church, Aaron ............Connecticut ..................1800
Church, Leman ...........Connecticut ..................1815
Church, Samuel ..........Connecticut—Chief Justice.....1806
Clark, Archibald .........Georgia ....................1800
Clark, Gibson ............Georgia ....................1804
Clark, Henry L............New York ....................1826
Clark, James .............Georgia ....................1820
Clark, Robert ............Georgia ....................1832
Clark, Peter ..............New Jersey ...................1811
Clayton, John M...........Delaware—L.L.D, Chief Justice;
U. S. Senator; Sec. of State..1817
Cleveland, Stephen ........New York ....................1815

| | | |
|---|---|---|
| Clifton, William C. | Georgia | 1825 |
| Clinton, George W. | New York | 1828 |
| Cockburn, William | New York | 1818 |
| Cogshall, Josiah H. | Massachusetts | 1809 |
| Coleman, John J. | Alabama | 1827 |
| Collier, John A. | Connecticut—M. C. New York | 1805 |
| Collins, Augustus | Connecticut | 1804 |
| Collins, Josiah, Jr. | North Carolina | 1826 |
| Cook, James C. | Connecticut | 1813 |
| Cook, Oliver D., Jr. | Connecticut | 1818 |
| Cooke, Roger W. | Connecticut | 1817 |
| Cooley, James | Massachusetts | 1799 |
| Cole, John | New York | 1810 |
| Cooper, Benjamin F. | New York | 1821 |
| Conkling, Thomas | Maryland | 1817 |
| Condit, Jacob A. | New Jersey | 1813 |
| Converse, Porter | Vermont | 1804 |
| Cowles, Samuel | Connecticut | 1802 |
| Cowles, Henry B. | New York | 1817 |
| Cowles, Sands G. | Connecticut | 1826 |
| Crawford, James | Vermont | 1832 |
| Crawford, Joel | Georgia—Member of Congress | 1806 |
| Croghan, William | Kentucky | 1815 |
| Crosby, Platt H. | New York | 1813 |
| Cruger, H. N., Jr. | South Carolina | 1821 |
| Cumming, Edward H. | New Jersey | 1826 |
| Cumming, William | Georgia | 1806 |
| Cunningham, Robert | South Carolina | 1810 |
| Cuthbert, John A. | Georgia—Member of Congress | 1807 |
| Cuthbert, Alfred | Georgia—United States Senator | 1804 |
| Cutler, George Y. | Connecticut | 1819 |
| Cutting, Brockholst | New York | 1823 |
| Cushman, Charles C. | Vermont | 1828 |
| Cushman, John P. | Conn.—M. C. and Judge N. Y. | 1808 |

## D

| | | |
|---|---|---|
| Dart, John S. | South Carolina | 1821 |
| Davidge, Francis H. | Maryland | 1815 |
| Davis, John | Virginia | 1811 |
| Davis, James | Maryland | 1816 |
| Davis, John H. | Delaware | 1817 |
| Davies, Henry | Maryland | 1809 |
| Davies, Israel W. | Massachusetts | 1811 |
| Davies, John B. | Virginia | 1815 |

| | | |
|---|---|---|
| Dawson, Lawrence | South Carolina | 1822 |
| Dawson, William C. | Georgia—Judge; U. S. Senator | 1817 |
| Day, Edgar B. | New York | 1826 |
| Delamotter, Jacob | Georgia | 1821 |
| DeMenou, Charles | Charge d'Affairs of France, D. C. | 1808 |
| Deming, Buel H. | Connecticut | 1825 |
| Denny, Thomas | Massachusetts | 1825 |
| Deveraux, Geo. P. | North Carolina | 1817 |
| Deveraux, Thomas | North Carolina | 1813 |
| Deveraux, Thomas P. | No. Carolina—Reporter Sup. Ct. | 1815 |
| Deas, Henry | South Carolina | 1818 |
| Dexter, Christopher C. | Rhode Island | 1813 |
| Doolittle, Amos B. | Connecticut | 1806 |
| Doan, Guy | Connecticut | 1814 |
| Downes, Appleton | Massachusetts | 1811 |
| Downman, John B. | Massachusetts | 1813 |
| Doyle, Francis | Georgia | 1822 |
| Dubois, Cornelius, Jr. | New York | 1830 |
| Dunbar, Daniel | Connecticut | 1798 |
| Dunbar, Miles | Connecticut | 1809 |
| Dwight, Henry W. | Massachusetts, Member Congress | 1809 |
| Dyer, Thomas | Connecticut | 1799 |

## E

| | | |
|---|---|---|
| Eastman, A. G. | New York | 1833 |
| Edwards, Henry P | Conn.—Judge Sup. Ct. N. Y. | 1828 |
| Edwards, Henry P. | New York | 1830 |
| Edwards, Henry W. | Conn.—U. S. Sen.; Gov. Conn. | 1798 |
| Edwards, John S. | Connecticut | 1798 |
| Edwards, Odgen | Conn.—Judge Sup. Ct. N. Y. | 1801 |
| Eickelbergger, Louis | Maryland | 1810 |
| Elgin, Hezekiah R. | Maryland | 1815 |
| Ellis, Grindall R. | New Hampshire | 1809 |
| Ellsworth, Henry L. | Connecticut | 1811 |
| Ellsworth, William W. | Conn.—Com. of Patents; M. C.; Governor; Judge Sup. Court | 1811 |
| Ellmaker, Amos | Pennsylvania | 1806 |
| Ellmendorf, Edmond B. | New York | 1826 |
| Ennis, William | Rhode Island | 1820 |
| Erwin, Isaac H. | Alabama | 1828 |
| Everest, Sherman | Connecticut | 1800 |

## F

| | | |
|---|---|---|
| Fairle, Frederick | New York | 1818 |
| Felder, John M. | South Ca rolina—Mem. of Cong. | 1805 |
| Fine, John | New York | 1813 |

GEORGE M. WOODRUFF

Reprinted the Catalogue, 1900

| | | |
|---|---|---|
| Fisher, Isaac, Jr | Maryland | 1811 |
| Fisher, Samuel | Massachusetts | 1810 |
| Fitch, John | Connecticut | 1803 |
| Fleming, Matthew | South Carolina | 1815 |
| Floyd, Joseph R. | Maryland | 1818 |
| Follet, Timothy | Vermont | 1812 |
| Folsom, Joshua | New Hampshire | 1811 |
| Foot, John A. | Connecticut | 1824 |
| Footman, William | Maryland | 1815 |
| Ford, William H. | South Carolina | 1826 |
| Foster, George | Massachusetts | 1812 |
| Foster, James | Massachusetts | 1812 |
| Foster, Thomas F. | Massachusetts—M. C., Geo. | 1816 |
| Fowler, James | Massachusetts | 1808 |
| Fowler, John D. | Massachusetts | 1813 |
| Francis, John B. | Rhode Island | 1813 |
| Franklin, Walter S. | Penn.—Clerk H. R. U. S. | 1818 |
| Frazier, Alexander G. | South Carolina | 1810 |
| Frisbie, Samuel | Connecticut | 1809 |
| Fuller, Henry H. | Massachusetts | 1812 |
| Fuller, William W. | Massachusetts | 1814 |
| Fullerton, Alexander N. | Vermont | 1826 |
| Fullerton, Thomas S. | Vermont | 1822 |

## G

| | | |
|---|---|---|
| Gantt, Samuel | South Carolina | 1817 |
| Ganesvoort, Peter | New York | 1810 |
| Gardner, Philip S. | Rhode Island | 1826 |
| Gibbs, David | Massachusetts | 1808 |
| Gibbs, Henry W. | Connecticut | 1808 |
| Gibbs, William C. | Rhode Island—Governor | 1810 |
| Gibson, William | Georgia | 1823 |
| Glover, Samuel | New York | 1820 |
| Gold, Thomas A. | Massachusetts | 1808 |
| Goodwin, Edward | Connecticut | 1823 |
| Goodwin, Hiram | Connecticut | 1829 |
| Gould, George | Conn.—Judge Sup. Court N. Y. | 1827 |
| Gould James R. | Connecticut | 1824 |
| Gould, William T. | Conn.—Judge, Georgia | 1818 |
| Graham, John L. | New York | 1814 |
| Grant, William | South Carolina | 1823 |
| Grant, William A. | Georgia | 1823 |
| Graves, Thomas C. | Kentucky | 1808 |
| Gray, Thomas | Connecticut | 1817 |
| Green, Caleb, Jr | New York | 1830 |
| Greene, Albert C. | Rhode Island—U. S. Senator | 1812 |

| | | |
|---|---|---|
| Greene, Benjamin D. | Massachusetts | 1813 |
| Green, Henry W. | Rhode Island—Justice Sup. Court and Chancellor New Jersey | 1823 |
| Greene, Richard W. | Rhode Island | 1812 |
| Greene, William | Rhode Island | 1817 |
| Griffin, George | Connecticut—L.L.D. | 1798 |
| Griswold, Shubal | Connecticut | 1809 |
| Groome, John C. | Maryland | 1824 |
| Gustin, Alpheus | North Carolina | 1819 |
| Gwathmy, Isaac K. | Kentucky | 1813 |
| Gunn, Frederick | Connecticut | 1812 |

## H

| | | |
|---|---|---|
| Hadnall, William B. | Maryland | 1819 |
| Hall, Ambrose | Massachusetts | 1802 |
| Hall, Gideon | Conn.—Judge Sup. Court | 1829 |
| Hall, Horace | Vermont | 1803 |
| Hall, Willis | New York—Attorney Gen. N. Y. | 1826 |
| Halsted, Oliver S. | New Jersey—Chancellor N. J. | 1813 |
| Halsted, Robert W. | New Jersey | 1827 |
| Halsted, William, Jr. | New Jersey | 1814 |
| Halsey, Hopkins | Georgia—Mem. of Congress | 1819 |
| Hand, Augustus C. | Vermont—Judge Sup. Ct. N. Y. | 1827 |
| Hamilton, Thomas | South Carolina | 1810 |
| Harrison, Tipton B. | Virginia | 1818 |
| Harvey, Leroy | Georgia | 1821 |
| Hasbrook, Abraham B. | New York—M. C.; L.L.D.; President Rutgers' College, N. J. | 1812 |
| Hassell, Bentley | South Carolina | 1825 |
| Hatch, Moses | Connecticut | 1801 |
| Hawkes, Francis L. | North Carolina—Clergyman; author N. Y. | 1818 |
| Hawkes, Benjamin B. | North Carolina | 1823 |
| Hawkins, Samuel | New York | 1798 |
| Hawley, Charles | Conn.—Lt.-Gov. Conn. | 1813 |
| Hayden, Moses | Massachusetts | 1804 |
| Head, George E. | Massachusetts | 1813 |
| Hepburn, Joseph L. | Pennsylvania | 1819 |
| Hiccox, Guy | Connecticut | 1806 |
| Hill, Joseph A. | North Carolina | 1819 |
| Hill, William R. | South Carolina | 1821 |
| Hillhouse, Augustus L. | Connecticut | 1812 |
| Hine, Homer | Connecticut | 1800 |
| Hines, Richard | | 1814 |
| Hinman, Royal R. | Conn.—Sec. State; historian | 1806 |
| Hitchcock, Samuel | Alabama | 1828 |

Holabird, William F. — Connecticut—Lt. Gov. Conn. — 1815
Hodges, William F. — Connecticut — 1812
Holcomb, Chauncey P. — Connecticut — 1824
Holley, John M., Jr. — Conn.—Mem. of Cong. N. Y. — 1823
Holt, George B. — Conn.—Judge in Ohio — 1812
Holt, Thaddeus G. — Georgia—Judge Sup. Court Ga. — 1816
Hooker, James — Connecticut — 1810
Hopkins, Abiather — New Hampshire — 1808
Hotchkiss, Minor — Connecticut — 1813
Houston, Patrick — Georgia — 1798
Houghton, Josiah — Maine — 1817
Howard, Benjamin Chas. — Maryland — 1812
Howard, John H. — Georgia — 1813
Howe, Samuel — Massachusetts—Judge — 1805
Hoyt, Henry S. — New York — 1829
Hubbard, Elijah — Connecticut — 1798
Hubbard, Elizur — Vermont — 1799
Hubbel, James — Vermont — 1802
Hudson, Jonathan T. — Connecticut — 1826
Hull, Hezekiah B. — Connecticut — 1813
Hunt, Hiram P. — New York—Mem. of Congress — 1817
Hunt, Jonathan — Connecticut — 1808
Hunt, Ward E. — New York—Chief Justice of N. Y.; Judge U. S. Sup. Court — 1830
Huntington, Jabez W. — Conn.—M. C.; U. S. S.; Judge Supreme Court — 1808
Humphrey, Joseph — Connecticut — 1812
Hurlbut, William — Connecticut — 1815
Huffington, William — Delaware — 1823
Hyde, John J. — Connecticut — 1829

## I

Ingersoll, Charles M. — New Hampshire — 1812
Ingham, Alpheus — Pennsylvania — 1825
Ives, Moses B. — Rhode Island — 1812
Ives, Henry C. — New York — 1831

## J

Jacobs, Cyrus — Pennsylvania — 1823
Jacobs, George W. — Pennsylvania — 1819
Jacobs, William C. — Pennsylvania — 1820
Jackson, Ebenezer, Jr. — Georgia—Member of Congress — 1814
Jackson, John P. — New Jersey — 1824
Jackson, Joseph — Georgia — 1817
Jackson, Oliver P. — New York — 1823

| | | |
|---|---|---|
| Jackson, Thomas L. | Georgia | 1823 |
| Janvier, Thomas, Jr. | Delaware | 1828 |
| James, Edward M. | New York | 1805 |
| Jarvis, Russell | Massachusetts | 1813 |
| Jenkins, Charles M. | New York | 1831 |
| Jessup, Ebenezer | Connecticut | 1825 |
| Jewell, Ezra | Connecticut | 1809 |
| Johns, Kensey, Jr. | Delaware—M. C.; Chancellor | 1812 |
| Johnson, Charles F. | Connecticut | 1824 |
| Johnson, Edwards | Connecticut | 1826 |
| Johnson, James | Georgia | 1816 |
| Johnson, William S. | Connecticut | 1816 |
| Johnston, James T. | Georgia | 1816 |
| Jones, Henry | Calcutta, East Indies | 1810 |
| Jones, Joel | Pennsylvania—L.L.D. | 1819 |
| Jones, John Q. | New York | 1817 |
| Jones, Robert | | 1813 |
| Jones, Rice | Louisiana | 1807 |
| Judson, Noah | Massachusetts | 1799 |

## K

| | | |
|---|---|---|
| Kaleb, William M. | Maryland | 1827 |
| Kaleb, J. A. Mc. | Maryland | 1829 |
| Kellogg, Edward | Massachusetts | 1823 |
| Kelso, Charles W. | Pennsylvania | 1828 |
| Kerr, Joseph C. | North Carolina | 1817 |
| Key, Phillip | Maryland | 1829 |
| Kilbourn, Austin | Connecticut | 1821 |
| King, Edward | New York | 1813 |
| King, George G. | Rhode Island | 1826 |
| King, James G. | New York—Mem. of Congress | 1810 |
| Kingsbury, Sanford | New Hampshire | 1801 |
| Kinnecutt, Thomas | Massachusetts—Lieut-Gov. | 1823 |
| Kirby, Reynold M. | Connecticut | 1809 |
| Kirkland, Chas. P. | New York | 1818 |
| Knight, Frederick | Massachusetts | 1812 |

## L

| | | |
|---|---|---|
| Lake, Joseph | Ohio | 1820 |
| Lamar, Lucius Q. C. | Georgia—Judge Sup. Court | 1817 |
| Langdon, Benjamin F. | Vermont | 1821 |
| Langsing, Leviness S. | New York | 1830 |
| Lathrop, Cyrus H. | Massachusetts | 1810 |
| Latham, Allen | Massachusetts | 1814 |
| Lashell, John | Pennsylvania | 1810 |

| | | |
|---|---|---|
| Lawrence, Augustus A. | New York | 1813 |
| Lawrence, Phillip K. | New York | 1814 |
| Lawrence, William B. | New York—Charge d'affaires, London | 1819 |
| Leavenworth, Elias W. | Mass.—L.L.D.; M. C.; Sec. of State N. Y. | 1825 |
| Leavenworth, Nathan | New York | 1813 |
| Leavenworth, William F. | Connecticut | 1822 |
| Leavitt, Harvey F. | New Hampshire | 1816 |
| Ledyard, Henry | New York | 1830 |
| Leonard, Cornelius | New York | 1810 |
| Lewis, John L. | Louisiana | 1825 |
| Lewis, Robert H. | Virginia | 1821 |
| Lewis, William | Louisiana | 1817 |
| Livingston, Carroll | New York | 1827 |
| Livingston, Henry W. | New York | 1820 |
| Livingston, James K. | New York | 1818 |
| Livingston, John R. | New York | 1823 |
| Livingston, Robert | New York | 1829 |
| Livingston, Walter | New York | 1820 |
| Lloyd, Joseph R. | North Carolina | 1818 |
| Lockwood, Ephraim | Connecticut | 1798 |
| Loring, Charles G. | Massachusetts | 1813 |
| Loring Edward G. | Massachusetts | 1822 |
| Lord, Daniel, Jr. | New York—L.L.D. | 1814 |
| Longstreet, Augustus B. | Georgia—L.L.D.; Judge Sup. Ct.; College President | 1813 |
| Lott, Adrain | New York | 1831 |
| Low, Cornelius | New York | 1812 |
| Lowndes, Benjamin | Virginia | 1825 |
| Ludlow, Alfred | New York | 1822 |
| Lundy, Etheldred | Virginia | 1818 |
| Lyman, Darius | Connecticut | 1811 |
| Lyman, Samuel F. | Massachusetts | 1819 |
| Lyman, Theodore | Massachusetts | 1811 |

## M

| | | |
|---|---|---|
| Marberry, John | Maryland | 1813 |
| Mack, Elisha | Massachusetts | 1805 |
| Magruder, Enoch | Pennsylvania | 1816 |
| Mackie, Peter | New York | 1813 |
| Mallory, Garrick | Penn.—L.L.D.; Judge Penn. | 1810 |
| Mann, George | Rhode Island | 1826 |
| Mann, Horace | Mass.—M. of C.; educator | 1822 |
| Mansfield, Edward D. | New York | 1823 |
| Markley, Benj. A. | South Carolina | 1806 |

| | | |
|---|---|---|
| Marvin, Ebenezer | Vermont | 1799 |
| Marsh, Charles, Jr. | Vermont | 1813 |
| Martin, Joseph F. | Rhode Island | 1818 |
| Martin, William D. | South Carolina—M. C. | 1810 |
| Mason, John Y. | Virginia—M. C.; Judge; Sec. of Navy; Mason and Slidell affair | 1817 |
| Mason, William J. | Virginia | 1821 |
| Mayson, Charles C. | South Carolina | 1814 |
| Mather, Nathaniel | Connecticut | 1811 |
| Maxwell, Robert | Maryland | 1817 |
| Maxey, Virgil | Rhode Island—Chg. d'affairs Belgium | 1805 |
| Mayer, Abraham | Pennsylvania | 1817 |
| Mayer, John B. | Pennsylvania | 1823 |
| Mayo, Harman B. | New York | 1821 |
| McCawley, Robert | Virginia | 1819 |
| McClean, James G. | Maryland | 1822 |
| McElhenny, James | South Carolina | 1822 |
| McFarland, William H. | Virginia | 1818 |
| Merwin, Elijah B. | Vermont | 1801 |
| Metcalf, Theron | Massachusetts | 1806 |
| Middleton, Henry A. | South Carolina | 1815 |
| Middleton, Henry | South Carolina | 1817 |
| Mills, Roger | Connecticut | 1798 |
| Mills, Michael F. | Connecticut | 1801 |
| Millar, Bowyar | Virginia—(Boyer F. Miller?) | 1817 |
| Miller, Charles | Connecticut | 1818 |
| Miller, Joseph | Connecticut | 1801 |
| Miller, Morris | Georgia | 1798 |
| Miller, Rutger B. | New York | 1824 |
| Miller, Solomon S. | Vermont | 1811 |
| Minturn, Thomas R. | New York | 1826 |
| Mitchell, Charles | Connecticut | 1804 |
| Mitchell, Henry A. | Connecticut | 1826 |
| Mitchell, Louis C. | Connecticut | 1807 |
| Mitchell, Louis | Connecticut | 1813 |
| Mitchell, Stephen M. | Connecticut | 1800 |
| Moffit, Thomas | Georgia | 1816 |
| Morris, Henry | New York | 1826 |
| Moore, Robert | Georgia | 1822 |
| Morrison, James | New Hampshire | 1809 |
| Morse, Sidney E. | Mass.—Founder N. Y. Observer | 1814 |
| Morson, Arthur A. | Virginia | 1823 |
| Moseley, Charles | Connecticut | 1806 |
| Mumford, William W. | New York | 1815 |
| Munger, Warren | Connecticut | 1811 |

Purchased the Judge Reeve Homestead

## N

Nash, Lonson ............ Massachusetts ................ 1803
Neill, George P............ Pennsylvania ................ 1829
Nesbit, Eugenius A........ Georgia—M. C.; Judge Sup. Ct. 1823
Nichols, Joseph H......... New York ................ 1827
Nichol, Edward ........... New York ................ 1813
Nicoll, John C............ Georgia—Judge; U. S. District Judge ................ 1814
Nixon, Henry G........... South Carolina ................ 1820
Nelson, Armstead ......... Maryland ................ 1814
Newcomb, Isaac M........ New York ................ 1828
Norton, Marcus .......... Mass.—Judge; Gov. Mass...... 1806
Norton, James C........... New York ................ 1819
North, Theodore .......... Connecticut ................ 1808
Nutall, William B.......... North Carolina ................ 1823

## O

Oakley, Jesse ............. New York ................ 1814
Ogden, Matthias B......... New Jersey ................ 1813
Olcut, Theophilus ......... New Hampshire ................ 1801
Oliver, Henry ............ Maryland ................ 1821
Oliver, Samuel W.......... Georgia ................ 1820
Olmstead, Charles C....... Connecticut ................ 1810
Ormsbee, Edgar S.......... Vermont ................ 1824
Orne, Henry .............. Massachusetts ................ 1811
Overton, Thomas B. ....... Pennsylvania ................ 1813
O'Hara, Arthur H......... North Carolina ................ 1814

## P

Page, Benjamin ........... Rhode Island ................ 1805
Page, Henry .............. Rhode Island ................ 1816
Painter, Alexis ........... Connecticut ................ 1817
Parker, Amasa ............ Connecticut ................ 1809
Parker, Aurelius D......... Massachussetts ................ 1826
Parker, Charles T.......... Massachusetts ................ 1828
Parker, William M.................................. 1820
Parrott, Abner B........... Georgia ................ 1821
Parson, Anson V. .......... Mass.—Judge Sup. Court Penn.. 1825
Pasteur, Edward G......... North Carolina ................ 1823
Patterson, Chris. S........ Pennsylvania ................ 1821
Patton, Robert ..................................... 1814
Payne, Elijah, Jr........... Vermont ................ 1815
Peck, William V.......... Cennecticut—Judge, Ohio ..... 1824
Pell, Duncan C............ New York ................ 1826
Penney, Samuel ........... New York ................ 1828

| | | |
|---|---|---|
| Perkins, Charles | Connecticut | 1813 |
| Perkins, Thomas S. | Connecticut | 1812 |
| Pettibone, Sereno | Connecticut | 1802 |
| Petet, Joel T. | Connecticut | 1800 |
| Petet, William W. | Ohio | 1815 |
| Phelps, Charles B. | New Hampshire | 1806 |
| Phelps, Edward A. | Connecticut | 1828 |
| Phelps, Elisha | Conn.—Mem. of Congress | 1801 |
| Phelps, Jedediah | Massachusetts | 1810 |
| Phelps, Samuel S. | Conn.—U. S. S.; Judge S. C. Vt. | 1811 |
| Pickett, Reuben | North Carolina | 1825 |
| Pickett, William D. | North Carolina—Judge Sup. Ct. Alabama | 1826 |
| Pierce, James | Connecticut | 1798 |
| Pierce, Levi | Maryland | 1815 |
| Pierce, William L. | Georgia | 1809 |
| Pierpont, John | Connecticut—Rev.; poet | 1809 |
| Pierpont, John | Conn.—Chief Justice Vermont | 1825 |
| Pierson, George | New York | 1830 |
| Pillsbury, William | Massachusetts | 1813 |
| Pitcher, John | New York—Lieut.-Gov. | 1815 |
| Pitcher, Phillip | New York | 1828 |
| Pitt, John R. | Georgia | 1816 |
| Player, Thompson T. | South Carolina | 1826 |
| Poe, Washington | Georgia—Member of Congress | 1823 |
| Polk, Thomas G. | North Carolina | 1811 |
| Porter, George B. | Penn.—Gov. of Michigan | 1812 |
| Porter, Timothy H. | New Hampshire—M. Congress | 1807 |
| Porteus, John | South Carolina | 1800 |
| Post, Albert L. | | 1832 |
| Potter, Ansel | Connecticut | 1805 |
| Potter, Asa | Rhode Island | 1826 |
| Prentice, Henry E. | | 1832 |
| Preston, Isaac T. | Virginia—Judge S. C. Louisiana | 1812 |
| Price, Benjamin | Maryland | 1820 |
| Pumpelly, George J. | New York | 1826 |
| Putnam, Austin | New York | 1828 |
| Putnam, Charles | Massachusetts | 1814 |

## R

| | | |
|---|---|---|
| Rankin, Robert G. | New York | 1827 |
| Raymond, Daniel | Connecticut | 1810 |
| Raymond, David H. | Connecticut | 1810 |
| Raymond, James | Connecticut | 1820 |
| Raynor, Benj. L. | Connecticut | 1824 |
| Read, John, Jr. | Delaware | 1824 |

Read, John D. . . . . . . . . . . . . .Delaware . . . . . . . . . . . . . . . . . . .1823
Read, William T. . . . . . . . . . . .Delaware . . . . . . . . . . . . . . . . . . .1812
Reed, George . . . . . . . . . . . . .Delaware . . . . . . . . . . . . . . . . . . .1808
Reed, John H. . . . . . . . . . . . . .South Carolina . . . . . . . . . . . . . .1809
Reeve, Aaron B. . . . . . . . . . . .Connecticut . . . . . . . . . . . . . . . . .1802
Reynolds, Walter. . . . . . . . . . .New York . . . . . . . . . . . . . . . . . . .1822
Richards, George H. . . . . . . .Connecticut . . . . . . . . . . . . . . . . .1809
Richards, Henry S. . . . . . . . .New York . . . . . . . . . . . . . . . . . . .1826
Richards, Robert K. . . . . . . . .New York . . . . . . . . . . . . . . . . . . .1829
Rideley, Greensburg . . . . . . .Kentucky . . . . . . . . . . . . . . . . . . .1816
Ridgate, Benjamin . . . . . . . . .Maryland . . . . . . . . . . . . . . . . . . .1814
Ridout, Addison . . . . . . . . . . Maryland . . . . . . . . . . . . . . . . . . .1813
Robbins, Samuel H. . . . . . . . .Connecticut . . . . . . . . . . . . . . . . .1817
Robbins, Silas . . . . . . . . . . . .Conn.—Judge, Kentucky. . . . . . .1808
Rogers, Archibald G. . . . . . . .New York . . . . . . . . . . . . . . . . . . .1823
Rogers, Artemas . . . . . . . . . .Connecticut . . . . . . . . . . . . . . . . .1811
Rogers, Charles W. . . . . . . . .Georgia . . . . . . . . . . . . . . . . . . . .1829
Rogers, Edward . . . . . . . . . . .Delaware . . . . . . . . . . . . . . . . . . .1810
Rogers, Henry A. . . . . . . . . . .Rhode Island . . . . . . . . . . . . . . .1821
Rogers, Henry B. . . . . . . . . . .Massachusetts . . . . . . . . . . . . . .1823
Rogers, Henry W. . . . . . . . . . .Connecticut . . . . . . . . . . . . . . . . .1810
Rogers, Henry . . . . . . . . . . . .Pennsylvania . . . . . . . . . . . . . . . .1823
Rogers, John . . . . . . . . . . . . .Delaware . . . . . . . . . . . . . . . . . . .1813
Rogers, Moulton C. . . . . . . . .Delaware—Judge, Pennsylvania.1807
Rogers, William M. . . . . . . . .Georgia . . . . . . . . . . . . . . . . . . . .1829
Ross, Thomas . . . . . . . . . . . .Pennsylvania . . . . . . . . . . . . . . . .1827
Ruggles, Heman . . . . . . . . . .Connecticut . . . . . . . . . . . . . . . . .1803
Ruggles, Henry J. . . . . . . . . . .New York . . . . . . . . . . . . . . . . . . .1832
Rutledge, Benj. H. . . . . . . . . .South Carolina . . . . . . . . . . . . . .1817
Rutherford, John . . . . . . . . . .Georgia . . . . . . . . . . . . . . . . . . . .1829
Rutherford, Robert . . . . . . . .Georgia . . . . . . . . . . . . . . . . . . . .1806

## S

Samuel, Beverly . . . . . . . . . . .South Carolina . . . . . . . . . . . . . .1819
Samson, John P. C. . . . . . . . .New York . . . . . . . . . . . . . . . . . . .1817
Sankey, Joseph S. . . . . . . . . .Georgia . . . . . . . . . . . . . . . . . . . .1826
Sanford, Rollin . . . . . . . . . . . .Connecticut . . . . . . . . . . . . . . . . .1831
Sargent, William F. W. . . . .Mississippi . . . . . . . . . . . . . . . . . .1817
Saunders, Curtis H. . . . . . . . .Tennessee . . . . . . . . . . . . . . . . . .1833
Schley, John T. . . . . . . . . . . . .Maryland . . . . . . . . . . . . . . . . . . .1828
Schell, Augustus . . . . . . . . . . .New York . . . . . . . . . . . . . . . . . . .1831
Schuyler, Robert . . . . . . . . . .New York . . . . . . . . . . . . . . . . . . .1818
Scott, John Ray . . . . . . . . . . .New York . . . . . . . . . . . . . . . . . . .1807
Scott, Jessup W. . . . . . . . . . .Connecticut . . . . . . . . . . . . . . . . .1822
Scudder, Phillip J. . . . . . . . . .New Jersey . . . . . . . . . . . . . . . . . .1813
Sedgwick, Harry . . . . . . . . . .Massachusetts . . . . . . . . . . . . . . .1807

| | | |
|---|---|---|
| Sedgwick, Philo C. | Connecticut | 1831 |
| Selden, Ulysses | Connecticut | 1802 |
| Sewall, William H. | Maryland | 1816 |
| Seymour, Henry | Conn.—M. of C.; Gov. of Conn. | 1829 |
| Seymour, Horatio | Conn.—L.L.D; U. S. Senator Vt. | 1798 |
| Seymour, Isaac G. | Georgia | 1825 |
| Seymour, Origen S. | Conn.—M. of C.; Judge and Chief Justice | 1824 |
| Seymour, Osias | Vermont | 1821 |
| Shaffer, Joseph L. | Georgia | 1825 |
| Shaumburgh, Charles W. | Louisiana | 1827 |
| Shaw, Henry | New York—Mem. of Congress | 1810 |
| Sheldon, Daniel | Connecticut | 1798 |
| Shelden, William | Connecticut | 1822 |
| Sheldon, Isaac | Connecticut | 1810 |
| Shelton, Stephen | Connecticut | 1809 |
| Shepard, Samuel | | 1799 |
| Sherman, Elkanah C. | New York | 1825 |
| Sherrell, Joseph | Massachusetts | 1815 |
| Sill, Theodore | Connecticut | 1798 |
| Simkins, Eldred | South Carolina—M. C.; Lt.-Gov. S. C. | 1803 |
| Sims, John G. | Pennsylvania | 1812 |
| Simons, Moses | South Carolina | 1810 |
| Simmons, Edward P. | South Carolina | 1815 |
| Skinner, John B. | Connecticut | 1820 |
| Skinner, Oliver | Connecticut | 1800 |
| Skinner, Richard | Conn.—Chief Jus. and Gov Vt. | 1798 |
| Skinner, Roger S. | Connecticut | 1815 |
| Sloan, Douglass W. | Massachusetts | 1804 |
| Slosson, Barazilli | New York | 1830 |
| Smith, Archibald | New York | 1814 |
| Smith, Charles | Massachusetts | 1810 |
| Smith, Henry B. | Massachusetts | 1809 |
| Smith James H. | North Carolina | 1818 |
| Smith, Joseph L. | Conn.—Judge Florida; U. S. | 1800 |
| Smith, Junius | Conn.—L.L.D; 1st ocean steamship, Tea grower | 1802 |
| Smith, Ira | Connecticut | 1809 |
| Smith, Lemuel | Massachusetts | 1817 |
| Smith, Levi B. | Pennsylvania | 1825 |
| Smith, Nathaniel B. | Connecticut | 1817 |
| Smith, Perry | Conn.—U. S. Senator | 1807 |
| Smith, Truman | Conn.—M. of C.; U. S. Senator | 1817 |
| Smallwood, William A. | District Columbia | 1824 |
| Spaulding, Richard B. | Georgia | 1809 |
| Sparks, William H. | Georgia | 1820 |

ORIGEN S. SEYMOUR

| | | |
|---|---|---|
| Spaight, Charles G. | Georgia | 1822 |
| Spires, Bracney T. | North Carolina | 1832 |
| Sprague, Peleg | Massachusetts—U. S. Senator | 1813 |
| Speed, Robert H. | Virginia | 1827 |
| Spencer, Alexander O. | New York | 1818 |
| Spencer, Oliver M. | Ohio | 1829 |
| Spooner, William | Massachusetts | 1813 |
| Stagg, Peter | New York | 1823 |
| Stansbury, G. A. | New York | 1827 |
| Stanley, Henry | New York | 1801 |
| Stark, Caleb, Jr. | Vermont | 1823 |
| Stark, Wyatt | South Carolina | 1811 |
| Starr, Ephraim, Jr. | Connecticut | 1803 |
| Starr, Henry | Connecticut | 1809 |
| Steele, William F. | Maryland | 1814 |
| Sterrett, John | Pennsylvania | 1822 |
| Sterrett, William P. | Georgia | 1821 |
| Stewart, Charles S. | New York | 1817 |
| Stiles, Joseph C. | Georgia | 1817 |
| Stiles, Richard | Georgia | 1822 |
| Stone, Gregory D. | New Hampshire | 1823 |
| Stoddart, John T. | Maryland | 1813 |
| Storrs, Juba | Connecticut | 1806 |
| Stevens, Henry W. | Connecticut | 1811 |
| Stevens, John L. | New York | 1823 |
| Stevens, Thomas | Georgia | 1823 |
| Strobel, Martin | South Carolina | 1806 |
| Strong, Elisha B. | Conneticut | 1810 |
| Strong, Martin | Connecticut | 1801 |
| Strong, Moses M. | Vermont | 1830 |
| Strong, Theron | Connecticut | 1822 |
| Stuart, Francis | South Carolina | 1809 |
| Stuart, Josephus B. | Massachusetts | 1812 |
| Sullivan, James | Massachusetts | 1822 |
| Sutherland, Josiah, Jr. | New York—M. C.; Judge Sp.Ct. | 1825 |
| Sweezy, Thomas | Massachusetts | 1811 |
| Swift, Benjamin | Vermont—U. S. Senator | 1801 |
| Swift, William | Vermont | 1817 |

## T

| | | |
|---|---|---|
| Tabor, William J. | Connecticut | 1813 |
| Tallifero, William F. | Virginia | 1813 |
| Tallmadge, Frederick A. | Conn.—M. C. from N. Y. | 1811 |
| Tatnall, Edward F. | Georgia—Member of Congress | 1810 |
| Taylor, Edwin M. | Massachusetts | 1832 |

| | | |
|---|---|---|
| Taylor, Hubbard | Kentucky | 1810 |
| Taylor, James S. | Virginia | 1818 |
| Taylor, John Gilman | Massachusetts | 1803 |
| Taylor, William | South Carolina | 1828 |
| Teakle, James D. | Maryland | 1817 |
| Tellfair, Josiah | Georgia | 1804 |
| Tellfair, Thomas | Georgia | 1806 |
| Tenney, William | New Hampshire—M. of C. | 1809 |
| Terry, Alfred | Connecticut | 1823 |
| Thayer, James | Massachusetts | 1815 |
| Thweat, Uriah | Georgia | 1802 |
| Thomas, Alexander | Georgia | 1810 |
| Thomas, Charles, Jr. | Delaware | 1812 |
| Thompson, Henry | Massachusetts | 1814 |
| Thorndike, Larkin | Massachusetts | 1809 |
| Todd, Charles | Kentucky | 1810 |
| Tolman, Thomas | Kentucky | 1813 |
| Torrey, Charles | Massachusetts | 1814 |
| Tracy, George H. | New York | 1830 |
| Treat, Selah B. | Connecticut | 1825 |
| Trescott, Henry | South Carolina | 1815 |
| Trotter, James G. | Kentucky | 1809 |
| Troup, Robert R. | New York | 1809 |
| Tucker, George J. | | 1824 |
| Tuthill, Cornelius | New York | 1815 |
| Twining, Thomas, Jr. | Massachusetts | 1814 |
| Tyler, Nathan | Connecticut | 1825 |

## V

| | | |
|---|---|---|
| Vandusen, William | Connecticut | 1803 |
| Vanderheyden, Samuel | New York | 1820 |
| Vandyke, Kensey J. | New Jersey | 1818 |
| Vanmeter, John J. | Virginia | 1821 |
| Van Wagener, Gerritt G. | New York | 1823 |
| Verplank, James D. | New York | 1827 |

## W

| | | |
|---|---|---|
| Wager, John | Virginia | 1823 |
| Wakeman, Jonathan | Connecticut | 1807 |
| Waldo, William B | New York | 1828 |
| Walburg, George M. | Georgia | 1815 |
| Walker, Charles | Massachusetts | 1822 |
| Walker, George J. S. | Georgia | 1826 |
| Wallace, James W | Pennsylvania | 1829 |
| Waring, Nathaniel F | New York | 1827 |

| | | |
|---|---|---|
| Ward, Isaac | New Jersey | 1813 |
| Ward, Richard R | New York | 1817 |
| Ward, Solomon | Massachusetts | 1802 |
| Warner, Eli | Connecticut | 1808 |
| Warner, Thomas | Massachusetts | 1809 |
| Waterhouse, Andrew O. | Massachusetts | 1811 |
| Watson, John B. | Connecticut | 1815 |
| Watson, Samuel | Massachusetts | 1826 |
| Watson, William | Connecticut | 1831 |
| Webber, Sumner A. | Massachusetts | 1823 |
| Weeks, Alfred A. | New York | 1823 |
| Wells, Ralph | Connecticut | 1812 |
| Welles, Thomas L. | New York | 1823 |
| Weems, James J. | District Columbia | 1820 |
| Wetmore, William | Connecticut | 1815 |
| Wheeler, Justice P. | Massachusetts | 1804 |
| White, John P. | Connecticut | 1799 |
| White, Thomas | Georgia | 1816 |
| White, William | New Hampshire | 1818 |
| Whiting, John C. | Massachusetts | 1823 |
| Whitman, John | | 1808 |
| Whitman, Lemuel | Connecticut—Mem. of Congress | 1805 |
| Whittlesey, Elisha D. | Connecticut—Mem. of Congress | 1813 |
| Whittlesey, Frederick | Conn.—M. of Congress; Judge Sup. Court N. Y. | 1819 |
| Whittlesey, Thomas T. | Connecticut—Mem. of Congress | 1818 |
| Wight, John L. | Virginia | 1824 |
| Williams, David | Louisiana | 1816 |
| Williams, Henry F. | Louisiana | 1818 |
| Williams, Jared W. | | 1820 |
| Williams, Lemuel | Massachusetts | 1806 |
| Williams, Thomas S. | Connecticut | 1797 |
| Williams, William G. | Massachusetts | 1799 |
| Wilkins, Edmond | North Carolina | 1817 |
| Wilkins, John L. | North Carolina | 1820 |
| Wilson, Andrew P. | Pennsylvania | 1825 |
| Winslow, Edward D. | North Carolina | 1831 |
| Winship, John C. M. | Massachusetts | 1810 |
| Wittich, Lucius L. | Georgia | 1824 |
| Wolcott, Oliver S. | Connecticut | 1818 |
| Wood, James | | 1798 |
| Woodbridge, William | Ohio—U. S. Senator | 1802 |
| Woodbury, Levi | New Hampshire—Gov. of N. H.; Sec. of Navy and Treas.; Judge of U. S. Sup. Court | 1809 |
| Woolridge, Thomas | South Carolina | 1815 |

Woodruff, George C.........Connecticut—Mem. of Congress.1825
Woodruff, Lewis B.........Conn.—L.L.D.; Judge Sup. Ct. Ct. of Appeal N. Y. and Judge of Circuit Ct. N. Y., Conn. and Vermont ....................1830
Worthington, Perry .......Maryland ....................1831
Wright, Augustus R .......Georgia—Judge Sup. Court....1833

## Y

Yates, Metcalf ............New York ....................1821
Yates, William ............New York ....................1824
Young, Charles C. ..........New York ....................1827
Young, Ebenezer ..........Connecticut—Mem. of Congress.1809

| | |
|---|---|
| Number on Catalogue.......... | 805 |
| Students previous to 1798...... | 210 |
| Whole number ............... | 1015 |

# Biographies

# BIOGRAPHICAL NOTES

OF

# LITCHFIELD COUNTY

# BENCH, BAR

AND

# COUNTY OFFICERS

# BIOGRAPHICAL NOTES

In the following sketches the compiler has endeavored to give in most cases only a very brief account of the legal history of the person with no attempt at genealogy, or comments upon the life or character. The information has been drawn from a great variety of sources and is believed to be in the main correct. It is, however, merely an index of the names of those who have contributed their lives and energies to make our Mountain County deserve its high and noble record of the past and to incite our present and future attorneys to uphold and maintain the lofty standard that their sires have bequeathed them.

"The lives of great men all remind us
That we can make our lives sublime
And dying leave behind us
Footprints on the sands of time."

ELISHA S. ABERNETHY, was a son of General Russell Abernethy, of Torrington, born October 24, 1805. He entered Yale College when sixteen years old and graduated in 1825. Admitted to the bar and practiced in Waterbury, removed to Torrington and afterwards to Bridgeport, where he was the Clerk of the Superior Court of Fairfield County from 1859 to the time of his death in 1869.

ANDREW ADAMS, LL.D., was born in Stratford in 1736 and graduated at Yale College in 1760, settled in Litchfield. He rose to the rank of Colonel in the Revolutionary War, was a member of the Council of Safety two years, of the State Council for nine years, a member of the Continental Congress three years and Speaker of the House of Representatives in 1779 and 1780. He was an associate Judge of the Superior Court for four years and the Chief Justice from 1793 to the time of his decease, November 27, 1797.

The Litchfield *Monitor* mentions it as a sad and singular coincidence that Governor Wolcott and Chief Justice Adams (the two highest official dignitaries of the State), both residing in the same village and on the same street should be lying apparently at the point of death at the same time. Governor Wolcott survived his distinguished neighbor only three days.

Upon a rapidly crumbling marble slab in the West burying ground in Litchfield, is the following epitaph of this eminent man:

"In memory of the Hon. Andrew Adams, Esq., Chief Judge of the Superior Court, who died November 27, 1797, in the 63d year of his age. Having filled many distinguished offices with great ability and dignity, he was promoted to the highest judicial office in the State, which he held for several years, in which his eminent talents shone with uncommon lustre, and were exerted to the great advantage of the public and the honor of the High Court in which he presided. He made an early profession of religion, and zealously sought to promote its true Interests. He lived a Life and died the Death of a Christian. His filial Piety and paternal tenderness are held in sweet Remembrance."

ELIJAH ADAMS, was a son of Chief Justice Adams. He studied law with Judge Reeve and was admitted to this bar in 1795, practiced his profession a few years in Litchfield and then moved to Geneva, New York.

SAMUEL ADAMS, was a native of Milford, Conn., but in early life went to Stratford, where he married Mary Fairchild. He became a prominent lawyer and a Judge of the Fairfield County Court. A few years before his death, which occurred November 12, 1788, in his 85th year, he removed to Litchfield and assisted his son, the Hon. Andrew Adams, in his extensive practice. His widow died August 29, 1803, in the 106th year of her age, having lived in three centuries.

JOHN Q. ADAMS, born in Cornwall, November 2, 1837. Was admitted to this bar in 1864, and located at West Cornwall, where he practiced until April, 1872, when he removed to Negaunee, Michigan, where he made a fortune by his practice and successful mining investments. He has held many and important political and executive positions and is widely known.

JOHN ADAMS, was born in Canaan June 22, 1785. He was admitted to this bar in 1825. He carried on a very large business in the iron industry at Woodville, in the town of Washington, and was interested in other iron works. It does not appear that he ever practiced law. He removed to Litchfield and from thence to Falls Village in the town of Canaan, where he died about 1871.

J. HENRY ADAM, only son of John Adams, was born at Woodville, town of Washington, December 29, 1822, graduated at Yale College 1842, and was admitted to this bar in 1844. Soon after he removed to New York City and began the practice of his profession, which he relinquished and became interested in the lighting of the city; was president of the gas company and acquired much wealth.

JOHN F. ADDIS, is a native of New Milford, Connecticut. Studied law with his uncle John S. Turrill, Esq., and was admitted to this bar in 1882. Resides and practices in his native town, and is Judge of Probate for the district of New Milford.

EDMOND AIKEN, was admitted to this bar in 1790 from Norfolk, Connecticut. He practiced in that town and was also engaged in keeping a country store. He died in 1807.

JOHN AIKEN was admitted to the bar in 1800 from Sharon.

JOHN A. ALBRO was admitted to this bar in 1821. He abandoned this profession and became a clergyman.

JOHN ALLEN.—A long biography of this eminent attorney will be found in Boardman's sketches, page 45 of this book.

On a simple headstone in the East Cemetery in Litchfield appears the following epitaph:

To the memory of JOHN ALLEN, ESQ.
Many years during a life of eminent usefulness, highly distinguished for his integrity and patriotism as a member of the Council and Supreme Court of Errors of Connecticut, and no less distinguished during a period interesting and critical to his country as a member of the Congress of the United States.
Born June 12, 1763.
Died July 31, 1812.
Aged, 49 years.

Henry J. Allen, Sheriff 1884-1895. He was born in Manchester, Connecticut, May 26, 1831. He came to Litchfield County in 1859, and engaged in the hotel business in the then village of "Wolcottville" as the proprietor of the well known "Allen House," which he kept until 1880. During much of this time he was employed as an agent or trustee in the management and settlement of large estates, and was very successful therein. He was also a constable and especially noted from his skill in collecting doubtful claims. He enjoyed political life and was a shrewd worker. In 1884 his party elected him Sheriff, which office he held until 1895, when he was defeated.

He had the unpleasant duty of carrying into effect the first and only execution of the death penalty of the century. His great executive ability was fully felt throughout the County. After his retirement he was active in the interests of the New York Mutual Life Insurance Company, of which he had been an agent for many years, and also in the management of various trust estates. He died October 9, 1899, and his funeral at Torrington on October 11 was remarkable for the attendance of many prominent citizens of the State. See picture, page 164.

Charles B. Andrews, LL.D., was born in Sunderland, Massachusetts, in 1834. Graduated at Amherst College in 1858. Admitted to the bar of Fairfield County in 1861, and began his practice in the town of Kent.

In 1863 he removed to Litchfield and formed a partnership with Hon. John H. Hubbard, then a member of Congress. He was elected Senator from the Fifteenth District in 1868 and 1869, and was chairman of the Judiciary committee in 1869, a member of the House of Representatives in 1878, and again chairman of the Judiciary Committee. Was elected Governor of the State of Connecticut in 1879, which office he held two years. Became a Judge of the Superior Court in 1882 and Chief Justice of the Supreme Court in 1889, which office he resigned October 1, 1901. He was unanimously elected by the electors of Litchfield member of the Constitutional Convention of 1902, of which body he was the presiding officer.

He died suddenly at Litchfield September 12, 1902. His legal obituary is in the seventy-fifth volume of Connecticut Reports, from which we quote the tribute paid to him by his successor, Chief Justice Torrance:

"This Court is fully sensible of the distinguished services rendered to this State by Chief Justice Andrews, and expresses its obligation to the Attorney General for the appropriate manner in which he has called the attention of the bench and bar to them on this occasion.

CHARLES B. ANDREWS.

"The Practice Act was enacted with the warm approval of Governor Andrews in 1879. Three years later, it became his duty, as a judge of the Superior Court, to aid in its administration,—a work which he continued on the bench of that and of this court for nearly twenty years. But the regulation of legal practice, however important, is but a small part of judicial labor. Chief Justice Andrews was an earnest student of law as a science,—of its fundamental principles, and philosophical development. Only such an one could have written such an opinion, for instance, as that from his pen, in the case of Wildman *vs.* Wildman, 70 Conn., 700, in which he analyzes with so much clearness and precision the nature of a cause of action.

"He was the seventeenth in the line of Chief Justices who presided in this court during the first hundred and seventeen years of its history, and of this number, only Judges Hosmer, Williams and Park held the office for as long a period.

"In a review of a history of the courts of Connecticut, on a public occasion, he once said this, 'In every government of laws, the courts hold the most important place. The legislature may be nominally higher than the judiciary, but in the actual experience of life, the courts touch the citizen more frequently and more nearly than the lawmaking power.'

"Acting under his conviction, he was deeply impressed by the responsibility which attaches to a judicial station. It was his ambition to discharge it with fidelity, and none of his associates on the bench failed to remark the earnestness of his convictions and the force and perspicuity with which he was able to set them forth. On the pages of our reports they have become interwoven with the jurisprudence of the State and of all the States."

CHARLES W. ANDREWS, only son and child of Judge Charles B. Andrews, was born in Litchfield November 21, 1874. Was admitted to the bar in 1902. He located in Hartford.

EDWARD WARREN ANDREWS, born at Windham, Connecticut, July, 1811, a son of Rev. William Andrews. Was at Union College but did not graduate, studied law and was admitted to this bar in 1834. He was for a time partner of the Hon. Truman Smith at Litchfield. He gave up the practice of law, studied theology and was settled in 1837 over the Congregational Chruch at West Hartford. About 1841 he went to New York to be pastor of the Broadway Tabernacle Church. After some years he went to Troy as the pastor of a Presbyterian church. He gave up preaching and established a school at Cornwall, Connecticut. He was sent to the Legislature in 1851. He then gave up teaching and resumed the practice of law in New York City. In the war of 1861 he was a captain and was made assistant adjutant general under General Morris at Fort McHenry, Baltimore. After the war he practiced law for a short time in West Virginia. He then returned to New York but soon left his profession. He died September, 1895, at Chicago, Illinois.

SAMUEL JAMES ANDREWS, son of Rev. William Andrews, born at Danbury, Connecticut, July, 1817. Graduated at Williams College in 1839. Studied law in Hartford and Boston and was admitted to this bar in 1842, was also admitted in New York City and removed to Ohio and was re-admitted there. In 1844 he left the law and studied theology, and was settled as pastor of the Congregational Church at East Windsor, Connecticut, 1848. Dismissed 1855. He became an author and student for some years. and in 1868 took charge of the "Catholic Apostolic" congregation in Hartford. He died in Hartford October, 1906. James P. Andrews the present reporter of the Supreme Court of Errors, is one of his sons.

CURTISS B. ATWOOD was born in Bethlehem in 1845. Was educated at Stamford Academy, New York, and at Brandon Seminary, Vermont. Studied law with Webster and O'Neil in Waterbury, and was admitted to the bar at New Haven in 1879. Now resides at Watertown but is not in active practice. Represented his town in the Legislature of 1905.

RALSAMON C. AUSTIN, was a son of the Hon. Aaron Austin, born in New Hartford, graduated from Yale College in 1801, and was admitted to this bar in 1808. He practiced a short time at Litchfield and then located in Peekskill, New York. He died at Washington, D. C., September 19, 1840.

ROGER AVERILL, born at Salisbury, August 4, 1809. Graduated at Union College, 1832. Admitted to this bar in 1834 and practiced at Salisbury until 1849, when he removed to Danbury, where he had a successful practice and held many important offices and was Lieutenant Governor of the State during the four years of the Civil war. He was one of the organizers of the American Bar Association. He died in Danbury, December 9, 1883. (Obituary in 50th Conn. Report.) See Warner's Reminiscences.

RUSSELL W. AYRES, of Waterbury, admitted 1869. He graduated at Yale, 1868, and afterwards at Harvard Law School. He was the founder of the shore resort at Woodmont, Connecticut. He died December 14, 1873.

ASA BACON, a native of Canterbury, Connecticut, born February 8, 1771, graduated at Yale College in 1793, and was admitted to this bar in 1795. After practicing in various places he removed to Litchfield in 1806, where for many years he held a leading position at the bar. He died in New Haven in 1857. (See Boardman and Sedgwick's sketches.) His picture appears in the Bacon group, page 62.

EPAPHRODITIS CHAMPION BACON, a son of Asa Bacon, born in Lichfield in 1810. Graduated at Yale College in 1833, and was admitted to this bar in 1840. He died at Seville in Spain, January 11, 1845. Picture on page 62.

GENERAL FRANCIS BACON was another son of Asa Bacon; born in Litchfield January 6, 1819, and graduated at Yale College in 1838. Was admitted to this bar in 1840; he was a young man of great promise, holding a high rank as a lawyer, and took great interest in military affairs, rising to the rank of Major General of the State militia. His death occurred September 16, 1849. Picture on page 62.

WILLARD BAKER was admitted to this bar in 1881. He located and resides in Sharon. He has a large office practice and real estate business.

BIRDSEY BALDWIN, born in Goshen, February 3, 1786. Studied law at Litchfield Law School and was admitted to practice in 1811.

He lived and practiced in his native town until 1841, when he removed to West Cornwall, where he died April 27, 1858. His picture is on page 115.

GEORGE BALDWIN, a native of Washington, Connecticut, was admitted to the bar in 1840. He relinquished the law for other pursuits.

GEORGE H. BALDWIN

GEORGE H. BALDWIN, Sheriff 1869-1878. He died in Litchfield December 2, 1879. The following obituary of him appeared in the Litchfield *Enquirer*:

"Our readers will notice, with deep regret, the death of ex-Sheriff George H. Baldwin, which occurred at his residence in this village on Tuesday morning. Mr. Baldwin was born on the 20th of September, 1827, and had entered upon his 53d year. His father, Captain Daniel Baldwin, was a man of great energy, and the son was of a similar nature. After a good education in our village schools, he served an apprenticeship in the Enquirer office. He subsequently published, for a short time, the Litchfield Republican, a democratic paper, and was the first publisher of the Sentinel. He was postmaster here for eight years, Judge of Probate for one year, and Sheriff of the county for nine years. He represented the town in the General Assembly in 1861, held the office of town clerk for five years, from 1858 to 1863, and was first selectman for several years succeeding. His friends were warmly attached to him, and he was noted for his generosity and neighborly kindness. In his family, he was a devoted husband and father, and his excellent widow and children have the heartfelt sympathy of the entire community."

ISAAC BALDWIN, was born in Milford, Connecticut, February 22, 1715-16. His father removed to Durham and subsequently to Litchfield.

He graduated at Yale College in 1735, and studied theology and was licensed to preach in 1737. He was never settled in this profession, but occasionally preached in neighboring churches.

He married a daughter of Parson Collins, the eccentric minister of Litchfield, bought a farm and went to farming. His services were soon demanded in public affairs and for many years he was a prominent man in town and county matters. He represented his town in the General Assembly ten sessions, and was town clerk for thirty-one years (1742-1773.)

He was clerk of the Probate Court for the district of Litchfield for twenty-nine years, and was the first clerk of the County Court, which office he held for forty-two years (1751-1793.) He died in Litchfield January 15, 1805.

Isaac Baldwin, Jr., born at Litchfield November 12, 1753. Graduated at Yale in 1774. Admitted to the bar and practiced at Litchfield until 1812, when he removed to Pompey, New York, where he died in 1830.

Roger Sherman Baldwin, born in New Haven, Connecticut in 1793. Was a member of the Litchfield Law School, and admitted to the bar of this county in 1813. He located in his native city, where he died February 19, 1863.

Probably no lawyer ever attained in Connecticut a higher rank at the bar than that which was generally conceded to Governor Baldwin by his professional brethren, and few men have filled more public offices than he. (For a more extended sketch of him see obituary in 30th Conn. Report.)

Samuel S. Baldwin was born in Litchfield, and graduated at Yale College in 1801. Was admitted to this bar in 1803 as of Litchfield. He died in 1854.

William Baldwin, lawyer at Salisbury 1842. (Conn. Register.)

Luther T. Ball was born in Salisbury, studied law with Judge D. J. Warner and at Ballston, New York, and was admitted to this bar in 1854. He removed to Illinois, where he acquired a good reputation as a lawyer. In the Civil War he was an officer of the Eighty-fourth Illinois regiment and was killed at the battle of Murfreesboro, December, 1862, and buried on the field.

Lorrin Barnes studied in the law school. Was admitted in 1807 and practiced a short time in Bristol.

Henry S. Barbour was a native of Canton, Connecticut. Born August 2, 1822. Studied law at Yale Law School and was admitted to this bar in 1849. He practiced at Torrington for twenty-one years, when he removed to Hartford, where he died September 21, 1891.

Sylvester Barbour was a brother of Henry S. Barbour and practiced law a short time about 1861 at New Hartford and is now in practice in Hartford.

ANSON BATES, admitted to the bar in 1820. The History of Hartford County says he practiced law at East Granby 1831-1869.

ROBERT C. BATES, admitted to the bar in 1811 as of Salisbury.

JOSIAH B. BATTELL, born in Woodbury March 1, 1776. Admitted to the bar in 1799 as of Torrington. Died May 7, 1843, in Torrington.

JESSE BEACH was born in Litchfield in 1769. He studied law with Judge Reeve and was admitted to the bar in 1791. The next year he married Sally Wheeler, of Derby, to which place he moved and practiced law there until 1801, when he removed to Redding, Connecticut.

J. GAIL BECKWITH, JR., was born in Litchfield in 1874. Graduated at Union College in 1896. Studied at Albany Law School and in the offices of Terry & Bronson and L. F. Burpee in Waterbury, where he engaged in practice for a short time. He served as Corporal of Company A, Tenth Battalion, First New York Volunteers, from April, 1898, to April, 1899. The regiment was ordered for service in the Philippines, but only went as far as Honolulu. Was admitted to the Litchfield bar in 1899. Was a deputy sheriff under Sheriff Middlebrook. Is engaged in journalism.

HEZEKIAH BEECHER, was born in Bethlehem, the son of Abraham Beecher. He was admitted to the bar in 1854. He removed to, and was an early settler of Fort Dodge, Iowa. Is now deceased.

PHILEMON BEECHER, a native of Kent, was born in 1775 and was admitted to this bar in 1800 as from Sharon. He soon removed to Lancaster, Ohio. Henry Howe in his Historical Collections says of him: "He represented this district in Congress from 1817 to 1827, and died about 1840. Was in politics a whig, and a man of fine address and presence. He it was who gave Thomas Ewing his first law business of any moment. The very elegant Henry Stanbery, who began his law practice in Lancaster, and lived there for many years, married for his first wife the daughter of Mr. Beecher. He later lived at Columbus and in the vicinity of Cincinnati, and ended his professional career as Attorney General of the United States under General Jackson."

TRUMAN BEECHER, admitted in 1818 from Kent. Was a student of the law school.

FREDERICK BEERS was born in Woodbury July 23, 1785 and was admitted to this bar in 1815. He died in Woodbury on December 6, 1828, at the age of 43.

George W. Beers was a son of Hon. Seth P. Beers and was born in Litchfield February 18, 1817. He graduated from Trinity College in 1839, and was admitted to this bar in 1842. He never practiced his profession, but was an assistant for his father in the care and management of the immense interests of the School Fund in the Western Reserve of Ohio. He died at Litchfield.

Lewis F. Beers was admitted in 1864 to this bar from Winsted. He studied with Judge Gideon Hall, and remained in his office in Winsted a short time after Judge Hall's death ,when he removed to South Norwalk, where he died February 15, 1872.

Seth P. Beers, a native of Woodbury, born July 4, 1781. Was a student of the Litchfield Law School from 1803 to 1805, when he was admitted to this bar and settled in the practice of his profession in Litchfield, where he died September 9, 1862. He had a large clientage and occupied many positions of trust. He was State's Attorney for the county 1820 to 1825. His principal work was commissioner of the School Fund of Connecticut from 1824 to 1849, a period of twenty-five years, during which time the settlement of a very large number of contested land claims and titles in the Ohio land, known as the Western Reserve, had to be adjusted by him. It is largely through his legal and financial ability that our present school fund of $2,000,000 exists. Died September 9, 1862 at Litchfield. (See Sedgwick's address.) Picture on page 92.

Frederick D. Beeman, was a native of Warren, graduated at Yale, class of 1842, and was admitted to this bar in 1846, and settled and began practice in Litchfield. In 1855 he was appointed clerk of the Superior Court, which office he held at the time of his death, August 1, 1860, aged 38 years. Picture on page 138.

Charles O. Belden, born in Montecello, New York, in 1827, was admitted to practice in 1848. After practicing a short time at Litchfield he removed to Milwaukee, Wisconsin. In 1861 he took an active part in the Civil War, organizing the Sixty-seventh New York Volunteers, of which he was the Lieutenant Colonel and was in several engagements. At the close of the war his health failed and he was unable to follow his profession. He died in Litchfield November 22, 1870.

Joseph H. Bellamy, a native of Bethlehem, was a grandson of the celebrated divine Joseph Bellamy, D. D. He graduated at Yale College in 1808, and was admitted to this bar in 1810 and resided and practiced in Bethlehem, where he died in 1848. (See Sedgwick's Address.)

Amos Benedict, born in Middlebury, Connecticut, July 6, 1780, graduated at Yale College 1800, studied law in the Litchfield Law

School and was admitted to practice in 1803. After practicing a short time in Litchfield he removed to Watertown, New York. He died in 1816 while on a visit to Litchfield.

NOAH B. BENEDICT, born in Woodbury, April 2, 1771. Graduated at Yale 1788. Admitted to the bar in 1792 and died July 2, 1831. He was one of the most learned and distinguished lawyers in the State. (See Boardman's sketches and Sedgwick's Address and note in 8th Conn. Report 426, also obituary in 15th Conn. Report.) His portrait is on page 58, taken from an old painting in the Woodbury Probate office.

MILO L. BENNETT, admitted in 1813, as of Sharon. Removed to Vermont and was a Judge of the Supreme Court of that State.

HEMAN BERRY, admitted 1796, as of Kent.

JOHN B. BETTS, admitted to this bar in 1882; practiced a short time in New Hartford; removed to the West. He died in Beatrice, Nebraska, and was buried in New Hartford, January 24, 1902.

WILLIAM W. BIDWELL, born in Colebrook in 1850 and admitted to this bar in 1858, located in Collinsville, where he practiced his profession and was killed by accident in 1894.

WILLIAM W. BIERCE was born at Cornwall Bridge in 1863; graduated at Williams College in 1885 and was admitted to this bar in 1891. Is now in practice at Torrington, where he was the town clerk and town prosecuting attorney, and is also one of the prosecuting agents for Litchfield County.

HENRY A. BILLS, admitted to this bar in 1851, practiced a short time in Winsted, Connecticut. Published for some years the Winsted *News*, and then followed other avocations. He died June 24, 1892.

HON. JOHN BIRD, born in Litchfield, November 22, 1768, graduated at Yale College in 1786, was admitted to this bar in 1789, and after a practice of five years removed to Troy, New York, where he resided until his death in 1806. During these few years he held many important positions and was a member of Congress.

EDWARD BISSELL, a native of Litchfield, born November 27, 1808, and admitted to this bar in 1832. He afterwards entered the United States naval service, and died January 24, 1876.

EDWARD BISSELL, born in Litchfield, December 16, 1827, and graduated at Yale College in 1851, and at the Yale Law School in 1853, and was admitted to this bar in 1853. He removed to Fond du Lac, Wisconsin, where he now resides.

FRANCIS BISSELL, born in Litchfield April 16, 1852, and admitted to this bar in 1875. He practiced a short time in New Hartford , then went into the insurance business, from which he retired, and is now engaged in agriculture at Bantam.

EBENEZER B. BLACKMAN, graduated at Yale College in 1817, admitted to this bar in 1822 and practiced at Sharon, whence he removed to Brookfield in 1840 and died there in 1863.

LEWIS J. BLAKE, admitted to this bar in 1874 and began practice in Litchfield, but soon removed west, and is now a law stenographer and teacher at Omaha, Nebraska.

J. W. BLAKESLEE, admitted in 1866, as of Plymouth.

SAMUEL C. BLAKELEY, admitted in 1800 from Roxbury.

WILLIAM H. BLODGETT, a native of Canaan. Admitted to this bar in 1903. He located in Winsted and is now Town Prosecuting Attorney. He was assistant clerk of the Connecticut House of Representatives in 1907.

DAVID SHERMAN BOARDMAN, born in New Milford in 1768, graduated at Yale in 1793 and admitted to this bar in 1795. He located and practiced all his lifetime in his native town, where he died December 2, 1864. President Porter, of Yale College, in his sketch of Mr. Boardman, published in the history of New Milford, says: "There have been few, if any of the inhabitants of New Milford since its settlement, who deserve to be more honored than this pure minded, sagacious and noble hearted man." He is the author of the sketches published herewith. See Sedgwick's Address.

GEORGE S. BOARDMAN, a native of New Milford, son of Hon. Elijah Boardman, born 1799, admitted to this bar in 1820 and died in New Milford 1825. (See Sedgwick's Address.)

WILLIAM WHITING BOARDMAN, another son of Hon. Elijah Boardman was born 1794 graduated at Yale College in 1812 and admitted to this bar in 1818. He removed to New Haven, where he had a large practice and held many public offices—member of Congress, etc. Died August 27, 1871.

WILLIAM D. BOSLER, born in New York City February 23, 1877. Studied law with L. J. Nickerson, of West Cornwall, and admitted to this bar in 1902. Commenced practice at West Cornwall, but in 1906 he removed to New York City, and is now connected with the District Attorney's office.

CHARLES BOSTWICK was born in New Milford, graduated at Yale College in 1796, and studied law under Judge Reeve, of Litchfield, begun to practice his profession but subsequently went into commercial pursuits in New York. Later he removed to Bridgeport, where he was elected mayor in 1840 and served afterwards as city judge.

JOSEPH A. BOSTWICK, of New Milford, admitted in 1804.

SAMUEL BOSTWICK was born in New Milford in 1755 and graduated at Yale College in 1780. He practiced law in his native town until his death, April 3, 1799.

HENRY A. BOTSFORD

HENRY A. BOTSFORD was born in Watertown in 1821 and died at Hartford, April 14, 1895. He was Sheriff from 1866 to 1869. He came to Litchfield from Salisbury, where he had been deputy sheriff for ten years and about 1870 he removed to Winsted and in 1872 to Hartford and engaged in the wholesale Chicago dressed beef business. He received the first car of that commodity from Chicago shipped to any point in New England, except to Boston. He was a genial, kind-hearted gentleman and made no enemies in his official and business life.

JOHN A. BOUGHTON was admitted to this bar in 1862. He soon removed to Bridgeport, Conn. He was for many years connected with the internal revenue service. Is not now in the practice of his legal profession.

JOHN BOYD was born in Winsted March 17, 1799. He graduated at Yale College in 1821 and was admitted to the bar of New Haven County in 1825, and to this bar in 1826. Representative in the General Assembly 1830 and 1835; County Commissioner 1840, 1849 and 1850; State Senator 1854, and President *pro tem;* town clerk of Winchester about thirty years and died in 1881.

He was Secretary of the State of Connecticut 1859, 1860 and 1861. One of the mottoes used in some of the political campaigns of the State was, "Give us your hand, honest John Boyd." He compiled and published the annals of Winchester. It is to him that the State is indebted for the preservation of so much as remains of the original charter granted by King Charles II. In 1698 the duplicate of the patent was by the Governor and council placed in the hands of Captain Joseph Wadsworth "in a very troublesome season when our constitution was struck at" and was safely kept and preserved by him until May 1715. This history is worth recording here.

"In 1817 or 1816, while Mr. Boyd was preparing for college at the Hartford Grammar School, he boarded in the family of Rev. Dr. Flint, of the South Church, Hartford.

"Coming one day from school he noticed on the workstand of Mrs. Bissell, the doctor's mother-in-law, a dingy piece of parchment, covered on one side with black letter manuscript. In answer to his inquiries Mrs. Bissell told him that having occasion for some pasteboard her friend and neighbor, Mrs. Wyllys, had sent her this. Mr. Boyd proposed to procure her a piece of pasteboard in exchange for the parchment, to which Mrs. Bissell consented. It was not, however, until six or eight years had elapsed when Mr. Boyd examined the parchment with care, when he learned for the first time that he had what he thought and was generally thought, until recently, was a duplicate of the charter."

The Colonial Record, Vol. IV., published in 1868, says:

"The original charter, which now hangs in the secretary's office at Hartford, is engraved on three skins. The duplicate was written on two. So much of the duplicate as remains being about three-fourths of the second skin, is now in the library of the Connecicut Historical Society, where it was placed by Hon. John Boyd, late Secretary of State."

Not long ago, however, search was made through the records in London and it was found that five pounds was the fee paid for drafting the original charter and twenty shillings for the duplicate. Examination of the documents showed that twenty shillings was written (probably a memorandum) on the supposed original charter and five pounds on the supposed duplicate so that now it is certain that the one saved by Mr. Boyd was the original and the one that hung for years in the secretary's office and has been recently hung in the State library is the duplicate.

The Mrs. Wyllys spoken of was related to the former Secretary of the State by that name and the parchment was probably found with his effects.

Connecticut lived under this charter until 1818, forty-two years after the Declaration of Independence."

Abraham Bradley, Jr., was born in Litchfield 1767. Studied law with Judge Reeve and was admitted to the bar in 1791. He located in the valley of the Wyoming, Pennsylvania. Soon after he accepted a position under Colonel Pickering, then the Postmaster

General of the United States at Washington. He removed to Washington, D. C., and was assistant postmaster general, under various administrations for nearly forty years. He and his brother, Phineas, were the real organizers of the postoffice department of the United States.

ALBERT P. BRADSTREET was born in Thomaston in 1846, graduated at Yale College in 1871, and Columbia Law School in 1873. He was admitted to the bar in 1874 and took up practice in Thomaston. He was a member of the General Assembly in 1872-78, and in 1881 and 1882 was elected to the Senate from the Sixteenth District, being the first Republican who was returned from that district for several years. He was town clerk of Thomaston from 1875 to 1891, and Judge of Probate from 1872 to 1890. In 1879 he was appointed deputy judge of the Waterbury district court and in 1883 he was elected Judge of the same court, being re-elected in 1887 and 1893. He is now in business in New York City.

NELSON BREWSTER was admitted from Cornwall in 1824. He resided in Goshen and had a very limited practice. He died in 1850.

JAMES T. BREEN was admitted from Winsted in 1881, located in the West.

DANIEL N. BRINSMADE

DANIEL N. BRINSMADE, of Washington, was the son of the Rev. Daniel Brinsmade, the second pastor of the Society of Judea, afterwards the town of Washington. He was born in 1750, graduated at Yale College in 1772, read law at Sharon and was admitted to this bar and settled in his native town, where he practiced his profession for more than fifty years. In 1787 he was a delegate to the convention at Hartford that ratified the Constitution of the United States. He was justice of the quorum and assistant judge of the County Court for sixteen years. He represented his town in the Legislature during forty-three sessions and was one session clerk of the House of Representatives. He died in 1826.

CLIFFORD E. BRISTOL was admitted to this bar in 1882 and began practice at Norfolk and then removed to Plainville. He now resides in Winsted and is engaged in mercantile business.

MERRITT BRONSON was admitted to this bar in 1855 from New Hartford.

BENNETT BRONSON was a graduate of Yale College in 1797 and admitted to this bar in 1802 as of Southbury. He was born November 14, 1775, in Waterbury. He became a prominent man in Waterbury, as lawyer and banker, and died there December 11, 1850.

CHARLES R. BROWN was admitted to the bar in 1816 from Sharon.

SAMUEL BROWNSON was one of the early settlers of New Milford and its town clerk from 1714 to 1733. He was its first justice of the peace and also Judge of the New Haven County Court and died in 1733. He acted as attorney for the town on several occasions and is said to have been an attorney in fact.

ROGER BROWNSON was a brother of Samuel and succeeded him in the office of town clerk in New Milford and was there justice of the peace for a number of years. He died in 1758.

NORTON J. BUEL, born in Salisbury September 13, 1813. Studied law wth General Sedgwick and Judge Seymour and was admitted to the bar in 1834. Removed to New Haven County and died in New Haven March 6, 1864. See Warner's reminiscences.

EPAPHRUS W. BULL, born in Danbury in 1805, and was admitted to this bar in 1825. He went South in 1830 and was reported to have been killed by the Indians in Texas in its war of 1840.

WILLIAM BURKE was born in Ireland in 1820, came to America in 1838 and following the example of Roger Sherman, settled in New Milford, and while earning his living by shoemaking, studied law and was admitted to this bar in 1868. He removed to Danbury in 1869, and resided there at the time of his death in 1890. The History of Danbury says of him: "In social matters his kindness of heart, his ever ready smile and cordial bearing, his bright and sunny disposition, and his uprightness and strength of character made him many warm friends, who will long cherish a pleasant memory of him."

WILLIAM M. BURRALL was a native of Canaan and admitted to this bar in 1808. He was associate Judge of the County Court from 1829 to 1836, and after that its presiding Judge for two years. He died in Canaan in 1851, aged 77 years. (See Sedgwick's Address.)

JUDSON CANFIELD

WILLIAM PORTER BURRALL, was a son of the Hon. William M. Burrall, born in Canaan September 18, 1806. Immediately after his graduation from Yale College in 1826 he began the study of law with his father, attended the Litchfield Law School and was admitted to this bar April, 1829. He practiced law in his native town until October, 1838, when he removed to Bridgeport, Connecticut, and assumed the presidency of the Housatonic Railroad Company, then just organizing, which office he held till 1853, when he resigned. He was connected with the New York, New Haven & Hartford Railroad Company during its construction and the earlier years of its operation. He was also treasurer and president of the Illinois Central Railroad. In 1862 he was chosen vice-president of the Hartford and New Haven Railroad and in 1868 was made its president, and upon consolidation became the vice-president of the New York, New Haven & Hartford Railroad Company, which office he held at the time of his death at Hartford, March 3, 1874.

CHARLES D. BURRILL, of Litchfield, was born in Charleston, South Carolina, in 1854. He entered the class of 1878, Yale, and after studying at the Columbia Law School, was admitted to the Hartford bar in 1884. He removed to Litchfield in 1891.

CALVIN BUTLER, born in Waterbury in 1772. He began to study at Williams College but left at the close of the sophomore year and began the study of law at Norfolk. He was admitted to this bar in 1799, and finally located at Plymouth in 1806, where he died in 1845. He held many of the town offices, was a member of the Constitutional Convention in 1818. In 1839 he was appointed a Judge of the County Court for Litchfield County.

CALVIN R. BUTLER was a son of Calvin Butler, Esq., and born in Plymouth August 6, 1809, and was admitted to this bar in 1843. He died October 16, 1844.

MALCOMB N. BUTLER was another son of Calvin Butler, Esq., and was born in Plymouth, June 26, 1826, and admitted to this bar in 1846. He died in Plymouth February 29, 1848.

S. MCLEAN BUCKINGHAM, born in Brooklyn, N. Y. October 3, 1876. Graduated at Yale 1899 and at Harvard Law School1902. Admitted to this bar 1903. Resides and practices at Watertown.

CURTISS W. CABLE was admitted to this bar in 1828.

DANIEL W. CADY, a native of Petersboro, New York, and a graduate of Cornell in 1878, was admitted to this bar in 1884. He removed to Kansas and was engaged as a law instructor until his death in 1885.

DAVID S. CALHOUN, born in Coventry, Connecticut, in 1827, graduated at Yale College in 1848. Studied law with Judge O. S. Seymour at Litchfield 1850-51, and was admitted to this bar December 18, 1851. Has practiced in Hartford County to the present time and for many years was Judge of the Court of Common Pleas for that county. He resides in Hartford.

GEORGE W. CAMP was admitted to the bar in 1882 from New Milford.

SAMUEL G. CAMP is a native of North Canaan. He was admitted to the bar in 1902. Resides and practices in his native village, and is largely interested in lime manufacturing.

EZRA CANFIELD was admitted to the bar in 1802 from Salisbury.

EDWARD T. CANFIELD was born in Thomaston, graduated at Yale College and Yale Law School in 1903, and admitted to this bar 1903. Practices his profession at Hartford, but resides in his native town, which he represented in the Legislature in 1907.

JOHN CANFIELD was born in New Milford in 1740 and graduated at Yale College in 1762; admitted to this bar in 1763 and settled in Sharon as the first lawyer who established himself in practice there. He was ten times sent from that town to the General Court and in 1786 he was a member of the Continental Congress and died the same year. He was State's Attorney for the county from 1772 until his death.

JOSEPH CANFIELD, JR., born in 1767 in Lyme, Connecticut, and removed with his father when he was young to Salisbury. He studied law with Colonel Strong and at the Litchfield Law School and was admitted to the bar in 1786. He located and practiced in Salisbury until his death in 1803.

JUDSON CANFIELD, born in New Milford January 24, 1759, and graduated at Yale College in 1782. He was admitted to the bar in 1785 and located and practiced in Sharon. He held many important official positions and was for many years one of the judges of the County Court. He was one of the purchasers of the school lands in Ohio and the county seat of Mahoning County was named after him. He died in New York City February 5, 1840.

HENRY J. CANFIELD was a son of Judson Canfield, born in Sharon, 1789, graduated from Yale College in 1806 and was admitted to this bar in 1810. In early life he removed to Ohio to take care of his father's interests in that State. Died November 27, 1856, at Canfield, Ohio.

SAMUEL CANFIELD was born in Milford and removed to New Milford early in its settlement. For many years he was the Justice

GEORGE CATLIN.

of the Peace and Town Clerk. Upon the organization of the county in 1751 he was one of the justices of the quorum for the county, and in 1754 was appointed the agent of the county for the building of the court house at Litchfield. He died December 14, 1754, aged 52. He was the father of Colonel Samuel Canfield, whose picture is shown on page 18. " But few men have a higher record than he at his age in the olden time."

ALBERT M. CARD, born in Amenia, New York, in 1845 and removed to Sharon while quite young. He was admitted to this bar in 1889. He represented Sharon in the Legislature in 1866 and in 1891. Is deceased.

LYMAN W. CASE was admitted to this bar in 1849 and resided in Winsted. He died May 9, 1892, at the age of 64, and the disposal of his large estate can be seen in the case of Pinney *vs.* Newton et al. in the Sixty-sixth Connecticut Reports.

ORRIN S. CASE, born in Canton and admitted to this bar in 1849. He practiced in Collinsville. In the war of the rebellion he was an officer in the Thirty-first Connecticut Volunteers and was killed before Petersburg, Virginia, August 6, 1864.

URIAH CASE, born in Canton in 1828, studied law with Elisha Johnson and was admitted to this bar in 1851. He practiced in Pine Meadow and Plainville, but finally removed to Hartford, where he now resides.

ABIJAH CATLING, of Harwinton, appears upon the records of the County Court as a practitioner in 1752.

GEORGE CATLIN, was a son of Putnam Catlin and was born in Wilkesbarre, Penn. He studied law in the Law School and was admitted to the Bar in 1817. After a few years practice in Pennsylvania he quit the profession and went to painting Indian portraits for which he has gained a world wide reputation. Our portrait of Judge Reeve is from Catlin's painting.

GEORGE SMITH CATLIN, born in Harwinton August 24th, 1808, and admitted to this bar in 1828. He practiced in Windham County from 1829 to 1853. He was a representative in Congress in 1843-45.

PUTNAM CATLIN, was born in Litchfield April 5, 1764 and admitted to the bar in 1786 and soon after removed to Pennsylvania and died at Great Bend in that state in 1842. He served in the revolutionary war and received a "Badge of Merit." He was the father of George Catlin the Indian painter.

ABIJAH CATLIN, born in Harwinton, Conn., April 1, 1805. Graduated at Yale in 1825 and was admitted to the bar in New Haven County in 1827. He practiced a few years in Georgia but returned in 1837 to Harwinton where he lived until his death, April 14, 1891. He held various public offices, representative to the General Assembly ten times, member of the Senate in 1844, Comptroller of the State 1847, 1848 and 1849, School Fund Commissioner 1852. Was Judge of the County Court a number of years. He was Chairman of the Bar Association for many years prior to his death and all his life an active participant in all reform matters of good citizenship. See his obituary in 60 Conn. Report.

JOHN D. CHAMPLIN, was born in Stonington, Conn. January 29, 1834, but in early life removed to Litchfield. He was admitted to this bar in 1859. After a very brief practice he engaged in newspaper work, publishing the Litchfield Sentinel, but disposing of that enterprise he removed to New York City, and has ever since been engaged in literary work.

ELMORE S. CHAFFEE, was born in Sharon April 26, 1810 and admitted to this bar in 1833, and died in 1834.

CHARLES Y. CHASE, was born in Sharon in 1784. Admitted to this Bar in 1808 and after a short practice abondoned his profession for the ministry, and removed to Ohio.

THOMAS CHIPMAN removed from Groton, Conn. to Salisbury in 1740 with five sons. He was a practioner of law and was appointed a Judge of the first County Court, but died before its first term. He was the grand-father of Hon. Nathaniel Chipman of Vermont.

FREDERICK CHITTENDEN was born in Kent, but died in Litchfield August 12, 1869, aged 65 years, and with one exception was the oldest practicing member of this Bar. He possessed good legal attainments, and at one time did a very extensive law business. He was of a very impulsive tempement, and sometimes made enemies, but he also had warm friends. He was given to acts of kindness and generosity. He resided at Woodville in the town of Washington and carried on a large Iron Works making bar and slitted iron.

AARON CHURCH, admitted to this Bar from Hartland in 1802.

LEMAN CHURCH, born in Salisbury, and was admitted to this Bar in 1816. He settled in Canaan where he died in 1849. He had an extensive practice and was State's Attorney for a number of years. (See Boardman sketches and Sedgwick's Address.)

Many years ago Truman Smith was called to try a case in North Canaan. The affair was one which called together a good many witnesses and others, and the rooms at the hotel were all taken. Mr. Smith, in his absentmindness had neglected to have a room assigned to him, and toward midnight, having spent the evening in preparation for the trial of the morrow, he made application to the landlord for a room. The host was quite taken back to find that more room was wanted, for every bed was occupied. It was finally decided that Mr. Smith would have to occupy the same bed with Judge Leman Church. Judge Church, as will be remembered by the men of those days, was of very small stature, not larger than the average boy of fourteen of fifteen; his head was round and small, albeit he was a very able jurist. Accepting the situation, Mr. Smith disrobed for sleep, turned down the bedclothes, and there beheld the Judge, up over on the back side of the couch, like a crooked-necked squash. "Humph!" said the senator, glancing around at the host, who was waiting to carry away the tallow-dip of those early days, "this is the first time I ever had to go to bed with an interrogation point!" (See Warner's Address.)

SAMUEL CHURCH, LL. D., born in Salisbury February 4, 1785. Graduated at Yale in 1806. Studied at the Litchfield Law School and was admitted to the Bar in 1806 and soon began practice in his native town. He was a member of the Constitutional Convention in 1818, a Judge of the Superior Court in 1832, Chief Justice of the Supreme Court in 1847. The latter part of his life he resided in Litchfield, where he died in 1854. (See Sedgwick's Address.) See Portrait on page 3.

GREGG CLARK was born in Iowa City, Iowa, February 5th, 1872. Graduated at Harvard 1893. Engaged as a teacher at "The Gunnery" in Washington, Conn., and studied law with Hon. Geo. A. Hickox, and was admitted to this Bar in 1899. Removed to New Jersey.

THOMAS M. CLARK, born in Winsted, January 4, 1830. Never

practiced. Noted as being a long time the spicy editor of the Winsted Herald, and afterwards a prominent manufacturer. He died at sea November 13, 1887, while returning from a voyage taken for his health.

CHESTER D. CLEVELAND, born in Barkhamsted, served in the 2nd. Conn. Heavy Artillery in the Rebellion, gaining the rank of Major. Admitted to this Bar in 1866. Removed to Oshkosh, Wis. where he was County Judge.

FRANK E. CLEVELAND, born in Salisbury May 18, 1853. Graduated at the University of Michigan and was admitted to the Bar at Ann Harbor, Mich. in 1873, and also to this Bar the next year. After a short practice he became totally blind. He moved to Hartford and was the publisher of law blanks and stationery. He was the secretary of the State Board of Education for the blind. He now, 1907, resides in Washington, D. C. and is engaged in education of the blind.

WILLIAM G. COE, born in Winchester September 10, 1829, admitted to this Bar in 1851, began his practice at New Britain, Conn., but in 1856 removed to Winsted and engaged in manufacturing. He was an active promoter of the then Connecticut Western Railroad Company and was its secretary. He died in Winsted May 31, 1872.

CHURCHILL COFFIN, born in Salisbury, admitted to this Bar. Died in Chicago in 1873.

GEORGE W. COLE, born in Warren, Conn. September 6, 1850. Was admitted to this Bar in 1876 and practiced about two years in Plymouth and removed to Torrington in 1878. He remained there until 1885 when he left the practice of law and became a professional librarian. He is now engaged in Bibliographical work in New York City.

RICHARD COOK, admitted in 1835 from New Hartford.

ROGER W. COOK, born February 10, 1797 in Litchfield. Admitted to this Bar in 1819 from Litchfield. Died at sea November 4, 1823 on a voyage to the West Indies for his health.

WILLIAM COGSWELL, was a native of Washington and admitted to this Bar in 1791. Was a Presidential elector in 1824 and died in 1825. He took great interest in military matters and was Colonel in the Militia. (See Sedgwick's Address.)

WILLIAM COTHREN, born in Farmington, Maine, November 28, 1819. Graduated at Bowdoin College in 1843. Came to Woodbury and studied law with Hon. Charles B. Phelps, and was admitted to this Bar in 1845. He located and always resided in Woodbury having an extensive practice until his death March 11th, 1898. His fame will rest principally upon his historical investigations and especially his History of Ancient Woodbury.

STEWART W. COWEN, born in Middlebury, studied law with James Huntington, of Woodbury, admitted to the Bar in 1885, now in practice in Mt. Vernon, N. Y.

EDWARD P. COWLES, born in Canaan January 16, 1815, admitted to the Bar in 1849. Practiced in Hudson, N. Y. and in New York City; was appointed in 1854 Justice of the Supreme Court of New York.

WALTER S. COWLES, born in Canaan February 23, 1819, admitted to the Bar in 1851. Located and practiced in Bridgeport, and removed to New York City, where he died in 1897.

SAMUEL COWLES, admitted to the Bar in 1803 from Norfolk.

EDWARD H. CUMMING, admitted in 1830.

ELI CURTISS, was born in Northbury, (now Plymouth) February 10, 1748. Graduated at Yale College in 1777, was active in the Revolutionary War where he reached the rank of Captain. He lost an arm in the service for which he received a pension. He was admitted to the Bar in 1781, and practiced in Watertown, but finally removed to Bristol, where he died December 13, 1821, and was buried in Plymouth east burying ground.

HOLBROOK CURTISS, born in Newtown, Fairfield County July 14, 1787. Graduated at Yale College 1807, admitted to this Bar in 1809. Began his practice in Litchfield County in 1815 at Watertown. He died February 21, 1858. (See Sedgwick's Address.)

WILLIAM E. CURTISS, was a son of Holbrook Curtiss, born in Watertown September 29, 1823, graduated at Trinity in 1843, studied law with William Curtiss Noyes in New York City and was admitted to this Bar in 1846. He practiced in New York City and was a Judge of the Superior Court of that State in 1871, and its presiding Judge in 1876. He died in Watertown July 6, 1880.

MEDAD CURTISS, admitted to this Bar in 1797 from Norfolk.

GEORGE Y. CUTLER, born in Watertown April 6, 1797. Graduated at Yale in 1816, admitted to this Bar in 1820 from Watertown. He practiced at Watertown till about 1828, when he removed to Illinois, where he was land agent, lawyer, merchant and farmer at Commerce, the place where the Mormons located in 1838 and changed the name to Nauvoo. He died there September 3, 1834.

SPENCER DAYTON, born in Winchester in 1820, and admitted to the Bar in 1846. Resides in Philippi, W. Va.

GILBERT DEAN, born in Dutchess County, N. Y. in 1819. Graduated at Yale College in 1841. Admitted to the Bar in 1842. Died in Poughkeepsie, N. Y. in 1870.

LEE P. DEAN, born in Canaan October 18, 1838. Admitted to the Bar in 1864. In 1886 he removed to Bridgeport, where he now resides engaged in other pursuits.

EUGENE C. DEMPSEY, born in Barkhamsted January 7, 1864, admitted to the Bar in 1886. Located in Danbury, where he now resides.

JEREMIAH W. DEXTER, a native of Salisbury, served in the war of the rebellion and was admitted to the Bar in 1866. Located and resides at Waverly, N. Y.

WILLIAM E. DICKINSON, was born in New York City May 30, 1824, but came to Litchfield when a child. He was admitted to this Bar in 1846. Located and practiced at Stonington, Conn., until 1850, when he removed to the Lake Superior regions and was engaged in important mining operations. Subsequently he went to Cuba in the same business and while there had charge of building the Daiqduria Pier for loading ore, the same pier used by the United States to unload troops during the Spanish-American War. He then removed to Wisconsin where he was District Attorney of Florence County for a number of years. He died at Florence, Wis., June 15, 1899.

WHEATON F. DOWD, born in New Hartford, August 21, 1867. Graduated at Yale Law School in 1894 and was admitted to this Bar the same year, and was appointed Assistant Clerk of the Superior Court. In 1901, after the decease of William F. Hurlburt, he was appointed Clerk of the Court of Common Pleas for Litchfield County which office he has since held. He resides in Winsted.

THEODORE W. DOWNS was admitted to this Bar in 1870 from Bridgeport. The following is taken from a Bridgeport paper of September 24th, 1907, "Former Consul dead. Theodore Waldren Downs former United States Consul to Quebec and prominent in national Democratic politics, died at his home in this city yesterday after a sickness of about seven weeks following a shock."

WILLIAM DRINKWATER, came to New Milford about 1730 from Ridgefield and for nearly thirty years was a prominent man there and was in the practice of law in 1753. He died in 1758.

DANIEL DUNBAR, was a native of Plymouth, admitted to this bar in 1798. Located and practiced in Berlin, Conn., 1803 to 1841.

MILES DUNBAR, was a native of Plymouth but was admitted to this bar in 1810 as from Sharon. The history of Ellsworth a part of the town of Sharon gives this notice of him. "Our first Dunbar was hardly representative of the household, for he came and went more like a comet than the staid and planetary bodies since representative. That was Miles Dunbar of Plymouth, Conn., lawyer, music teacher and jack-at-all-trades. About 1812 he departed from Sharon."

WHEATON F. DOWD.

HENRY M. DUTTON, was a son of Ex-Governor and Judge Dutton (who was born in Litchfield), and practiced law in Litchfield in 1861 with his uncle Henry B. Graves, Esq. Upon the breaking out of the war he entered the service of his country and received a commission as Lieutenant in the 5th Connecticut Infantry, and was killed in the battle of Cedar Mountain, Va., August 9th, 1862.

RUFUS EASTMAN, admitted to the Bar in 1796 from Washington.

DAVID EDMUNDS, admitted to the Bar in 1806 from Newtown.

OGDEN EDWARDS, born in 1781, a student of the Law School in 1801, admitted to the Bar in 1802 as from New Haven. He removed to New York where he was a prominent man and a leading attorney for many years; a Judge of the Superior Court, Surrogate, etc.

FREDERICK EGGLESTON, admitted in 1834 from Cromwall.

NATHANIEL B. ELDREDGE, admitted in 1811 from Salisbury.

JOHN ELMORE, was a son of Col. Samuel Elmer of Revolutionary war fame, and born in Sharon. Settled in Canaan in 1793 and died in that town December 10th, 1849, aged 84 years.

JOHN ELMORE, JR., was admitted to the Bar in 1819 from Canaan. He died at East Canaan, June 12th, 1857, in his 65th year. See Warner's Reminisences.

HENRY LOOMIS ELLSWORTH was a son of Chief Justice Oliver Ellsworth, and after studying with Judge Reeve in the Law School, he was admitted to this Bar in 1812 from Windsor. After a practice in Hartford he was appointed Commissioner of Indian affairs under President Jackson. He was also Commissioner of Patents for ten years. He died in 1858.

WILLIAM H. ELY, admitted to the Hartford Bar in 1879, but located at Winsted and then removed to New Haven, where he now resides and has a large practice.

JAMES ENSIGN, born in Canaan February 2, 1819, graduated at Yale 1842, and admitted to this Bar in 1848, from Canaan. He practiced law but a short time when he engaged in farming. He died in Salisbury, February 3, 1883.

FRANK W. ETHERIDGE, of Thomaston, was born in Montville in 1858. He was educated at the Hartford High School and pursued his law studies with the late firm of Johnson & Prentice, of Hartford, being admitted to the Bar in 1880. He settled in Thomaston and has held a number of town offices. He has been Judge of Probate since 1890. In 1896 he was appointed Health Officer for the County which office he has since held. He was a member of the last Constitutional Convention. He is also the publisher and editor of the Thomaston Express, a weekly newspaper.

WILLIAM W. ELLSWORTH was born in Windsor in 1781, the third son of Oliver Ellsworth, the second Chief Justice of the United States, graduated at Yale in 1810, studied law with Judge Reeve and was admitted to this Bar in 1813, and began his practice in Hartford, where he died January 15th, 1868. He was a member of Congress five years; Governor of the State four years; a judge of the Superior Court and the Supreme Court fourteen years. Rufus Choate said of him "If the land of the Shermans and Griswolds, and Daggetts and Williamses—rich as she is in learning and virtue—has a sounder lawyer, a more upright magistrate, or an honester man in her public service, I know not his name." (See obituary in 34th, Conn.)

DANIEL EVERETT, born in Bethlem in 1748, and began practice of law in New Milford in 1772, where he resided until his death in 1805. (See Boardman's Sketches.)

SHERMAN EVERETT, was admitted to this Bar in 1801 as from Cornwall. He seems however, to belong to Sharon, where he was born April 20, 1781, lived there and died October 5, 1870. The Ellsworth History says, "The major became captain of militia was early sent to the legislature, surveyed almost every bit of this town, and much of other towns, was a justice of no mean record, rose to the rank of major in the war of 1812, was treasurer of this (Ellsworth) society, commissioner of the common land and founder of the library which now bears his name.

JOHN R. FARNAM, was admitted to this Bar in 1871, practiced a short time at Litchfield and also published the Litchfield Sentinel. In 1877 he located in Danbury, Conn., from whence he removed in 1884 to Washington, D. C.

AMOS H. FARNSWORTH, was admitted to this Bar in 1849.

AUGUSTUS H. FENN, born in Plymouth January 18, 1844. In the Civil War he gained the rank of Major of the 2nd Conn. Heavy Artillery. At the battle of Cedar Creek he was wounded and suffered the amputation of his right arm at the shoulder. He was a graduate of Harvard Law School and was admitted to this Bar in 1867 and began his practice at Plymouth removing to Waterbury and thence to Winsted at which place he resided at his death, September 12, 1897. In 1887 he was elected Judge of the Superior Court, and in 1893 he was promoted to the Supreme Court of Errors. (See his obituary in Vol. 67, Conn.)

The following tribute to Judge Fenn was given by his associate Judge David Torrance at the Annual Meeting of the Army and Navy Club in 1898:

"I trust, that you will pardon me if I say a few words about him who was my friend and companion for some years in the highest court of this state, whom all of you know and loved, and who, when he died was the honored president of this club.

The best legacy that a man can leave to his children and to his fellow men, is the inspiring example of a well spent life; a clean life, nobly lived for noble ends. Happy the man who dying leaves behind him the record of such a life; and to the full measure of such felicity, as far as human facility will permit, my friend and yours attained.

His war record, young as he was, is as brilliant as it is inspiring. Entering the army in July, 1862, when he was eighteen years old, as a member of the gallant Second Connecticut Heavy Artillery, he served with distinction as lieutenant, as captain, as brevet major and brevet lieutenant-colonel, till the close of the war and after.

When wounded and disabled by the loss of his arm at Cedar Creek in 1864 he refused to be discharged and reported for duty within seven weeks after he was wounded. Most men would have regarded the loss of a good right arm as sacrifice enough for one's country, but our comrade, in this respect, as in some others, was not like most men. Since the war what a busy useful life he led, as student, as lawyer, as the trusted judge of probate for years in Plymouth and Winchester, as member of the Legislature, as member of important committees for the revision of our laws, as an active participant in political contests, as lecturer in the Yale Law School, as the eloquent orator on Memorial Days, and at Grand Army meetings innumerable, as the trusted friend, the wise counsellor, and burden bearer, in local matters and affairs, and finally as judge of the superior court and of the supreme court of errors of this state. What a deal of work he crowded into his fifty-four years of life. What a useful life it was to his country and to his fellow men! How unselfishly and unstintedly he gave himself to all things that tended to help men and make them better citizens, and in the midst of all its stir and activity and storm and stress, what a clean and noble life it was! He was the architect of his own fortunes. About all he inherited from the past was the blood of a vigorous ancestry, but blood will tell, and in him it made the desert of adverse circumstances the very vantage ground of succeess, and caused its barren wastes to blossom as the rose.

He was successful because he merited success. He won his promotions in the army, without the aid of influential friends, by sheer force of character, by his bravery, and his proved fitness to fill every position to which he was assigned.

In civil life he attained position and influence by his sterling integrity and his own unaided ability. He worthily filled every office he ever held, and worthily fulfilled every one of the many trusts that were reposed in him. His was on the whole a successful life, in a high sense a joyous victorious life, and now that death has put a period to it, while yet the infirmities of old age were afar off, he may, with the wise old Greek, call it a happy life, worthily ended."

ELLIOTT J. FENN, was born in Plymouth September 1, 1855, and studied law with Augustus H. Fenn in Plymouth, and was admitted to this Bar in 1874. He began practice in Waterbury in 1875, and died there in 1888.

FREDERICK J. FENN, was a native of Washington, Conn., but was admitted to this Bar in 1821 as from Canaan. He removed to Harrisburg, Penn.

LINUS FENN, was a native of Plymouth and studied with Judge Reeve and was admitted to practice in 1794 and persued his profession in his native town. He died in 1852.

GEORGE L. FIELD, was born in Watertown December 4, 1828. He studied law with John W. Webster in Waterbury, and was admitted to this Bar in 1856, and after a brief practice in Watertown he opened his office in Waterbury. He was one of the earlier Judges of the city court, and also the Mayor of the city. During the last few years of his life he was totally blind. He died in Watertown, October 22, 1879.

JOHN A. FOOTE, was admitted to this Bar in 1825, having attended the Law School. The following taken from Howe's Historical Collections of Ohio, is of interest regarding Mr. Foote:

"Much gratification was derived at this time in Cleveland by a call upon Mr. John A. Foote, an old lawyer an octogenarian, of whom I had all my life heard but never met until now. He was a brother of Admiral Foote and a son of that Governor Foote of Connecticut who introduced a resolution, historically known as 'Foote's Resolution' which led to the debate between Daniel Webster and Mr. Hayne, of South Carolina.

"Mr. Foote first came here from Cheshire, Connecticut, in the summer of 1833, and was for years a member of the eminent law firm of Andrews, Foote & Hoyt. He was born in 1803 on the site of the Tontine Hotel in New Haven, but his home at the time of leaving was in Cheshire. That town was overwhelmingly Democratic, and he was a Whig, but as the State Legislature was in session but for a few weeks his townsmen irrespective of politics gave him and a Mr. Edward A. Cornwall, prior to their departure for the distant wilds of Ohio, as a parting compliment the privilege of representing them in that body. So they went down to Hartford and passed a few weeks pleasantly among the 'Shad Eaters' as in the humorous parlace of the time the members were called, from the fact that they met in May, the season of shad-catching in the Connecticut.

"The year 1883 came around when Foote and Cornwall, after a lapse of fifty years, in company visited the Legislature of Connecticut at Hartford and were received with great *eclat.*

"The House passed some complimentary resolutions, signed by the speaker (Charles H. Pine) and by the clerk (Donald H. Perkins) expressive of their high gratification. 'Passed February 22, 1883. Washington's birthday.' These Mr. Foote with commendable pride pointed out to me framed on his parlor wall."

EBENEZER FOOTE, was born in Watertown (then Westbury) July 6, 1773. Studied law at Judge Reeve's school and was admitted to the Bar in 1796. He located at Lansingburgh, N. Y., and with the increase of his business moved to Troy and later to Albany. He was one of the leading attorneys of the state, an active and influential politician. He was the founder and promoter of the celebrated Albany Female Academy. He died July 21, 1814, at Troy, New York.

JARED B. FOSTER, born in Albany, N. Y., 1820, was admitted to this Bar in 1848 and located and practiced in New Hartford until his death in March 3, 1895. He held many town offices and was Judge of the District Court for Litchfield County for the term of three years. He was a very bright man and a witty lawyer and a great many pleasant stories and recollections are told of his practice. (See picture, page 107.)

WALTER S. FRANKLIN, born in Lancaster, Penn. in 1799. Studied at the Litchfield Law School and was admitted to this Bar in 1820 and practiced law in York, Penn. He was Clerk of the House of Representatives in Washington, D. C. from December 2, 1833 to his death September 20, 1838. Major General Wm. B. Franklin was one of his sons.

GEORGE A. FREEMAN was born in Boscowen, N. H. in 1876, fitted for College at Phillips Academy, Andover, graduated at Yale Scientific School in 1897, studied law with Huntington & Warner, and was admitted to the Bar in 1901. Mr. Freeman resides and practices in Waterbury.

SAMUEL FRISBIE, admitted to the Bar in 1811 from Waterbury, where he practiced a few years and then removed to Indiana.

HENRY I. FULLER, admitted in 1846 from Kent and removed to the State of New York.

JEROME FULLER, admitted in 1832 from Kent.

RUFUS FULLER, born in Plymouth in 1810, graduated at Union College in 1835, was admitted to this Bar in 1836, located in Kent, where he practiced his profession for a quarter of a century, and retired therefrom in consequence of ill health.

FLORIMOND D. FYLER, born in Torrington in 1834, graduated at Yale Law School in 1860, admitted to this Bar in 1864, located at Winsted, was a Judge of the District Court for Litchfield County, 1878-1882. Returned to Torrington, and from ill health quit his practice and became extensively engaged in the poultry business on his ancestral home, where he died after a protracted illness, August 22, 1905.

FREDERICK GAYLORD, admitted to the Bar in 1853 from Goshen.

AMMI GIDDINGS, born at Sherman, Conn., in 1822 and graduated at Yale Law School and was admitted to this Bar in 1849. He practiced at Plymouth until 1866, when he removed to Kalamazoo, Mich., returning to Connecticut in 1872. He died at his birth-place, February 13, 1882.

VAN RENSSALAER C. GIDDINGS, born in New Milford in 1833 and after attending Yale Law School was admitted to this Bar in 1861. After practicing in this County a while he removed to Bridgeport in 1869 and was the City Attorney for Bridgeport.

JAMES P. GLYNN, a native of Winsted was admitted to this Bar in 1895. Practices in Winsted and was for some years the Town Clerk of Winchester, and also Prosecuting Attorney of the Town Court. In 1901 was appointed by President Roosevelt, Postmaster of Winsted, which office he now holds.

GEORGE R. GOLD, admitted to the Bar in 1856 from Cornwall and removed to Michigan.

THOMAS R. GOLD, born in Cornwall in 1764, graduated at Yale College in 1786, admitted to this Bar in 1788 and removed to Central New York, where he held a leading position as a lawyer. Was a member of Congress for twenty years. He died in 1827.

JAMES GOULD, born in Branford, Conn. December 5, 1770, graduated at Yale College in 1795, attended the Litchfield Law School and was admitted to this Bar in 1798. He assisted Judge Reeve in the Law School and after the retirement of Judge Reeve conducted it himself until its close in 1833. He died in Litchfield May

11, 1838. He was a Judge of the Supreme Court of Errors, and author of Gould's Pleadings, published in 1832. (See Boardman and Sedgwick Sketches.)

JAMES REEVE GOULD, a son of James born in Litchfield November 2, 1803. Graduated at Yale College in 1824, was admitted to this Bar in 1826, and removed to Augusta, Georgia, where he died October 11, 1830.

GEORGE GOULD, a son of James born in Litchfield September 2, 1807, admitted to this Bar in 1829. ' Removed to Troy, N. Y., where he died February 11, 1868. He had been Mayor of Troy and a Justice of the Supreme Court of New York from 1855 to 1863.

WILLIAM TRACY GOULD, another son of James and born October 25, 1799, graduated at Yale College in 1816, and admitted to this Bar in 1820. He removed to Augusta, Georgia, where he became a distinguished Judge and prominent citizen. Died July, 1882.

HIRAM GOODWIN, born in New Hartford May 5, 1808, admitted to the Bar in 1830. Located at Riverton in the town of Barkhamsted. Was a Judge of the Litchfield County Court 1851 to 1855. Died February 5, 1885. His obituary is in 52d Conn. Reports.

LYMAN GRANGER, admitted to the Bar in 1821. He was a native of Salisbury or Canaan, and graduated at Union College in 1820. After a short practice in Salisbury he removed to Rutland, Vermont and associated with Moses Strong, having a large law practice. He died in 1839.

ELIJAH PHELPS GRANT, born in Norfolk, 1808. Practiced in Winsted in 1835 and 1836, when he removed to Canton, Ohio, where he died December 21, 1874.

FRIEND GRANT, born in Litchfield September 14, 1740. Graduated at Yale 1761, and practiced in Litchfield a year or two, and died in 1764.

MILES TOBEY GRANGER, was born August 12, 1817 in New Marlboro, Mass. By his own exertions as a farmer boy and at country school teaching he graduated at Wesleyan College at Middletown in 1842. The next year he went to Louisana as a family teacher and began studying law and was admitted in that State in 1845. Returning to the North he was admitted the same year to this Bar, and soon located in North Canaan, making that his residence, until his decease October 21, 1895.

Judge Granger was a Democrat in his political views, and in 1857 represented his town in the General Assembly, and in 1867 and 1868 he was State Senator from his district and chairman of the Judiciary Committee, and was appointed a Judge of the Superior Court. In 1876 he was advanced to the Supreme Court of Errors which office he held until 1887, when he resigned to accept an election to Congress. In 1893 he was appointed a State Referee, which position he held at the time of his death.

Bro. Hickox in his obituary of Judge Granger published in the 66th Conn. Reports, ends with a sentence with which every member of the Bar fully concurred. "A grave, honest, shrewd man, he inspired confidence and respect, while his sense, wit and kindly nature won him general esteem, and his loyalty, many lasting friends." (Picture on page 156.)

HENRY B. GRAVES, born in Sherman, Conn. in 1822 and admitted to this Bar in 1845. He began his practice in Plymouth, but after a couple of years removed to Litchfield where he had for more than forty years a large and lucrative practice, frequently representing the town in the General Assembly. The Judicial History says of him, "He was a typical lawyer of the old school. In figure he was tall, handsome and striking. He had great keenness of preception, splendid capacities for analyis and was a compact and logical thinker. He was a man of most kindly feelings warm and ardent in his friendships, generous and helpful to all and never vindictive even to his opponents." He died in Litchfield August 10, 1891. Obituary in 60 Conn. Reports. Picture, page 152.

G. W. GRISWOLD, was in practice in Winchester in 1831, but was not admitted at this Bar.

FREDERICK GUNN, admitted in 1813 from New Milford. Died in New Milford November 23, 1852, aged 65.

WARREN W. GUTHRIE, admitted to this Bar in 1855, began practice in Seymour, Conn., but in 1856 removed to Atkinson, Kan., and was Attorney General of Kansas for a number of years.

NATHAN HALE, was an Attorney at Sharon in 1777 and an assistant Judge of the County Court for eighteen years.

BENJAMIN HALL, admitted to this Bar in 1797.

ELANATHAN S. HALL, admitted in 1846 from Fairfield County.

GIDEON HALL, born in Winchester May 1, 1808, graduated at Litchfield Law School and was admitted to the Bar in 1832. He always resided in Winsted and had a large practice until 1866, when he was appointed a Judge of the Superior Court, which office he held at the time of his death December 8, 1867. (See Warner's Reminiscences.) Picture, page 113.

ROBERT E. HALL was born in Morris, Conn. in 1858, graduated at Yale Law School in 1882 and was admitted to the Bar in New Haven County, has practiced principally in Waterbury. Is not now in practice.

JACOB B. HARDENBURGH, born in New York State in 1833, was admitted to the Bar in 1854 and practiced at Kingston. In the war of the rebellion he served nearly five years and was Colonel of the 80th N. Y. Vols. In 1867 he located at North Canaan taking Judge Granger's practice. In 1883 he was appointed County Coroner which office he held at the time of his death, April 4, 1892.

JOHN HARPER, admitted to this Bar from Winsted in 1850. He removed South and located at Alpalechicola, Fla. about 1851. He was an officer in the Confederate service during the rebellion.

JULIUS B. HARRISON, was born in Cornwall in 1819, was admitted to this Bar in 1843 and located at New Milford. Was State Attorney in 1852 and died in New Milford October 10, 1854, aged 35 years.

MOSES HATCH was born in Kent in 1780, graduated at Yale in 1800, admitted to this Bar in 1802, settled in Danbury where he died in 1820.

CHARLES R. HATHAWAY, a native of Winchester. Admitted to this Bar in 1880, now in practice in Manchester, Conn. Is now the Record Commissioner of Connecticut.

WILLIAM HAWLEY, born in Redding, Conn., graduated at Yale College in 1780, was admitted to this Bar in 1791; he removed from Fairfield County in 1798 to Woodbury, and soon thereafter abandoned his legal practice for mercantile pursuits.

CHARLES GORDON HAYES, eldest son of the Rev. Gordon Hayes, born in Washington, Conn. January 20, 1830. Graduated at Yale in 1851. Admitted to this Bar in 1855. Removed to Rock Island, Ill., and to Muscatine, Iowa. Died at DesMoines, Iowa, April 8, 1878.

LOUIS M. HEMINWAY was born in Watertown in 1875. Was fitted for College at the Cheltingham Military Academy, graduated at Lafayette College in 1896 and at the Law School of the University of Virginia in 1899 and admitted to this Bar in the following year. He is largely engaged in the hotel business.

JOSHUA HENSHAW, was admitted to this Bar in 1797, from New Hartford.

PHILO M. HEACOCKS, born February 8, 1784, admitted to the Bar in 1810, and practiced in New Milford until his death April 20, 1825.

SAMUEL A. HERMAN, born in Canaan 1855, and was admitted to this Bar in 1878. He located at Winsted in company with the late Judge Fenn, and they had a large and lucrative practice. He has attended strictly to his profession, doing very little non-professional work. He was State Senator in 1897. He was an active promoter of the Torrington & Winchester Electric Road, and its Secretary. He resides at his farm residence in the town of Torrington, but continues his practice at Winsted.

GEORGE A. HICKOX.

GEORGE A. HICKOX was born in Washington in 1830, graduated at Trinity College in 1851, was admitted to this Bar in 1853 and located at Litchfield. In 1866 he purchased the Litchfield Enquirer, which he published for a quarter of a century, editing it with marked ability and profound scholarship.

In 1895 he removed to his ancestral home at Washington, where he died, June 6, 1903.

RICHARD T. HIGGINS was born in Washington in 1865, was educated at St. Francis College, Brooklyn, New York. Studied law with Hon. James Huntington of Woodbury and admitted to this Bar in 1890. Resides in Winsted and has for several years been the County Coroner. (See Coroner page 165.)

BERNARD E. HIGGINS, born in Woodbury January 31, 1872, admitted to the Bar June, 1897. Resides and practices in Torrington, Conn. Was Borough Clerk for three years. Is now (1907) Prosecuting Attorney for the town.

HOMER HINE was admitted to the Bar in 1800 from New Milford.

CHARLES W. HINMAN, born in Southbury in 1829, admitted in 1853. Before he had begun to practice he received an appointment as one of the librarians of Congress and removed to Washington, D. C.

EDWARD HINMAN was born in Southbury, then a part of Wood-

SAMUEL A. HERMAN.

bury in 1740 and practiced in Southbury. He was familiarly known as Lawyer Ned. He is said to have been a very able lawyer. He was very corpilent man, weighing something over four hundred pounds.

ROBINSON S. HINMAN was born in South Britain in 1801. Was admitted to this Bar in 1825. In 1827 he removed to Utica, N. Y., but returned to Connecticut in 1828 and was appointed Clerk of the Superior Court for New Haven County in 1831, holding that office seven years. He died in New Haven in 1843.

ROYAL R. HINMAN was born in Southbury, graduated at Yale College in 1804 and was admitted to practice in 1811 and practiced for twenty years at Roxbury. In 1835 he was elected Secretary of State and held that office for seven years. He was largely engaged in compiling and publishing matters relating to the early history of the State, and in other historical and genealogical labors. He subsequently removed to New York City.

SIMEON HINMAN, graduated at Yale College in 1784, was admitted to this Bar in 1790 and engaged in his profession in Southbury, where he died in 1825.

ROLAND HITCHCOCK, one of the Judges of the Superior Court, was a native of Burlington in Hartford County. He was admitted to this Bar in 1844 and located in Winsted, where he died on April 28th, 1889. Picture, page 114.

The following was published at the time of his death:

"Roland Hitchcock, ex-judge of the Superior Court, died Sunday afternoon at his residence in Winsted, aged 66. He was a native of Burlington and wrote the history of that town for the Memorial History of Hartford County. He studied law with Lieutenant-Governor Holabird in Winsted, which town he afterward made his residence. He was clerk of the House of Representatives in 1852 and 1853, postmaster from 1853 to 1861, and judge of probate six terms. He was appointed on the Superior Court bench in 1874, by Governor Ingersoll, and served until 1882. His last public service was as representative from Winchester in 1883, when he served on the judiciary committee. Since that time he has been engaged in the practice of law in Winsted."

ELKANAH H. HODGES was born in Torrington in 1812 and was admitted to this Bar in 1837. He was one of the pioneers of California and died in that State in 1862.

WILLIAM S. HOLABIRD was born in Canaan in 1794 and attended the Litchfield Law School. Was admitted to this Bar in 1816 and commenced his practice in Colebrook, removing to Winsted in 1824. He was District Attorney under President Jackson's administration. In 1842 and 1844 he was Lieutenant Governor of this State. Died May 22, 1855.

MARCUS H. HOLCOMB was born in New Hartford, Litchfield County November 28, 1844. He received his higher education at Wesleyan Academy and studied law with the late Judge Jared B. Foster. He was admitted to the Litchfield County Bar in 1871 and soon after removed to Southington, where he has since resided. He has been Judge of Probate for more than thirty years and Treasurer of the County of Hartford since 1893; a Commissioner of the State Police since its creation; was a member of the Constitutional Convention in 1902; he has been representative and senator several times in the General Assembly and was unanimously elected speaker one term. He holds many offices of trust and responsibility in Southington and is closely identified with all its business interests. Is now the Attorney General of Connecticut. (See page 167.)

WALTER HOLCOMB, born in New Hartford October 13, 1853. Admitted to this Bar in 1881, removed to St. Paul, Minn., where he practiced until 1896 he then returned to Connecticut and located in Torrington, where he now resides. Is Judge of the Borough Court.

DAVID F. HOLLISTER, born in Washington March 31, 1826, graduated at Yale in 1851 and was admitted to the Bar the same year. He commenced practice in Salisbury, removing in 1854 to Bridgeport, where he resided and died May 4, 1906. He held the office of Collector of Internal Revenue for Connecticut a number of years. The following notice is from the Bridgeport Standard:

The death of the Hon. David F. Hollister removes another of the older citizens of Bridgeport who had been a prominent factor in its development and in all the reputable and admirable elements of its progress. Mr. Hollister distinguished himself by his probity and ability in every station which he filled and as a government official, occupying an important place for many years he made a record that is hardly paralleled in that department for accuracy, efficiency and thoroughness. As a citizen he answered every obligation; as a professional man he was honorable and able and in every walk in life he set an example to be emulated. He lived a long and useful life and he leaves a memory to be cherished with affection and respect by all who were associated with him.

JOHN B. HOLLISTER, born in Litchfield in 1860, the only son of Gideon H. Hollister; was admitted to the Bar in 1884. Has never practiced.

JOHN M. HOLLY, born in Salisbury and graduated from Yale College in 1820 and was admitted to this Bar in 1824. He removed to western New York, became a member of Congress and died in Florida while holding that position.

GEORGE B. HOLT, born in Norfolk in 1790, attended the Litchfield Law School and was admitted to practice in 1812 and removed to Dayton, Ohio in 1818, where he became a very prominent man in the prosecution of its system of internal improvements. He was Judge of the Circuit Court of Ohio and its President Judge for fourteen years.

GIDEON H. HOLLISTER, born in Washington in 1817, and graduated from Yale College in 1840, and was admitted to this Bar in 1842, and soon after located in Litchfield, but has resided and practiced at various times in other places. He was Clerk of the Courts 1844 to 1845, and from 1847 to 1850. Under President Andrew Johnson he was the United States Minister to Hayti. He is best known of from his literary work, being author of several Historical novels and plays. He was singularly gifted in making and delivering addresses on public celebrations and anniversary occasions. In 1855 he published the History of Connecticut in two large volumes. He died at Litchfield March 21, 1881. His obituary is in Vol. 48, Conn. Reports.

URIEL HOLMES, born in Hartland in 1765, graduated at Yale in 1784 was admitted to the Bar and located at Litchfield. He was State Attorney from 1807 to 1814. A member of the General Assembly from Litchfield nine times; Judge of the County Court from 1814 to 1817; a member of Congress in 1817 and 1818. He died May 18, 1827.

SAMUEL MILES HOPKINS, L. L. D. was born in Waterbury 1772, but in early life removed to Goshen, studied at Yale, but refused graduation, studied at Judge Reeve's Law School and was admitted to this Bar in 1793. He removed to the State of New York and was engaged in large real estate transactions. He was a member of Congress and held many other high official positions. He died at Geneva, N. Y. October 8, 1837.

SAMUEL B. HORNE, of Winsted was admitted to the Bar in 1869 from that town, having served through the Civil War where he gained the rank of Captain. He was an aide on the staff of Governor Phineas Lounsbury and was Commander of the Connecticut Dept., G. A. R. He was United States consul under President Harrison. Labor Commissioner for Connecticut from 1895 to 1899. He now resides and practices at Winsted; holds a Medal of Honor Badge. His practice is mostly confined to recovering estates from foreign countries.

F. H. HORTON, admitted to the Bar in 1846.

ISAAC M. HORTON, admitted to the Bar in 1882 from Harwinton.

SAMUEL C. HOSFORD, admitted to the Bar in 1850 from Canaan; never practiced; became a teacher and removed to New Jersey, where he died.

JOHN D. HOWE, studied law with Judge Hitchcock in Winsted, admitted to the Bar in 1866 from Winsted and soon after his admission removed to St. Paul, Minn. where he holds a large practice as a railroad attorney.

EDWARD J. HUBBARD, born in Bethlehem, studied with Wm. Cothren, was admitted to this Bar in 1864 and removed to Trimdad, Colorado, where he is now in practice.

JOHN T. HUBBARD, born in Litchfield in 1856, graduated from Yale College in 1880, studied law at Yale Law School and was admitted to the New Haven Bar in 1883. Now resides at Litchfield. Represented his native town in the General Assembly 1901 and 1903; is now, (1907) Judge of Probate for District of Litchfield.

JOHN H. HUBBARD, born in Salisbury in 1804 and admitted to this Bar in 1826. He began practice in his native town, but in 1854 removed to Litchfield. Was elected member of Congress from his district in 1863 and 1865. Was State Attorney of the County in 1844 and again in 1849. He enjoyed a lucrative practice and was one of the leading lawyers of the State. He died July 30, 1872.

The following notice of the death of this distinguished member of our Bar, is from the Litchfield paper and written by his neighbor and friend, Hon. Henry B. Graves:

The Hon. John H. Hubbard died in this village on the 30th of July, 1872. The deceased was born in Salisbury in November, 1804 and was therefore at his death past sixty-seven years of age. He was admitted to the Litchfield County Bar in April 1826 and soon after commenced practicing law in his native town, in the village of Lakeville, where he continued in a very successful business until about seventeen years since when he removed to Litchfield. Here he was constantly occupied in his profession, being engaged in most of the important causes tried in our higher courts until his election

COL. SAMUEL B. HORNE

to Congress in 1863, from this District. He was again returned to Congress in 1865. Having served his four years in Congress, he again returned to the practice of the law and continued it till within a few weeks of his death.

He was very industrious, energetic, and perserving; never discouraged by an adverse decision, where there was an opportunity to pursue the cause of his client further, and was often victorious in the court of review, where he had been overruled in the inferior courts.

In the course of his professional career he had a lucrative practice and for many years was one of the more prominent lawyers in this county. He served five years as State Attorney of the county in which position he gave general satisfaction; he was also State Senator from the 17th District two terms and served in various other public relations and in all of them acquitted himself with honor. He was a good citizen; liberal, kind, and generous to the poor, and always ready to contribute his full share to all objects of worthy charity. As a husband and parent, he could not do enough for those so nearly connected to him, and his affections knew no bounds or limit. The deceased leaves a widow, three sons, and a daughter, surviving him, to mourn his loss. Though his death had been expected for several days, owing to the character of his disease, yet our community was not prepared to meet with so great an affliction and deeply sympathize with the stricken family in their great sorrow. Picture on page 107.

FRANK W. HUBBARD, born in Litchfield in 1861, graduated at Yale College in 1888 and from Yale Law School in 1890 and was admitted to the Bar. After a few years practice in Torrington he removed to Flushing, N. Y., and is Attorney for New York City Railway Co.

FRANK L. HUNGERFORD of New Britain was born in Torrington in 1843 and entered the University of Vermont in 1860. From 1862 to 1864 he studied law in the office of Senator Edmunds, and graduated at the Harvard Law School in 1865 being admitted to the Bar in Burlington in 1865 and to this Bar in 1866. He practiced in Torrington for three years, then removed to New Britain, where he has been Judge of Probate as well as City Attorney.

LEVI HUNGERFORD, admitted to this Bar in 1854 from Sherman. He was a Lieutenant in the 28th C. V. and died in service August 9, 1863.

JOSEPH D. HUMPHREY, admitted to the Bar in 1812 from Goshen. He was born in Goshen March 15, 1780, and after admission settled in practice in Torringford, a part of Torrington, for a few years, when he removed to Norton, Summit County, Ohio, where he died February 4, 1839.

VAN R. HUMPHREY, admitted to the Bar in 1820. Was born in Goshen July 28, 1800. Soon after his admission to the Bar he removed to Ohio, where he became a Judge and a very prominent man. He died in Hudson, Ohio September 5, 1864.

HIRAM HUNT, a native of Canaan, was admitted to this Bar in 1820; removed to New York City.

REUBEN HUNT, a native of Canaan, admitted to this Bar in 1812, and removed to Illinois.

ROBERT HUNT is on Connecticut Register, 1859 as Attorney in Falls Village.

JABEZ W. HUNTINGTON, born in Norwich in 1788, graduated at Yale College in 1806, studied at the Litchfield Law School and was admitted to this Bar in 1810. He located in Litchfield until 1834, when he removed to Norwich. He was a Judge of the Superior and Supreme Courts. He was elected a member of Congress several terms, and United States Senator in 1840. He died in 1874. (See Boardman's Sketches, page 64.)

JAMES HUNTINGTON was born in Coventry, Tolland County, Connecticut, June 4th, 1833, the son of Edward G. and Eliza Clark Huntington, and died at his residence in Woodbury, Litchfield County, May 2nd, 1908.

Mr. Huntington received a high school education and taught school in his native town. Later he attended Wilbraham Academy, and the New York Conference Seminary at Charlottsville, N. Y., and in 1857 was graduated, with the degree of L. L. B., from the State and National Law School at Poughkeepsie, at which time he was admitted to the Bar of the State of New York.

Subsequently he entered the law office of Alvin P. Hyde and Loren P. Waldo at Tolland, Connecticut, and was admitted to the Bar of Tolland County in April, 1859.

After being admitted to the Bar in the spring of 1859 he opened an office in Woodbury, where he continued in active, honorable and successful practice up to the time of his death, at which time he was, and for a long number of years had been president of the Litchfield County Bar and Law Library Associations.

In April, 1861 he was elected Judge of the Probate District of Woodbury, comprising the towns of Woodbury, Bethlehem and Southbury, which office he retained continuously, with the exception of one term, until disqualified by age limitations in 1903. His wise and judicious administration of the office of Judge of Probate for a period of over forty years won for him a high standing as a probate lawyer, and the unqualified confidence and esteem of his fellow men.

On July 4th, 1874 he was appointed State's Attorney for Litchfield County, filling that office with marked ability until June, 1896,

JAMES HUNTINGTON.

nearly a quarter of a century, and during that time tried many important cases, and became renowned as a States Attorney in his tireless effort to eradicate crime and bring criminals to justice; some of the most bitterly contested cases being in connection with liquor prosecutions, and yet at all times he displayed the commendable disposition of tempering justice with mercy. At the close of his twenty-two years of service as States Attorney the members of the Bar of Litchfield County presented him with handsomely engrossed resolutions expressive of their high regard and esteem for him in the conduct of that important and off-times unpleasant office.

He was appointed a member of the Commission of State Police at the time of its organization in 1903, and took a great interest in the workings of that police power, in the detection and punishment of crime, up to the time of his death.

Mr. Huntington always took an active interest in public affairs, and in politics was a democrat, representing the town of Woodbury in the Legislature in 1874-5, and was Senator from the old sixteenth district in 1877-8. In 1904 he was a candidate for Secretary of State on the Democratic ticket.

Mr. Huntington was married January 6th, 1863 to Miss Rebecca Huntley Hurd, of Honesdale, Pa., who died February 28th, 1865, leaving one daughter, Rebecca. On June 11th, 1868 he married Miss Helen Elizabeth Parker, of Woodbury, who survived him, together with two daughters, Rebecca Huntington and Eunice Huntington Tomlinson, and one grandson, James Huntington Tomlinson.

For over a quarter of a century, Judge Huntington was engaged in nearly all the large legal battles in Litchfield County, and was considered one of the giants of the Litchfield County Bar, always honest with the court, fair to his opponents and faithful to his clients.

He was not a great orator, but his honesty of purpose, integrity of character and thorough familiarity with the law and facts of the case on hand, together with his clear, concise and logical presentation, made him a tower of strength in the courts, and especially before a Litchfield County Jury. He abounded in quaint simile, and many times the studied argument of his opponent would fall before some simple homley illustration, delivered at the oppertune time, in his inimitable style.

While always firm, and sometimes stern, in the performance of his duty, he possessed a most generous disposition, and was ever courteous and obliging to his brother lawyers and especially to the younger members of the Bar, to all of whom he became endeared, and was affectionately known as "Uncle Jim." He loved his profession and the members of the Bar, and their honest and oft expressed love and esteem for him, was a matter of great comfort to him in his declining years.

His commanding form and genial presence were in evidence at nearly every official meeting of the Bar, and were among the most pleasant features of the annual Bar banquets.

Socially, Mr. Huntington was of a domestic nature, and delighted in the companionship of his home, family and surroundings, believing in the simplicity of the nineteenth century customs rather than the pomp and glitter of twentieth century fads. He was a great lover of nature and would spend hours at a time roaming through the woods, fields and gardens where every tree, plant and flower had for him a noble sentiment to reveal, and he took an active interest in their growth and protection.

Mr. Huntington was a member of the school board and did much to build up and strengthen the educational system of the town of Woodbury. He was always active in his support of the Episcopal Church to which religious denomination he belonged. The high esteem in which Mr. Huntington was held by the citizens of Woodbury was in a measure evidenced by the memorial services held in that town on the evening of June 28th, 1908, and the proposed memorial fountain to be erected to his memory.

As a practicing attorney Mr. Huntington stood in the front ranks, not only of the Bar of Litchfield County, but also of the State of Connecticut, and yet the characteristics which stand forth most prominently to commemorate his memory, were his nobility of character, sincerity of purpose, lofty ideals and generous disposition; born of New England ancestors, reared in a New England climate, he lived and died an illustrous example of christian manhood.

WILLIAM F. HURLBUT, born in Winsted, Conn., January 27, 1835, and was admitted to the Bar in 1859. He resided in Winsted and was the Clerk of the District Court and Court of Common Pleas for Litchfield County since 1872, excepting three years during which time he was County Health Officer. He died at Winsted, April 11, 1901, aged 66. (See picture on page 142.)

HENRY C. IVES, admitted in 1832.

GEORGE W. JACOBS, admitted to the Bar in 1820.

DANIEL JAQUA, JR., admitted to the Bar in 1819. Practiced in Connecticut about twenty years.

GEORGE P. JENKS, admitted to the Bar in 1856.

EBENEZER JESUP, JR., admitted to the Bar in 1826.

EZRA JEWELL, admitted to the Bar in 1810 from Salisbury.

FREDERICK A. JEWELL, admitted to the Bar in 1881 from Salisbury. He removed to New Hartford, where he is now in practice. Is Judge of Probate. He represented the town in the General Assembly, 1907.

AMOS M. JOHNSON, born in Southbury, October 21, 1816, admitted to the Bar in 1851. Died at the Old People's Home in Hartford, April 6, 1879.

ELISHA JOHNSON, born in Barkhamsted, May 1, 1818. Graduated at Trinity College in 1835. Attended the Yale Law School and was admitted to this Bar in 1840. He practiced in Plymouth until 1855 when he removed to Hartford. He was Clerk of this Court from 1850 to 1851. He died in Hartford, February 18, 1891.

SOLON B. JOHNSON was born in Cornwall, admitted to this Bar in 1863. He published the Litchfield Sentinel from 1866 to 1873, then removed to his farm in Cornwall, where he died, May 30, 1890, aged 51 years.

WALTER W. JOHNSON was admitted in 1866. He never practiced.

SYLVESTER JOHNSON, admitted in 1813 from Cornwall, of which town he was a native.

H. ROGER JONES, JR., born at New Hartford, June 22nd, 1882, attended public schools in New Hartford and Gilbert School, Winsted, graduated from the latter, June, 1901. Entered Cornell University Law School at Ithaca, N. Y., September, 1903 and graduated June, 1906. Became a member of the New York Bar in September, 1906 and the Connecticut Bar February, 1907. At present is editor and proprietor of the New Hartford Tribune, and engaged in the practice of law at New Hartford.

WALTER S. JUDD was born in Litchfield in 1859, graduated at Yale Law School in 1882 and was admitted to the New Haven Bar that same year. Settled in Litchfield and was Clerk of the Court of Common Pleas from 1894-7. Was in the Legislature in 1891 and 1893, serving on the judiciary committee the last named year. Now resides in New York City.

GEORGE H. JUDSON was a native of Woodbury, admitted to the Bar in 1845 and removed to Texas.

S. W. JUDSON was a native of Cornwall and a graduate of Union College. Was admitted to practice in 1836. He located in New York City. It is said of him, "As a lawyer he is more distinguished for his learning, integrity and honesty, than for his brilliancy as a pleader. If lawyers were more generally of his style, we should have fewer law-suits and more justice."

CHARLES A. JUDSON was a native of Washington. Held the office of Sheriff from 1835 to 1838. After his term of office he removed to New Haven and engaged in mercantile business.

JAMES D. KEESE was born in the City of New York, entered Yale College, but did not finish his course of studies there; came to

Litchfield and studied law with Judge Seymour, and was admitted to this Bar in April, 1852. He immediately set up practice in Woodbury, but in less than one year removed to Birmingham, Conn., where he died.

EBENEZER B. KELLOGG was a native of Norwich, Conn., and for some years was a school teacher coming to Litchfield from Naugatuck, where he had been Principal of the schools. He studied law with George A. Hickox, and was admitted to the Bar in 1879. After a brief practice in Litchfield he removed to Denver, Colorado, where he died.

WILLIAM KELSEY practiced law in Winchester in 1850, and in 1856 removed to Cheshire, where he died.

DWIGHT C. KILBOURN was born in Litchfield, October 9th, 1837. He read law with Seymour & Seymour and Henry B. Graves, of Litchfield, and after a three years service in the war of the Rebellion was admitted to the Bar in April, 1866. Practiced in Litchfield until 1887 when he was appointed Clerk of the Superior and Supreme Courts of Connecticut for Litchfield County, which office he now holds.

GEORGE KINGSBURY, admitted to this Bar as of Canaan in 1794. Mr. Boyd in his annals of Winchester, refers to him as being assessed in that town in 1796 for his faculty as attorney-at-law, being the "first legal luminary that shed its light on this benighted town. His stay seems to have been as brief as a comet's visit." He removed to Poultney, Vt., where he died, April 30, 1803.

JOHN KINGSBURY, born in Norwich, West Farms (now Franklin), December 31, 1762. Graduated at Yale, 1786, and 1788 entered the Law School at Litchfield, and was admitted to this Bar in 1790, and the next year opened an office in Waterbury and soon became a leading citizen of that town. He was seventeen times in the Legislature. He was Judge of the County Court about twenty years. He died August 26, 1844. He was the grandfather of Frederick J. Kingsbury, Esq. of Waterbury, the distinguished banker and historian.

DANIEL M. KING was admitted to this Bar in 1870 from Watertown. He located in the West and died there.

EPHRAIM KIRBY, born in Litchfield in 1756, in a part of the town now included in Washington. See Article "First Law Reports" for his biography.

REYNOLD M. KIRBY was a son of Ephraim Kirby and was admitted to this Bar in 1810.

PHILEMON KIRKUM, admitted to the Bar in 1799, resided at Winsted. In Boyds Annals of Winchester is a very interesting account of this eccentric man.

WILLIAM KNAPP was a member of the Fairfield County Bar, but practiced in New Milford a few years prior to 1880, when he removed to Denver, Colorado.

FREDERICK M. KOEHLER, admitted to the Bar in 1885, resided in Litchfield, but soon removed with his family to Montana.

EDWARD A. KUNKEL, practiced at Torrington a year or two prior to 1878 and at a later period was at Thomaston.

JOHN R. LANDON was born in Salisbury, September 14, 1765, and married in Litchfield, Anna Champion, daughter of Rev. Judah Champion, January 10, 1796, and settled at Litchfield. He was Sheriff from 1801 to 1818. After his term of office expired he removed to Castleton, Vt., where he died, February 27, 1851. Mr. Landon during his term also had unpleasant duties. Here is sentence that he had to execute:

"Whereas Samuel Whitmore, of New Milford, in said county, before the Superior Court holden at Litchfield in said county, on the 1st Tuesday of February 1804, was legally convicted of *Adultry*, and, on consideration, was by the Judges of said Court sentenced and adjudged to be whipped on his naked body *Ten Stripes*, and to be stigmatized or burnt on his forehead with the letter "A" on a hot iron, and to wear a halter about his neck on the outside of his garments during his abode in this State of Connecticut—and as often as he shall be found without his said halter, worn as aforesaid, upon information and proof of the same before any Assistant or Justice of the Peace, to be whipped not exceeding thirty stripes, and to pay the cost of this prosecution, etc." All these sentences were thus executed to the letter, as appears from sheriff's returns. In executions for horse stealing, the prisoners were sentenced to be twice set astride a wooden horse and kept there an hour and then whipped fifteen stripes on the naked body, with an interval of a month between two punishments. A man convicted of forgery in 1788 was sentenced to stand twice in the pillory, and was "disenabled to give any evidence or verdict in any court or before any Magistrate or Justice of the Peace."

JOSEPH LAKE, admitted in 1822.

EDGAR M. LANDON of Salisbury, admitted in 1824.

HOWARD F. LANDON of Salisbury was born in Sharon in 1869 and graduated at the Amenia Seminary. He studied law with Hon. Donald T. Warner in Salisbury and graduated at the Albany Law School in 1890. He was admitted to the Litchfield Bar the following year and formed a partnership with Mr. Warner in Salisbury. As Senator from the 19th district he made an enviable record in the session of 1901.

HIRAM P. LAWRENCE of Winsted was born at Norfolk in 1833. He fitted for Yale College at Norfolk Academy, studied law with Judge F. D. Fyler in Winsted and was admitted to the Litchfield Bar in 1873. Died August 9, 1908.

ISAAC LEAVENWORTH, admitted to this Bar in 1815. Settled in Roxbury where he practiced for twenty years. In 1837 he removed to New Haven and engaged in other business. (See Sedgwick's fifty years.)

BRADLEY D. LEE, born in Barkhamsted March 24, 1838. Served in the War of the Rebellion as Quartermaster of the Second Connecticut, Heavy Artillery. Admitted to this Bar in 1856 and removed to St. Louis, Mo., where he became a leading attorney. Died in that city May 10, 1897.

CHAUNCEY LEE, D. D., born in Salisbury November, 1763. Graduated at Yale College in 1784, was admitted to this Bar in 1786. He practiced a few years and then relinquishing his profession, entered the Ministry and became a very learned and impressive preacher. He was author of "Revival Sermons," "Triumphs of Virtue," a metrical paraphrase of the Book of Job, an arithmetic, and several pamphlets. He died in Hardwick, N. Y., 1842.

REV. ALONZO NORTON LEWIS, M. A., born at New Britain September 3, 1831. Graduate of Yale, class of 1852. For several years a teacher of public schools and academies. Principal of Litchfield Academy 1852-4. Studied law with Hollister and Beeman and afterwards with Judge Charles B. Phelps of Woodbury, whose youngest daughter, Sarah Maria he married November 28, 1860. Admitted to the Bar at Litchfield September, 1857. Ordained an Episcopal clergyman in 1866. Rector at Bethlehem, Connecticut, Dexter, Maine, New Haven and Westport, 1866 to 1891. From 1891 to 1907 was rector of Christ Church, Montpelier, Vt. He died in New Haven September 12, 1907. He had been Secretary of the Masonic Veteran Association of Connecticut for many years. Was a member of the Society of the Cincinnati of Connecticut.

DANIEL W. LEWIS was a native of Farmington. Studied law with Judge Reeve, graduated at Yale College in 1788, and was admitted to this Bar in 1796.

JAMES LILLEY, admitted in 1809 as from Sharon.

FRANK D. LINDSLEY, admitted in 1882 from North Canaan. He located at Philmont, New York.

CHARLES D. LONGFELLOW was a native of Maine, but studied with Mr. Cothren in Woodbury and was admitted to this Bar in 1861. He located in Pennsylvania.

JOHN J. LORD, admitted in 1823 from Sharon.

LYNDE LORD was the second Sheriff of the County, holding the office from 1771 to 1801, about thirty years. He was born in Lyme, Connecticut, and died in Litchfield June 16, 1801, aged 68 years.

That he had some unpleasant duties to perform the following returns on Executions attest:

The execution in this case is dated 1779 and signed by Geo. Pitkin, Clerk of the Superior Court. The statute of blasphemy then in force reads as follows:

That if any person within this state shall presume wilfully to blaspheme the name of God the Father, Son or Holy Ghost, either by denying, cursing or reproaching the true God, or his government of the World; every person so offending shall be punished by whipping on the naked body, not exceeding forty stripes, and sitting in the pillory one hour; and may also be bound to his good behavior, at the discretion of the Superior Court, who shall have cognizance of the offence.

The nature of the punishment inflicted will most concisely appear from the following return of the officer setting forth what he did in pursuance of the sentence of the court:

LITCHFIELD, 23d August, 1779.

Then by virtue of the within Execution took the within named Samuel Tousley from the common Goal in Litchfield to a Gallos, viz, erected for that purpose, and set him thereon with a Rope round his Neck for the space of one full hour, and then I branded him with the capital Letter B with a hot iron on his forehead, and then tied him to a tail of a Cart, and caused him to be whip'd thirty-nine Stripes in his Naked body, in the whole,—at four of the most public places in the Town of Litchfield and then returned him to the Goal from whence he came.

Test,

LYNDE LORD, Sheriff.

Three days after execution of the sentence Tousley paid the cost in the case, amounting to £153, 8 shillings and six pence, or $531.42. This would imply that Tousley must have been a man of considerable property, but these costs were probably payable in paper money worth at that time hardly a twentieth of its face value in specie.

It seems that tramps were not unknown in Connecticut in our early history. A transient person who, "not having the fear of God before his eyes, but being moved and seduced by the instigation of the devil" burnt some buildings in Sharon, "contrary to the law of this colony and the rights of mankind." The fellow was duly convicted and sentenced, and the following sheriff's return shows the nature of his punishment. After being duly "bull dozed" at the cart's tail by the sheriff, he was remanded to jail till he could procure sureties for future good behaviour and had paid the costs of his prosecution:

LITCHFIELD, 21st Feb., 1776.

Then by virtue of the within Execution I caused the within named John Thomas to be taken from the common Goal in Litchfield to the place of Execution and there Set upon a Gallos with a Rope Round his neck for the full Term of one hour and Then tied to the Tail of a Cart and Transported to four of the most public places in the Town of Litchfield and there whipped on his naked body Thirty-nine stripes in the whole, according to the within Directions.

Fees 40s. Test,

LYNDE LORD, Sheriff.

GEORGE LOVERIDGE was admitted in 1840 and practiced a short time in New Milford.

JOHN P. LOVERIDGE. This name appears on the Connecticut Register of 1842 as an attorney at New Milford.

ROMEO LOWERY, born in Farmington in 1793, graduated at Yale in 1818, studied at the Litchfield Law School and was admitted to this Bar in 1820. He settled in Southington and was a highly respected member of the Hartford County Bar and a Judge of the County Court. He died in 1856.

BENEDICT E. LYONS was born in Thomaston, June 13, 1883. Graduated from Yale College in 1905 and from the Law School in 1908, and was admitted to this Bar in 1908. Located at Hartford. Represents Thomaston in the General Assembly of 1909.

DARIUS LYMAN was a son of Col. David Lyman, born in Goshen July 19, 1789. Was admitted to this Bar in 1812 and removed to Ravenna, Ohio. He died at the residence of his son-in-law, W. S. C. Otis, Esq., of Cleveland, Ohio December 13, 1865.

DAVID LYMAN was admitted to this Bar in 1841, and after a practice of five years he relinquished the profession and entered the Ministry of the Methodist Episcopal Church.

SAMUEL LYMAN was a son of Ensign Moses Lyman, born in Goshen January 25, 1749. He graduated from Yale College and studied Theology and afterwards studied law and was admitted to this Bar in 1773. He commenced practice at Hartford with flattering prospects of success, but relinquished that for a military appointment and removed to Massachusetts. Here he became a Judge of the Circuit Court of that State and was a member of the first Congress convened under the Constitution of the United States. He died at the age of 55 years.

WILBUR G. MANCHESTER was born in Winchester in 1860. Graduated at the Yale Law School and was admitted to the Bar in 1896. resides and practices in Winsted, and has been active in Grange and Prohibition circles.

THEODORE M. MALTBIE, born in New York in 1842, admitted to this Bar in 1863 from Norfolk where he practiced a short time and then removed to Hartford where he now resides.

CYRUS MARSH, practiced law in Kent in 1761 and was afterwards a Minister of the Gospel of that place.

FRANK W. MARSH, born in New Milford in 1855, graduated at Yale College in 1879, admitted to the New Haven Bar in 1882, removed to New Milford where he now resides.

SAMUEL MARSH, born in Litchfield in 1765, graduated from Yale College in 1786, admitted to this Bar in 1788 and removed to Norfolk, Va.

GEORGE A. MARVIN was born in Norfolk in 1870, graduated from the Yale Law School in 1901 and was admitted to this Bar. He resides and practices in North Canaan.

REYNOLD MARVIN was born in Lyme, Conn., and graduated at Yale College in 1748. He located in Litchfield on the formation of the New County, and was the first lawyer in that town. He was appointed King's Attorney in 1764, which office he held eight years. After this period he does not appear to have been active in legal matters. He died at Litchfield in 1802.

NICHOLAS MASTERS, born in 1758, graduated from Yale College in 1779, admitted to this Bar in 1780, resided in New Milford, where he died in 1795.

CHARLES S. MASTERS, admitted to this Bar in 1812 from New Milford.

PETER J. MCDERMOTT was born in Torrington, and graduated from Yale Law School in 1905 and was admitted to this Bar.

JAMES H. MCMAHON, born at New Milford, June 24, 1839; son of John and Sophia Wells McMahon. He received an acedemic education, but did not enter College. He studied law at the Albany Law School and was admitted to the Litchfield County Bar in November, 1863. Judge McMahon was a well-known lawyer in Western Connecticut, and for many years was engaged on one side or the other in most of the important cases in that section. He was elected Judge of Probate for the District of New Milford in August, 1864, and held his first term of probate, August 30th, of that year. He continued in office until the first Monday in January,1897. In 1873 and 1875, he was a member of the General Assembly. He died at New Milford, August 9,1906. His funeral was very largely attended by lawyers from Litchfield, Fairfield and New Haven Counties, in all of whose courts he had been an active practioner, and also by the members of the Odd Fellows, and the Masonic bodies of which he had been a member.

He gave in his will the sum of $1,200 to the Litchfield County Bar Association, to be divided between each of the Law Libraries at the Litchfield, Winsted and New Milford Court houses. His picture may be found on page 136.

WILLIAM H. McMORRIS was admitted to the Litchfield Bar in 1904. He removed to Pennsylvania.

WALTER S. MERRILL, born in New Hartford in 1829, admitted to this Bar in 1852 and located in Southington, where he resided until his death, January 10, 1901.

PAUL E. MEAD was born in Westbrook, Maine, October 27, 1878. but came when quite young to Falls Village, Conn. Studying at Exeter and at Brown's University, he entered the Yale Law School, from which he graduated in 1904, and was admitted to this Bar.

CHESTERFIELD C. MIDDLEBROOKS was Sheriff of Litchfield County from 1903 to 1907. He was born in Sharon, Conn., July 24, 1860. In 1880 he went to Winsted and entered the employ of the Gilbert Clock Company, where he continued for fourteen years. He was for several years at the head of the police force in Winsted, and was a constable of the Town of Winchester, in which offices he showed great executive ability. In 1894 he was appointed deputy sheriff under Sheriff Henry J. Allen, and in 1903 was elected sheriff by a good majority. At the expiration of his office in 1907 he was appointed by the Judges of the State, one of the Jury Commissioners for Litchfield County.

EDWARD S. MERWIN, admitted to the Bar in 1870 from New Milford.

T. DWIGHT MERWIN, born in New Milford. Graduated from Yale College in 1877. After a short practice in New Milford, he removed to New York City, where he is now in practice.

MICHAEL F. MILLS, born in Norfolk in 1786, admitted to this Bar in 1801. He located in Norfolk, dying there in 1857. (See Sedgwick's Address.)

ROGER MILLS was admitted to this Bar in 1798 from Norfolk and settled in New Hartford about 1800.

ROGER H. MILLS was a son of Roger Mills and was admitted to this Bar in 1836 and located at New Hartford. Was Secretary of State in 1849-1850, after which he removed to Beloit, Wis., where he died, November 11, 1880, aged 67.

JOSEPH MILLER, a graduate of Williams College, studied at the Litchfield Law School and was admitted to this Bar in 1802. He located at Winchester, was a member of the Constitutional Convention in 1818. In 1835 he removed to Richland, Mich. He was a member of the Michigan Constitutional Convention and also U. S. Attorney for the District of Michigan.

MATTHEW MINER, JR., born in Woodbury in 1781, graduated from Yale College in 1801 and was admitted to this Bar in 1804. Practiced in Woodbury, which town he represented in the General Assembly in 1830-1832, and was also Senator of his district in 1837. Died at Woodbury, December 11, 1839.

GILBERT S. MINOR, a native of Cornwall, admitted to the Bar in 1848. He removed to Alexandria, Va., where he died about 1880. (The compiler of this work pursued his law reading while in the U. S. service in the Civil War, from books borrowed from this gentleman's library.)

PHINEAS MINER, born in Winchester 1777, studied at Litchfield Law School, admitted to this Bar in 1797, began practice in his native town, but removed to Litchfield in 1816, was representative in Congress in 1832. Died at Litchfield, September 16, 1839. (See Boardman's Sketches.)

JOHN G. MITCHELL, practiced in Salisbury. (See Warner's Reminiscences.)

HENRY A. MITCHELL. The Connecticut Register says, he was a lawyer in Plymouth in 1832. He removed to Bristol. Was States Attorney for Hartford County, 1836 to 1838. Was editor of the Hartford Times.

JOHN G. MIX, admitted to this Bar in 1815 from Woodbury.

HENRY S. MORRILL, born in New Hampshire in 1840, graduated at Wesleyan College in 1866, was admitted to this Bar in 1870, and for a few years thereafter he was engaged as a teacher, but finally removed to Waterbury, where he was a Judge of the City Court. He died in Waterbury, July 12, 1884.

T. DWIGHT MORRIS, born in Litchfield in 1817, graduated from Union College in 1838, and was admitted to this Bar in 1839 and located at Bridgeport. Was Colonel of the 14th Connecticut Infantry in the Civil War, United Statets Consul at Havre, France, 1865 to 1869, Secretary of State, 1876. Died at Bridgeport, September 26, 1894.

NATHAN MORSE, a graduate of Amherst College, practiced in New Hartford in 1876, and removed to Akron, Ohio.

CHARLES E. MOSS, born in Litchfield and admitted to the Bar in 1843. Practiced in Waterbury until 1847, when he removed to Iowa. He was engaged in the Mexican War as a Sergeant of the 3rd United States Dragoons, and in the War of the Rebellion as a Lieutenant-Colonel of an Iowa Cavalry Regiment.

WILLIAM P. MULVILLE, born in Norfolk February 23, 1879. Graduated at Yale Law School in 1906, and was admitted to this Bar. Located at New Canaan, Connecticut.

WARREN MUNGER, admitted to this Bar in 1812 from Norfolk.

FRANK B. MUNN, born in West Stockbridge, Mass. November 16, 1860. Graduated from Dartmouth College in 1887, admitted to this Bar in 1891. Resides in New Hartford and practices in that town, and also has an office in Winsted. He is now, and has been a Referee under the United States Bankrupt Law since its passage.

HARRIS B. MUNSON, born in Middlebury in 1812, admitted to this Bar in 1850, finally located at Seymour, where he died, February 2, 1885.

THADDEUS MUNSON, practiced in Canaan in 1809.

FREDERICK E. MYGATT, a native of New Milford, studied at the Yale Law School, admitted to this Bar in 1892. Now practices in New York City.

EDWARD A. NELLIS held the office of Sheriff of Litchfield County from 1895 to 1903. He was born in the State of New York, but in early life came to Winsted, where he has since resided. For many years he carried on a tinware manufacturing and jobbing business. He was a soldier in the Civil War, a member of the 6th Connecticut Volunteer Infantry, he was wounded at the siege of Petersburg in 1864 and suffered an amputation of his left foot. (See picture on page 162.)

LEONARD J. NICKERSON of West Cornwall was born in that town October 23, 1857. He graduated from the Alger Academy and studied law with Hon. Arthur D. Warner, being admitted to this Bar in 1879. In 1883 he represented Cornwall in the General Assembly, and has been very active in town affairs. He has an extensive practice throughout the State. Picture, page 162.

MAJOR A. NICKERSON, a native of Cornwall, admitted to this Bar in 1834. After a brief practice, mostly in Berlin, Connecticut, he removed to New York State and entered the Ministry.

MAJOR A. NICKERSON, born in Cornwall and admitted to this Bar in 1868. For some years, owing to poor health he did not practice, but about 1888 opened a law office in Plainville, Conn. Died suddenly in his office, April 25, 1891.

MIKKEL NEILSON, a native of Denmark, studied law in Litchfield and was admitted to the Bar in 1881, and removed West.

CHARLES NETTLETON was born in Washington, Conn. October 2, 1819, and after studying law at Litchfield was admitted to the Bar. He opened an office in Naugatuck and was for a time in New Haven, but not meeting with satisfactory clientage he removed to the city of New York and made a specialty of conveyancing and for some years was a pension attorney. He was a great collector of the session laws of all the different States and it was claimed that he had the largest and fullest library in this line in the country. For the help of the Tilden-Hayes Electoral Commission, the Library of Congress moved to Washinton all this part of Mr. Nettleton's library. He died in New York May 5, 1892.

THEODORE NORTH, born in Goshen March 2, 1780. Graduated from Williams College and was admitted to this Bar in 1809. Member of the Constitutional Convention in 1818. Removed to Elmira N. Y. in 1823. Died April 21, 1842.

JONATHAN T. NORTON was admitted to this Bar in 1847 and practiced a short time in West Cornwall, when he removed to Brooklyn, N. Y.

JAMES H. NORTON, born in Goshen in 1823, admitted to this Bar in 1846 and soon removed to Pennsylvania. Entered the field of journalism and was connected with the New York City daily papers. Resided at Middletown, N. Y. Died in 1894.

WILLIAM H. O'HARA, born in Washington October 15, 1859 and was educated at the "Gunnery"; admitted to this Bar in 1880.

Practiced in Bridgeport. In 1893-4 was an Alderman in Bridgeport and the latter year president of the Board and Acting Mayor. In 1902 removed his office to New York City.

JAMES L. ORR, born in Hudson, N. Y., studied with Hon. John H. Hubbard, was admitted to the Bar in 1845. He practiced at Sharon and then removed to Michigan. His health failing him he returned to Salisbury, where he died.

SAMUEL D. ORTON, born in Bridgewater. Admitted to the Bar in 1830. Practiced a number of years in New Milford.

EUGENE O'SULLIVAN practices law in Torrington.

CHARLES A. PALMER, born in Goshen in 1859, graduated from Williams College. Admitted to this Bar in 1885. Practiced a few years at Sharon and then removed to Torrington. Now resides in Goshen, and is not in the practice of law.

JOSEPH M. PALMER, born in New Milford in 1788. Was admitted to the Fairfield County Bar, but located at Woodbury, where he practiced until 1816, when he removed to Fredericktown, Md. He was a Judge of one of the higher courts in that State.

SOLOMON M. PALMER was admitted to the Bar in 1811.

JONATHAN EDWARD PARMALEY, admitted to the Bar in 1790, resided and practiced in Bethlehem.

DAVID PARMALEE, a lawyer in Litchfield, 1797. (Connecticut Register.)

COL. AMASA PARKER, born in 1784 in the limits of the present town of Washington. Graduated from Yale College in 1808. Attended the Litchfield Law School and was admitted to the Bar in 1810. He removed to Delhi, Deleware County, N. Y.

ANSON V. PARSONS, admitted to the Bar in 1826.

DANIEL PARSONS, admitted to the Bar in 1847 from Sharon.

WALTER M. PATTERSON, admitted to the Bar in 1860, practiced a short time in Sharon.

CALVIN PEASE, a lawyer in New Hartford, 1799. (Connecticut Register.)

WILLIAM K. PECK, JR., born in Harwinton and admitted to the Bar in 1847 from Norfolk. He located in Norfolk and removed to Winsted in 1864. He removed from Winsted to Michigan in 1869, and died at Grand Rapids, Mich. in 1870. The following paragraph is from a highly complimentary notice of the stump labors of Wm. K. Peck, Esq. which we find in the *Western New Yorker* published at Warsaw, November, 1867:

"The series of meetings held in this county by W. K. Peck, Esq., of Connecticut, have been among the most successful and satisfactory ever known here. The appointment for the Court House on

Saturday evening drew together an audience that packed the room full. Mr. Peck is a man of fine presence and genial manners with a remarkably good voice and excellent qualities as a popular speaker. For perfect candor and fairness, for strong points sharply put, for earnestness and agreeable humor, and to sum it all up—for *a good effect* in a political speech, Mr. Peck ranks with the best men on the stump. We hope to have him here again."

NATHANIEL PERRY was a native of Woodbury and was admitted to the Fairfield County Bar in 1816. He began practice in Woodbury, removing to New Milford in 1823. He died in Kent in 1849, aged 60 years.

GEORGE W. PEET was born in Salisbury in 1828 and after admission to the Bar he practiced in Canaan. The latter part of his life was devoted chiefly to financial operations. He was president of the Iron Bank of Falls Village, etc. He died at North Canaan in 1882.

HUGH F. PETERS, graduated at Yale College in 1849; admitted to the Bar in 1851.

JOHN THOMPSON PETERS, graduated at Yale College, 1789; admitted to the Bar in 1791. Was Judge of the Superior Court from 1818 to 1834. Died August 28, 1834. Resided at Hartford. (See Sedgwick's "Fifty Years.")

JOEL T. PETTET, admitted to the Bar in 1801 from Sharon. He was a young man of great promise, but died of consumption, September 13, 1807, aged 32.

AUGUSTUS PETTIBONE, born in Norfolk February 19, 1766, a son of Col. Giles Pettibone. Attended the Litchfield Law School and was admitted to the Bar in 1790. He settled in Norfolk, was a member of the Constitutional Convention in 1818 and Judge and Chief Judge of the County Court from 1812 to 1831 He died October 4, 1847. (See Sedgwick's "Fifty Years.")

COL. GILES PETTIBONE, born in Simsbury December 9, 1735. His name appears as an attorney in the early records of the County Court. Resided in Norfolk and died there March 17, 1810.

SAMUEL PETTIBONE, the first King's Attorney of Litchfield County was born in Simsbury July 26, 1798. He began to practice law as early as 1730. He removed to Goshen prior to 1740 and was active in the formation of the County in 1751. Upon the establishment of the County Court he was appointed King's, or as we now term it, State Attorney, which office he held several years. He was prominent in the town affairs of early Goshen and represented the town in the General Assembly a number of times. He died in 1787.

SERENO PETTIBONE was a brother of Augustus Pettibone and born in Norfolk November 9th, 1778; graduated at Williams College in 1800, and was admitted to this Bar in 1803. He practiced a few years at Norfolk, and died there, November 16th, 1826, "just in the prime of life, a man of fine ability and promise."

JOHN PIERPONT, 1851.

JOHN PIERPONT, born in Litchfield April 6, 1785. Graduated at Yale College in 1804. Studied law at the Litchfield Law School and was admitted to this Bar in 1810. He removed to Newburyport, Mass., where after a short practice of law he became an Unitarian Minister. He edited a large number of school books; the old fashioned National Precepter, being perhaps the best known of them. He was also a poet, and his "Stand, the ground's your own my braves!" has been the standard for boyhood declamations, during the last three-quarters of a century. His poem delivered at our Centennial celebration in 1851, has also become classical. In his earlier years he, like many of the Boston celebreties, was not fastedious in his dress, and the portrait we publish of him is said by all our old men to be a characteristic one. The second, near the close of this book, looks as he did in later life, when he held a clerical position in one of the Government departments in Washington. He was the ancestor of John Pierpont Morgan, the noted banker and financier. Mr. Pierpont died at Medford, Mass., August 27, 1866.

CHARLES B. PHELPS was born in Chatham, now Portland, Connecticut in 1788 and pursued his professional studies under Judge Reeve and Noah B. Benedict, Esq., and was admitted to the Bar in September, 1809. Entered into practice at Woodbury, and there continued the exercise of his profession to the time of his death, December 21, 1858. He was Judge of Probate for nearly thirty years and was an authority on Probate Law. He was a member of the House of Representatives in 1831, 1837, and 1852 in which latter year he was elected its Speaker. In 1843 he was elected to the Senate and was its President pro tem. In 1850 he was elected Judge of the County Court, holding the office three years. In Mr. Cothren's history of Woodbury, will be found a lengthy biography of this honest lawyer. Picture, page 94.

RALPH P. PHELPS, attorney in Winchester, 1832. (Connecticut Register.)

E. FRISBIE PHELPS, graduated from Yale Law School, and was admitted to this Bar from Harwinton in 1866. He soon removed from the State. Is now in New York City in the insurance business.

ELISHA PHELPS, born in Simsbury. Graduated from Yale College in 1800; attended the Litchfield Law School and was admitted to this Bar in 1802. Settled in his native town, where he died in 1847.

AMOS PIERCE (PEARCE), graduated at Yale, 1783. Died in Woodbury, 1798.

JAMES PIERCE was admitted by the County Court in 1799.

JOHN PITCHER was admitted by the County Court in 1816. Lieutenant-Governor of New York.

JOHN PIERPONT, born in Litchfield September 10, 1805; member of the Law School; admitted to the Bar in 1826. He removed to Vergennes, Vermont. Was Judge of the Supreme Court and held other important offices in that State.

ORVILLE HITCHCOCK PLATT was admitted to this Bar in 1850. He was born in Washington, Conn., and his early life was that of a hard working farmer boy. Both parents being of good New England stock, earnest in religion, patriotic, and having the courage of their convictions, he inherited that breadth of mind and strength of character for which he became so prominent. Beginning in the old red school house, and afterward attending the Academy, in which he later on taught, he was still further furnished, by close and persistent study at home. Having chosen the law as his profession he entered the office of Gideon Hollister and Fred. Beeman in Litchfield in 1848 and in due time was admitted to this Bar. He began his practice at Towanda, Penn., but in a short time returned to Connecticut and settled at Meriden, where he soon became a prominent attorney and citizen. In 1855 he was Clerk of the Connecticut Senate and in 1857 was Secretary of State. He was repeatedly elected to represent his town in the General Assembly of the State, serving in the Senate in 1861-2, and in the House of Representatives in 1864 and 1869 and was given important positions in the deliberations of those bodies. In 1877 he was appointed State Attorney for New Haven County. In 1879 he was chosen United States Senator by the General Assembly, a position which he occupied continuously until his death at his summer residence at Washington, Connecticut, April 21, 1905.

In an address delivered by him to his townsmen just before starting for Washington to take his seat in the Senate, he said, "Just now everything is new and seems unreal. I can scarcely appreciate the future; how I shall walk in the new part in which I am set, time will show. I do know that I shall try to do right as I see the right."

He took his seat March 18, 1879, and for more than a quarter of a century gave his best thought and untiring industry to all matters of legislation and gradually won his own place in the front rank.

He served eighteen years on the committee of patents, eight of those years as chairman. He was regarded by all, as the best authority on patent law in the Senate. For sixteen years he was a member of the committee on Indian affairs, and no one was more alive than he to the true welfare of the Indians. No man in official life was ever a more practical and useful friend of these wards of the nation.

For twelve years he was a member of the committee on Territories, six years as chairman, and while such chairman six states were admitted into the Union, viz: North Dakota, South Dakota, Montana, Washington, Idaho and Wyoming.

For ten years and up to the time of his death, he was a member of the committee on finance. For four years he was chairman of the committee on Cuban Relations, and was the author and father of the noted Platt Amendment—that great bulwark and mainstay of the Cuban Republic against foes, foreign and domestic. In the investigation of this subject he accumulated a large and exhaustive library relating to Cuban and Philippine matters, probably the largest in the country, which has been given by his heirs to the State Library at Hartford, Conn.

He was for twelve years a leading member of the Judiciary Committee, and at the time of his death was chairman of that committee. On this great committee, on account of his skill and learning as a lawyer, and his industrious prudence and conservative character, he was one of the most active, useful and safe members, favorable to all reasonable innovations, but strongly set against revolutionary or doubtful schemes or measures. No man in the Republican party was oftener consulted by both Presidents, Mc-

ORVILLE HITCHCOCK PLATT

Kinley and Roosevelt upon vital questions, not only of party policy, but of material and international importance. The last great service he rendered, was in presiding over the Senate as a Court of Impeachment in the case of Judge Swain. The care, dignity and impartiality with which he performed that difficult task proved him to be a master mind in that eminent body.

Senator Teller of Colorado said of him: "He was a party man with a strong partisan spirit, because he believed his party was best calculated to secure the highest degree of progress and prosperity it was possible for a nation to attain. While he was a partisan and defended the principles of his party with intelligence and vigor, he recognized that there were two political parties in the country, and that there might be wisdom and patriotism in those differing with him. He was a good type of Americanism, and his aspiration for his country was for all parts and all the people within its borders."

Probably the obsequies of no eminent man of Litchfield County were ever attended by so many distinguished public men as were his when he was laid to rest amid the scenes he loved so well on April 24th, 1905, in the cemetery at Washington, Connecticut.

HENRY B. PLUMB, a native of Wolcott, Conn., born in 1857, was admitted to this Bar in 1879. He has never practiced law—but is Secretary of the Eagle Lock Company of Terryville, with office in New York city, and resides in Terryville.

E. LEROY POND, born in Terryville, Town of Plymouth, Dec. 26, 1883. Graduated at Yale College 1904, and from the Law School in 1906. Admitted to this Bar February, 1907, and opened an office in Terryville.

CHARLES J. PORTER, born in Goshen, January 27, 1839; was sheriff from 1881 to 1884. He was in the Civil War for three years in the First Connecticut Heavy Artillery in which he was a Quartermaster Sergeant. He resided in Goshen Center where he was Post Master and carried on a large general store business. He represented his town in the Legislature in 1866 and 1893. He died Dec. 19, 1907. (See picture, page 160).

PETER B. PORTER, born in Salisbury. Graduated from Yale College in 1791, admittd to this Bar in 1793. Removed to the State of New York and died at his home at Niagara Falls in 1844. He was in Congress in 1810 and was Secretary of War under John Q. Adams' administration.

JOEL B. POTTER, admitted in 1803 from Sherman. He died October 7, 1806.

NATHAN PRESTON, born in Woodbury in 1758. Graduated from Yale College in 1776. He served in the Continental Army until 1780. In 1782 he was admitted to the Bar and settled in his native town having a large practice and enjoying many political honors until his decease in September, 1822.

William Preston. He was born in Stratford in 1676, but when quite young removed with his father's family to Woodbury. He became a leading man in the town and colony. He was a member of the General Court thirty-five sessions, and stood high in the militia, having attained the rank of Colonel. He was justice of the quorum eleven years from 1740. On the formation of Litchfield County in 1751, he was appointed its first judge, which office he held till his death in 1754. He was a man of fine talents and commanding influence—of sterling integrity and unflinching determination.

In another place will be seen a cut of his tombstone in fine preservation in the cemetery at Woodbury.

William L. Ransom was born in Granville, Mass., March 28, 1822. He studied law with Judge Hiram Goodwin of Riverton and was admitted to this Bar in 1854. Three years later he came to Litchfield and associated with Hon. John H. Hubbard in the practice of his profession until 1859, when he was appointed Clerk of Superior and Supreme Courts for Litchfield County from which position he resigned in 1887 after an honorable service of twenty-nine years. He now resides in Litchfield.

From the history of the Ransom family I quote the following well deserved tribute: "William L. Ransom was tendered the position of Clerk of the Superior Court and the Supreme Court of Errors which his experience and methodical habits eminently qualified him to fill. He accepted the appointment and for twenty-eight years he continued to discharge the duties of the office with honor to himself and the tribunal of which he was a trusted official. Patience and courtesy secured for him the well grounded regard of the clientage that had 'their day in court' and Bench and Bar alike held him in the highest esteem."

Timothy C. Ransom was a brother of William L. and born September 22, 1824, and was admitted to the Bar in 1858. He practiced a few years in Meriden, Conn., and then removed to North Dakota where he died.

David Raymond admitted to the Bar in 1812 from Montville, Connecticut.

James Raymond admitted to the Bar in 1834 from Canaan.

John Reed. This gentleman was undoubtedly the earliest attorney in the territory embraced in Litchfield County. He graduated at Cambridge in 1697 and entered the ministry and preached at Waterbury, Stratford and other places. He became interested in the Stratford colony of settlers who went to the region now called New Milford, and obtained a large tract of land now the center of that town, and built a residence near the present Ingleside School, where he resided and held religious services in his house. In 1708,

THOMAS F. RYAN

while living there, he was admitted as an attorney by the General Court and in 1712 he was appointed Queen's Attorney for the Colony. Mr. Reed had plenty business of his own to attend to, for the Milford settlers claiming a superior title to the New Milford lands, over the Stratford title, occupied some of the 26,000 acres, and Mr. Reed sued them for trespass, and after sixteen trials, fifteen of which he won and lost the sixteenth, became discouraged and gave up the effort, and removed to a large tract of land he obtained in the present town of Redding where he resided until 1722, when he went to Boston, and soon became the most eminent lawyer in the Colonies. He was Attorney General for several years and also a member of the Governor and Council. He was known there as "Leather Jacket John." Many anecdotes are told of this eccentric attorney which this compilation does not care to repeat. Knapp's Biographical Sketches says of him: "One act alone should give him immortality. He, from his own high responsibility reduced the quaint, redundant and obscure phraseology of the English deeds of conveyance, to the present short, clear and simple form now in use. His influence and authority must have been great as a lawyer, to have brought these retrenched forms into general use. The declarations which he made and used in civil actions, have, many of them, come down to us as precedents, and are among the finest specimens of special pleading that can be found. Story has preserved some of his forms, and Parsons says that "many other lawyers had assumed his work as a special pleader as their own; and that honors due him had by carelessness or accident, been given to others, who had only copied his forms."

He married Ruth Talcott, daughter of Col. John Talcott of Hartford and sister of Governor Joseph Talcott. One of his sons was the celebrated Col. John Reed of the "Lonetown Manor," Redding, Connecticut. He died in 1749, leaving a large estate.

John G. Reid was a son of Rev. Adam Reid of Salisbury and was admitted to this Bar in 1857 and located at Kent. He did honorable service in the War of the Rebellion, and afterwards removed to Chicago.

Aaron B. Reeve was a son of Hon. Tapping Reeve, graduated from Yale in 1802, was admitted to the Bar in 1808, began practice in Troy, New York, where he died in 1809.

Tapping Reeve, born in Southhold, Long Island, October, 1744. Graduated from the College of New Jersey in 1763. In 1784 he opened the Law School at Litchfield which continued until 1833. In 1798 he was appointed Judge of the Superior Court and in 1814 he became the Chief Justice of the State. He died at Litchfield, December 13, 1823. See Boardman's "Early Lights," Law School, etc.

James Richards was admitted to the Bar in 1862. He then resided at Litchfield where he had been preaching for some years. He afterwards removed to Charleston, W. Va., where he died.

Francis X. Richmond was born in New Milford, admitted to the Litchfield Bar in 1897, and practiced for a short time in Waterbury. He removed to New Milford, and later returned to Waterbury, where he died in 1906.

Edward Richmond, admitted in 1815 from Washington.

Clark Richter, graduated from Yale in 1856, admitted in 1861 from Salisbury.

William H. Rood, admitted in 1845. Practiced in Winsted, was a Judge of Probate there, removed to Lynn, Mass., where he died.

Edward Rockwell, born in Colebrook June 30th 1801. Graduated at Yale College 1821. Admitted to this Bar in 1827 as from Sharon. He located in Youngstown, Ohio. Was the Secretary of the Cleveland and Pittsburg Railroad Company until 1867, when he resigned that office and removed to New York City, where he died in 1874.

Julius Rockwell was born in Colebrook, graduated at Yale College in 1826, admitted to this Bar in 1829 and located at Pitsfield, Mass. He was a member of Congress and also a Judge of the Supreme Court of Massachusetts.

The following extract shows the proceedings taken by the Berksire County Bar upon the death of Judge Rockwell in 1888:

"The Superior Court opened here this morning. Chief Justice Brigham presided at a memorial meeting of the Berkshire Bar in honor of the late Judge Julius Rockwell. There was a large attendance of lawyers, prominent citizens of the county and ladies. Attorney General Waterman offered resolutions adopted at a meeting of the Bar yesterday, gave a short sketch of Judge Rockwell's career and moved the adoption of the resolutions. Judge Tucker seconded the resolutions, and speeches were also made by the Hon. Marshall Wilcox, T. P. Pingree, Senator Dawes and Judge Brigham. The resolutions were ordered spread on the records of the court and as a mark of respect to Judge Rockwell's memory the court adjourned until to-morrow morning."

William Rockwell was born in Sharon in 1804. Graduated at Yale College in 1822, and admitted to this Bar in 1824. Located in Brooklyn, N. Y. Was a Judge of the Superior Court of King's County.

Alberto T. Roraback was born in Sheffield, Mass. in 1849. Acquiring a good academic education; in 1872 began the study of law with Judge Donald J. Warner in Salisbury and was admitted to this Bar in 1872. He located at North Canaan and was for a

DAVID C. SANFORD

quarter of a century a leader of the affairs of north western Connecticut. From 1889 to 1893 he was the Judge of the Court of Common Pleas for Litchfield County. In 1895 and 1896 he represented his town in the General Assembly, and in 1897 was appointed a Judge of the Superior Court. He was in 1907 promoted by the Legislature to be a Judge of the Supreme Court of Errors to take effect in September, 1908. His picture is shown on page 133.

J. CLINTON ROARBACK, a son of Judge A. T. Roarback was born in North Canaan. Graduated at Yale University and at the Yale Law School. Was admitted to this Bar in 1905. He resides and practices in North Canaan.

J. HENRY ROARBACK was born in Sheffield, Mass. in 1870, and admitted to practice in 1892 at this Bar. He located at North Canaan in company with his brother Judge A. T. Roarback to whose law business he suceeded upon the latter's elevation to the bench in 1897. He has been a very active politician, holding the position of a member of the Republican State Central Committee for several years. Is the Postmaster at North Canaan. He is also extensively engaged in the lime business of that region.

WILLARD A. RORABACK was born in New Marlboro, Mass. March 12th, 1860 and admitted to this Bar in 1883. Locating in Torrington, he has held many of the town offices, representing the town in the Legislature of 1895. Has been Judge of the Borough Court, and is now Judge of the Probate Court of that District.

ELBERT P. ROBERTS was born in Litchfield in 1863 and was admitted to this Bar in 1884. Resides and practices in Litchfield. He has a large real estate business, and has for many years been the Secretary of the Board of Education of Litchfield.

WILLIAM J. ROBERTS was born in New Milford and graduated in Yale College in 1859. During the War of the Rebellion he was a Captain of Company I, Eighth Regiment of Connecticut Volunteers. He was admitted to the Bar in 1866, and died in New Milford, June 30, 1870.

WILLIAM R. ROGERS, of Georgia, a graduate of the Litchfield Law School, was admitted to this Bar in 1831.

SAMUEL ROWLAND, admitted to this Bar in 1794, resided in Fairfield, Conn. and died there in 1837.

PHILO RUGGLES was born in New Milford in 1765 and admitted to the Bar in 1791. Began practice in New Milford and then removed to Poughkeepsie, and afterwards to New York City where he died in 1829.

JOHN H. RUSSELL, a native of Canaan, admitted to this Bar in 1849 and settled in Salisbury. He devoted most of his time to farming. He died at Lakeville in 1871.

JOSEPH RYAN, admitted to practice in 1858 from Norfolk, went to Illinois.

TIMOTHY RYAN, admitted in 1861 from Norfolk. Located in Illinois.

THOMAS F. RYAN was born in Ireland, March 6, 1872. He was educated at St. Mary's College, Troy, N. Y. and graduated from Yale Law School in 1897, and was admitted to this Bar. He began to practice at Torrington, but soon went to Tucson, Arizona, where he combined law and mining. He returned to Connecticut in 1901 and located in Litchfield in 1905.

DAVID C. SANFORD, born in New Milford in 1798, was admitted to the Bar in Fairfield County in 1820. He removed to Litchfield, where he practiced till 1832, when he went to Norwalk, but soon returned to New Milford, where he resided at the time of his death in 1864. In 1854 he was elected a Judge of the Superior Court, which office he held at the time of his decease.

GEORGE A. SANFORD, born in Simsbury, 1852; educated at Union College, was admitted to the Litchfield County Bar in 1903. He resides and practices at Winsted. Is an active member of the School Board of Winchester.

ROLLIN SANFORD was born in Cornwall, Vt. of Litchfield, Conn. ancestry. Graduated from Yale College in 1831 and was admitted to this Bar in 1833. He abandoned the legal profession and engaged in the mercantile business in New York City, where he died, December 2, 1879.

HENRY SEYMOUR SANFORD died at his home in New Milford on Saturday November 2, 1901 at the age of 69 years. He was the son of the late Judge David C. Sanford and of Amelia S. (Seymour) Sanford, a member of the distinguished Seymour family of Litchfield. He was born in Norwalk, Conn., March 1, 1832. He entered Yale College in 1848 and graduated in the class of 1852. He then took the two years' course at the Harvard Law School. After his admission to the Bar he spent one year in Washington, D. C., as private Secretary for Ex-Judge Seymour, then a member of Congress. Returning to New Milford, he became associated with his father in his well established law practice, and when his father was elevated to the supreme bench, the son carried on the practice with ability.

At the age of 29 years he met with a serious accident that disabled him physically for life, placing him at a great disadvantage when in the full strength of youth he was entering upon an unusually promising career. But with remarkable pluck and bravery he rose superior to a misfortune which would have discouraged an ordinary man from attempting to do anything noteworthy, and for many years with rare perseverance and patience successfully pur-

HENRY SEYMOUR SANFORD

sued his chosen calling, although unable to go about except in a wheel-chair, and what was more remarkable still, he retained his naturally high spirits and genial disposition.

Mr. Sanford moved to Bridgeport in 1869 and was a well known attorney there for thirty years. He was at one time the leading lawyer of the Fairfield county Bar, and he was associated with or opposed to the foremost lawyers of his city and state in many important cases, a number of which came before the Supreme Court. He was aggressive, able and brilliant as a lawyer and liked nothing better than to cross swords with a foeman worthy of his steel.

One of the last and most gracious acts of Mr. Sanford's life was to donate the rare and valuable collection of law books which had belonged to him and his distinguished father to the law library in New Milford for the use of the members of the Litchfield County Bar which the two Sanfords, father and son, had both honorably and ably represented.

HENRY S. SANFORD, a son of Henry Seymour Sanford, was born in Bridgeport August 5, 1873. Graduated from Yale Law School in 1895. He was admitted to the New Haven Bar in the same year, and admitted to the New York Bar in 1898. Practiced in New York until 1905. Soon after the decease of his father he removed to New Milford, where he now resides and practices.

ALBERT SEDGWICK was born in Cornwall in 1801. He held the office of Sheriff 1834 and 1835 and also from 1838 to 1854 in which latter year he resigned the office, having been appointed School Fund Commissioner of Connecticut which office he held for twelve years during which time he resided in Hartford. He was an ardent and active politician, with a genial pleasing way and won many voters to his side at the polls. He died in Litchfield at the residence of his daughter Mrs. Thomas M. Coe in 1878. He at one time was greatly interested in developing the mining of Nickel in the western part of Litchfield, but the opening of the civil war and discovery of the rich silver deposits in the great West ruined this industry in Connecticut.

FREDERICK A. SCOTT, born in Plymouth in 1866, graduated from Yale 1889, from Yale Law School in 1891 and admitted to this Bar the same year. Resides at Terryville, practices at Hartford. Has been Clerk of the different branches of the General Assembly and in 1901 was Clerk of Bills in that body. Represents Plymouth in the General Assembly of 1909.

HOMER R. SCOVILLE was born in Harwinton in1865, graduated at Williams College in 1890, the New York Law School in 1892, and was admitted to that Bar the same year. After a few years practice in New York City, he removed to Torrington, Conn., and was admitted to this Bar in 1900. He is now in active practice in Torrington.

CHARLES F. SEDGWICK. The following obituary of this distinguished member of our Bar is taken from the 50th Conn. Reports, for which it was prepared by his colleague and friend Bro. Donald J. Warner:

Charles F. Sedgwick was born in Cornwall, Litchfield County, Connecticut, Septemeber 1, 1795. His grandfather Gen. John Sedgwick, was a major in the Revolutionary army, and a major-general of the State Militia. His ancestory is traced to Robert Sedgwick, one of Cromwell's Generals.

He was a brother of the late Albert Sedgwick, and a cousin of the renowned Gen. John Sedgwick, of the Sixth Corps of the Army of the Potoma.

After graduating at Williams College, 1813, he took charge of an academy in Sharon, Conn. and at the same time studied law, and was admitted to this Bar in March, 1820. He immediately located in Sharon, and there continued in the practice of his profession, and ended there his life's work.

He married Betsy, daughter of Judge Cyrus Swan, of Sharon, October 15, 1821.

He was early a member of the Legislature in both branches, a Judge of the Court of Probate for the District of Sharon, and from 1856 to 1874 was States Attorney for the county.

He inherited and manifested a special admiration for military affairs, and was appointed Brigadier General of the State Militia in 1829, and afterwards Major General of the Third Military Division of the State. Physically, he was a remarkable man; large, tall, and erect, his appearance in and out of the court room was attractive and commanding. As a lawyer not arrogant, not brilliant, always courteous, a ready, fluent advocate, presenting his views of the case on trial with force and zeal, commanding the respect of the court and jury.

In the discharge of his duty as a public prosecutor, the administration of his office was characterized by the application of the principle "that ninety-nine guilty persons should escape, rather than one innocent person should suffer." His habits were exemplary; tobacco and intoxicants in all their forms were to him abhorrent.

The current events of the day were all noted by him, and he delighted in works of history, biography and genealogy. His wonderfully retentive memory, bodily vigor, and genial nature made him a delightful talker in the social circle, and eminently useful in furnishing information of and concerning persons and their affairs. If it became necessary to find a collateral or other heir to an estate, or to insert a branch in the genealogical tree of a family in Western Connecticut, Gen. Sedgwick was referred to as a living compendum of the required information, and his detailed reminiscences of the peculiarities and characteristics of persons always interested his hearers and often excited their merriment.

His centennial address and history of the town of Sharon in 1865, is a valuable depository of knowledge for the inhabitants of the town. He lived soberly, he waited for death calmly and died in communion with the Congregational Church at Sharon, March 9th, 1882, in his 87th year. Picture on page 70.

EDWARD WOODRUFF SEYMOUR, a Judge of the Supreme Court of this State, died at Litchfield, on the 16th day of October, 1892. He was born at Litchfield, August 30th, 1832 the oldest son of Chief Justice Origen S. Seymour. His mother was a sister of George C. Woodruff, Esq., of Litchfield, a prominent lawyer there, and Judge Lewis B. Woodruff of New York. He graduated at Yale in 1853, and was admitted to the Bar in Litchfield in 1856, where he continued to practice until 1875, when he removed to Bridgeport, and formed a partnership with his younger brother, Morris W. Seymour, with whom he was associated until 1889, when he was appointed a Judge of the Supreme Court of Errors. He was for several years Judge of Probate in the Litchfield district. He represented Litchfield in the State Legislature in 1859-60-70-71, and was a member of the State Senate in 1876. He represented his district in Congress from 1882 to 1886. He was one of the representatives of the diocese of Connecticut in the general conventions of the Protestant Episcopal Church of the United States.

As a lawyer he was thorough, quick in perception, sound in reflection, pleasing and effective in speech. He prepared his causes conscientously. His knowledge of men, his quick wit, his rare apprehension of humor and humorous things, his abounding good judgment, his intellectual alacrity in emergencies, and his courage in a crisis gave him a fine outfit for practice. He cross-examined a witness always with skill, and sometimes with genius. But no tempation to score a point ever led him into the petty tyranny of abusing a witness. He wore the golden rule on his heart and remembered that the man in the witness box was a brother.

As a Judge, without being hortatory he warmed his opinions with wholesome morals. Such ethics, for instance, as we find in the opinion in Coupland vs. Houstonic Railroad Company, in the 61st Conn., make good reading. His career as a lawyer and Judge strengthens our attachment to our profession which he adorned.

Judge Seymour is mourned by the Bar and by the bench of the State with a common and tender grief. Years of closest intimacy bound many manly hearts to him with a love which may not be told, but which must be undying. His grave is the tomb of hope and promise and of a life broken when it was strongest. He was buried in the afternoon of a gentle October day, when the sun shone through the clouds and brightened the gold and scarlet and crimson of fading nature, and he was buried in love.

From Henry C. Robinson's sketch in the 62d Conn. Reports.

## A TRIBUTE BY JUDGE FENN.

Yesterday morning, at Litchfield, there passed from week-day toil into Sunday rest, from work so consecrated that it was worship into eternal peace—as pure a soul, and as gentle, as ever parted from earth to enter heaven. One who speaks from a torn heart because he loved him living, and loved him dead; one who met him in delightful social intercourse four days last week, (the last time on Friday), in seeming health, full of life and its interests, and to whom the telegram announcing his sudden death came with shocking agony, can neither be silent or speak with a calm, dispassionate utterance, in such an hour. Edward W. Seymour lies dead at the age of sixty, in the town in which he was born, and on the street where he has always lived. The oldest son of the late Chief Justice, Origen S. Seymour, he inherited the rare judicial temperament, the calm, candid, impartial judgment, the love of mercy-tempered justice, so essentially characteristic of his father. Educated at Yale College, a graduate of the famous class of 1853, studying law in his father's office, entering into partnership with him, early and frequently called to represent his town, and later his senatorial district in the General Assembly, a useful member of Congress for four years, having in the meantime, by devotion to his profession, as well as by natural ability, become the acknowledged leader of the Bar in the two counties of Litchfield and Fairfield; certainly it was the principle of natural selection which three years ago led to his choice as a member of our highest judicial tribunal—the Supreme Court of Errors of this State. While of his services upon that Court this is neither the time, or place, to speak with fullness, it has been the privilege of the writer to know them somewhat thoroughly, and because of such knowledge he can the more truly bear witness to the rare spirit of fidelity to duty, to justice, to law, as a living, pervading and beneficent rule of action, with which, whether upon the bench listening to, and weighing the arguments and contentions of counsel, in private study, in the consultation room, or in the written opinions of the Court, which bear his name, the high duties of that great office have been sacredly discharged. When Chief-Justice Seymour died, Governor Richard D. Hubbard, in a public address, declared: "I think we can all say in very truth and soberness, and with nothing of extravagance in eulogy, that we have just lost the foremost, undeniably the foremost lawyer, and take him for all in all, the noblest citizen of our State." If it be too much to say this of a son, whose years were almost a score less than those of the father, surely it is not too much to affirm that never did son tread more worthily in the footsteps of an honored parent, and never did untimely death break truer promise than this which has deprived our State of those years of ripened usefulness, which would have made the career of the son as fruitful in honor, and all good, and good to all, as that of the sire. But God knows best, and doubtless what is, is for the best. Certainly to him who lies crowned with the beautiude of Christ, upon the pure in heart, it is well.—AUGUSTUS H. FENN.

Picture on page 130.

MOSES SEYMOUR, JR. was born in Litchfield on June 30th, 1774. He held the office of Sheriff from 1819 to 1825. He gave little personal attention to it, being actively engaged in business,—and deputizing his brother Ozias who was his deputy, to attend to the Court duties. He was for a while Postmaster at Litchfield. He gave the site on which the Court House is now located to the County to be used only for County purposes. He was a large landholder, and engaged largely in the exchange and sale of real property. He died in Litchfield, May 8, 1826. (See Sedgwick's Address.)

ORIGEN S. SEYMOUR, born in Litchfield February 9, 1804, graduated from Yale College in 1824, admitted to this Bar in 1826 and located in his native town in which he resided until his decease, August 12, 1881. He frequently represented the town of Litchfield in the General Assembly and was elected Speaker of the House in 1850. In 1851 he was elected to Congress and again in 1853. In 1855 he was elected one of the Judges of the Superior Court, which office he held eight years. In 1864 and 1865 he was nominated for Governor by the Democratic Party. In 1870 he was elected a Judge of the Supreme Court of Errors and in 1873 was its Chief Justice, which office he held until retired by the Constitutional limitation of age in 1874. After his retirement he was engaged most of the time as a referee. The new code practice adopted by the Legislature in 1879 was prepared by a Commission over which he presided. He received the degree of L. L. D. from Trinity College in 1866 and from Yale, 1873.

The obituary notice and tributes to his great worth published in the 48 Conn. Report are but faint expressions of the feelings of all of the legal fraternity and leading citizens of the State of Connecticut regarding this distinguished member of our Bar.

The following obituary notice was published by the New Haven Register at the time of Judge Seymour's death: "This distinguished citizen of Connecticut died at his home in Litchfield, this morning, after a comparatively brief illness, in his 78th year. Possessed of a fondness for study, he prepared for college, and entered Yale at the age of sixteen, graduating in the class of 1824. His chosen profession was the law, and by his assiduity and natural gifts he speedily arrived at the highest rank at the Bar. Though devoted to his profession he engaged astivily in politics, espousing the Democratic cause. He was a member of the House of Representatives of Connecticut in 1842, 1843, 1849 and 1850, being Speaker in the latter year. In 1851 he was elected to Congress from the 4th District, and at the expiration of his term was re-elected. In 1855 he became a Judge of the Superior Court, continuing in office until 1863. In 1870 he was promoted to the Supreme Bench. He was Chief Justice from June 5, 1873, to February 9, 1874, when he became disqualified by reason of having reached the age of 70 years, and retired from the Bench, which he had greatly adorned. Upon his retirement from the Bench he resumed the practice of the law, being consulted in a great number of important cases. He served on various State Commissions, one of which was that appointed to settle the disputed boundaries between New York and Connecticut. His most important recent public duty was that upon the commission to revise the Civil Practice in the State courts. Of this commission he was the chief part, and the report adopted by the commission, of which he is the reputed author, was ratified by the Legislature and is now the established law of the commonwealth. The series of brilliant lectures delivered by him before the Yale Law School and members of the New Haven Bar, in advocacy of the adoption of the revised civil practice, had much to do with its final adoption. Though advanced in years he was elected a member of the House of Representatives of Connecticut in 1880, and was a controlling spirit in that body, although his usefulness was impaired latterly by ill health.

Born of a family distinguished both in law and in politics, Judge Seymour was one of its most brilliant scions. He was a cousin of

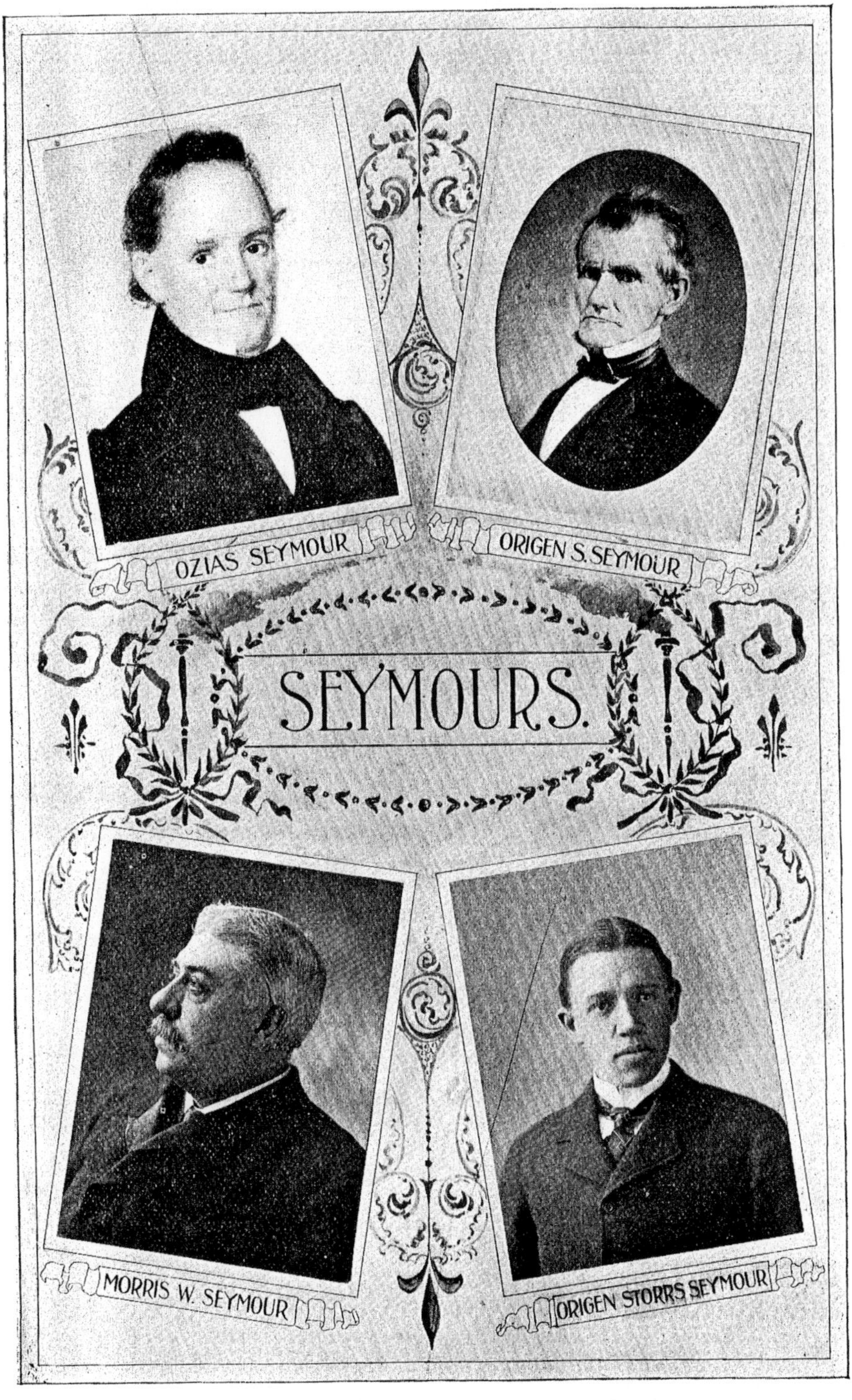
OZIAS SEYMOUR
ORIGEN S. SEYMOUR
SEYMOURS.
MORRIS W. SEYMOUR
ORIGEN STORRS SEYMOUR

Horatio Seymour of New York, a relative of Ex-Governor Thomas H. Seymour of Connecticut, and leaves behind him two sons at the Bar, Morris W. Seymour of Bridgeport and Edward W. Seymour of Litchfield; another son, Rev. Storrs O. Seymour is a prominent Episcopal clergyman in Litchfield. In politics Judge Seymour was a consistent, unflinching and earnest democrat. In religion he was an Episcopalian, being a devout and devoted Churchman.

While Judge Seymour was prominent in all the walks of life, whether in church affairs, politically or socially, he will be chiefly remembered as a great lawyer and a good man. By his qualities of mind and training he was specially fitted to ornament the Bar. His intellect was clear and cloudless; he grasped the salient points of a controversy with remarkable ease and quickness; in statement he was luminous, perspicacious and strong. His style of oratory was simple unornamental but pellucid and most convincing. Those who heard him argue a case were convinced in spite of themselves that Judge Seymour reasoned from internal conviction of the truth of his cause and they felt that the argument flowed from his intellect as a logical sequence of established facts. Hence he was, while unrhetorical, a most persuasive speaker. By his death the Bar of the State loses its brightest luminary, his party an able and effective, advocate, the church a pious and noble member, and society one who was amiable, gentle and affectionate, and who loved mankind because he recognized in them something akin to divinity. Viewed in every aspect his death must be regarded as a public calamity. That he will rest in peace needs no assurance. With such a noble life, such lofty aspirations, such a pure purpose, and with such noble fulfillments of the promises of his early manhood, he leaves behind him a record which, while it is the honor and glory of his family, is also a delight and blessing to the public. Judge Seymour was a good and great man. He needs no further eulogy.

His portrait is on page 210.

Ozias Seymour was born in Litchfield July 3, 1776, was a brother of Moses Seymour, Jr. He held the office of Sheriff from 1825, when he succeeded his brother in that office, to 1834. He was the father of the late Chief Justice Seymour. He died in Litchfield. His picture is included in the Seymour group.

Morris W. Seymour, son of the late Chief Justice Origen S. Seymour and brother of the late Supreme Court Judge, Edward W. Seymour, was born in Litchfield in 1842, was a member of the class of 1866 Yale, graduated from Columbia Law School in 1868 and was at once admitted to the Litchfield County Bar. Mr. Seymour began practice in Bridgeport and was soon elected successively city clerk, city attorney and corporation counsel. In 1881 and 1882 he was a member of the State Senate and was chiefly instrumental in establishing the State Board of Pardons of which he has been for many years, a valued member. He has been lecturer on law at Yale

University and has given especial attention to admirality and patent cases in the highest courts of the nation. Mr. Seymour's summer residence is at the old homestead in Litchfield.

ORIGEN STORRS SEYMOUR, is a son of Morris W. Seymour, graduated from Yale College in 1894 and from Yale Law School in 1896 and was admitted to this Bar in 1896. Is in practice in New York City.

FRANK W. SEYMOUR, born in Colebrook in 1871, graduated from Yale College in 1892 from Yale Law School in 1894, admitted to this Bar in 1894. Resides in Winsted and is Judge of the Winchester Town Court, and Judge of Probate of that district.

JAMES P. SHELLEY was born in Torrington in 1859 and admitted to this Bar in 1889. Resides and practices at Winsted. Has a large practice in Pension matters and Government claims.

GEORGE F. SHELTON was a native of Southbury, but was admitted to this Bar in 1851. He located at Seymour and soon became interested in extensive manufacturing operations in that town. He was very active in State Military matters and at one time held the office of Major General. He was also very prominent in political affairs. He died at Seymour, October 17, 1902.

GEORGE F. SHELTON was born in Southbury and graduated from Yale College in 1877. He studied law in Woodbury and was admitted to this Bar in 1880. His professional life has been in the Western States very much interested in railroad litigation. He is now in practice in Butte, Montana, and is one of the counsel for Senator William A. Clark in his extensive mining industries.

STEPHEN SHELTON was admitted to this Bar in 1811 from Plymouth.

DANIEL SHERMAN, of Woodbury, born August 14, 1721, was perhaps the most distinguished man that had arisen in the town previous to his day. He was a descendant of Samuel Sherman, of Stratford who emigrated to this country from England, in company with his brother, Rev. John Sherman, and his nephew, Capt. John Sherman, ancestor of Hon. Roger Sherman. He was a justice of the quorum for twenty-five years, a Judge of the Litchfield County Court for five years from 1786. For sixteen years he was Probate Clerk for the district of Woodbury, and Judge of that district for thirty-seven years. He represented his native town in the General Assembly sixty-five sessions, retaining the unbounded confidence of his fellow-citizens. This was by far the longest period of time any one has ever represented the town. He was a member of the Council of Safety from 1777 to 1781. He was a man of commanding powers of mind, of sterling integrity, and every way qualified for the various public trusts confided to his care. He died at Woodbury, July 2, 1799, full of honors, and was followed by the affec-

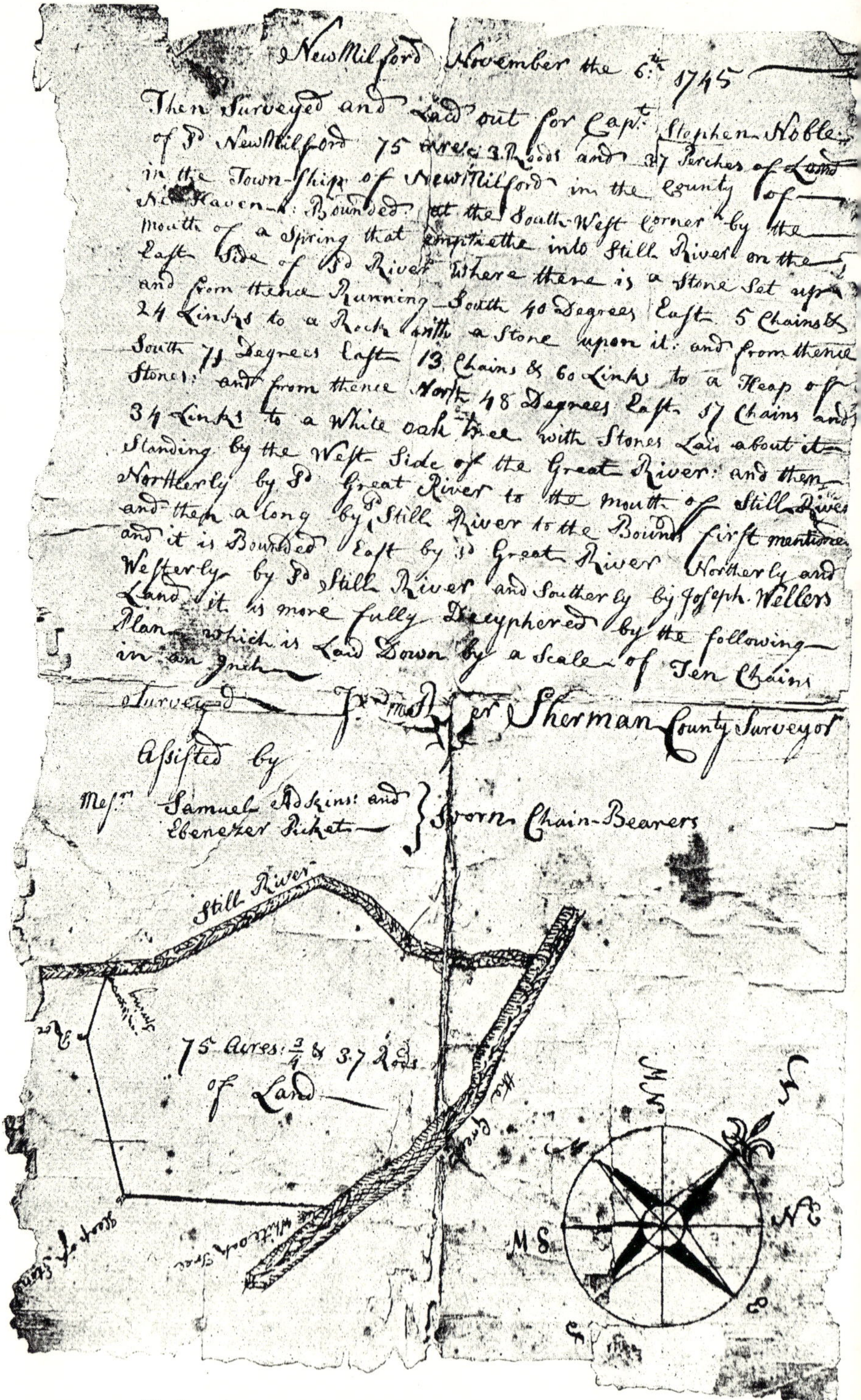

New Milford November the 6th 1745

Then Surveyed and Laid out for Capt. Stephen Noble of sd New Milford 75 Acres 3 Roods and 37 Perches of Land in the Town-Ship of New Milford in the County of New Haven: Bounded at the South-West Corner by the mouth of a Spring that emptieth into Still River on the East Side of sd River where there is a Stone Set up and from thence Running South 40 Degrees East 5 Chains & 24 Links to a Rock with a Stone upon it: and from thence South 71 Degrees East 13 Chains & 60 Links to a Heap of Stones: and from thence North 48 Degrees East 17 Chains and 34 Links to a White oak tree with Stones Laid about it Standing by the West Side of the Great River: and then Northerly by sd Great River to the mouth of Still River and then a long by sd Still River to the Bounds first mentioned and it is Bounded East by sd Great River Northerly and Westerly by sd Still River and Southerly by Joseph Wellers Land it is more fully Decyphered by the following Plan which is Laid Down by a Scale of Ten Chains in an Inch

Surveyed pr me Roger Sherman County Surveyor

Assisted by

Messrs Samuel Adkins: and Ebenezer Piket } Sworn Chain-Bearers



Reduced Facsimile of Layout of Land by Roger Sherman.

*Compliments of D. C. Kilbourn.*

*Insert in Bench and Bar Book.*

tionate recollections of the inhabitants of the town among whom he had so long lived. (History of Woodbury). He was the ancestor of Major-General William T. Sherman, and of Hon. John Sherman, M. C.

ROGER SHERMAN, a signer of the Declaration of Independence in 1776, was born in Massachusetts, and came to New Milford in 1750. He was admitted to this Bar in 1754 and in 1761 removed to New Haven where he lived until his death, July 23, 1793. See article on Signers of the Declaration, page 172.

OLIVER SKINNER, born in Litchfield July 18, 1782, and admitted to this Bar in 1803.

RICHARD SKINNER, LL. D. was born in Litchfield May 30th, 1778, the son of General Timothy Skinner and Susannah Marsh, his wife. He was admitted to the Bar in 1800, and removed to Manchester, Vt.

At the deidcation of the Mark Skinner Library in that town July 7, 1897, the following sketch of Richard Skinner was given by his townsman, Judge Loveland Munson: "It was in the year 1800 that Richard Skinner, then 22 years of age, and fresh from the Litchfield Law School, became a resident of Manchester and commenced the practice of his profession. He was appointed State's Attorney for Bennington County in the second year of his practice, was elected Judge of Probate for the District of Manchester five years later, and was continued in those offices until called to more important fields of service. He was a member of Congress from 1813 to 1815, three times chosen Governor of the State, a Judge of the Supreme Court of the State for eight years, the first Chief Judge of the Court as now organized. The esteem in which he was held is sufficiently attested by the fact that for twenty-eight years, and until his voluntary retirement, he was continuously in the public service." His death occurred in Manchester May 23, 1833.

ROGER SKINNER was a brother of Richard Skinner, and was born in Litchfield June 10, 1773, and admitted to the Bar in 1793. He began practice in Litchfield but removed to the State of New York. He was Judge of the United States Court in the Northern District of that State.

ROGER S. SKINNER graduate from Yale College in 1813 and was admitted to this Bar in 1816.

BARZILLAI SLOSSON graduated from Yale College in 1791, was admitted to the Fairfield County Bar in 1793, and settled in Kent, where he died in 1843. (See Boardman's Sketches).

JOHN SLOSSON, a son of the foregoing was admitted to this Bar in 1801. Resided in Kent where he was a prosperous merchant.

WILLIAM SLOSSON was admitted to this Bar in 1800 from Kent.

AARON SMITH was a son of Gen. David Smith of Plymouth, graduated at Yale in 1790, studied at Reeves Law School and was admitted to this Bar in 1793. In 1809 he located in Litchfield, where he held many official positions and died there in 1834.

CHAUNCEY SMITH, was a lawyer in Sharon in 1819, 1820. (Conn Reg.)

ERASTUS SMITH of Plymouth was admitted to this Bar in 1828, and located in Hartford about 1833 and practiced there for forty years. He died in 1878.

JAMES W. SMITH admitted to this Bar in 1884. He went to Kansas and practiced a few years and in 1895 returned to Winsted where he is now in practice.

JOHN COTTON SMITH, born in Sharon February, 12, 1765, graduated from Yale in 1783, admitted to this Bar in 1786. He located in his native town where he died December 7th, 1845. His whole life was one continual employment in public official capacity, was reppesentative in Congress four terms; Judge of the Superior and Supreme Courts of Connecticut; Governor of Connecticut 1813 to 1817. It is impossible in this brief statement to mention all of his other positions. A memorial biography of his life was published. See Boardman's Early Lights.

JOHN COTTON SMITH, JR., born in Tivoli, N. Y., graduated from Yale in 1830, admitted to the Bar in 1832. He resided in Sharon and is known much better as a politician than lawyer. He held a very influential position in the Democratic party for many years. He died at Sharon, November 21, 1879, aged 68 years.

JOSEPH L. SMITH, born in New Britain, Conn., May 28, 1776, located in Litchfield about 1802, where he practiced until the war of 1812. He married one of Ephriam Kirby's daughters. In consequence of the active part he took in the 6th of August Festival 1806, he lost most of his practice. He was appointed by the administration a Major in the war of 1812, remaining in service till 1818, when he removed to Florida. From 1823 to 1827 he was a Judge of the United States District Court for Florida. He died at St. Augustine May 24, 1846. Gen. Ephriam Kirby Smith who was the last Confederate General to surrender his command was a descendant of the above.

JUNIUS SMITH was a son of Gen. David Smith and a brother of Aaron Smith, born in Plymouth October 2, 1780. He graduated at Yale College in 1802, and then attended the Litchfield Law School, and was admitted to the Bar and began his practice in New Haven, but soon became interested in mercantile business which necessitated his removal in 1805 to London, England, and in which he was engaged until about 1832.

During this period Robert Fulton had demonstrated the practicability of using steam for propelling vessels and Smith conceived the idea that steam could be used in Ocean Navigation. It was a preposterous scheme at that time. The little boats would move on narrow rivers outside of waves and winds but on the broad bosom of the ocean Neptune's power could not be withstood, and Smith's efforts were laughed at as fancies of an idle dreamer. He persevered, however, after many rebuffs both in England and America some of which were strangely laughable; he succeeded in chartering a trial vessel but no one would take any stock in his building one. After six years the Sirius a small craft of seven hundred tons steamed out of the harbor of Cork on April 4, 1838, bound for America or as the papers of the day had it for destruction, but in nineteen days steamed into the bay of New York.

The arrival of this craft under steam in New York opened the new era of commerce and it was not long before a company was formed and a new steamship called the British Queen was built and soon Smith received great honors, Yale College adding an L. L. D. to his name.

He subsequently bought a plantation in South Carolina and began the culture of the tea plant which he imported from China, and proved the possibility of growing it successfully in the United States.

NATHANIEL SMITH was born in 1762, within the limits of the present town of Washington, then a part of Woodbury. He commenced life a farmer and cattle dealer, with scarcely the advantages of a common education. Such, however, was the impulse of his powers, he surmounted all obstacles. Studied law with Ephraim Kirby and Judge Reeve, at Litchfield, and was admitted to the Bar in that county in 1787. He commenced the practice of law at Woodbury and rose more rapidly to the highest grade of his profession than almost any other man has done. His powers of thought and elocution gave him almost unlimited dominion over his audienec. He was a member of the House of Representatives in the State Legislature October 1789, October 1791, May 1792, October 1794 and May 1795. In 1797 he was elected a representative from this State in the Congress of the United States. Having served in that capacity two terms he declined a re-election in 1801. In 1802, he was elected to the Council or Upper House of the Legislature of this State; a situation he resigned in 1804. In 1805, he was appointed States Attorney for the County of Litchfield, and

Judge of the Supreme Court, in October, 1806. In the latter office he continued until 1819. He died March 8th, 1822.

NATHANEL B. SMITH, born in Woodbury December 1795, graduated from Yale College in 1815 and admitted to this Bar in 1818. He began practice at New Haven but soon removed to Woodbury. He continued in practice only a few years. He died in Woodbury.

COL. NATHANEL SMITH, a son of Nathaniel B. Smith, born in Woodbury in 1831, admitted to the Bar. Never engaged in the practice of law and during the rebellion was appointed Major of the 19th Conn. Infantry and was promoted to be its Lieutenant Colonel, resigning therefrom for disability May 6, 1864. He died at Woodbury August 26, 1877.

NATHAN SMITH was born in Roxbury in 1770 and was admitted to this Bar in 1792 and located in New Haven. He became one of the most celebrated lawyers in the State, and had a very extensive business. He was United States Senator and died while holding that position in the City of Washington, December 6, 1835.

PERRY SMITH was born in Washington, Conn., studied law at the Litchfield Law School and was admitted to the Bar in 1807 and settled in New Milford, where he died in 1852. He was a United States Senator for six years from March 4, 1837.

PHINEAS SMITH, JR. was a younger brother of Hon. Truman Smith, born in Roxbury, graduated from Yale College in 1816, admitted to this Bar in 1818 and removed to Vermont, where he died.

RICHARD SMITH was born in Roxbury in 1769, graduated from Yale College in 1797, admitted to this Bar in 1801 and died in 1805.

RICHARD SMITH, a native of Sharon graduated from Yale College in 1825, admitted to the Bar in 1830, died in Sharon, December 21, 1878, aged 76.

TRUMAN SMITH was a son of Phineas and Deborah Ann (Judson) Smith and was born in Roxbury, Conn. on the 27th of November, 1791.

Mr. Smith graduated at Yale College in the class of 1815, was admitted to the Bar in 1818, and located in Litchfield where he resided until 1854 when he removed to Stamford, residing there until his death, May 3rd, 1885.

Two of his uncles, Nathaniel Smith and Nathan Smith had attained fame and rank at the Bar and in public life, and it seems natural that Truman Smith should be a successful practioner and be honored with many political offices. He was a member of the State Legislature in 1831, 1832, and 1834. He was a member of the 26th and 27th Congress (1839-43) for the 5th District and of the 29th and 30th (1845 to 1849) for the 4th District. He was chairman of the National Committee in the Taylor campagin and offered a seat in the Cabinet which he declined. From 1849 to 1854 he was a member of the U. S. Senate. This honor he resigned and opened an office in the city of New York, and continued in practice there until the 16th day of May, 1871, when he handed over all his business to a younger lawyer, Cephas Brainerd, retaining in his own hands but two cases, known as the Lockwood and the Humaston cases.

President Lincoln appointed Mr. Smith Judge on the part of the United States of the Mixed Court at New York, established under the treaty of 7th of April, 1862, with Great Britain, and he held that position until the abrogation of the treaty in 1870.

At the Litchfield School where he acquired the preliminary knowledge of his profession, he was under the instruction of Tapping Reeve and James Gould; and among his fellow students were John M. Clayton of Deleware and John Y. Mason of Virginia.

Upon entering Congress, Mr. Smith at once took a prominent position. He was a member of the Committee to which were finally referred some of the questions arising in regard to the famous New Jersey Election case and he drafted the minority report upon that case. This the majority in Congress refused to print, but it was printed in New Jersey and largely circulated. His associates in the minority report were Millard Fillmore, John Minor Botts and Benjamin Randall. The discussion was conducted with the greatest acrimony and John Quincy Adams in his Diary says, "Mr. Smith made a speech of three hours in answer to Fisher's most disingenuous speech."

It was Mr. Smith's habit all through his Congressional career to discuss *in extenso* some of the more important measures pending in the various sessions, and these speeches he always circulated among his constituents, his feeling being that they ought to know from the printed speeches as well as from the votes of their representatives what they were actually doing and saying in Congress.

Mr. Smith was deeply interested in legislation looking to the improvement of the means of communication in the country, hence he was exceedingly active in regard to the construction of the Sault Ste. Marie canal. Perhaps it may be safely said that the initiation and construction of the canal was more due to him than to any other one person. One of his last speeches in the Senate was in advocacy of a railroad and telegraph line connecting the two oceans.

Shortly before he resigned from the Senate he made his speech famous at that time and since, in reply to Douglas and against the repeal of the Missouri Compromise.

Mr. Smith came to New York at the age of sixty-three, probably too late in life to attain at that Bar a success correspondent to his talents and learning. The most important case which he conducted there was *Lockwood vs. The N. Y. Central Railroad* which is reported in 17 Wall. 321. The question presented was whether it was competent for a common carrier to secure exemption from liability for negligence by a stipulation in a ticket to that effect. The particular action was in favor of a drover who was taking cattle over the road under what was called a drover's pass. The courts of New York had decided in favor of the exemption. Mr. Smith's action was brought in the United States Circuit Court and Mr. Justice Smalley overruled the defense and the jury returned a verdict for $25,000. This verdict was set aside by Mr. Justice Nelson on appeal as excessive. The case came on for a second trial before Mr. Justice Woodruff who also overruled the defense and the jury found a verdict for $17,500.

The case was then taken to the Supreme Court of the United States and argued on the 15th and 16th of January, 1873. Mr. Smith attended upon this argument and opened the case in an address of an hour on behalf of the respondent. He argued the case upon a most elaborate brief which examined all the authorities bearing upon the question and it was most carefully reasoned. The Supreme Court, speaking by Mr. Justice Bradley, sustained the judgment below and a most elaborate opinion was written; in fact this is the leading case upon the subject in this country today.

The other case which Mr. Smith retained in his hands, the Humaston case, was tried before a jury, beginning on November 15th, 1871 and continuing for thirteen days. This suit was against the Western Union Telegraph Company. Mr. Smith had as his opponents John K. Porter, George Gifford, Grosvenor P. Lowry and Charles Francis Stone. It involved first, a very important question respecting the interpretation of the contract between the parties and, secondly, the value of the inventions under discussion over and above the cash which had already been paid upon them. Mr. Smith opened the case in an address of two hours in which he explained in detail the various inventions for the transmission of messages by telegraph and the case proceeded. Mr. Smith was alone in the case save only a young assistant whose chief business was to read papers and extracts from authorities.

During the progress of the case the question of the construction of the instument arose and was argued at length, Mr. Smith occupying practically an entire day, under the suggestions of the presiding Justice, in developing his view of the case. The presiding Justice afterwards remarked that considering Mr. Smith's age, it was the most remarkable exhibition of physical and mental power he had ever witnessed. The case was closed and the jury went out about six o'clock on the 13th day of the trial, Judge Porter having occupied the first part of the day in summing up for the defense and Mr. Smith the latter part in summing up for the plaintiff. The jury found a moderate verdict in favor of the plaintiff for $7,500.

The Humaston was a remarkable case in that Mr. Smith, who became eighty during the trial, was able to stand that amount of work without exhibiting any diminution of force at any time during the trial. That case also went to the Supreme Court of the United States and was argued there on the 30th of March, 1874, Mr. Smith closing the argument. That court however sustained the ruling of Judge Woodruff on the interpretation of the contract, and defeated Mr. Smith.

Mr. Smith was very effective before juries, his commanding presence and voice, his great moral force, his readiness in retort, his wit, his courage and his capacity as an actor and his elaborate preparation made him a very dangerous adversary.

Always a believer in the essential doctrines of Christianity, as taught in the churches of New England, late in life he became a communicant in the Presbyterian Church of Stamford.

WELLINGTON B. SMITH, born in New Hartford June 3, 1856, was admitted to practice at this Bar in 1877. He resides and practices in Winsted, Conn. He was a member of the Constitutional Convention in 1902. He was for many years a prosecuting agent for Litchfield County engaged in the suppression of the illegal sale of intoxicating liquor and was the moving spirit of the liquor trials a brief account of which can be found on page 155. He has represented the town of Winchester in the Legislature and was on Governor Chamberlain's Staff as Judge Advocate holding the rank of Colonel. His portrait appears on page 158.

SAMUEL J. SOUTHMAYD, a native of Watertown studied in the Litchfield Law School and admitted to the Bar in 1795. Practiced in Watertown, where he died in 1813. (See Boardman's Sketches.)

LEMAN B. SPRAGUE was a native of Salisbury and was admitted to the Bar in 1841. He soon after located in Woodbury and died there August, 1845.

RUFUS STANLEY, of Litchfield, admitted in 1790.

SETH P. STAPLES, graduated from Yale in 1797, admitted to this Bar in 1799, located in New Haven, where he died in 1861.

DANIEL STARR, born in New Milford, admitted to the Bar in 1800. Died May 1, 1826.

ANSEL STERLING, born in Lyme, 1782, admitted to this Bar in 1805, located in Sharon in 1808, where he died November 6, 1853. (See Sedgwick's Address).

ELISHA STERLING, born in Lyme, graduated from Yale in 1787, admitted to the Bar in 1790, in the following year located in Salisbury, where he lived until his death in 1836. (See Boardman's Sketches).

JOHN M. STERLING, son of Gen. Elisha Sterling, born 1800, in Salisbury, graduated at Yale in 1820. Admitted to the Bar in 1823.

In 1827 he removed to Cleveland, Ohio. Was a noted anti-slavery reformer. He died in Philadelphia in 1880.

HENRY W. STEVENS, admitted to the Bar in 1811 from Canaan.

JAMES STEVENS, born in Stamford in 1768, admitted to this Bar in 1797, located in his native town where he held many public offices and was elected to the 16th Congress. Died April 4, 1835.

BENJAMIN STILES, a native of Southbury, graduated from Yale in 1740. Practiced law in his native town of Southbury.

BENJAMIN STILES, JR. was born in Southbury, August 28, 1756, graduated from Yale College in 1776, was admitted to this Bar in 1781, and practiced in Woodbury, having a very large office practice. He died July 12, 1817.

ELIAKIM S. STODDARD, JR., admitted to the Bar in 1847 from Sharon. Died in Sharon May 14, 1865, aged 42 years.

HENRY STODDARD was a native of Woodbury and born in 1786. He was admitted to this Bar in 1815, and began to practice in Kent. In 1818 he left Kent and went "west" with George B. Holt of Norfolk, a young member of this Bar who became so distinguished in his later years in Ohio. They journeyed on horseback till they reached Dayton, Ohio, then a little village of five or six hundred inhabitants. Here they located, Holt to become an honored Judge and citizen, and Stoddard a millionare.

ROBBINS BATTELL STOECKEL of Norfolk was born in New Haven in 1872, fitted for college at Hopkins Grammar School, graduated from Yale with honors in class of 1893 and Columbia Law School two years later being admitted to the Litchfield Bar in 1896. Mr. Stoeckel resides and practices in Norfolk where he has been Judge of Probate for several years.

COL. ADONIJAH STRONG, Judge Church says, "He was unique in genius and manner, of large professional business, sound practical sense and many anecdotes of his sayings and doings are still remembered and reported in the County."

The following vote appears upon the Bar Record: "At a Bar meeting Decr. Term 1804 the following resolution was passed unanimously viz, That Adonijah Strong, Esqr. on account of his great emminence as a lawyer and eloquence as an advocate be considered as a member of this Bar for the purpose of instructing students, although he shall not continue to practice. Attest Amos Benedict, Clerk." (See Warner's Reminiscences.)

JOHN STRONG, JR., born in Woodbury December 31, 1786, graduated from Yale College in 1806 and admitted to this Bar in 1808. He opened an office in Woodbury and continued in the active discharge of his professional duties till his death in November, 1834.

FRANK H. TURKINGTON

Few men have occupied a higher place in the confidence and affections of the community. Was Judge of Probate and represented the town in the General Assembly a number of years.

JEDEDIAH STRONG, born in Litchfield, Connecticut in 1738, graduated from Yale College in 1761. He represented his town in the General Court for thirty sessions. Was a member of the Continental Congress and Secretary of the Convention which adopted the Constitution of the United States. He died in Litchfield in 1802.

MARTIN STRONG, a son of Col. Adonijah Strong, admitted to this Bar in 1801 and located in Salisbury. He was Judge of the County Court and one of its most active magistrates. (See Sedgwick's Address).

THERON R. STRONG was a son of Hon. Martin Strong, born in Salisbury in 1802, admitted to this Bar in 1823. He located at Rochester, N. Y. He was a member of Congress in 1839 and a Judge of the Supreme Court of New York, 1851 to 1858, and afterwards a Judge of the Court of Appeals. He died in New York City, 1873.

CYRUS SWAN was a native of Stonnington, studied in the Litchfield Law School and admitted to the Bar in 1798. He settled in Sharon and died there in 1835, aged 65. ((See Sedgwick's Address).

BENJAMIN SWIFT, admitted to the Bar in 1802.

HEMAN SWIFT, admitted to the Bar in 1819 from Kent.

MILTON H. SWIFT, a native of Kent, admitted to the Bar in 1838. Removed to Ottawa, Illinois.

JABEZ SWIFT, Judge Church says of him, "He was the first lawyer ever settled in Salisbury and was a native of Kent. He built the stone house of Town Hill. Upon the breaking out of the war of the Revolution he joined the army in Boston and there died."

GEORGE E. TAFT, born in Sheffield, Mass. November 4th, 1854, admitted to this Bar in 1883 and soon after located at Unionville in Hartford County, where he is now in practice. Has been a member of the School Board there and Judge of Probate.

ROBERT S. THAREN was born in Lebanon in 1714 and upon the formation of the County in 1751 was in practice at New Milford. He died January 9th, 1786. (See Boardman's Sketches).

JOHN Q. THAYER was admitted to this Bar in 1869 and after practicing a short time in New Milford he removed to Meriden, Conn., where he is now in practice. He served four years in the Civil War, 1861, and in 1899 was Judge Advocate of the Department of Connecticut G. A. R.

JAMES THOMPSON was born in Woodbury, March 4, 1767, graduated from Yale College, 1789, and was admitted to this Bar in 1791. He settled at New Durham, N. Y. About 1800 he left his profession and entered the Episcopal Ministry. He died August 18, 1844.

JUDSON B. THOMPSON, admitted to the Bar in 1811.

HEZEKIAH THOMPSON was born in New Haven in 1734, studied law in Stratford, and was admitted to the Bar in Litchfield in 1763. He located in Woodbury. Died May 1803. "He stood well as a lawyer and magistrate, and was a gentleman of the old school." 6th Conn. Reports.

MARTIN H. THOMAS, admitted to the Bar in 1808 from Salisbury.

JUDSON B. THOMAS was in 1810 in Colebrook. Admitted to the Bar in 1808 from Salisbury.

F. R. TIFFANY, admitted to the Bar in 1879.

GEORGE TOD, graduated from Yale College in 1795 and admitted to the Bar in 1797.

OLIVER A. G. TODD, born in Plymouth October 1812, admitted to the Bar in 1833, practiced law in Waterbury, Litchfield, New Milford and Danbury in which latter city he died August 14, 1886.

DAVID TOLMAN, admitted to this Bar in 1792 from Woodbury.

URIAH TRACY, appointed States Attorney, 1794 to 1800. He was born in Franklin, (now Norwich), Conn., February 2, 1755, and graduated at Yale College in 1778, and read law with Judge Reeve at Litchfield, where he was admitted to the Bar in 1780, and settled in that town where he rose to a high eminence in his profession. He was very largely engaged in duties of a public nature, and often represented his adopted town in the Legislature, and was Speaker of the House in 1793. Was a representative in Congress from 1793 to 1796, when he entered the Senate and was a member until his death in 1807, serving part of the time as President *pro tem.* He died at Washington, D. C. July 19, 1807, and was the first person buried in the Congressional burying ground.

AMOS S. TREAT, born in Bridgewater, February 5, 1816, admitted to this Bar in 1843, practiced in Fairfield County and died at Bridgeport April 24, 1886.

SELAH B. TREAT, D. D., born in Hartford February 19, 1804, graduated at Yale 1824, admitted to this Bar in 1826. Practiced at East Windsor and Penn Yan, New York. In 1835 he entered the ministry and was Secretary of the American Board of Commissioners for Foreign Missions many years. Died at Boston, March 28th, 1877.

FRANK H. TURKINGTON, the present Sheriff of the County, was born in Morris, then a part of Litchfield, June 11, 1854. Receiving a common school education, he associated with his father in an extensive cattle and stock buying business, and butchering for the wholesale trade at East Morris, carrying their meats mostly by teams to Waterbury, Conn. He was very much interested in political affairs, and represented his town in the Legislature twice—although he was a Republican in a strong Democratic town. In 1906 he was elected Sheriff. He is also a farmer on a large scale, owning more arable land which he successfully cultivates than any other person in Litchfield County.

JOHN S. TURRILL was born February 8, 1825, attended Law School at Balston Springs, N. Y. and was admitted to this Bar in 1851. Located in New Milford, enjoying a large practice until his death, July 19, 1889. He was one of the Committee who prepared the Revision of the Statutes of 1875.

STEPHEN TWINING, graduated at Yale College in 1795, was admitted to this Bar in 1797, located at New Haven, where he died in 1832. He was Steward of Yale College from 1819 to 1832.

CHARLES TUTTLE, admitted to the Bar in 1856 from North Colebrook.

NOAH WADHAMS, a native of Goshen, studied law at Litchfield Law School and was admitted to the Bar in 1793. Removed to Pennsylvania and was admitted to the Bar of Luzerne County, Pa. in 1800.

ALBERT WADHAMS, born in Massachusetts June 19, 1819, graduated at Norwich University, Vermont, and was admitted to the New York Bar. Removed to Goshen and began the practice of law about 1865. He died in Goshen, May 1884.

GEORGE WADSWORTH, born in Litchfield, was admitted to this Bar in 1851. He located in Buffalo, N. Y., where he died March 19, 1907, aged 77.

FREDERICK T. WALLACE, admitted to the Bar in 1844.

THOMAS J. WALL, born in Torrington, February 19, 1879. Graduated at Yale Law School and was admitted to this Bar, June 26, 1906. Practices in Torrington, and he writes me that he is kept very busy between law-book agents and mercantile collection agencies.

ARTHUR D. WARNER, born in Southbury August 2, 1848, admitted to this Bar April 1872. After eleven years practice at West Cornwall he removed to Woodbury, where he is now in practice. He was Judge of the Court of Common Pleas for this County one term of four years.

Donald J. Warner, born in Salisbury September 15, 1819, was admitted to this Bar in 1843, settled at Salisbury, where he deceased May 31, 1904. He was Judge of the District Court and Court of Common Pleas eight years, and until he was retired by reason of Constitutional limitation of age. His adress on the occasion of the Centenial Celebration in Litchfield 1898, was exceedingly interesting and a considerable portion of it is included in this compilation.

Donald J. Warner, son of Donald T. Warner, and grandson of Judge Donald Warner, was born in Salisbury July 24, 1885. Graduated at Yale College in 1905, and from the Law School 1908, when he was admitted to this Bar.

Donald T. Warner, son of Judge Donald J. Warner, was born in Salisbury December 15, 1850. Was admitted to the Bar in 1873. He resides in Salisbury, and has held the office of States Attorney since 1896. In 1902 he was a leading member of the Constitutional Convention of Connecticut. He was a member of the State Senate in 1895 and 1897, in which latter year he was chairman of the Judiciary Committee.

Lyman F. Warner, a native of Roxbury, admitted to the Bar in 1848 and removed west.

Milton J. Warner was born in Salisbury, graduated from Williams College, was admitted to this Bar September, 1867, and located at Waverly, N. Y. Afterwards removed to Santa Fe, New Mexico, wher he died.

Thomas G. Waterman, a native of Salisbury studied law with Gen. Elisha Sterling and was admitted to this Bar in 1809. He became a prominent member of the Bar in Binghamton, N. Y., where he died in 1861. Author of Waterman's Digests.

Douglass Watson, born May 12, 1821 at Canaan, admitted to the Bar in 1845.

Daniel F. Webster, born in Litchfield March 14, 1853, graduated from Dartmouth College in 1874 and admitted to this Bar in 1876. Located and practiced in Waterbury until his death in 1896.

Frederick C. Webster, born in Litchfield October 17, 1850. Graduated from Yale College in 1874 and was admitted to the Bar in 1876. Practiced law in Litchfield a short time, then removed to the West. He resides at Missoula, Montana, of which city he has been Mayor. He is now a Judge of one of the Districts of that State.

Gideon H. Welch, born at East Haddam, Conn., September 22, 1844. Graduated at Yale College 1868, and from Yale Law School in 1870, and immediately located at Torrington, succeeding the late

FREDERIC M. WILLIAMS

Henry S. Barbour, Esq. He had a lucrative practice, and held numerous town offices and represented the town in the General Assembly in 1881 and the District in the State Senate in 1897. In 1897 upon the appointment of Judge Roraback to the Superior Court he was appointed by the Governor, Judge of the Court of Common Pleas, which action the Legislature confirmed for another term of four years, and is now (1907) in office. Picture on page 141.

RALPH WELLS, admitted in 1813 from Hartford.

FRANCIS W. WESSELLS, admitted in 1870. Resides in Omaha, Neb.

SAMUEL WETMORE, admitted in 1803.

N. WETMORE, admitted in 1808.

LEVERETTE W. WESSELLS was born in Litchfield in 1819. Held the office of Sheriff for twelve years from 1854 to 1866, succeeding Hon. Albert Sedgwick, under whom he was a Deputy Sheriff for nine years. Was Post Master of Litchfield, 1850 to 1854, a representative in the General Assembly in 1879 and again in 1887, was Quarter Master General of the State in 1879 and 1880. In 1862 he was commissioned a Colonel by Governor Buckingham and by his skillful management organized the 19th Infantry Regiment, afterwards the 2nd Connecticut Heavy Artillery. This was a Litchfield County Regiment and won a leading record for its valor in the war of the Rebellion. Colonel Wessells resigned his commission by reason of ill health in 1863 and was immediately appointed Provost Marshall of the Fourth District of Connecticut which office he held until the close of the Rebellion. "To his old friends in the Commonwealth and beyond its limits the thought that they are to see his face no more must needs be a sad one: but to him the end came as a happy release from the house of pain. He had lived beyond all expectation and filled the measure of his years, had done a man's work in the world, and long since assured for himself an honorable place in the remembrance of his town and State." He died at Dover, Del. April 4th, 1895.

GEORGE WHEATON, of Cornwall,—The following is the notice of his death from a county newspaper:

"George Wheaton, Esq., the oldest and one of the most respected members of the Litchfield County Bar, died at his residence in Cornwall, on Friday evening, Nov. 24th, 1865. He was born in East Haven in 1790, and was, therefore, in his 76th year. He removed to Salisbury about 1810 where he studied law with Judge Church, then a practicing lawyer. He was admitted to the Bar in 1813, when he made Cornwall his place of residence. Mr. Wheaton was a well-read, exact lawyer, a prudent business man, and a close reasoner. He was a valuable man in town affairs, and enjoyed the respect and confidence of his fellow-citizens. He had long been a member of the Congregational Church, and he was known and beloved as a consistent Christian. His funeral was attended at Cornwall last Sunday by a large number of people, among whom were many of the prominent members of the Litchfield and Fairfield County Bars."

JOSHUA WHITNEY,—He was one of the early settlers of Norfolk coming there from Canaan. He was a lawyer and was first King's Attorney of the new County in 1751, appointed thereto by the new County Court. He was very prominent in town affairs in Norfolk until about 1763 when it is said that he removed back to Canaan. I suppose him to have been the same Joshua Whitney who served from Canaan all through the Revolution and was a "Leftenant."

SOLOMON WHITNEY, from Canaan admitted to the Bar in 1763.

CHARLES WHITTLESEY, born in Salisbury, graduated from Williams College in 1840, admitted to this Bar in 1844. Began practice in Cheshire, removed to Middletown and in 1855 to Hartford, Conn. Was States Attorney for Middlesex County for six years. Was Captain of Campany I 22nd Conn. Vols. He died in Alexandria, Va., in 1874.

ELISHA WHITTLESEY, a native of Washington, was admitted to this Bar in 1781 and soon removed to the Connecticut Reserve. In 1823 he was elected member of Congress which position he held for eighteen years. In 1841 he was appointed Auditor of the Treasury for the Post Office Department and in 1849 first Comptroller of the Treasury of the United States.

ROGER WHITTLESEY, born in Newington, 1767, graduated from Yale in 1787; studied at the Litchfield Law School and was admitted to the Bar in 1790. He practiced at Southington and died there October 5, 1844.

THOMAS T. WHITTLESEY, born in 1794, graduated from Yale College in 1817; admitted to this Bar in 1820. He located in Danbury. He was representative in Congress in 1827 and 1829 and died in 1868.

GOVERNOR OLIVER WOLCOTT

EDWIN A. WHITE, born in Cornwall, graduated from Wesleyan University; admitted to this Bar in 1882. Removed to the State of New York and after a practice of a few years abandoned the law and became an Episcopal Clergyman. He is now in Bloomfield, N. J. He is the author of a standard work on Episcopal law and is engaged in codifying the Church laws of the State of New Jersey.

HUBERT WILLIAMS was born in Salisbury, September 10, 1853. Graduated from Columbia Law School in 1873; was admitted to the Bar in 1875 and resided in Lakeville, his native town. He was Post Master in that village a number of years. He died suddenly September 24, 1906.

FREDERIC M. WILLIAMS, born in Washington, Conn., November 27, 1862. He prepared for college at the Upson School in New Preston and graduated from the Yale Law School in 1887; also studying with Hon. Simeon E. Baldwin. He was admitted to the New Haven Bar in 1887 and later moved to New Milford. He has been very prominent in the affairs of his town and is a most efficient Prosecuting Agent for Litchfield County.

WILLIAM G. WILLIAMS, born in Stockbridge, Mass. Admitted to this Bar in 1800 and located at Sharon until 1809 when he removed to New Hartford, where he died in 1838, aged 59.

THOMAS WILCOX, admitted in 1799 from Canaan.

ANDREW B. WILSON, admitted in 1865 from Cornwall. Practiced a short time at Newtown and removed to Bridgeport, where he engaged in manufacturing.

GEN. OLIVER WOLCOTT was the first Sheriff of the County, holding the office for more than twenty years. (See articles on Signers of the Declaration on page 174.)

OLIVER WOLCOTT, JR., L. L. D. was born in Litchfield January 11, 1760, and was the son of Oliver Wolcott, the Signer of the Declaration of Independence. At the age of thirteen he was prepared for and entered Yale College, but by reason of taking frequent vacations to go into the Revolutionary Army, did not graduate till 1779. He was admitted to this Bar in 1781. His whole life was devoted to the public service and affairs. He was successively Comptroller of this State, Auditor and Secretary of the United States Treasury, Judge of the United States Circuit Court, President of the Bank of America, President of the Constitutional Convention of Connecticut, and Governor of his native State from 1817 to 1827. He was one of the most illustrious statesmen of the early days of the Republic, the intimate friend and adviser of Washington, Adams and Hamilton; and for some time previous to his decease in New York, June 2, 1833, he was the last surviving member of Washington's cabinet. The departure of few men from the world ever produced a more deep and general feeling of sorrow.

DANIEL WOOD, admitted in 1799 from Sharon.

JOHN WOODBRIDGE, JR., admitted in 1851 from New Hartford.

EZEKIEL WOODRUFF, a native of Farmington, graduated from Yale in 1779 and was admitted to this Bar in 1781. He located at Middletown and in 1789 removed from the State.

GEORGE C. WOODRUFF was born on the first day of December, 1805 in Litchfield in that part of the town which is now the town of Morris. He was the eldest son of Maj. Gen. Morris Woodruff, who was for 11 years a Judge of the County Court. George C. graduated at Yale in 1825, studied law at the Litchfield Law School under Judge Gould and was admitted to this Bar in 1827. He soon located in Litchfield where he resided until his death on the 21st day of November, 1885. He took a leading position at the Bar of Litchfield County, gradually rising until he became its acknowledged head and was chairman of the Bar Association for many years. In his early life he was daily thrown into conflict with those giants of the profession—the two Churches, Huntington, Bacon, Smith and others of their able contemporaries. He held almost every office of the town and county—justice of the peace, grand juror, postmaster, town treasurer, town clerk, bank director and president, clerk of the superior court, Colonel in the Militia, member and clerk of the General Assembly, judge of probate, member of the Thirty-Seventh Congress—the duties of each in turn performed with that rigid exactness and scrupulous integrity which marks the perfect man. To him the state at large owes many of the best features of the revision of our statutes adopted in 1875. As a lawyer, Mr. Woodruff was prominent in those branches where certainty is possible. It was in the trial of questions of law, the dryer and more abstruse the better that his most consummate skill was shown. In the Supreme Court of Errors not infrequently his entire argument was written out with the most painstaking care.

In whatever relation of life one looks at him as citizen, as neighbor, in private life or public station, as counsellor or judge he was one of the best products of our American civilization.

(Condensed from obituary in 54, Conn. Report).

GEORGE M. WOODRUFF was a son of Hon. George C. Woodruff of Litchfield and enjoys the distinction of being, through his father and mother, a member of the only two families in the county who have for three successive generations practiced before its courts. In fact it might be said for four generations as Mr. Woodruff's grandfather on one side was county judge and on the other sheriff. He was born in Litchfield, 1836 and has been extremely active in state as well as town affairs. He prepared for college at Phillips Academy, Andover, graduated at Yale in 1857, the Harvard Law School in 1859 and was admitted to the Litchfield Bar in the same year. He was in the Legislature in 1863, 1865 and 1872, serving on the Judiciary Committee the first two terms. He was town treasurer 1866 to 1906 and Judge of Probate since 1868 with the exception of one year. He was one of the state railroad commissioners from 1874 to 1897 and chairman of the Board from 1875. Mr. Woodruff was commissioner for this state to the Universal Exposition at Hamburg in 1863 and a member of the State Board of education from 1865 to 1877. He is an active member and Deacon in the Congregational church and has been president of the Savings Society since 1885. He is also president of the First National Bank and Vice-President of the Colonial Trust Company of Waterbury.

James P. Woodruff is a son of Hon. George M. Woodruff, born in Litchfield October 30, 1868, graduated from Amherst College in 1891 and from Yale Law School in 1893 and was admitted to this Bar in 1893. Resides and practices at Litchfield in company with his father. He represented his town in the Legislature of 1899-1903.

Hon. Lewis B. Woodruff, L. L. D., son of Gen. Morris Woodruff and brother of Hon. George C. Woodruff, was born in Litchfield (South Farms) June 19, 1809. Preparing for College at the then noted Morris Academy, he graduated with high honors from Yale College in 1830. In the fall of that year he entered the Litchfield Law School, where under the instruction of Judge Gould, then at its head, he laid the foundation of the scholarly learning which secured his success at the Bar and so distinguished his judicial career. On completing his studies in that school he was admitted to the Bar of Connecticut in 1832. In October of that year he removed to the city of New York, and after a successful practice at the Bar he was, in 1850, called to the Bench, and thereafter held successively the offices of Judge of the Court of Common Pleas, Superior Court, Court of Appeals and United States Circuit Court for the Second Judicial Circuit, which latter position he filled at the time of his death. A devoted lover of his native State it was especially pleasing to him that Connecticut was a part of his Judicial District, maintaining a residence in Litchfield a portion of the year and he died at his home in that place September 10, 1875, esteemed, revered and beloved by all who new him. His great learning, his remarkable power of analysis, and his deep discernment and excellent judgment, reinforced by habits of profound study and indefatigable industry, and his sterling integrity insured his high reputation on the Bench.

Dignified, in his bearing, he was in the family circle tender and affectionate, everywhere generous, kind and helpful. Devoted to his home joys, genial and cordial, he was the delight of the social circle, and his loving welcome, hospitable board and ever open door, kept warm hearts constantly about him.

It was said of him:—"He went to the very bottom of every subject with which he undertook to deal. He cared not for the multiplicity of details, they never clogged his perception of a general bearing, and never one of them was deprived of the exact degree of weight to which it was relatively entitled. Law was to him what Music or Art is to some natures, it engrossed him, and was a province in which he moved a King and a Master."

In 1860, Columbia College of New York conferred upon him the honorary degree of Doctor of Laws.

He married a daughter of Chief Justice Hornblower of New Jersey. Of his three children, the eldest, Charles H. Woodruff, adopted his father's profession, practicing in New York and maintaining as a summer home his father's country residence; and he also has contributed two sons, Lewis B. and Frederick S., to the Bar of New York.

He purchased the Judge Tapping Reeve residence in Litchfield for his summer home. His portrait appears on page 206 in connection with the Law School.

MORRIS WOODRUFF was for many years one of the Judges of the County Court, and apparently a standing committee for the lay-out of highways and the transaction of matters of a similar nature. He was a Major General of the State Militia and held very many town and county public offices. His two sons, George C. and Lewis B. became Attorneys of the highest standing, while his only daughter was the esteemed wife of the late Chief Justice Seymour. He was born in Litchfield in 1777 and died in 1841.

PITKIN COWLES WRIGHT was born in Canaan May 1835. Graduated at Williams in 1852 and admitted to practice in 1855. He removed to Iowa. He was the Grand High Priest of Iowa in 1868-9. He died at Somerville, Tenn. September 15th, 1896.

JOHN F. WYNNE, born at Sandisfield, Mass., 1860. Admitted to the Bar in 1881. Settled at Unionville in the town of Farmington which town he represented in the Legislature in 1886. Subsequently he removed to New Haven where he is now in practice.

JOHN D. YALE, Sheriff of the County from 1878 to 1881. He was born in Canaan in 1826. At the close of his term of office he resided in Winsted and was employed as a commercial traveler. He removed to Hartford, and retired from active business pursuits. He died in Hartford April 24, 1905.

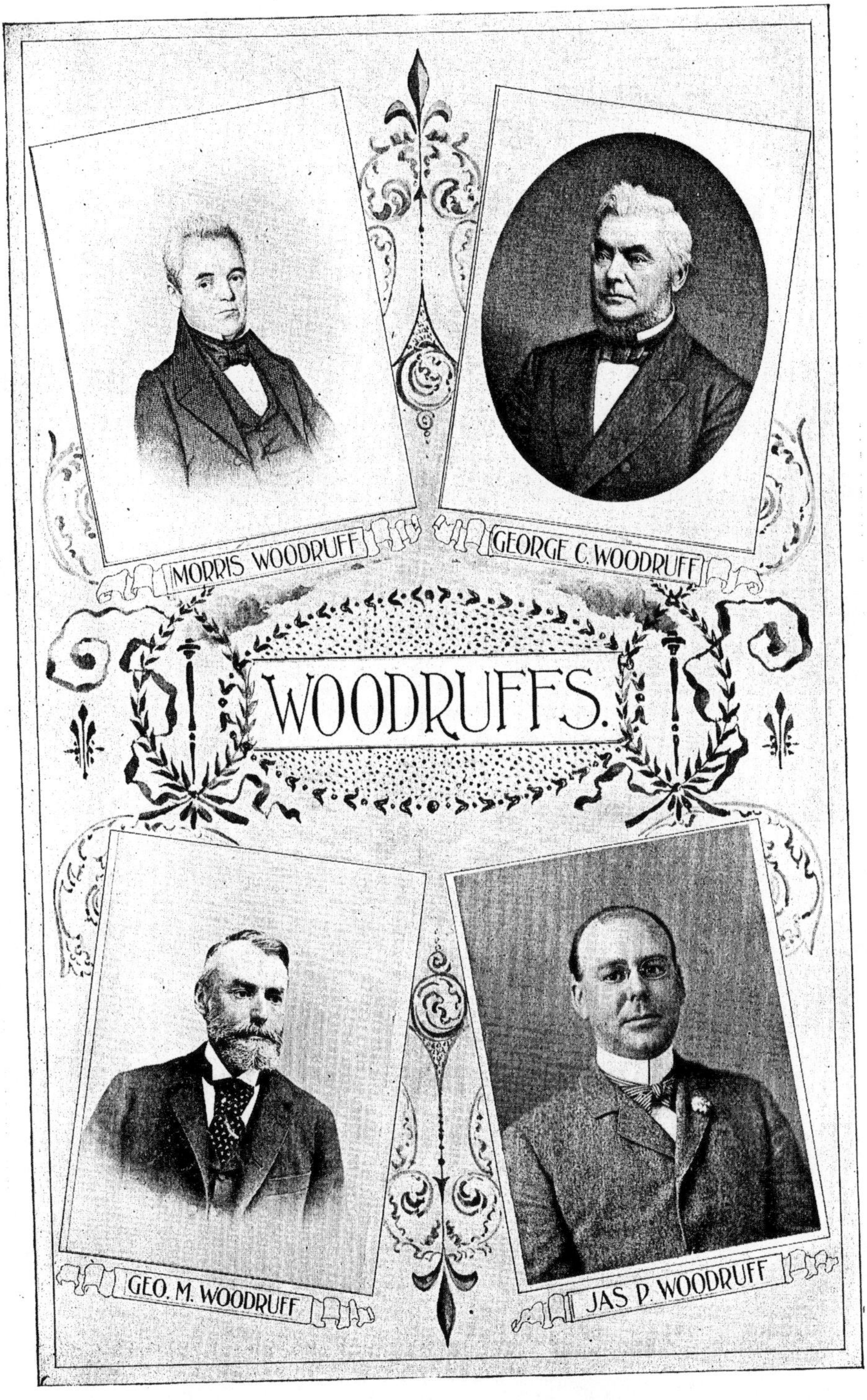
MORRIS WOODRUFF
GEORGE C. WOODRUFF
WOODRUFFS.
GEO. M. WOODRUFF
JAS P. WOODRUFF

# LIGANS

MAY IT PLEASE THE COURT.

# MAY IT PLEASE THE COURT

In the preparation of this volume the compiler has collected many items not exactly apropos to the general scheme of the book. They are, however, papers and documents of such general interest that they should be preserved, and I have printed them herein under an old law term, that they may be available at some future time. I have not aimed at any particular arrangement, and the reader if he is a lawyer, may demur to them, plead in abatement, move to strike out, erase, or for a more particular statement, just as he pleases. There will be no charge beyond the price of the book whether he wins or loses his motion; if he is a layman he may omit them altogether. I have included a number of pictures which may add to the interest of the book.

"This world is but a fleeting show,
And soon grim death will jerk us;
So let's be happy as we go,
And all enjoy the circus."

EX-GOV. CHARLES B. ANDREWS.

In the earlier preparation of this volume I was promised an original article by the late Hon. Charles B. Andrews, but his lamented decease prevented me from obtaining one in his own writing. Of course those who read the Connecticut Reports are familiar with his legal opinions as found in those Reports. Judge Andrews was, however, a writer on many other subjects besides legal opinions. The following is an address which he delivered, which will serve to show his style of thought and composition, and is also a review of many of the matters contained in this volume. He gave it to me as his contribution to one of our banquets.

# AN ADDRESS BY EX. GOVERNOR CHARLES B. ANDREWS

You give it, Mr. President, as the result of your reflections, that the judicial power is the highest in the trinity of the governmental powers. I apprehend that most thoughtful persons will agree with you for the reasons you have given. In every government of laws, the courts hold the most important place. The legislature may be nominally higher than the judiciary; but in the actual experience of life, the courts touch the citizen more frequently and more nearly, than the law-making power.. The legislature ordinarily does no more than make rules in the abstract; the courts apply them to concrete cases. To the parties in any given case, that seems only to be the law, which the court decides to be law, for the reason that the court must pass upon the facts, as well as interpret the rule made by the legislature.

In one of those fervid bursts of eloquence, for which Mr. Rufus Choate was so widely known, he exclaimed: "Let us repose secure under the shadow of a learned, impartial and trusted judiciary, and we need no more. Given that, and it matters little what constitution you have, or who makes the laws."

Thinking only of that former time, when no one living was connected with the courts, I cherish the belief that the judiciary of Connecticut has measurably fulfilled for the people of that state, such an high idea. To some extent, doubtless, this is due to the fact that there has been no great city in the state, so that the questions, vexatious and dangerous, liable to rise from a vast, divergent and largely unlearned population have never brought disturbance into the courts. Perhaps, also, the cities of New York on the one side, and Boston on the other, have drawn from us other sources of trouble. In another degree good fortune has come from the character of its people. Connecticut was a Puritan colony, even more so than Massachusetts. It has always been a Puritan state. The Puritan, with all his wilfulness, his self-assertion, his theology and his dogmatism, was a conservative citizen. Respect for the powers that be was a part of his creed. To be sure, he intended to have the powers on his side most of the time, and never scrupled to quarrel with them if they were not; but notwithstanding, he had the thrifty habit of economy; and the money-making man is compelled to have a respect for law; and this respect for the law has continued to this day to be a character of the people of the state. But mainly the result has come from the judiciary itself. In the original frame of government of that state all judicial power was exercised by the legislature. The legislature continued to hear cases on appeal until the year 1784.

CHARLES B. ANDREWS, C. J.

In that year it was enacted that the Lieutenant Governor and the Council should constitute the Supreme Court of Errors. In 1793 the Governor was added to the court, and made the presiding judge. Eight members were necessary to form a quorum. It was soon the subject of complaint, that the members of this court were chosen with reference to their qualifications as legislators rather than as judges. In 1806 an act was passed which transferred all the judicial power of the Governor and Council to the then Superior Court, and it was made the Supreme Court of Errors. That was the origin of the Supreme Court of Errors as it now exists. Jesse Root was at that time Chief Justice. Including its then members, and all who have since been appointed, there have been forty-four members of that court. Thirteen of its deceased members have been Chief Justices—Jesse Root, Stephen Mix Mitchell, Tapping Reeve, Zephaniah Swift, Stephen Titus Hosmer, David Daggett, Thomas Scott Williams, Samuel Church, Henry Matson Waite, William Lucius Storrs, Joel Hinman, Thomas Belden Butler and Origen Storrs Seymour.

These were notable men in their day, and came up to the full standard of being learned, impartial and trusted. The memory of every one of them is cherished by the people of Connecticut with affectionate pride and veneration. They were no more than a fair indication of the other members of the judges. It is little wonder, then, that the people of that state have reposed secure under the shadow of their own trusted magistracy. Nor is it a wonder that the court held a creditable place among other like courts in the nation.

Of the individual character of these and other of the judges, and of the later court, others can speak much better than myself.

Prior to 1819, all the judges were appointed annually. There was a statute which provided that the judges should hold office during the pleasure of the legislature; but the legislature continued to manifest its pleasure by annual elections, until the adoption of the constitution, in 1818. By that constitution the judges of the Supreme and Superior Courts were to hold office during good behavior, subject to impeachment and to be removed by advice of two-thirds of each house of the general assembly. Another clause of the constitution declared that no judge or justice of the peace should be capable of holding office after he arrived at seventy years of age. These two provisions of the constitution have given rise to the suspicion that in Connecticut a man cannot behave well as a judicial officer after he is seventy years old.

In 1855 there was a change by which the judicial term was made eight years. The legislature has always elected all judges. Another change in 1880, has so made it that the legislature elects the judges upon the nomination of the Governor.

In the general field of law, the state of Connecticut deserves at least a passing notice. Every lawyer in the country has heard of the Litchfield Law School. More than to any other, and perhaps more than to all other agencies, it is owing to that law school, that the law in these United States has so much uniformity, consistency and symmetry as it has. That school was founded by Tapping Reeve in 1784. When Mr. Reeve became a judge of the Superior Court, in 1789, he associated with himself James Gould as a teacher. They continued the school together till 1820. Judge Reeve died in 1822. Judge Gould continued it till 1833. During its existence there were educated nearly two thousand young men, coming from every one of the then states. Among the number were those who afterward became judges, chief justices and prominent lawyers and statesmen in most of the states—Chief Justice Baldwin, of Georgia; John C. Calhoun; John M. Clayton, of Deleware; Daniel S. Dickinson, of New York; Levi Woodbury, of Maine; Theron Metcalf, of Massachusetts; William Halstead, of New Jersey; Washington Poe, and very many others.

The earliest volume of reports of decided cases published in America was in Connecticut, by Ephraim Kirby, at Litchfield, in 1789. It has erroneously been said, that the first volume of Dallo's reports was the earliest. Dallo's first volume was not published until 1790.

Of Tapping Reeve I should speak a little more. He was much more than an ordinary man. He was born at Brookhaven, L. I., in 1744; graduated at Princeton in 1763. He studied law with Jesse Root, at Hartford; settled at Litchfield in 1772, and began his law teaching in 1784. He was a born teacher. Every one of the pupils who came under his instruction became at once inspired with a love of study, with the grandeur of the science and the dignity of the profession. Jesse Root, who was the instructor of Judge Reeve, was himself a distinguished man. He was born in Coventry, Conn.; graduated at Princeton, in 1756. He was a preacher until 1763, when he became a lawyer in Hartford. He raised a company for the army and became a colonel. He was a member of the Continental Congress for four years. He was a judge of the Superior Court after 1788. He published two volumes of reports. Another Chief Justice was Zephaniah Swift, who was the author of Swift's Digest. The older lawyers in all those states, which founded their law upon the common law, have doubtless heard of this book. It was exceedingly valuable as an introductory book for beginners, and an excellent hand-book for professional work.

The work of the court in Connecticut is recorded in the volume of reports which I have mentioned, in five volumes of Day's Reports, and in fifty-seven volumes of Connecticut Reports. In them there are no startling cases. They record the litigated cases of a people usually happy, and intent on the arts of peace; but I feel sure that they teach constantly the principles of that science of which Lord Erskine said: "They are founded in the charities of religion, in the philosophy of nature, in the truths of history, and in the experience of common life."

# A DEMURRER

## AN ARGUMENT ON A DEMURRER.

Argument of Hubert Williams, Esq., in the case of Arthur Goodman vs. The Town of Salisbury,.tried in the court of Common Pleas before Hon. Arthur D. Warner, Judge.

The lease ran in the name of Arthur Goodman, agent for the Kickapoo Indian Company. A plea in abatement was filed on the claim that the suit should have been in the name of the real party, instead of the agent. To this plea in abatement the plaintiff filed a demurrer.

MR. WILLIAMS: If the Court please, I appear in behalf of the plea in abatement and against the demurrer. This is a demurrer to a plea in abatement in the case nominally of Arthur Goodman against The Town of Salisbury, but actually of the Kickapoo Indian Medicine Company against said town.

It would be a waste of words for me to tell your Honor that I am like necessity—that I know no law. There are, however, a few facts in relation to this demurrer which I would like to present to the Court. And in passing, I would like to ask your Honor what you are here for? As I understand it, I am here to give your Honor the facts, and you are here to apply the law to those facts. It would be presumptious in me to attempt to instruct your Honor as to what the law is, because if you don't know, you ought not to be here, and I assume that because you are here, you do know the whole law.

Coming back to the question at issue in this case, what are the real facts? In order to obtain a proper comprehension of the case it will be necessary to begin our recital of facts back in the dawn of tradition, and I will begin at the time when the great Creator placed our common forefather, Adam, in a deep sleep in the Garden of Eden, and from his side drew forth and fashioned that which has ever since been the solace and joy of mankind in all ages,—WOMAN, but, after all, Eve was only a side issue, and that is all I am in this case.

Taking up now the lease, for the breach of which this action is instituted, and examining it carefully, your Honor will see that it gives to the Kickapoo Indian Medicine Company the exclusive use of the town hall of Salisbury with all its appurtenances for one week *or longer,* an absolute deed in fee, at the option of the Medicine Company, in perpetuity, so that no longer shall we be able to transact the ordinary affairs and business which appertain to the town of Salisbury, for the oratory of the yeomen will be blended with the shrill cry of the Indian warwhoop, and the beat of the festive tom-tom. They can build their wigwams and campfires any where in the town building. Whether this lease includes the town vaults, I know not, for the town officials still hold the keys thereto. But any citizen getting the keys to the vaults and desiring to examine the probate, land or town records, could only obtain access to them after stumbling over tall drunken chieftains, squalling pappooses, fat squaws and ill-smelling dogs.

Not only that, but your Honor will see that it includes the town hall and its appurtenances. Among other appurtenances we have a lockup. Under the language of this lease which is set forth in the complaint, we will no longer be able to apprehend offenders and keep them in close confinement in that lockup until they may be brought before proper authority, because, forsooth, Arthur Goodman, representing the Kickapoo Indian Medicine Co., has the exclusive lease of our lockup. And God and your Honor know that if these Kickapoo Indians flock into our beautiful, peaceful town and get on the rampage, after filling up with their own medicine or the white man's fire-water, there will be immediate need for a lockup.

Another appurtenance connected with our town hall, and dear to the heart of every son of Salisbury, is a cemetary immediately in the rear of that hall, where repose the bones and ashes of many of our honored dead. Under the terms of this lease, your Honor, it is possible that when Time shall have filled the measure of Eternity, and new ones shall have been born, still that hallowed ground which we love so much will be given over to Indians and tape-worms, and the graves strewn with feathers.

# SOUND ADVICE

Albert Wadhams, Esq. practiced law in Goshen, coming to this County from Vermont. He never had an extensive clientage and held some peculiar views relative to law and particularly to railroad trusts, but did not live long enough to see the trusts all abolished according to his ideas. I found in his papers a good many queer things, some of which were very sensible. The following good advice is I think, worthy of preservation.

## MAXIM FOR A LAWYER

**OR**

## *"Quantum Meruit"*

**Always be sure, in regard to the payment of your Fees, before your Services are Rendered.**

This is an act of justice to your clients, as well as to yourself. I will suppose you do not make this provision, but render voluntary services, trusting to the supposed honor of your clients, after benefiting them, to remunerate you. There are times, when your chances are, that they will imitate "Annanias and Sapphira" partly, or in full, thereby treating you discreditably, and placing no proper estimate on what you may have accomplished. It is equally a wrong, if excessive fees are received. In order to compensate yourself fairly in the first case, you can seldom do it, only as you give the delinquents a sting, "a la mode" "Peter vs. Annanias and Sapphira," in which case you loose your client probably, and the mutual benefit is at an end. Doubtless your client suffers equally with yourself in the final result, which might have been avoided by you in the commencement, by providing for your fee. Your services are either of value, and should be adequately paid for, or they are of no value. It is said that a stone fitted for a wall, will not be left in the way, and in a like manner your compensation for services can be secured, before you are placed in a required position. If this cannot be done *generally,* then you had better leave the undertaking, and follow some more appropriate calling, by which you can be maintained. Therefore, legal services, freely rendered, without adequate provision for remuneration, are, as to yourself, your clients, or any one, both impolitic and unwise. A wise lawyer, for any services he may have rendered, will *seldom* permit a client, or any one, to define his *"Quantum Meruit."*

This Notice, you can post up in your office, or hang it out doors, by the side of your shingle.

*A. W.*

Albany, N. Y., Feb. 1st, 1865.

# The Annual Banquets

The one hundredth anniversary of the establishment of the Litchfield County Bar Association was observed by a Centennial Celebration at Winsted, on the 18th of November, 1898, at the Beardsley House, then kept by George Spencer. And since that time the Bar has held an Annual Banquet at about the same time of the year, they being holden in different places in the county as accomodations could be secured. They are generally attended by between forty and fifty members of the Bar. The exercises consist of after-dinner speeches, with a good deal of singing interspersed, and all of them have been very enjoyable.

It is impossible to give a full account of these yearly gatherings. I have, however, already included in this book some of the good things which have been said on these occasions, and now present a few more.

The invitation to the Centennial was as follows:

YE INVITATION.

GREETING:

By authority of the Litchfield County Bar you are summoned to appear at Winsted on Friday evening, November 18, 1898, then and there to answer in a complaint wherein it is complained and said.

FIRST COUNT.

1. The Superior Court for Litchfield County was established within and for Litchfield County in 1798.

2. At a meeting of the "Barr" of said County it was voted to commemorate said event at Winsted, Conn.

3. James Huntington, Wellington B. Smith, Leonard J. Nickerson, and Dwight C. Kilbourn were appointed a Committee to carry said vote into effect.

SECOND COUNT.

1. Such commemoration will be held at the Beardsley House, Winsted Conn., November 18, 1898, and consist of a Banquet and other exercises commencing at 8:30 P. M.

2. Your prompt acceptance of this invitation is requested that the Committee may be able to guarantee the requisite accommodations.

3. Damages are assessed at $2 per plate.

The plaintiff is found to be of sufficient ability to provide for your comfort and pleasure.

Hereof fail not but due appearance make, or immediately signify cause to the contrary.

Winsted, Nov. 4, 1898.

THE COMMITTEE,

By James Huntington, Chairman.

Dwight C. Kilbourn, Sec'y.

·YE·BANQUET·

## YE SENTIMENT.

"Come back to your mother, ye children, for shame,
Who have wandered like truants, for riches or fame,
With a smile on her face, and a sprig in her lap,
She calls you to feast from her bountiful lap.

Come you of the law who can talk if you please
Till the man in the moon will allow its a cheese,
And leave the old lady who never tells lies
Asleep with her handkerchief over her eyes."

## YE MENU.

---

Little Waramaug Clams
Celery
"We have met the Enemy and they are Ours."—*Oliver H. Perry,* 1813

---

Puree of Litchfield Mushrooms
Salted Almonds Stuffed Olives
"The Law: It has honored us; may we honor it."—*Daniel Webster,* 1847

---

Steamed Twin Lake Salmon
"Pinch Gut Plain" Potatoes "Dibble Hill" Sauce
"We Surgeons of the Law do desperate deeds, sir."—*Beaumont and Fletcher*

---

Supremes of Sweetbreads
Sturges Case style
"Oh! 'tis a blessed thing to have rich clients."—*Beaumont and Fletcher*

---

Probate Punch
"Protect me from the sin
That dooms me to those dreadful words:
'My dear, where have you been?' "—*O. W. Holmes*

---

Mount Riga Patridges, Roasted, Stuffed with Torrington Chestnuts
" 'Fore God, my intelligence
Costs me more than my share oft comes to."—*B. Jorison*

---

Knowles Salad, "Move to Erase" Dressing
"Importance is one thing and learning's another;
But a debate's a debate, that I assert."—*Congreve*

---

Canaan Ice Cream, with original R. and R. flavor
" 'Tis better belly burst than good food be lost."

---

Crackers Cheese

---

Coffee

"Whilst we together jovial sit,
Careless, and crowned with mirth and wit,
We'll think of all the friends we know
And drink to all worth drinking to!"—*Charles Cotton*

## PRESIDENT HUNTINGTON'S ADDRESS

The after-dinner speaking was opened by the Hon. James Huntington,—for many years the beloved and honored president of the Bar Association, and who has recently deceased,—and his speech shows in a measure the felicitous and happy manner of "Uncle Jim," as he was familiarly called by his brethren of the Bar during the later years of his life.

"Brethren of the Bar of Litchfield County: We have met this evening to celebrate the 100 years of the existence of the Superior Court of Litchfield County. To you younger members of the Bar it may seem a great ways back to 1798, but to me, who has practiced at the Bar two-fifths of the time (and I don't tell you now how old I am) it seems but a step back to the beginning. I suppose that some of my brethren here tonight will give something of the history and reminiscences of the Bar either specially or in the county generally, but for myself, I wish to say but a few words in regard to this celebration. I wish to direct your attention to a few of its peculiarities and characteristics, and the first characteristic that I wish to mention after the practice of two-fifths of a century at this Bar, is that it has the reputation of being a fighting Bar, that the lawyers of Litchfield County are persistent tryers and fighters, they never let the ground go un-hoed in a case. As a Judge of the Court said to me not long ago "If a Judge comes to Litchfield County and expects that it will be a sort of a vacation, after he has been to Litchfield, and from Litchfield to Winsted and from Winsted down to New Milford and back again two or three times, he will go home thoroughly convinced that it is no vacation to come to Litchfield County and hold a long term."

Another characteristic of this Bar is its good fellowship. It has been so for forty years and I presume it was for the sixty years before; it is now and I trust it ever will be.

It is remarked by attorneys from other counties in this State and from other States, that they never came to a Bar where there is such good fellowship as there is in this Bar. They never address one another by more than half of their first name. And when one of the boys becomes a Judge of the Superior Court they with pride and pleasure address him as His Honor, it is ten chances to one that when night comes and he comes off the Bench, that they address him as Tobey or Ed or Jerry or Bert or Gid. And he feels as much honored to come down to that fellowship off from the Bench as he is by being respectfully addressed while on it by the members of this Bar.

I say it is peculiarly characteristic of the Bar of this County and I trust it will remain so another 100 years.

Another characteristic is their self-reliance, we have to rely on ourselves and it has made self reliant lawyers.

Another thing, they are a tough lot physically as well as mentally. And they must necessarily be so. They come up to these shire towns in summer's heat and winter's cold. We start out early in the morning and go 7 or 8 miles and try a justice case all day long and come home in the rain and cold at night, together singing songs and telling stories. We are called in the night season to go miles away to make the wills of the dying, we are called upon day after day to take depositions in kitchens by the kitchen stove, and instead of sitting down to such a fine feast as this to eat we are satisfied with the smell of the onions and the turnips and cabbage that are boiling on the stove for the family to eat. Our lives are spent in that way and it has made a tough lot of us physically. We are called upon as lawyers in the country to become all-round men and to do all kinds of work. A country lawyer is called upon to do everything almost that can be done except writing sermons and writing Doctor's prescriptions although some Cornwall gentlemen can write those, I am told.

If anyone asks what kind of lawyers does it make to practice in that manner, my answer is if you take the Connecticut Reports from Kirby to the 70 Conn., you read the work of Litchfield County lawyers clear through the 70 volumes of those reports. Yes, further, it is the same kind of men that you are, gentlemen, that 13 of them have represented the Bench of the Superior Court of this State, 10 of them the Supreme Court Bench and three of them as Chief-justices, they were men of the same experience and the same kind of practice; and how well hey have filled their places the records of the Supreme Court, the opinions, that have been written by them through all the Connecticut Reports will tell you. So we may well be proud of our County and of our County Bar, and I ask, when my time has come to join the innumerable caravan that moves, that there can be nothing better said of me than that Jim Huntington was a respectable member of the Litchfield County Bar.

My brethren, I said to you that 40 years practice, two-fifths of a century, two-fifths of the time of this Superior Court went back to where one could almost say it was a step back to the beginning. We have with us tonight a brother whose tall form and snowy hair are known to you all and who has practiced law in the Superior Court over one half its time, who is a connecting link with the beginning of this court; who practiced law with men who were members of the Bar when the Superior Court was organized, and it is with exceeding great pleasure, nothing could give me more pleasure, that I introduce to you our venerable and honored brother, Donald J. Warner.

To him it may be said, as Holmes wrote to Whittier on his 80th birthday.

Dear friend, whom thy fourscore winters leave more dear
Than when life's roseate summer on thy cheek burned in the flush
of manhood's earliest year,
Lonely, how lonely! is the snowy peak
Thy feet have reached after many a year!
Close on thy foot-steps 'mid the landscape drear
I stretch my hand thine answering grasp to seek
Warm with the love no rippling rhymes can speak.
Look backward! from thy lofty height survey
Thy years of toil, of peaceful victories won
Of dreams made real, large hopes outrun!
Look forward! brighter than earth's morning ray
Streams the pure light of Heaven's unsetting sun,
The unclouded dawn of Life's immortal day.

For Judge Warner's address see his reminiscences, page 101.

Many letters were received from the absent brethren regretting their inability to attend; the one from the Hon. Wm. L. Ransom, who for nearly thirty years was Clerk of the Courts enclosed as his response an excuse from the late Judge Granger for not attending a Banquet at the Island Hotel to which he had been invited, and is as follows:

Dear Ransom, were my legs as limber
As they were in days of yore,
When I snared the festive sucker
On the Whiting River shore,—
Silvery stream,—that murmers sweetly
Through fair Wangum's peaceful vales,
Kissed by morning's slanting sunbeams,
Fanned by evenings pleasant gales.

When I chased the obese woodchuck
O'er the hills and sandy knoll
When I snatched the sluggish bull heads
Wriggling from their muddy holes,
When with dog and gun by moonlight
Through the swamps and reedy fens
I pursued the scented polecat
Terror of the matron hens.

Gladly would I climb Mount Pisgah,
Mystic mountain of the East,
For the fun of being with you
At your Island Hotel feast.
But, Oh! Ransom, tempus edax
Unremitting night and day
Seventy years has gnawed our muscles
Till they're in a—bad way.

Youthful hose well saved or ragged
Serve but to hide our spindle shanks,
And our shin bones sharp and jagged
Play us now rheumatic pranks.
Accoutered thus Dear Rans, you see,
The feast you spread is not for me,
Whatever things the Gods deny us,
Is for the best. Good night. Tobias.

Leonard W. Cogswell, the Official Stenographer, offered the following original

POEM:

Oh, sacred soil of Litchfield Hills,
Where Winter's winds howl drear;
The country's best and bravest men,
Have found their birth-place here.

The plain and simple life they led
Upon these rugged hills,
Gave vigorous health and mental strength,
Brave hearts and sturdy wills.

Senators, Governors, Judges Preachers,
Found here congenial soil,
And worked their way to high renown
With most incessant toil.

Then let us all fresh courage take,
And till Death our warm blood chills,
We'll bless the Fate that gave us birth
On these rock-ribbed Litchfield Hills.

At one of our banquets the following interesting letter was received from Rev. A. N. Lewis:

Montpelier, Vermont, Dec. 11, 1902.

To the Members of the Litchfield County Bar, in annual reunion convened:

Gentlemen:—I regret exceedingly my inability to be present at your festive gathering. Forty-five years ago at the September term of the Superior Court, Judge Seymour presiding, I was admitted an attorney and counsellor. F. D. Beeman, Esq., was Clerk of the courts, and Hollister, Graves, Hubbard, Toby Granger, George C. Woodruff, Judge Phelps, Sedgwick, Sanford, et al., were the leading barristers. "There were giants in those days." The Litchfield Bar was second to none in the state.

The condition of things was very different than the present. Litchfield was an inland town, accessable only by stage and private conveyance. The lawyers, litigants and witnesses came to stay. The Mansion House, U. S. Hotel and Wheeler House were thronged with guests. The open hotel fires in the hotel offices were scenes of mirth and jollity. William Deming, Sr., Stephen Deming, Harry Bissell and other notables were usually in attendance with stories, jokes and repartees worth recording.

"Uncle" Stephen Deming had been in his younger days a tavern keeper. A certain deacon, professedly a temperance man, but suspected of selling "the ardent" on the sly, took up his parable and said, "Uncle Stephen, when you reflect upon your rum-selling days, the widows and orphans you have made and the misery you have caused, how do you feel?" Uncle Stephen paused a moment and said, "Deacon————, when I think of myself, by myself, I feel like putting my hand upon my mouth and my mouth in the dust and crying unclean, unclean, God be merciful to me a sinner. But, Deacon, when I compare myself with my neighbors I thank God and take courage."

A Plymouth farmer had a case in Graves' hands which had been running for years. Term after term Graves had charged continuance fee $7; and the farmer becoming discouraged had tried to get the case taken out of court, but all in vain. One day he was sitting on the piazza of the U. S. Hotel rehearsing his grievance to the lawyers, when Graves went past. The farmer ejaculated, "I hope to G—d Graves won't go to hell!" "Why not," asked one of the listeners. "Because," answered the farmer, "Because he'd make trouble there."

The writer of this talk was a student in Hollister & Beeman's office and was often employed in copying pleadings, etc. In one of the documents occurred the following sentence: "And whereas this case has been brought by regular continuances to this court, etc." In the copy made by the writer it read thus: "And whereas this case has been brought by regular contrivances to this court!" The blunder (?) caused a ripple of merriment on the bench and in the bar. It was too true.

A petition for a divorce was submitted to a referee or commissioner who made his report thereon to the court. It was charged by the petitioner that her husband on a certain occasion when she had returned from a drive with the co-respondent had composed and recited to her and her escort before the children the following lines:

"William Johnson went to ride,
With Sarah Wilkins for his bride,
Returning home I heard them say,
We've had a dam good ride to-day."

Imagine Hollister reading with solemn face this poetical gem to the court!

A Litchfield lawyer, whose name I have forgotten, was pleading a case of little importance before a jury. He was very pathetic and solemn, so much so that when he concluded the opposing counsel arose and said, "May it please your Honor, hadn't we better sing a hymn?"

The Hon. Charles Chapman of Hartford was journeying to Litchfield to attend court, in the Hartford and Litchfield stage. It was winter. The stage was an open pung, the snow was falling and a northwest wind drove it directly into the faces of the passengers. Chapman and "Dick" Hubbard, a brother lawyer, were sitting on the first seat and took the full force of the storm. No one had spoken for some minutes, when Chapman broke the silence with "I say Hubbard, I had rather *facit per alium* than *facit per se!*"

Gentlemen:—Some of us have outlived our contemporaries. We are nearing the setting sun; our places must soon be filled by another generation; soon we shall be summoned to the court of last resort. May we respond to the summons, bearing with us the record of a well-spent life and the hope of a blessed immortality.

Yours fraternally,

A. N. LEWIS,

Pastor of Christ's Church, Montpelier, Vermont.

---

## HURLBUTISMS

The late William F. Hurlbut, Clerk of the Court of Common Pleas, gave me considerable assistance in the preparation of this work. The following items are some which he thought would interest members of the Bar.

One of the learned Judges of the Superior Court, after setting through a long, tedious trial of a case, to charge the jury commenced with the following remark:

"Gentlemen of the Jury! If you know anything about this case, God knows that you know more about it than I do."

On the trial of a prisoner for shooting a man whom he thought was stealing his chickens, the judge charged the jury very forcibly against the accused, but the jury brought in a verdict of "Not Guilty." The Judge continued the laborious work of sharpening his pencil in which he was engaged when the jury gave the verdict. After a considerable length of time had elapsed he suddenly exclaimed, "S———, you have escaped as by fire." The members of the Bar have never been able to understand the nature of that escape.

The Hon. Truman Smith closed an argument made in a little case appealed from a Justice of the Peace, in which the matter in demand was very trivial, and the action of the opposing counsel had been very erratic, with the following comments. "If your Honor please: I had prepared with considerable care a brief with the intention of filing it with the court. After I had finished it I said to myself, if I live fourteen years from the 26th day of next October I shall be one hundred years old; now is it worth while at my time of life to come into court with an enormous bomb shell just to annihilate a musquito? and I said to myself it was not—the game was not worth the powder."

There are a multitude of odd and funny things connected with our profession. I am obliged to exclude almost everything of that sort, but will save a few. Some of them I have taken from Brother Cogswell's brief before the "Supreme Court of Eaters" and others from various sources.

SCENE, Criminal Court in Canaan. Alonzo B. Garfield, C. J. on the bench. Crime, prisoner charged with robbery of a drunken woman. Clint Roraback, acting State's attorney.

Mrs. Nora Smith (complainant) sworn.

Ex. by Mr. Roraback:

Q. Were you down in the defendant's house near Pine Grove?

A. Yes.

Q. Did you have some money there?

A. Yes.

Q. Did you lose it?

A. Yes. It was stolen from my pocketbook which I carried inside my corsets, as I lay on the bed drunk.

Q. You think the prisoner stole it?

A. Yes, and I come up to see Hen. Roraback the next day, and he said he'd see I had justice done. Hen. is all right since "he growed up."

MR. RORABACK:—That is all the testimony we have, your Honor, and it is enough. Don wants him bound over.

GARFIELD, C. J.—We hain't got much evidence ag'in' the prisoner, and I don't think he is guilty; that is, not much; but what Don says goes in this court, and so I'll bind him over.

SCENE, Superior Court at Litchfield, October Term, 1906. Hon. Ralph Wheeler, J. Prisoner, Franceski Balcyss, charged with robbing a Swede of $165.

DONALD T. WARNER, to complainant, Mr. Gustafson: Did you have a Hungarian at work for you? A. I did; he is what they call a Pole, and I can do a day's work, or yump over the moon quicker than I speak his name, but I have it writ down on a piece of paper, and you can tear off what you want and make a dictionary of the rest. I had a German, and an Irishman, and a nigger to work for me at the same time, and at first I thought one of them took it, but our Northfield detective says this is the man.

Don took the paper and attempted to read the following name—but he didn't—but asked Kilbourn to: Czyrkstecheltzkoxtcheldoszleffski.

T. F. RYAN (counsel for prisoner, to prisoner on the stand):

Q. If you had any of your countrymen in Waterbury, who were they and where are they now?

THE PRISONER (through a Waterbury interpreter):

Petrovsky, Oskaloffsky, and Nevereffski,
To Siberia were sent;
Kitoffsky, Rubonoffsky, and Wallereffsky,
In a dungeon cell were pent.

Milarodovitch and Tetrovitch,
Kostolovitch and Rostomaroff
They imprisoned or swung them off;
But when is gone,
He never is missed.

That is what it says in a Polish letter written in Russian script.

THREE OTHER INTERPRETERS EMPLOYED BY THE COURT TO WATCH THE FIRST:—That is wrong, he says what not so it.

THE COURT: Keep still.

DON: Wait.

RYAN: Sit down.

THE COURT: Mr. Stenographer, what did the witness say?

THE STENOGRAPHER: I don't know, your Honor.

THE COURT: This is the worst Babel of a case I ever heard.

Brother Ryan got the $165.

✠

(Answer to complaint for divorce between Hungarians, received from Hungary by Kilbourn.)

DR. GROSZ DEZSO
Lawyer
S. A. UJHELEY
Hungary.

HIGH ESTEEMED COURT:

Janos Zsarnay, seated at Torrington, Conn., according to the writ of summon of Litchfield County, ss. dated from 1906, 12 September, and being handed to me on the day of 20ktober, claims that the marriage, bound between me and the plaintiff in the year of 1873, should be devorced upon the ground, that I should have wilfully deserted him and totally neglected all the duties of marriage.

All this complains of the plaintiff are not true. I did not desert him but he left me 10 years since, flying secretly. Within this time he did not wrote a single line, nor supported me and our children. Therefore he is who neglected the duties of marriage and not I am who has deserted him.

I being now a 55 years old women, unable to earn, do not agree, that our marriage should be devorced. On the contrary: I entreat the jury that Janos Zsarnay should be convicted to pay a 20 dollar monthly rate as to support myself and the children.

I give, further, to acknowledge to the court, that a verdic of devorce returned in the U. S. A. has no power ther in Hungary and even if the jury should devorce him, according to our laws, I remain in links of marriage, still he can live married in the U. S. A. That would be very unlawful.

Faithfully,

## AN ENOCH ARDEN CASE

"All's Well that Ends Well,"—
On Mt. Riga as well as in Shakespeare.

The happy ending of St. Valentine's night, February 14th, 1908, of the tragical story of Lovie ———— of Mt. Riga, deserted with her baby in her arms by her husband in 1882, who was reported dead a few years later, and thereafter remained unheard of until August, 1907, when, like Enoch Arden, he appeared to find his wife happily married to Charlie ........ with two stalwart children by her side, but unlike Enoch of old did not conveniently sink into obscurity again.

Divorced February 14th, 1908, from the resurrected husband and married the night of the same day to her true husband, according to the following form:—

Both Lovie and Charlie your right hands unite
Before witnesses here St. Valentine's night.
You, *CHARLIE,* do promise to take Lovie to wife,
To love her and cherish her the rest of your life.
You, *LOVIE,* do promise Charlie as husband to take,
And, cleaving only to him, each and all others forsake.
Now, each having promised the other to wed,
To Have and to Hold, till Life's journey be sped,
For richer, for poorer, in sickness and health,—
By force of the Law of our good Commonwealth,
I PROCLAIM you to be lawful Husband and Wife.

*L' ENVOI.*

May your joys be many, and your sorrows be light,
And the memories sweet of St. Valentine's night.
And ever, as the circling years roll on,
Keep a kindly thought of the Justice,—Don.

THE MAKING OF A JUROR.—Judge Ralph Wheeler had had his patience sorely tried by lawyers who wished to talk, and by men who tried to evade jury service. Between hypothetical questions and excuses it seemed as if they never would get to the actual trial of the case. So when a puzzled little German, who had been accepted by both sides as a juror, jumped up, the Judge was exasperated.

"Shudge!" cried the German. "What is it?" demanded the judge. "I tink I like to go home to mein Frau," said the German. "So would I, but we can't," retorted the Judge. "Sit down." "But, Shudge," persisted the German, "I tink I not make a good shuror." "You're the best in the box," said the Judge. "Sit down." "What box?" said the German. "The jury box," said the Judge. "Ach, Himmel, I thought it was ein bad box what beoples get in somedimes. But, Shudge," persisted the little German, "I don't speak goot English already yet."

"You don't have to speak at all," said the Judge. "Sit down."

The little German pointed to the lawyers to make his last desperate plea. "Shudge," said he, "I can't make noddings von what dese fellers say." It was the Judge's chance to get even with the lawyers for many annoyances. "Neither can anyone else," he said. "Sit down." With a sigh, the little German sat down.

✠

Here is a sonnet which the Clerk received, which perhaps may be slightly sarcastic.

"For the love of God and humanity,
To avoid both wrath and profanity,
To enable the executor to pay legacies and debts,
Send along that certificate in Selleck vs. Betts."
Yours very truly,

Judge Miles T. Granger was very much addicted to poetry; one of his specimens has been for many years a classic. More than fifty years ago when Fred D. Beeman was Clerk and Mr. Granger was simply a practicing attorney, Sheriff Sedgwick got Beeman to write an epitaph on Granger, which was as follows:

"When Toby died—dire groans were heard,
His friends were in commotion.
For Heaven refused to own the bird
And Hell declined the portion."

Taking this epitaph into another room the Sheriff folded it up and presently returned to the court room where Mr. Granger was at the table, trying a case, and handed the note to him. Upon reading it, Mr. Granger turned it over and wrote upon the back the following, upon Mr. Beeman:

"And when the Clerk of Hell rose up
To publish to the legions
The reason why the bird was barred
A place in those dark regions,
A bright red glow about his head
Revealed to all those poor damned souls
The face and form of Beeman."

Lines Composed by Judge Granger while on the Bench trying a Sheep-stealing case.

Alas for Winters, all forlorn,
He husked for Hod, the Rustling Corn
And through the woods when night was dark,
He raided on the sheep of Clark,
And one small lamb out of the flock
He slew and skinned, without a shock
Of conscience, or a thought of wrong,
But took the mutton right along.

The picture of Judges evidence shows how the witnesses impress a judicial mind. It is a reproduction of a paper left by a learned judge upon his desk after a tedious trial. Other similar papers are in my possession, many of them utterly unintelliglble. The State pays an enormus sum for Stenographers, but their notes are little value during a trial and the translating of them is too expensive for an ordinary suit. The attic of the Court House contains many pounds of their hieroglyphic papers, and are practically worthless, as different systems are used, and seldom one shorthand writer can read anothers notes. To make our present system of taking evidence of full use, the notes should be transcribed during the trial and placed in the hands of the Court and Counsel. Until that is done lawyers and judges must take their own notes as best they can.

### THE LAWYERS' WAYS.

"I've been list'nin to them lawyers
  In the court house of the street
An' I've come to the conclusion
  That I'm most completely beat.
First one fellow riz to argy,
  An' he boldly waded in
As he dressed the tremblin' pris'ner
  In a coat o' deep-dyed sin.
Why, he painted him all over
  In a hue o' blackest crime,
An' he smeared his reputation
  With the thickest kind o' grime,
Tell I found myself a-wond'rin,
  In a misty way and dim,
How the Lord had come to fashion
  Such an awful man as him.
Then the other lawyer started,
  An' with briming, tearful eyes,
Said his client was a martyr
  That was brought to sacrifice,
An' he gave to that same pris'ner
  Every blessed human grace,
Till I saw the light o' virtue
  Fairly shining from his face.
Then I own 'at I was puzzled
  How such things could rightly be;
And this aggrevating question
  Seems to keep a puzzling me.
So will some one please inform me,
  An' this mystery unroll,
How an angel an' a devil
  Can possess the self-same soul."

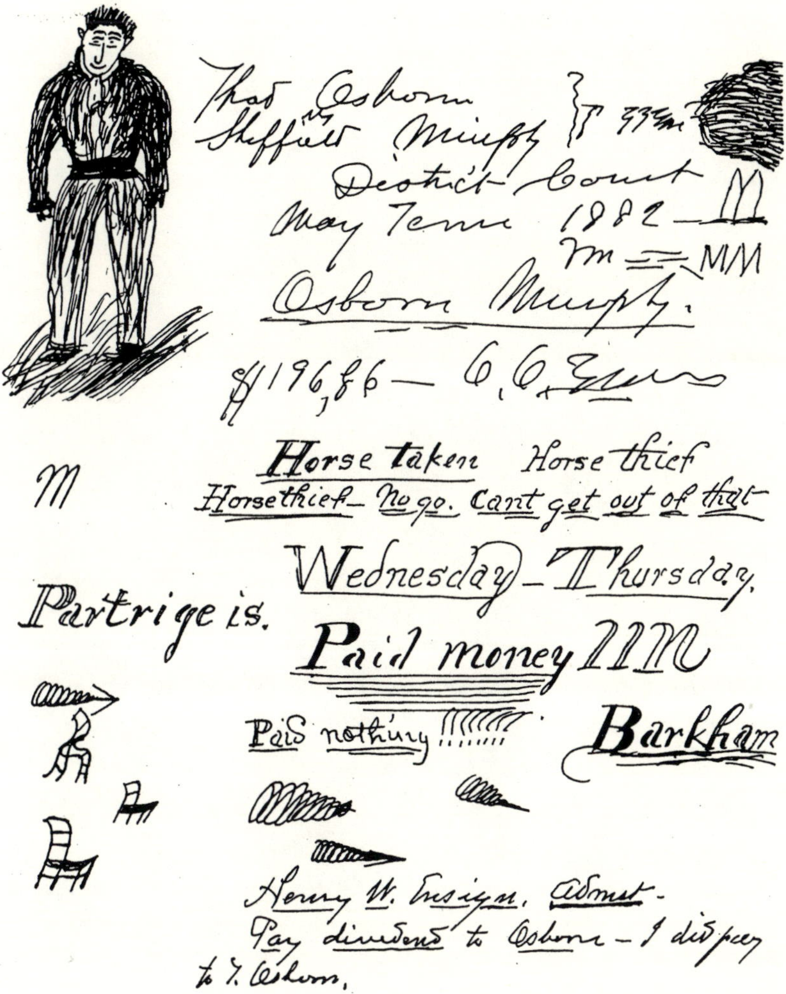
Thad Osborn
Sheffield Murphy
District Court
May Term 1882
Osborn Murphy.
$196,86 — 6,6,
Horse taken Horse thief
Horsethief — No go. Cant get out of that
Wednesday — Thursday.
Partrige is.
Paid money
Paid nothing
Barkham
Henry W. Ensign. Admst —
Pay dividend to Osborn — I did pay
to T. Osborn.

THE JUDGE'S NOTES OF EVIDENCE

Showing the workings of the Judicial mind

MR. WILLIAM GRIMES.
("OLD GRIMES")

## "OLD GRIMES."

One of the characters connected with our legal fraternity was William Grimes, universally known as "Old Grimes." It is generally supposed that he was a mythical character but he was not. He was a run-away slave who came to Litchfield probably about 1808, and was a general servant to the students at the Law School. He was born in Virginia and was the body servant of a man by the name of Grimes, whose name, in after years, he adopted; by the fortunes of business adversities his master was obliged to dispose of him and he fell into the hands of cruel masters from whose barbarous treatment he ran away to the land of Liberty, which at that time was Litchfield. Judge Reeve had acquired quite a reputation for defending fugitive slaves and Litchfield was thought by them to be the home of the free. Grimes was thrifty, frugal and acquired some little property and owned a piece of land between the present residence of George Kenney and the Fire Department building, to which he moved a small building for a barber shop. Some of the Southern students of the Law School ascertained his status, made matters unpleasant for him by notifying his master who took steps to recover him and he was obliged to dispose of his property through his friends Dr. Abel Catlin and William H. Thompson, who took the proceeds to purchase his freedom. His last appearance on Litchfield Land Records was August 6, 1824. In the latter years of the Law School, Grimes removed to New Haven, where he acted in the same capacity as he had at Litchfield to the students at Yale College. He published in a little pamphlet a sketch of his life, containing the portrait of which a copy is here given. He died about 1850 in New Haven.

His great notoriety consists in the the well-known lines "Old Grimes is Dead," the history of which as given to me by an old resident of Litchfield, and from other data which I have secured is as follows: Albert G. Green, of Rhode Island, who afterwards became a distinguished man, United States Senator, etc., was a student of the Law School in 1812, and was very fond of making rhymes about all manner of things, and upon all occasions, and Grimes importuned him to make some poetry for him, the result being the lines above referred to, a few stanzas of which are here given.

### OLD GRIMES.

Old Grimes is dead—that good old man,
  We ne'er shall see him more;
He used to wear a long black coat
  All buttoned down before.

His heart was open as the day,
  His feelings all were true;
His hair was some inclined to gray—
  He wore it in a queue.

Whene'er he heard the voice of pain
His breast with pity burned;
The large round head upon his cane
From ivory was turned.

Kind words he ever had for all,
He knew no base design;
His eyes were dark and rather small,
His nose was aquiline.

He lived in peace with all mankind,
In friendship he was true;
His coat had pocket-holes behind,
His pantaloons were blue.

But good old Grimes is now at rest,
Nor fears misfortune's frown;
He wore a double-breasted vest,
The stripes ran up and down.

He modest merit sought to find
And pay it its desert;
He had no malice in his mind,
No ruffles on his shirt.

His neighbors he did not abuse,
Was sociable and gay;
He wore large buckles on his shoes,
And changed them every day.

Thus undisturbed by anxious cares
His peaceful moments ran,
And everybody said he was
A fine old gentleman.

## GEORGE CATLIN'S PORTRAIT

[redacted]e in this book is from an old oil painting that he made of himself when he was about twenty-five years old and is now in the possesston of his daughter in New York city who kindly loaned it for reproduction.

# COMPLIMENTARY DINNER TO JUDGE O. S. SEYMOUR

On the 29th of January, 1874, the Bar of Fairfield County gave a complimentary dinner to Chief Justice Origen Storrs Seymour, on the eve of his retirement from the Bench—under the provisions of the Constitution.

Many distinguished guests were present; many pleasant and interesting things were said, some relating to our Bar and though all are worthy of preservation we have the space for only a few.

The President, Hon. James C. Loomis, introduced the exercises by saying:

GENTLEMEN:—I feel confident that nothing has transpired in the history of the Fairfield County Bar during my long connection with it, which has given more pleasure to its members than the opportunity which this occasion affords, to express to our Chief Justice on the eve of his retirement, our high appreciation of those exalted qualities which characterize and adorn his life, and which has made him so eminently useful and so universally esteemed, and our deep regret that, in the midst of his usefulness and in the full possession of all his intellectual powers, he is compelled to retire from his high official station and discontinue his invaluable services under the stern provisions of our Constitution, which makes 70 years of age the limit of judicial life in Connecticut.

I assure you, gentlemen, it affords me unfeigned pleasure to assemble with you around this festive board and unite with our distinguished friends, His Excellency, the Governor of the State of Connecticut; His Honor, the Chief Justice elect, and his honorable associates of the Supreme Court; the distinguished Judge of the Circuit Court of the United States for the district of Connecticut; the Judges of our Superior Court and of other courts, and other officials who have honored us with their presence, in paying this well-merited tribute of respect to one who so emiently deserves it.

From the time of a generation at least Judge Seymour has been a star of the first magnitude in the civil, political, judicial and, I may say, religious constellations of the State. He has deservedly won for himself a name that will be known, honored and loved, not only in his day and generation, but so long as the public records endure.

There is no human standard by which we can measure the exact amount of good which results to a State from a busy, active and well spent life in the public service Even the great Amazon is swallowed up in the bosom of the fathomless deep; nevertheless its influence, unmeasured and immeasurable in all its magnitude and power is there, and the great ships which float the treasures of the nations on "Old Ocean" float more or less securely, however unconsciously, upon the foundations, which this mighty river has contributed to establish and maintain; so, though we cannot define with mathematical precision the exact quantity of good, which has resulted to our commonwealth and its citizens from the eminent services of our distinguished friend, yet no one will doubt but his long, active and useful life spent in the administration of the local affairs of his immediate neighborhood—in the advocacy of the rights of the citizens at the Bar—in the promotion of the public weal in the councils of the State and nation—and in the maintenance of the great principles of justice and equity, according to established authority upon the Bench, have greatly contributed to the stability and prosperity of our institutions and given additional security to the rights of person and property so eminently and so universally enjoyed.

It has been my privilege to have been honored with the personal acquaintance and I believe friendship of eight of the predecessors of our Chief Justice in that high office—Hosmer, Daggett, Williams, Church, Waite, Storrs, Hinman, Butler—glorious names! They were all high-minded, learned, impartial judges, uncorrupted—incorruptible! They have gone down to their graves crowned with honors, having transmitted the ermine of the judicial robes spotless and when that emblem of purity and incorruptibility fell upon the shoulders of him who now so gracefully wears it—*it touched nothing less spotless.* He will soon transmit it to his successor stainless, to be borne by him through his judicial life unsoiled and then transmitted in all purity to another, thence to descend from generation to generation, I hope to the latest generation of man, without a spot or blemish.

It would afford me great pleasure to dwell for a few moments, did time permit, upon the many virtues which embellish and adorn the private life of our Chief Justice; to speak of his devotion to the welfare and happiness of his family and friends—of his tender sympathies with the unfortunate and afflicted, of his gentlemanly deportment everywhere and on all occasions, of his manly practice at the Bar, of his patience and suavity on the Bench, of his hospitality, his generosity, his integrity, his incorruptibility—but time fails me. I can only say that in all the relations of private life, Judge Seymour has been and is the Christian gentleman, acknowledged and appreciated as such by all who know him most, by those who know him best.

Daniel Webster, speaking of himself at a public dinner given him in the city of Boston some years since, said: "If public life has its cares and trials, it sometimes has its consolations; if the approbation of the good is fit to be pursued, it is fit to be enjoyed; if it be, as it undoubtedly is, one of the most stirring and invigorating motives which can operate upon the mind, it is also among the richest rewards which can console and gratify the heart."

In the spirit of these sentiments of this pre-eminently distinguished statesman—in the name of the Fairfield County Bar—in the presence of this large circle of distinguished friends, and from the lowest depths of my heart, let me say to you, Mr. Chief Justice, in conclusion, you have experienced the cares and trials of public life;

you have secured the approbation of the good; you have won a crown; it is fit that you should enjoy it. Console and gratify your heart with this rich reward and when you ascend from your present high position to the bosom of your family and to the circle of your loving and beloved friends, there to enjoy the honored evening of your useful life in tranquil repose, may the soul stirring and invigating consolation cheer and animate you to your latest breath, intensified with the comfortable hope that beyond there is prepared an immortal crown, which neither time nor Constitution can take away.

Chief Justice Seymour responded to the toast "Our Chief Justice" as follows:

I stand here to-night on the eve of separation from pursuits to which during a long life I have been devoted. I have enjoyed my professional life at the Bar and on the Bench, and I do not and cannot look with indifference upon my approaching separation from these duties.

I, however, make no quarrel with the constitutional provision under which my retirement takes place. "The days of our age are three score years and ten;" when those years are accomplished, nature craves a brief period of repose between, on the one hand, the active duties of life and its final close on the other.

I submissively bow, therefore, to the law of the land, believing it to be in harmony with the law of nature, but at the time I cherish the memories of professional life, and part from it with fond regret, and I will occupy your time a few moments this evening in suggesting some particulars wherein the lawyer's life among the varied pursuits of mankind is regarded by me as a favored one.

I was admitted to the Bar in my native County of Litchfield in 1826, and I at once found myself in possesion of a privilege which I then thought might be peculiar to myself, but which I afterwards found was common to all young lawyers,—the privilege of fellowship on free and easy terms with the elder brethren. I well remember the pleasure of these associations and the help I derived from them. It is pleasant to recall the names of the giants in those days, when I was a stripling, Bacon, Miner, Huntington, Beers, Boardman, the Churches, Smith. When I found myself in a snarl, and that happened to me semi-daily, I always found relief in the ready and cheerfully-given counsel of these my venerable seniors.

It is truth familiar to us all that lawyers, young and old, high and low, rich and poor, associate together with great freedom, not perhaps that we love one another more than the medical faculty, but our business brings us constantly into association with our brethren, our labors are not isolated but performed in public and in each other's company, whereby we become thoroughly acquainted with each other. No man can conduct a complicated cause in court without showing his brethren what manner of man he is. If he has mind industry, learning and culture, he shows it; his temper and disposition will show themselves. If he has integrity and truthfulness in him, they will appear. If on the contrary, he is a sham, everybody will see it. The practice of changing partners as associate counsel, brings lawyers into the most intimate relation with each other.

It is amusing to notice gentlemen who are opposed to each other in the morning almost to personal altercation, in the afternoon engaged as associates, and at once as familiar and intimate with each other as the Siamese twins. We become, therefore, thoroughly acquainted with each other and wear no masks in each other's society.

In this connection, if time allowed, I would like to describe the bar meetings of olden time which had a lingering existence 50 years ago, but those old-fashioned gatherings could not be conducted on temperance principles and upon the advent of the temperance reformation, they "took the chills" and died out. But the attraction of the profession lies in the inherent dignity of the law itself, controlling as it does by its silent power, the moving masses in all their various relations and interests—in the equity, calm wisdom and dispassionate justice of its precepts—in its noble history in the past and in the services and accomplishments of its living professors.

The bar has always drawn to itself the best talent and highest culture of the country, and hence the contests of the Bar conducted by skillful and learned counsel, furnish scenes of instructive interest. The marvelous and varied powers of the human mind are in these contests called for and developed in a manner and to an extent unequaled in any other arena.

I readily recall many such scenes as lively and dramatic as the inventions of Shakespeare's genius. I would not be understood however, as saying that the court room is exactly paradise regained. The scenes are generally animated, spirited and varied; sometimes, however, dull and stupid; sometimes disgusting, exhibiting human nature of its most revolting form and the members of the Bar have much thankless labor, many sleepless nights and bitter disappointments.

But it is in his library that the true disciple of the law finds his highest satisfaction. He can here interrogate the masters of jurisprudence, ancient and modern upon the matters he has in hand, and will seldom fail of getting an appropriate answer. I yield no blind obedience to authorities and precedents. Law is a progressive science. When it is said that law is the perfection of reason, it is not to be understood that all the utterance of judges and jurists are such. There are mistakes and errors in the past that the present may correct, and there are mistakes and errors in the present which it is to be hoped the future will correct, but taken as a whole a law library is replete with sound truths applicable, more or less directly, to the various living issues pending before the courts, not mere abstract truths worked out in the closet, but truths upon which learned arguments have been heard at the Bar, and learned consultations had by the Bench, so that all available learning on the subject is brought forward and receives its due weight. It is difficult to overestimate the value of the well weighed opinions of such chancellors as Hardwick, Eldon and Kent, and of such Judges as Mansfield, Ellenborough and Marshall.

Among the most cherished memories of my professional life is the intimate acquaintance which I have enjoyed with all the eminent jurists who have adorned the bench of the State during the fifty years. I need not recite their familiar names in this assembly, but you will permit me, occupying the position I do, to repeat the names of those who have filled the high office I am about to lay down, *nomina clara* each of which upon bare mention suggests all the virtues pertaining to their high judicial position.

When I came to the Bar the Chief Justiceship was held by the learned Hosmer followed in quick succession by Daggett, Williams, Church, Waite, Storrs, and Hinman, and then by my immediate predecessor, the lamented Butler, companion, friend, brother. In this, his native county, he needs no eulogy from me. In the reports of his judicial opinions he has raised to himself a monument *aere pernnius*. Allow me, in conclusion, to propose as a toast, "The memory of the honored dead of the Bench and Bar of this State."

The toast "The Bar of Litchfield County" was responded to by Hon. Gideon H. Hollister, as follows:

It is difficult to name a portion of this Continent that might with more propriety have been called a wilderness than was Litchfield County at the time of its first settlement, nearly a century after Hartford was founded. The site of the present village of Litchfield was overgrown with alder. It needed an emigrant's faith to foresee the changes that human industry under the guidence of good principles could bring about in the face of wintry skies and in defiance of steep hills.

In 1772, about fifty years after the organization of the town, Tapping Reeve, son of a clergyman of Brookhaven, established himself in this remote and obscure place which had nothing but a Court House, Jail and Meeting House to form a centre for the few towns that clustered around it. He could not have driven to the village in a carriage to save his life, for two reasons there were no wheeled vehicles and had there been any, there were no roads that could have been safely traversed by them. This interesting adventurer was a graduate of Princeton, and was then only twenty-eight years old. He was a delicately formed slender man of classical features, pale complexion and large bright eyes. With him went Sally Burr, his wife, daughter of President Burr of Princeton, sister of Aaron Burr, and grand-daughter of Jonathan Edwards—one of the most beautiful and accomplished women of her time. They took up their abode in South Street, in a house where I spent four happy years and which now belongs to Judge Woodruff, who is our distinguished guest this evening. Mr. Reeve established himself here as a lawyer and soon attained to the highest distinction in his profession. After continuing in it for twelve years, in 1784, when the Revolutionary War was scarcely over, he instituted the Litchfield Law School in which he was the sole instructor until 1797, a period of fourteen years, when he associated with him James Gould, who was afterwards so renowned in the history of American jurisprudence. This school educated young men from all parts of the Union, among whom were John C. Calhoun, Levi Woodbury, John M. Clayton, Roger S. Baldwin, Samuel S. Phelps, Nathaniel Smith, William Elliot, Origen S. Seymour, Lewis B. Woodruff, Truman Smith and other distinguished men, whose names have shed lustre upon the annals of our country. Two of these graduates have been judges of the Supreme Court of the United States, fifty of them members of Congress, forty have been judges of the highest State courts and several have been foreign and Cabinet ministers.

Tapping Reeve was not a mere pedagogue, nor was he a mere lawyer. He was a man of genius, and in middle age when his feelings were enlisted in the trial of a cause, he often exhibited powers of eloquence, which from the suddenness with which they flashed upon the minds of his audience and from his impassioned manner, produced an overwhelming effect. He was very unequal in the exhibition of his powers. He was a man of ardent temperament, tender sensibilities and of a nature deeply religious. His sympathies led him to espouse the cause of the oppressed and helpless. He was the first eminent lawyer in this country who dared to arraign the common law of England for its severity and refined cruelty in cutting off the natural rights of married women, and placing their property at the mercy of their husbands to squander it at pleasure. His sentiments did not at first meet with much favor, but he lived long enough to see them gain a foot hold in this and other States. His principles did not die with him, but are perpetuated in his "Domestic Relations," and in the jurisprudence of his country. He was an ardent Revolutionary patriot of the Federal school. His fervent piety, well-timed charities, noble impulses, thoroughness, simplicity of character, and disinterestedness all served to render him a general favorite in a widely-extended circle of friends and acquaintances. He died in 1823, in the 80th year of his age. Such was the head and founder of the Litchfield Bar.

The next distinguished member of this Bar if we are to follow the order of birth, was Andrew Adams, born in 1736, who was successively King's Attorney, member of Congress and Chief Judge. He was a man of clear mind and of great learning. After him Major-General Uriah Tracy, born in 1755. From 1796 to 1807 he was a Senator from Connecticut, leader of the Federal party, an intimate friend of Hamilton, Fisher Ames and Morris, and was a man of great legal acumen and particularly famed for his wit.

Then follows Col. Ephriam Kirby, born at Litchfield in 1757, an officer in the Revolutionary army who carried to his grave a frightful wound that he received in the struggle. He was a faithful and accurate lawyer. In 1789, he published a volume of "Reports of the Supreme Court of Errors." This was the first volume of law reports ever published on this continent. Upon the organization of Lousiana, he was appointed by President Jefferson a judge of the newly acquired territory of Orleans, and died on his way to his place of destination in the 48th year of his age.

After him in the order of birth comes Nathaniel Smith, who was born about the year 1763 and who, after severe struggles with poverty and imperfect, early education, rose so rapidly in his profession that soon after he commenced the study of law under Judge Reeve, he was sitting by his master's side on the bench of the Supreme Court of Errors. Judge Church and Judge Wiillams have both told me that he was in their opinion the most gifted man ever born in the State. I will not attempt any sketch of him, but if you will allow me I will quote a passage from a letter written to me by David S. Boardman who knew Mr. Smith and how to estimate him. He says:

"His voice was excellent, being both powerful and harmonious, and never broke under any exertion of its capacity. His manner was very ardent and the seeming dictate of a strong conviction of justice of his cause, and his gestures were the natural expression of such a conviction. Mr. Smith's style was pure and genuine Saxon, with no attempt at classic ornament or allusion. His train of reasoning was lucid and direct, and evincive of the fact that the whole of it was like a map spread out in his mind's eye from the beginning. His integrity was always felt and dreaded by his opponent. He spoke with much fluency but with no undue rapidity, he never hesitated or haggled at a word, nor did he ever tire his audience with undue prolixity; or omit to do justice to his case for fear of tiring them; and indeed there was little danger of it."

There is only one brief specimen of the style of this eloquent man handed down to us. This is a part of his argument in the case of Jedediah Strong and wife before the General Assembly, and which is to be found in a volume of our reports. In arguing against the theory advocated by Judge Reeve in favor of married women, he took the opposite or common law ground and expressed himself as follows:

"But the manners have led the law and the law the manners, until every barrier is broken down and we seem about to bury in oblivion forever the rule that the wife has no separate existence."

Last in order of birth of the truly great men who can be particularly dwelt upon in this hurried outline, is James Gould, born at Branford in 1770, and one of the most elegant scholars and terse writers who have adorned the profession in this country. He studied law under Judge Reeve, and joint professor and delivered lectures to the students in this institution for thirty-five years; at the end of which time, there had been educated at the Litchfield Law School one thousand and twenty-five lawyers from all parts of the United States. Gould's pleading is one of the most condensed and critical pieces of composition to be found in our language and is of an original character. He had at first contemplated a more extended treatise, but while he was preparing material for it, the announcement of Chitty's work on the same title induced him to change his plan. As it was presented to the public, Gould's "Pleading" is therefore only a summary of the original design but for clearness and logical percision it is surpassed, if at all, only by the Commentaries on the laws of England.

Judge Gould carried to the Bar the same classical finish which appears in his writings. It would have been impossible for him to speak an ungrammatical sentence, use an inelegant expression or make an awkward gesture. His arguments were expressed in the most brief forms in which a speaker can convey his thoughts to his hearers. He seldom spoke longer than half an hour, and in the most complex and important cases never exceeded an hour. He could shoot a quiver full of shafts within the circle of the target with such certainty and force that they could all be found and counted when the contest was over.

As a Judge, his opinions are unsurpassed by any which appear in our reports for clearness and that happy moulding of thought so peculiar to him at the Bar and in social conversation.

The position of this eminent jurist and his venerable master and associate, was truly enviable. To them flocked from every State in the Union the youth who were to shape the jurisprudence of the western world. They looked upon these renowned teachers with as much reverence as the young men of Athens regarded the philosophers who prepared their minds for the strifes of the Agora, the debates of the council or the shades of contemplative retirement.

As I have before said, all attempts at particular description of the members of the Litchfield Bar, must end here. I might speak of John Allen, Gov. John Cotton Smith, Holmes, Boardman, Huntington, Benedict, Sterling, Swan, Asa Bacon, Samuel and Leman Church, Mills, Phelps, Minor, Strong and others—and but for the presence in which I stand, I might attempt some brief sketch of the character and career of the venerable man whose retiracy from public life has been the occasion of this meeting, which, though a festival in form, has suffused our eyes with tears. I am one of his oldest students here present and have known him well. You will all join me in the prayer that his declining years may be like his professional and judicial life, serene as they are pure, and that no clouds of sorrow may settle down between him and a better world.

LITCHFIELD
CHAUNCEY J. BUEL.

WINSTED
WILLEY T. SMITH.

NEW MILFORD
LEWIS W. MOSHER.

THE MESSENGERS, 1908.

# WATERTOWN MURDER TRIAL

New principles of law are presented in the case of State vs. William McLaughlin, who was indicted by the Grand Jury at the April term, 1908, for murder in the first degree. The facts, over which there was no particular contest, were as follows:

On the morning of April 12, 1908, a few men were gathered upon the depot platform at Watertown. Some of them were attaches of the railroad, but most of them were on their way to church. The accused, a man of forty-six years, accosted the deceased in a manner which the latter regarded as offensive. One word led to another, and the victim of the tragedy, Robert Downs, a young man of nineteen, pushed McLaughlin over so that he fell on the platform, breaking a bottle of whiskey which he had in his pocket. More angry words followed, and the combat, so far as the knowledge of those on the platform went, was over. Robert Downs retired to a distance on the westerly side of the depot platform from where the wordy dispute took place, and McLaughlin went around the opposite corner of the building and threw out the broken glass from his pocket, and then, unseen by anyone, drew a pocket knife, and going up to Downs struck him with it in the neck, severing the carotid artery, from which wound Downs died within a few minutes.

The trial before the Superior Court was at the October term 1908, in Litchfield, before Judge Edwin B. Gager, lasting into the third week. The prisoner was defended by Thomas F. Ryan, Esq., assisted by Elbert P. Roberts, Esq., both of Litchfield. The State prosecution was by State Attorney Donald T. Warner, assisted by Howard F. Landon, Esq. The principal question was as to the degree of the crime, the State contending that there was time for premeditation and deliberation and that all the elements of murder in the first degree were present. The defense claimed that the chronic alcoholism of the accused, as shown by his previous history, and by the medical testimony of the defendant's expert, Dr. John L. Buel, rendered the accused incapable of the deliberation and premeditation under all the circumstances of the case necessary to constitute the crime of murder in the first degree.

The jury after long deliberation returned a verdict of murder in the second degree, and the prisoner was sentenced to State Prison for life.

While chronic alcoholism, as a defense is known in the law, it has been so seldom resorted to, in cases of this character, that unusual interest was manifested by the legal fraternity in this case.

An interesting case not heretofore mentioned, is that connected with the successful installation of The New Milford Power Company.

# NEW MILFORD POWER CO.

About twenty-five years ago the Hon. Nicholas Staub, of New Milford and a former Comptroller of the State, conceived the idea that the great water power of the Housatonic river ought to be utilized. He interested a few other persons with him in the matter and they decided to incorporate a company for that purpose, and a charter was granted by the General Assembly of 1893, forming the New Milford Power Company. The matter laid dormant for a long time. There was plenty of power in the river, but there were no mills or factories requiring it. The scientific development of electrical energy and more particularly the availibility of transmitting it without material loss over long distances to be applied wherever power was required, opened up the way for the Company to begin operations. Many hydro-electric engineers advised that there could not be fall enough obtained to develop sufficient power to make such a plant, considering the large expense of the transmission line, profitable. Walter S. Morton, an eminent hydraulic engineer, now the consulting engineer of the New York City Water Supply Commission, saw at once how the power of the water at Bulls Bridge could be doubled, and acting under his suggestions the company proceeded to erect a small dam in the gorge at Bulls Bridge, and dug a canal over two miles long to convey the water to a point in the town of New Milford, where they obtained a fall of one hundred and fifteen feet, with an average of two thousand horse power.

The incorporators employed Frederic M. Williams, Esq., of New Milford to attend to the legal part of the business. The charter had to be amended, giving the company various powers not originally included therein. After the charter was perfected and the stock of $1,000,000. subscribed, the dam was built, the canal dug and the power house, with four immense dynamos was erected. These were all matters of mechanism, but the real interesting part to us attorneys was the proceedings relating to the acquisition of the flooded territory. Lands bordering on the river suddenly rose in value, and but little could be purchased, consequently condemnation proceedings under the charter were instituted by Mr. Williams, to acquire them. Nothing like these proceedings appear upon our records, in number or in accuracy. Committees were appointed consisting of Hon. Geo. M. Woodruff of Litchfield, James Alldis, Esq., of Torrington and Edward S. Roberts, Esq., of North Canaan, and long hearings were had before these gentlemen, and it is an interesting fact that no exceptions were taken during the three weeks of the hearings by either party. The report of the Committee was accepted by the Superior Court, and no appeal was carried in any case to the Supreme Court of Errors. Lines of wire were erected and power successfully transmitted to Waterbury, and other cities. Several electric roads are run by it, and ultimately the New York and New Haven and Hartford Railroad Company obtained the control of the plant.

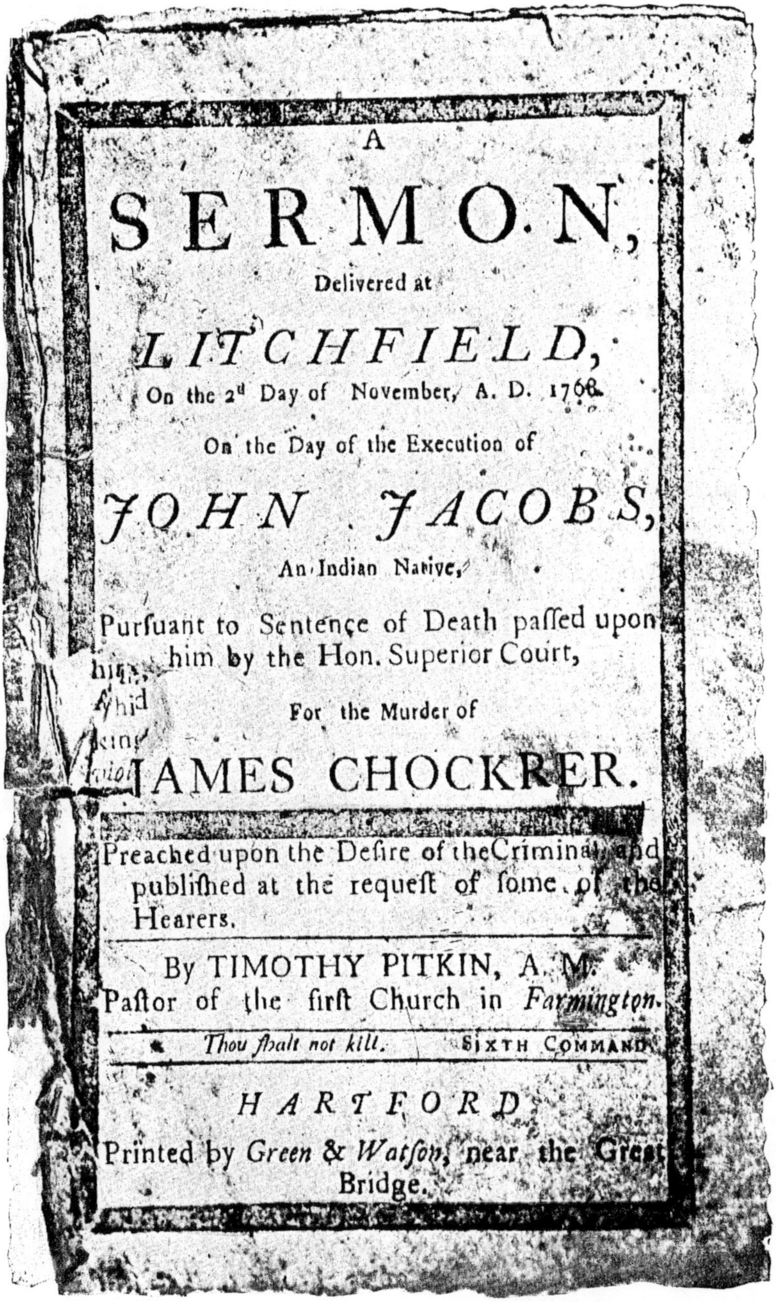

A

SERMON,

Delivered at

*LITCHFIELD*,

On the 2d Day of November, A. D. 1768.

On the Day of the Execution of

*JOHN JACOBS*,

An Indian Native,

Pursuant to Sentence of Death passed upon him by the Hon. Superior Court,

For the Murder of

JAMES CHOCKRER.

Preached upon the Desire of the Criminal, and published at the request of some of the Hearers.

By TIMOTHY PITKIN, A. M.
Pastor of the first Church in *Farmington*.

*Thou shalt not kill.* SIXTH COMMAND.

*HARTFORD*:
Printed by *Green* & *Watson*, near the Great Bridge.

(Reproduction of title page of sermon).

# OLD SERMON

The compiler has in his library a copy of a sermon delivered at Litchfield, in November, 1768, on the execution of John Jacobs for murder of James Chockrer, both Indian natives, the title page of which is herewith reproduced. This is the first trial for murder in the county, and must have been of unusual interest to have called forth a sermon from so eminent a divine as Timothy Pitkin, pastor of the Church at Farmington. I will quote a few choice extracts therefrom.

The text was:

NUMBERS XXXV. 16.

AND IF HE SMITE HIM WITH AN INSTRUMENT OF IRON, (SO THAT HE DIE) HE IS A MURDERER: THE MURDERER SHALL SURELY BE PUT TO DEATH.

After a long sermon on the text addressed to "Men and Brethren," and ending with "There is no way for sinners, but to repair to Christ; to Christ we must go, or to hell," the learned Divine proceeds, "My discourse now turns to the poor prisoner, under sentence of death,"—with the following soothing language, "JOHN JACOBS. It was your request, that this last advice, by me should be given to you, and therefore by help of divine grace, I shall speak to you, with great plainess, and O! that I may address you, with that warmth and faithfullness, which your present case calls for; this being the last sermon you will ever hear.

"When I see a poor criminal, under sentence of death, when I view your aggravated crimes, and you standing upon the edge of time, and just launching into an unalterable and eternal state; O! prisoner what shall I say to you! O! my hearers, what words shall your preacher choose!

Prisoner, attend! The great God hath made a law, *that he that sheddeth man's blood, by man shall his blood be shed.* And in our text, *if* one *smite* another *with an instrument of iron, so that he die, he is a murderer, the murderer shall surely be put to death.* GOD had an infinite authority to make this law, and annex this penalty; and, JOHN, this is your case: you smote one of your fellow creatures in malice and rage, *with an instrument of iron so that he died;* therefore you are a *murderer,* and you stand *chargable* with guilt of blood, 'tis just that you be put to death, for by the statute of heaven, by the law of GOD, you ought to die.

Prisoner, attend! You deserve to suffer the eternal pains of hell, it is just in God to send you to the hopeless regions of the damned; you was a sinner and have been a prayerless malicious creature, therefore GOD, against whom you have sinned and whose laws you have violated, may justly damn you." There is a considerable more of this kind of consolation.

# TRUMAN SMITH

The biographical notes on Truman Smith, which I have heretofore given, were prepared by a distinguished lawyer of New York City, who had been associated with Mr. Smith in his practice, and mostly relate to matters outside of Litchfield County. The Humaston case, however, was one in which the plaintiff, Mr. Humaston, was a native of Litchfield, and was in the employ of the Western Union Telegraph Company when he invented a process of sending a number of messages simultaneous upon the same wire, and the Telegraph Company claimed that it was their property. To prevent other telegraph companies from using this invention they pensioned Mr. Humaston during his lifetime.

During Mr. Smith's residence in Litchfield he was one of the leading, if not the leading lawyer in Litchfield County, in certain classes of cases, and used the forcible, brow-beating method of trial. He was a terror to witnesses in cross-examination, and many stories are told about him. Previous to the great fire in 1886 the compiler had in his office a massive cherry table which once belonged to Mr. Smith, who frequently came into the office, as he visited Litchfield, and would go up to the old table and after examining it a little would say, "Old fellow, I have pounded you a great many times!"

I well recollect the last case which Mr. Smith tried in this court, and probably the last one he tried in any court. It was a case which was brought by Mr. Cothren for some man in Woodbury against Mr. Nathan Smith of Roxbury, a brother of Truman Smith. It appeared during the trial that the plaintiff never authorized the bringing of the suit, which was over some very trivial dispute of account, nor did the party who was recognized to prosecute, enter into any recognizance. The case came before Judge Hovey, and Mr. Smith moved that it be erased from the docket, and made an argument of about two hours in support of his motion. He was then nearly eighty years old and too infirm to stand during his argument, so he would stand part of the time, then sit for a time, and never did an attorney receive such a scoring as did Mr. Cothren, who withdrew the suit. The whole performance was the most impressive exhibition of ancient legal warfare I have ever witnessed.

C. F. Sedgwick, Esq. of Sharon, Conn., said in an article in the Leavenworth Genealogy, P. 26, that "Up to Mr. Smith's time, the eminent men of the county were a kind of privileged class, never mingling with the common people—but Mr. Smith welcomed to his acquaintance and sympathy good men of all conditions in society no matter how humble or obscure the man might be. He never took advantage of his social position to obtain preferment for himself—never asked for a nomination—never solicited the vote of any man—his weight of character, eminent fitness and great abilities always marked him as the man for the place and his nominations were made with great unanimity."

GEORGE C. HARRISON

BYRON TUTTLE

CHESTERFIELD C. MIDDLEBROOKS

ANDREW G. BARNES

JURY COMMISSIONERS

Mr. Smith, in the latter part of his life, lived in Stamford, and for a number of years was actively engaged in the suppression of intoxicating liquors, writing and publishing several pamphlets relating thereto and often appearing before the General Assembly in support of temperance legislation.

## JURY COMMISSIONERS.

On page 129 the method of drawing jurors is outlined. I have obtained the pictures of all of the Jury Commissioners since this way of selecting the Jury was provided and who act with the Clerk as the board of selection in July.

George C. Harrison was appointed in 1895 and died while holding the office, February 25th, 1907. He was born in Cornwall, May 19th, 1840, and resided in his native town all his life, holding nearly all the honors its citizens could give him regardless of party in the town offices. Was Judge of Probate many years. He was often appointed by this Court as a Committee to lay out roads, appraise property, assess damage, etc. As a Jury Commissioner he was very conscientious and at the sessions of the board he always had his list carefully marked and checked as to the fitness of each nominee.

Byron Tuttle was also appointed in 1895 and resigned soon after Mr. Harrison's death. He was also exceedingly careful and fair in the discharge of his duty. He died in Plymouth September 25, 1908, aged 83. He was in early life an active business man and a noted manufacturer of carriages which industry he discontinued soon after the close of the civil war. He held many of the most important offices of the town of Plymouth; Selectman and Judge of Probate. He did a good deal of law business such as conveyancing, drawing wills, contracts and the like. He was especially fond of assisting attorneys in preparing a case for trial by looking up the evidence, witnesses and exhibits, and felt great pride saying that he never lost a case that he prepared as he desired.

Andrew G. Barnes was appointed Jury Commissioner in 1907. He is a native of Sherman Conn., born November 15th, 1838, but has resided in New Milford nearly his whole life where he is an extensive farmer, dairyman, cattle breeder and large grower of tobacco. Has held many town offices and represented New Milford in the Legislature of 1895 and 1903, and was Senator of his district in 1907, and is re-elected Senator for 1909.

Chesterfield C. Middlebrook was appointed a Jury Commissioner in 1907. He has been Sheriff of Litchfield County and possesses a large acquaintance all over the County, peculiarly fiitting him for exercise of his present office.

## COUNTY COMMISSIONERS.

The office of County Commissioner was established more than half a century ago and a large variety of duties are assigned to them in relation to County affairs, such as providing for the care of the County buildings, their repair, providing for the maintenance of the jail, etc. Probably their most arduous duty is that relating to the excise, or granting of licenses for the sale of spirituous and intoxicating liquors. Their salaries at present are $600 a year and mileage. They hold their office for four years from their appointment. The present Commissioners are as follows

Hubert B. Case, the Chairman is a native of Barkhamsted, born April 3rd, 1856. He is a merchant, has been a member of the General Assembly from his town, and has held many town offices. His term of office expires October 1, 1911.

Howard M. Guernsey was born in Thomaston January 9, 1877. He has been for several years engaged in the manufacture of lumber. His mills are now in operation in New Hampshire and Vermont. He has represented Thomaston in the Legislature. His term of office expires October 1, 1911.

John J. Karl was born in Goshen, N. Y. March 1, 1864, but has resided since his boyhood in Litchfield. He is a teacher, composer and publisher of music. Is very active in political affairs, and is Town Clerk of Litchfield, and Clerk of the Probate Court of Litchfield District. His term of office expires October 1, 1913.

## COURT MESSENGERS

One of the busy men in Court is its messengers. The duties are various, and not defined by statute. The theory is they are to regulate the temperature, lighting and ventilation of the Court room; to get reference books as required from the library for use in the Court, and attend to the multitudinous errands of the lawyers engaged in the trial of a cause.

They are appointed by and hold their office during the pleasure of the judge.

The present messengers are at Litchfield, Chauncey J. Buel. He is also the Janitor of the building. In Winsted, Dr. Willey T. Smith, a dentist by profession, rests his nerves in the forensic eloquence of the attorneys. In New Milford, Lewis W. Mosher, a veteran of the Civil war, enjoys the strifes and conflicts of the opposing parties.

HUBERT B. CASE

JOHN J. KARL

HOWARD M. GUERNSEY

COUNTY COMMISSIONERS

J. Pierpont
Æt. 79 yrs

## JUDGMENT.

One hundred years have brought their bloom and fruit,
Since "every one who had a cause or suit,"
Might "come up hither" and present his claim,
With no misgivings, that, whoever came,
With a good cause, good witnesses, good men
Upon the bench as judges, and, again,
With twelve good honest jurors; if he saw
That well-feed "counsel learned in the law,"
Had courage, after half dozen fights,
Would—stand an even chance to get his rights,
And then at least the controversy o'er,
The case all settled, to be tried no more.
Those hundred years, as onward they have swept,
Have seen how calm the litigants have slept:—
Judge, jury, counsel, parties have withdrawn,
And to a higher bar together gone,
Where every right decree is ratified
And every wrong reversed and set aside.

JOHN PIERPONT.

IN RE
IN THE MATTER OF
THE LITCHFIELD COUNTY
BENCH AND BAR.

JANUARY 1, 1909

Be it remembered that this cause having been pending for a century and a half, and the parties having been duly heard, by their witnesses and counsel, and having examined the foregoing exhibits, which are made a part of this record. It is considered and ordered that the foregoing judgment presented fifty years ago to the citizens of Litchfield County by John Pierpont in his Centennial poem is hereby accepted and approved.

DWIGHT C. KILBOURN,
*Clerk.*

# INDEX

NAMES

## C

## D



## E

**I**



**J**

**N**



**O**



**P**

**T**

# REPRINTS OF LEGAL CLASSICS PUBLISHED BY THE LAWBOOK EXCHANGE, LTD.

## LEGAL EDUCATION

**Hicks, Frederick C.** *History of the Yale Law School to 1915*. With a new introduction by Morris L. Cohen and a new index. New Haven: Yale University Press, 1935-1938. 301 pp. Illustrated. Reprinted 2001 by The Lawbook Exchange, Ltd. LCCN 2001016436. ISBN 1-58477-175-5. Cloth. $75.

* The only history of the early years of Yale Law School, a chronological history from its founding to 1915, with historical information and colorful anecdotes not found elsewhere. Hicks, the author of *Materials and Methods of Legal Research*, was the librarian at Yale Law School from 1928-1944. From 1935-1938 Yale University Press issued the work in four paperbound volumes that were not widely distributed. This edition combines the four volumes (*The Founders and the Founders' Collection; From the Founders to Dutton 1845-1869; 1869-1894 Including The County Court House Period; and 1895-1915 Twenty Years of Hendrie Hall*) into one, and is prefaced by a new introduction by Morris L. Cohen, who was Professor of Law and head of the law libraries at Harvard and Yale, and is the author of many well-known works including *Bibliography of Early American Law*.

**Hilliard, Francis.** *The Elements of Law; Being a Comprehensive Summary of American Civil Jurisprudence. For the Use of Students, Men of Business, and General Readers.* Boston: Hilliard, Gray, and Company, 1835. xv, 345, v pp. Reprint available 2002 by The Lawbook Exchange, Ltd. LCCN 2001041395. ISBN 1-58477-188-7. Cloth. $75.

* Hilliard [1806-1878] was a New England lawyer and prolific legal writer whose works set the standard for later law texts. "At the time that he wrote, judges and lawyers lacked legal treatises which cited American decisions and showed how far the English common law had been followed by American courts or modified to suit new conditions. Textbooks presenting cases from all states were needed in order to encourage the development of national judge-made law rather than particularistic local doctrines. Hilliard was one of the first and most voluminous of the authors who met these needs." *DAB* V:53.

His vast legal knowledge is aptly employed in this important early textbook which provides a summary of the basic principles of American law. His success with this first work, which went into a second edition, led Hilliard to go on to write numerous other well-regarded treatises, many of which went into numerous editions, including *The Law of Torts* (1859), the first English treatise on the subject. *Dictionary of American Biography* V: 53-54. *Catalogue of the Library of the Law School of Harvard University* (1909) I: 925. Cohen, *Bibliography of Early American Law* 5393.

**Kalman, Laura.** *Legal Realism at Yale, 1927-1960.* Chapel Hill: University of North Carolina Press, 1986. xii, 314 pp. Reprinted 2002 by The Lawbook Exchange, Ltd. ISBN 1-58477-203-4. Cloth. $85.
* The history of the concept of legal realism as it evolved at Yale University Law School is in fact a history of the development of legal education in this country during the years 1927-1960, as Kalman shows in this important study. The realists' attention toward the importance of the role of litigation, the practitioner, judges and judicial reasoning, and the judiciary in a societal context represented a departure from the scientific casebook method espoused by C.C. Langdell at Harvard University Law School in the 1870s, and later supported by Roscoe Pound.

**Kilbourn, Dwight C.** *The Bench and Bar of Litchfield County, Connecticut 1709-1909: Biographical Sketches of Members. History and Catalogue of the Litchfield Law School. Historical Notes.* Litchfield, Conn.: Published by the Author, 1909. xiv, 344, [3], viii pp. Illustrated. Reprint available 2002 by The Lawbook Exchange, Ltd. LCCN 2001038974. ISBN 1-58477-213-1. Cloth. $80.
* Litchfield Law School, the first American law school, was founded by Tapping Reeve in 1782. The work is composed of materials relevant to the school and related personages, and contains historical notes, biographies, photographs, accounts of important trials, and the following reprints: Litchfield County: Historical Address Delivered at Litchfield, Conn., On the Occasion of the Centennial Celebration, 1851, by Samuel Church; Sketches of the Early Lights of the Litchfield Bar by David S. Boardman (1860); Fifty Years at the Litchfield County Bar by Charles F. Sedgwick (1870); and Reminiscences of the Litchfield County Bar, Delivered at the Centennial Banquet, November 18, 1898, by Donald J. Warner.

**Langdell, C.C.** *A Selection of Cases on the Law of Contracts. With References and Citations. Prepared for Use as a Text-book in Harvard Law School.* Boston: Little, Brown & Co., 1871. xvi, 1022 pp. Reprinted 1999 by The Lawbook Exchange, Ltd. LCCN 99-28293. ISBN 1-58477-001-5. Cloth. $120.
* The landmark work that introduced the revolutionary idea of the "case system" to legal education, which Langdell [1826-1906] instituted in his position as Dean at Harvard law School. A response to the European educational practice of the expository textbook as the basis of study, Langdell invented herein the use of original authorities to teach legal principles in his classes at Harvard. He posted lists of leading cases on the bulletin boards or announced them in class beforehand. The students prepared for class by going to the library, taking down the reports, and studying them. The process was both injurious to the library collection and inconvenient for the students. It was very soon apparent to Langdell that having done away with the traditional textbook, the law library was not a satisfactory alternative. No library had, or could afford, the number of duplicate volumes of the court reports that were required so that all students could have easy and equal

access to the cases. Langdell's solution was the casebook. This innovation in legal education publishing led to the proliferation of casebooks that continue today. Walker, *Oxford Companion to Law* 714. Marke, *A Catalogue of the Law Collection of New York University* (1953) 423. *Dictionary of American Biography* V:585-586.

**Lieber, Francis.** *On Civil Liberty and Self-government. Enlarged edition in one volume.* Philadelphia: J.B. Lippincott & Co.. 1859. xix, [15]-629 pp. Reprinted 2001 by The Lawbook Exchange, Ltd. LCCN 99-056928. ISBN 1-58477-070-8. Cloth. $100.

* "In these volumes Lieber presented the first systematic works on political science that appeared in America... he retains credit as a notable pioneer with wide influence in more than one generation." DAB VI:236-238. Widely read and used as a textbook, this is the best known of Lieber's work. Lieber [1800-1872], a German scholar and political activist who suffered persecution from the Prussians, was early associated with the historian Niebuhr. He immigrated to the United States in 1827, and his writings, among them an encyclopedia that was the foundation of the *Encyclopedia Britannica*, advanced his reputation. He became professor of history and political economy at South Carolina College, and was later appointed to the same chair in Columbia College. In 1865 he moved to Columbia Law School, where he was known to be a prominent political philosopher and consultant to the Union government, due to his influential writings on military law. Enlarged edition in one volume, having first been published in two volumes in 1853. Cohen, *Bibliography of Early American Law* 3369. Sabin, *A Dictionary of Books Relating to America* 40974. *Catalogue of the Library of the Law School of Harvard University* (1909) I:1176. *Dictionary of American Biography* VI:236-238.

**[St. Germain, Christopher].** *The Doctor and Student or Dialogues Between a Doctor of Divinity and a Student in the Laws of England Containing the Grounds of Those Laws Together with Questions and Cases Concerning the Equity Thereof Revised and Corrected by William Muchall, Gent. to which are added two pieces concerning Suits in Chancery by Subpoena.* Cincinnati: Robert Clarke & Co., 1874. xiv, 401 pp. Reprinted 1998 by The Lawbook Exchange, Ltd. LCCN 98-11338. ISBN 1-886363-49-8. Cloth. $65.

* Written originally in Latin in 1523, this work contains two dialogues between a doctor of divinity and a student of English law, and is known for putting into popular form canonist learning regarding the nature and object of law, the religious and moral standards of law, the foundations of the common law and other discussions regarding the jurisdiction of Parliament. A very important work in the development of equity, *Doctor and Student* appeared in numerous editions. It was frequently cited and influenced generations of legal writers down to Blackstone and later. Marke, *A Catalogue of the Law Collection of New York University* (1953) 38. *Catalogue of the Library of the Law School of Harvard University* (1909) II:516-517.

**Stevens, Robert.** *Law School: Legal Education in America from the 1850s to the 1980s.* Chapel Hill: The University of North Carolina Press, [1983]. xvi, 334 pp. Reprinted 2001 by The Lawbook Exchange, Ltd. ISBN 1-58477-199-2. Cloth. $85.

* Comprehensive history of over a century of legal education in America. Examines the law school institution and its impact on the legal profession and the society it serves. This highly lauded work won a Certificate of Merit from the American Bar Association upon its original publication. Stevens' distinguished career in education and law includes his seventeen-year term as professor of law at Yale University and nine-year term as president of Haverford College, during which tenure this work was published. Well-annotated and indexed, with a thorough bibliography.

**Walker, Timothy**. *Introduction to American Law. Designed as a First Book for Students.* Ninth Edition. Revised by Clement Bates. Boston: Little, Brown, and Company, 1887. Reprint available 2002 by The Lawbook Exchange, Ltd. LCCN 2001038955. ISBN 1-58477-214-X. Cloth. $120.

* A systematic outline of American law, written to fill a void in this area, and "...for many years was used as a textbook for American law students." Marke, *A Catalogue of the Law Collection at New York University* (1953) 250. Based on lectures given by Walker [1802-1856] while a law professor at Cincinnati College.

**Warren, Charles.** *History of the Harvard Law School and of Early Legal Conditions in America.* New York: Lewis Publishing Company, 1908. Three volumes. xiv, 543; iv, 560; 397 pp. Illustrated. Reprinted 1999 by The Lawbook Exchange, Ltd. LCCN 99-29193. ISBN 1-58477-006-6. Cloth. $275.

* The definitive history. Warren provides a fascinating account of law studies, lawyers, legal practice and legal conditions in America from 1640 to 1817--the year of the foundation of the Harvard Law School. This is followed by a comprehensive history of the Harvard Law School from 1817 to 1908. Volume three contains a complete, detailed biographical Alumni Roll for the Harvard Law School, with selected class pictures and an alumni index. Marke, *A Catalogue of the Law Collection of New York University* (1953) 201. **The set is also available in handsome quarter calf with raised bands, gilt-stamped lettering-pieces and gilt embellishments, over marble boards for $750.**